Living Media Ethics

Winner of the Clifford G. Christians Award for Research in Media Ethics, Michael Bugeja's *Living Media Ethics* posits that moral convergence is essential to address the complex issues of our high-tech media environment. As such the book departs from and yet complements traditional pedagogy in media ethics. Bugeja covers advertising, public relations and major branches of journalism, as well as major schools of philosophical thought and historical events that have shaped current media practices.

Examining topics including responsibility, truth, falsehood, temptation, bias, fairness and power, chapters encourage readers to develop a personal code of ethics that they can turn to throughout their careers. Each chapter includes exercises, as well as journal writing and creative assignments, designed to build, test and enhance individual value systems. Unlike other texts, this media ethics book ends with an assignment to create a digital portfolio with a personal ethics code aligned with a desired media position or company.

Michael Bugeja is a professor and former director of the Journalism and Communication School at Iowa State University, USA. He won the 2015 Scripps Howard Award for Outstanding Administrator of the Year and the 2017 Distinguished Service Award from the Iowa Newspaper Association. His teaching honors include an AMOCO Foundation Outstanding Teacher Award and two University Professor Teaching Awards, all bestowed by student bodies of research institutions. He is the author of 24 books, including *Interpersonal Divide in the Age of the Machine* (2018) and *Interpersonal Divide: The Search for Community in a Technological Age* (2005). Before entering academe, Dr. Bugeja worked as a state editor for United Press International. He holds a master's degree from South Dakota State University, USA, and a doctorate from Oklahoma State University, USA.

Living Media Ethics

Across Platforms

Second Edition

Michael Bugeja

NEW YORK AND LONDON

Second edition published 2019
by Routledge
711 Third Avenue, New York, NY 10017

and by Routledge
2 Park Square, Milton Park, Abingdon, Oxon, OX14 4RN

Routledge is an imprint of the Taylor & Francis Group, an informa business

Library of Congress Cataloging-in-Publication Data
Names: Bugeja, Michael J., author.
Title: Living media ethics : across platforms / Michael Bugeja.
Description: Second edition. | London ; New York : Routledge, 2019. |
    Includes bibliographical references and index.
Identifiers: LCCN 2018021777 | ISBN 9781138322608 (hardback :
    alk. paper) | ISBN 9781138322615 (paperback : alk. paper) |
    ISBN 9780429451928 (ebook : alk. paper)
Subjects: LCSH: Mass media—Moral and ethical aspects.
Classification: LCC P94 .B85 2019 | DDC 175—dc23
LC record available at https://lccn.loc.gov/2018021777

First edition published by Oxford University Press 2007

ISBN: 978-1-138-32260-8 (hbk)
ISBN: 978-1-138-32261-5 (pbk)
ISBN: 978-0-429-45192-8 (ebk)

Typeset in Giovanni
by Apex CoVantage, LLC

For All My Current and Former Media Ethics Students

Table of Contents

About the Author   xi
Acknowledgments   xiii
Permissions   xv
Preface   xvii

CHAPTER 1   Overview: Ethics Across Platforms   1
               Aspire to Live Media Ethics   1
               Ethics Are Not in the Cloud   2
               Emphasize Motives over Medium   3
               Make Platforms Truthful Again   4
               Commit to Truth Now, Not Later   8
               Know Standards Across Media   10
               Moral Literacy Enhances Credibility   13
               Personal and Communal Journal Exercises—"Media
               Literacy: Motive vs. Motivation"   18

PART I •   Building Your Ethical Base   23
CHAPTER 2   Influence: Who Shaped Your Values?   25
               Develop Ethical Values   25
               Shortcuts Compromise Ethics   26
               Ethics Can Be Taught   28
               Revisit "Family Values"   30
               Learn a Few Philosophical Tenets   34
               Know Right From Wrong   38
               Remember Who Molded Your Morals   42
               History Matters More Than You Think   49
               Language Shapes Perception, Too   59
               Sharpen Insight and Attain Balance   65
               Personal and Communal Journal Exercises—
               "Deprogramming Your Influences"   68
CHAPTER 3   Responsibility: Take or Forsake It   75
               Right and Wrong Differ from Good and Bad   75
               "Justification" is Just an Excuse   77
               Be Accountable for Behavior   80
               Accountability Means Having to Say You're Sorry   81
               Seek Role Models and Mentors   86
               Recognize Responsibilities   90
               Responsibility Creates Trust   92
               Some Things Are Almost Always True   94
               Personal and Communal Journal Exercises—"What
               Are Your Moral Absolutes?"   98
CHAPTER 4   Truth: Levels, Shades and Hues   103
               Be a Font of Truth   103

	Objectivity is a Process	104
	Truth is Subject to Proof	106
	Truth Should Be Transparent	111
	Make Appropriate Disclosures	114
	Exercise Good Judgment	115
	Satire is Truth Everyone Knows but Won't Admit	122
	Truth Can Be Mythic, Too	125
	Personal and Communal Journal Exercises—"Your Highs, Lows and Turning Points"	129
PART II •	Testing Your Ethical Base	133
CHAPTER 5	Falsehood: Lie at Your Own Risk	135
	Lies Undermine Trust	135
	Lies Have Consequences	137
	Detect the Many Types of Lies	139
	Quote-Making Can Be Untruthful	144
	Pictures Can Lie, Too	149
	Crossing the Line in Photojournalism	150
	Question Every Lie	152
	Personal and Communal Journal Exercises—"Just How Truthful Are You?"	156
CHAPTER 6	Manipulation: Feel It, Spot It, Bust It	161
	Remember How Manipulation Feels	161
	Manipulators Violate Conscience	162
	Manipulators Exploit Media	164
	Hoaxes Rewrite History	166
	Media Pull Stunts, Too	171
	Expose and Defuse Manipulation	172
	Personal and Communal Journal Exercises—"Your Biases, Fears, Desires and Convictions"	181
CHAPTER 7	Temptation: Brace for It to Strike	185
	Temptation Strikes Without Warning	185
	Temptation Invites Conflict	187
	Resist the Urge to Plagiarize	190
	You Can Detect and Prevent Plagiarism	195
	Avoid Conflicts of Interest	200
	Personal and Communal Journal Exercises—"Your Own Conflict Resolution"	219
CHAPTER 8	Bias: Recognize and Resist It	223
	Are You Acknowledging Diversity?	223
	Recognize Misperceptions About Race	225
	Explore Bias Across Platforms	227
	Cultural Biases Taint the Workplace	229
	Know the History of Inclusion in Media	231
	Diversify News- and Boardrooms	233
	Stereotypes Perpetuate Bias	234
	Identify and Resist Stereotypes	241

	Personal and Communal Journal Exercises—"Taking Stock: Your Personal Bias Barometer"	244
Part III •	Enhancing Your Ethical Base	249
CHAPTER 9	Fairness: Level the Playing Fields	251
	Fairness Means Continuous Improvement	251
	Fairness Pivots on Viewpoint	253
	Fairness Makes Lasting Impressions	255
	Familiarize Yourself with Fairness Concepts	258
	"To Err is Human," by Clarence Page, *The Chicago Tribune*	266
	Personal and Communal Journal Exercises—"Do You or Others Play Fair or Foul?"	267
CHAPTER 10	Power: Apply as Needed	271
	Power Expresses Values	271
	Empowerment: *You Can Claim It*	290
	"A Case of Sexual Harassment," Anonymous, former account executive	294
	Nurture Compassion	295
	"Lasting Moments," Therese Frare, photojournalist	303
	Personal and Communal Journal Exercises—"Your Path to Empowerment"	305
CHAPTER 11	Value Systems: Create Your Own	311
	Commit to Ethical Living	311
	Values Reinforce Work Ethic	314
	Our Rights Have Historic Roots	315
	Values Foster Teamwork	317
	Create a Code You Can Live By	320
	Personal and Communal Journal Exercises—"Your Own Code of Ethics"	325
	Selected Bibliography	327
	Index	331

About the Author

Michael J. Bugeja is an ethicist and author of 25 books, including *Interpersonal Divide in the Age of the Machine* and *Interpersonal Divide: The Search for Community in a Technological Age*, Oxford University Press. He is co-author of *Vanishing Act: The Erosion of Online Footnotes and Implications for Scholarship in the Digital Age*. He twice won the prestigious Clifford G. Christians award for Research in Media Ethics. He is a regular contributor to *The Chronicle of Higher Education* and *Inside Higher Ed*. He directed the Greenlee School of Journalism and Communication at Iowa State University and now teaches media ethics there as a professor.

Dr. Bugeja is a frequent source about media, technology and ethics, interviewed by *The New Yorker, The New York Times, The Washington Post, The Christian Science Monitor, USA Today, International Herald Tribune, Newsday, American Journalism Review, Columbia Journalism Review* and other media outlets. His creative and scholarly works have appeared in a variety of publications, including *The Chronicle Review, Journalism Educator, Journalism and Mass Communication Educator, Journal of Mass Media Ethics, New Media and Society* and *Journalism Quarterly*, among others. His awards include the Scripps Howard Foundation Outstanding Administrator of the Year, the Iowa State University Outstanding Administrator Award, Iowa Newspaper Association Distinguished Service Award, a National Endowment for the Arts fellowship, and a National Endowment for the Humanities grant. Dr. Bugeja is an elected member of the Accrediting Council on Education in Journalism and Mass Communications. He has received several teaching honors, including an AMOCO Foundation Outstanding Teacher Award and two University Professor Teaching Awards, all bestowed by student bodies of major research institutions. Before entering the academe, Dr. Bugeja worked as a state editor and national correspondent for United Press International.

Acknowledgments

This book could not have been written without the help of dozens of professional journalists and practitioners from newspapers, broadcast outlets, online media, advertising and public relations agencies, magazines, professional associations and universities. Acknowledging every contributor here would fill several pages. Readers may not recognize their names but their places of employment. You will find contributors from broadcast outlets such as ABC, CBS, NBC, CNN, National Public Radio, British Broadcasting Corporation; news companies such as Gannett, Hearst, Lee Enterprises, Reuters, Associated Press; corporations and communication agencies such as Meredith, Weber Shandwick, Edelman, Raytheon, Leo Burnett, Ketchum; magazines such as *Esquire, Newsweek, Time, Better Homes & Gardens, Good Housekeeping*; newspapers such as *The Denver Post, Des Moines Register, Miami Herald, St. Louis Dispatch, The Chicago Tribune, The New York Times, The Washington Post*; and associations and foundations such as American Advertising Federation, Public Relations Society of American, Freedom Forum, Knight Foundation, Newseum, Nieman Foundation and Scripps Howard Foundation.

Journalists and practitioners who worked at these outlets and organizations, in addition to dozens more employed in a wide array of online and traditional media, share their values and work ethic. My spouse, photojournalist Diane Bugeja, also deserves special credit, not only for helping illustrate the book, but also for enduring my long absences from the family while I was interviewing and writing the work. Melissa Garrett, former teaching assistant in media ethics at Iowa State University, also helped in identifying library sources for citation in the text. No book reaches its potential without constructive criticism. Comments and suggestions by external reviewers were especially appreciated. The author is grateful for the support of Erica Wetter, publisher; Mia Moran, senior editorial assistant; and external reviewers who critiqued and helped assemble the text.

Permissions

The photos, "Dandelion Boy" and "Roadside Marker," are reprinted with permission of the copyright holder, Diane Bugeja, all rights reserved.

The following photographs—"Flight Nurse," "Marine Funeral," "Couple Kissing," "Magdalena" and "Lanier"—are reprinted with permission from the copyright holder, Dennis Chamberlin, all rights reserved.

The photo, "Final Moments," and accompanying essay, "Lasting Moments," are reprinted with permission from the copyright holder, Therese Frare, all rights reserved.

The photo, "Grieving Family and Friends," is reprinted with permission from the copyright holder, Morris L. Manning, all rights reserved.

The photographs, "Brian" from the Pulitzer Prize-winning series "21" and "A Policeman's Torment," are reprinted with special permission from the copyright holder, John Kaplan, all rights reserved.

Michael Bugeja's *Living Ethics: Developing Values in Mass Communication* was originally published by Pearson Allyn & Bacon in 1995. A later edition titled *Living Ethics across Media Platforms* was published in 2007 by Oxford University Press.

Additionally, small sections of chapters are based on essays of Michael Bugeja as published in *Aviso, The Chronicle of Higher Education, The Department Chair, Editor & Publisher, Inside Higher Ed, Media Ethics, The Quill, Tactics* and *Writer's Digest* along with research papers accepted for presentation at various conferences, including the Association for Education in Journalism and Mass Communication and the International Communication Association. Bugeja is the sole owner of the copyright.

Preface

This edition of *Living Media Ethics* comes with a preface or brief statement by the author, explaining how the updated text was assembled. The text has a long publication history spanning a quarter century of research and updates. This latest edition is a substantial revision of a 2007 text *Living Ethics across Media Platforms* published by Oxford University Press. That work, in turn, was a major revision of the 1995 text, published by Allyn & Bacon under the title *Living Ethics: Developing Values in Mass Communication*. The current work contains more than 20 years of research and interviews. While media events change daily and technology, almost as rapidly, the thematic content of each edition is grounded in philosophical and historical underpinnings that inform our conscience and consciousness, dual aspects of the human condition. While each of the editions maintains the original approach to media ethics, grounding our sense of right and wrong in the conscience, and consequences for our actions in consciousness, the scope of each book has broadened to cover a diversity of people as well as media. That approach further affirms the concept of "living ethics," developing ever stronger virtues and standards. The new edition builds, tests and enhances personal values and work ethic, exposing readers to issues and approaches encountered in print, electronic and photojournalism and in advertising and public relations.

By necessity, an ethics book analyzes and explores moral decision-making at the workplace. Doing so, this text cites other books, articles and online materials across media platforms. Such analysis is an act of criticism covered by fair use standards of U.S. copyright law. Although the works of several authors are cited here, only as much content as necessary has been used to make a point or clarify an issue. While most online citations were accessed during 2017–18, dozens of links were retrieved much earlier. These and earlier links may cease to work now or in the future because domains lapse or web page formats change. This phenomenon, known as linkrot, is examined at length in *Vanishing Act: The Erosion of Online Footnotes and Implications for Scholarship in the Digital Age* (Litwin Books, 2010), co-authored by Michael Bugeja and Daniela Dimitrova, Iowa State University professors.

In her book *Cyberliteracy*, a rhetorical analysis of the internet, Laura J. Gurak articulates a similar methodology. She quotes from books to make an observation or embellish an argument and cites works according to fair use.[1] "If anything," she writes, "examples used in this book bring positive value to the original by pointing readers to these sources."[2] (Books cited in *Living Media Ethics* also are recommended as outside reading.) Because hers is an act of criticism, Gurak has not chosen to seek permissions, especially on use of web material:

> For one, the Web pages contained herein are used for criticism. In addition, when a person or organization makes a Web site available to the world, that person or organization knows full well that the resulting Web page will be uploaded onto thousands of computer screens, linked to by other Web sites, and printed out on desktop laser printers. None of these uses require written permission, and a book, especially an act of criticism, is hardly different.[3]

With few exceptions, listed in the permissions section, this is also the case in *Living Media Ethics*.

Additionally, readers may notice that several quotations in the work contain no reference notes. These were interviews conducted via email, telephone or in person. Sources were sent this interview request:

> The new edition of *Living Media Ethics* has three sections and ten chapters:
>
> **Section I:** *One*: Influence, *Two*: Responsibility and *Three*: Truth, to develop ethical awareness;
> **Section II:** *Four*: Falsehood, *Five*: Manipulation, *Six*: Temptation and *Seven*: Bias, to test values;
> **Section III:** *Eight*: Fairness, *Nine*: Power and *Ten*: Value Systems, to enhance ethical values.

The last chapter discusses personal and professional standards and explains how to create a code to reflect those—a living document, requiring regular updating, throughout one's career.

The chapter headings above are broad and conceptual. But *Living Media Ethics* makes those abstractions concrete and applicable. For instance, your professional mentors or work ethic might fall under influence; obligations to the audience or clientele, under responsibility; fact-checking or objectivity, under truth; testimonials and fabrication, under falsehood; racism or sexism, under bias; hoaxes or product tampering, under manipulation; plagiarism and conflict of interest, under temptation; apologies and corrections, under fairness; privacy and taste, under discretion; profit motive or sexual harassment under power, and so forth.

You may want to email me a few sentences, paragraphs or pages, share a personal case study, or otherwise add your voice to such issues, based on research and/or experience. Or I can telephone you and arrange an interview via that method.

You can approach the issue another way, by asking and then responding to these questions:

> *   *What are the pertinent issues—the basics—that every journalism student should know (pick one) concerning influence, responsibility, truth, falsehood, bias, manipulation, temptation, fairness, discretion and power?*

- *What issue do you contend with on a regular basis?*
- *What was the most difficult? What do you wish you handled differently and so on?*

Some contributors preferred to be interviewed by phone, others in person and still others via email. Some preferred not to be interviewed at all but to provide statements for inclusion in this volume. For the most part, each of these options has been treated like interviews, with comments excerpted, cast in quotations and inserted where appropriate in the new work, often in several chapters. This was done for readability and is not standard procedure in news reporting, of course. Neither is fact-checking with sources to ensure that their quotations have been used in context. This, too, was done when possible throughout the text as standard procedure in the creation of a book-length work whose goal is to present as much accurate information as possible to engage readers for as long as possible in a dialogue about moral convergence complementing the technological one.

As in other texts, *Living Media Ethics* illustrates professional standards by referring to case studies submitted by journalists and practitioners responding to a call for contributions. However, the method of analysis regarding case studies in this text differs from many other ethics books whose authors ask readers with little work experience to judge decisions of experts acting in crisis situations. Anecdotes of professionals cited here are meant to enhance lessons about value systems and work ethic—not to judge whether readers would act differently in their cubicles, newsrooms or conference rooms. The purpose is to spark meaningful discussion and critical evaluations about ethical concepts in the text. Used in this manner, case studies help us appreciate moral decision-making, understand the context in which those decisions were made, analyze consequences and reconcile polar viewpoints.[4] However, as ethicist Deni Elliott notes, when case studies are misused, their strengths become weaknesses. "The purpose of an ethics discussion is to teach discussants how to 'do ethics'—that is, to teach the processes by which they can practice and improve their own critical decision-making abilities."[5]

That is the objective in this book. The challenge is to convey a modicum of the pressure that journalists and practitioners felt in challenging situations. No analysis, however perceptive, can convey to readers the sleepless nights and anxious moments that media employees endure when they have nothing left to rely on except their values. Moreover, rarely are such ethical dilemmas "black or white"; they are mostly complex and gray. Professionals, especially ones who have worked across media platforms, realize this. "I have to admit when I was a student at Oklahoma State University I was a little naive about ethics," says Linda DiJohn, who began her career as a reporter at the *Tulsa World* and then switched to public relations, working for such prestigious firms as Leo Burnett, Edelman and Weber

Shandwick. According to DiJohn, "I figured such dilemmas were black and white, presenting a clear choice: good vs. evil. But I've found that ethical dilemmas rarely present themselves so boldly. Instead, ethics come into question in subtler ways."

Several case studies depict those subtleties. *Living Media Ethics* also includes ones that augment the theme of "moral convergence." That is a fancy way of stating that this book does not put forth journalism ethics as distinct from advertising or public relations ethics. Neither does it ignore those practices. Rather, it focuses on ethical concepts that apply across *all* platforms. Examples from other sources—textbooks and articles, for instance—were cited on the same criteria. Several books and case studies were eliminated from inclusion when they failed to convey ethical approaches that applied across platforms. Journalists and practitioners also contributed real rather than theoretical case studies, usually through personal interviews. Finally, sources were asked when they realized that they were in an ethical situation, what they felt during those pressure-packed moments, and how they went about resolving dilemmas according to lessons that apply across platforms.

Some of the practical tasks associated with assembling a new edition of a work are to decide which content from the previous edition to keep, which to delete, what new material to add, and how to represent all that in the updated text. Here is how this has been handled in *Living Media Ethics*. When content from a variety of sources was still relevant, including interviews, no special notation calls attention to that fact. Some sources were re-interviewed or asked to update their case studies. A few journalists and practitioners in the previous edition were asked to revisit what they shared years earlier and state how, if at all, their perspectives had changed or evolved. This also illustrates how one "lives" his or her ethics.

Finally, *Living Media Ethics* employs an applied pedagogy, grounding abstract values in concrete situations across media emphases. This approach puts a premium on professional ethics and, as such, does not overly associate methods with philosophical concepts that require readers to memorize arcane definitions and translate concepts before addressing everyday matters on the job. Philosophy is important and undergirds several chapters in *Living Media Ethics*. When proper, philosophical terms will be explained or discussed, especially in introductory chapters, but not to such extent that each chapter requires a glossary to be learned by heart, understood and then applied. Several media ethics texts deal with professional practices through the filters of philosophy, and they are worth reading. However, *Living Media Ethics* does not overemphasize this type of scholarly framing. Rather, this book embraces the view that modern-day media are equally as influenced by Supreme Court decisions as well as U.S. charter documents and the Constitutional founders who created them. And while it is true that those founders might have ascribed to the "natural law" philosophy of John Locke, these early American leaders also had political motives that reverberate to this day and which are embedded in our laws, standards and practices. *Living Media Ethics* pays as much attention to Benjamin Franklin, Thomas Jefferson, James Madison, Alexander Hamilton, John Jay, Frederick Douglass, Abraham Lincoln, Martin Luther King and other influential figures as to Plato, Aristotle, Locke, Immanuel Kant, René Descartes, Jeremy Bentham, John Stuart Mill, Arthur Schopenhauer, Martin Heidegger and other truth-seeking counterparts. Again, these and other Greek, German and English philosophers are worth studying in addition to their multicultural equivalents such the ancient Lao Tzu and Confucius or the contemporaries Kwasi Wiredu and Kwame Gyekye. However, the notion here is that extensive references to such scholarship belong in a conceptual philosophy text rather than in an applied media ethics text that attempts to unify communication principles in a fast-changing technological environment.

So much has been written about that technological environment in recent years. Those interested in how technology is impacting moral principles should read *Interpersonal Divide in the Age of the Machine*, which discusses the ethics of data analytics and artificial intelligence. This latest edition of *Living Media Ethics* takes into account changes that have led to a technology-driven media, particularly social media. Unlike other texts, *Living Media Ethics* does not focus on the technological aspects of advertising, journalism and public relations, but their impact on ethical standards and practices, striving for a unified set of principles that will guide readers through their careers across a multitude of platforms.

NOTES

1 Fair use involves the purpose and character of the use (commercial vs. educational), the nature of the copyrighted work (published vs. unpublished), the amount and substantiality of the portion used in relation to the copyrighted work as a whole (qualitative vs. quantitative), and the effect of the use on the potential market or value of the copyrighted work (adverse vs. no effect). See *The First Amendment Handbook*, 6th ed., (Arlington, Va.: The Reporters Committee for Freedom of the Press, 2003), 91.
2 Laura J. Gurak, *Cyberliteracy: Navigating the Internet with Awareness* (New Haven, Conn.: Yale University Press, 2001), 162.
3 Ibid.
4 Deni Elliott, "Cases and Moral Systems," in *Media Ethics: Issues and Cases*, 5th ed., by Philip Patterson and Lee Wilkins (New York: McGraw-Hill, 2005), 18.
5 Ibid.

CHAPTER 1

Overview: Ethics Across Platforms

ASPIRE TO LIVE MEDIA ETHICS

What does "living media ethics" mean? Ethics are not studied; they are lived through personal and professional experience, with updates to our moral compass made on a regular basis. You will learn methods to do and measure that by completing personal journal exercises at the end of each chapter. Some of those exercises apply to you; others are more communal, engaging your class instructor or group discussion leader. Moreover, those exercises also are designed for you to engage an audience, perhaps via a personal blog or in social or multimedia, showcasing the continued emphasis on ethics in mass communication. You can use interactive technology to discuss and document your ethical journey of discovery and learn by doing as well as by reading.

You may also learn that you cannot "live ethics" without a thorough self-examination revealing your influences and biases. You may have role models or mentors who have shaped your values. Perhaps family or religion played a major role. Or you may admit, reluctantly perhaps, that you have not been sufficiently introspective to heed your moral values, acknowledging that your beliefs have been influenced by an array of celebrities, politicians, icons, trends and fads. We promise you this, though: If you approach *Living Media Ethics* with an open mind, you not only will experience revelations about your character but will be better able to discern the character of others and the ethics that apply across platforms. Nothing is more important than that if you aspire to leadership positions in media. Moreover, you have the option to apply this knowledge personally in the last chapter, which explains how to create professional ethics codes, a process that helps identify who or what shaped your values so that you can decide whether those characteristics are advancing or hindering you in communication careers. Including such a code as a tab in a digital portfolio can play a key role in securing media internships and employment.

Codes of ethics are living documents that should be reviewed and renewed regularly so that you can chart your moral development. Codes also illustrate that moral relativity—the notion that "anything goes" concerning values—does not exist at the typical workplace. When you take a position, you must follow corporate, association or government guidelines. Should you decide to create an ethics code for your digital clipbook or portfolio, you can use it to identify and apply for a position at a company or an organization that shares values similar to yours—a practice that can jump-start your career so that you can work enthusiastically for your readers, viewers or clients. You can also visit this URL for a sampling of codes created by students now in the work force: https://myethicsclass.com/portfolios/

ETHICS ARE NOT IN THE CLOUD

Living Media Ethics cautions journalists and practitioners not to look "out there" on social media or "up there" in the digital cloud for ethical advice, relying on friends, experts or websites for information about moral choices. Admittedly, you may benefit in the short term by crowd-sourcing friends or emailing ethicists who offer meaningful recommendations in person, in print or online; however, the impulse to consult with them "on demand" or impulsively is misguided and usually associated with a culture of instant, electronic communication. With a click of a mouse or touch of a keypad, we have become accustomed to accessing answers, especially about choices. For millennia, however, ethics have been associated with contemplation and introspection, and *Living Media Ethics* reminds us about and helps develop those abilities in each section. While it is true that patience and meditation are difficult to exercise on the job, it is fallacious to assume that they cannot be introduced into our daily routines. The average person looks at screens—mobile phones, computers, television, etc.—nearly 11 hours per day with much of that done while multitasking, including driving. Those who choose to make time for ethical analysis often reap the benefits thereof, assuming leadership positions. According to reporter Sam Amico in the *Houston Chronicle*, ethics and behavior on the job are important in as much as they ensure high morale and teamwork, essential for profitability and business success.[1] Career advancement is no reason to embrace ethics, of course; but it does show that employees who live their ethics are in demand at the workplace. Moreover, surveys show that Millennials, in particular, want to work for employers committed to values and ethics that "have a positive impact on the world."[2]

Ethically speaking, journalists and practitioners using today's high-tech communication tools have more obligation than ever to assess their actions before taking them and to prepare themselves to do so by shutting off computers, smartphones and tablets during "down time" and evaluating their work-related motives and choices. This may be difficult to do initially. After all, journalists and practitioners in their everyday professions are trained to look "out there" for answers, scouring databanks and sources for information, photographs and clients. In developing one's conscience and honing one's consciousness—the twin objectives of *Living Media Ethics*—communicators can perform their tasks with reasonable assurance that they have acted in the best interests of the audience or clientele. Doing so there will be less time wasted in corrections, apologies and revisions to the official record or corporate accounts. That is why ethical employees soon find themselves in leadership positions in industry or non-profit associations. They know how to use technology to gather information and when to put it aside and meet face-to-face with a colleague, source or client. Technology filters and alters our intentions. In dubious situations, when ethics matter most, this can prove troublesome. That is why the medium not only is the message but also the moral, too.

Because technology blends the various media platforms, *Living Media Ethics* must deviate from standard ethics books to assess global media from a moral rather than conventional perspective. Typically, when discussing media, educators focus on the technology, noting how programs and mobile applications incorporate the brands of newspaper, radio, television and more, from augmented to virtual reality. Moral convergence, on the other hand, collapses boundaries between standards and practices of all media and technology as used in advertising, journalism, public relations and other forms of traditional and online mass communication. Additionally, moral convergence applies not only to journalists and practitioners but also the several technology companies that partner with media outlets, agencies and organizations. This is further complicated by non-journalists and amateur practitioners using the same technologies, contributing to the global media environment. According to the Center for Journalism Ethics at the University of Wisconsin-Madison, that "mixed" environment is chaotic "across many media platforms," requiring "a new mixed media ethics – guidelines that apply to amateur and professional whether they blog, tweet, broadcast or write for newspapers."[3] This is the focus of the latest edition of *Living Media Ethics*.

EMPHASIZE MOTIVES OVER MEDIUM

To create a new ethic for the global media environment, the focus must be on motive rather than on medium. Once we establish a motive for our own or others' actions, we can discern how to respond according to philosophical or historical tenets that apply to everyone. This approach is more inclusive, inviting a variety of viewpoints, and also provides you with an opportunity to investigate the notion of moral convergence in a technological world, applying core concepts of ethics to any form of communication regardless of the medium that transmits it. "My first thought as I considered the notion of 'Living Ethics,' and pondered issues associated with moral convergence, is that the very existence of new platforms, new possibilities, is itself a morally uplifting phenomenon," states Geneva Overholser, former editor of *The Des Moines Register* and chair of the Pulitzer Prize Board who has served on the editorial board of *The New York Times* and as ombudsman of *The Washington Post*. Overholser believes that putting the emphasis on moral convergence can help return the news media to their public service role, especially after "years of struggle with the high-profit, low-reinvestment model, which has demoralized so many in the business."

To serve the public in advertising, journalism and public relations, we might acknowledge what motivates us to do so, especially if we aspire to careers in government and politics. We are living in an era of "fake news" in which it becomes increasingly difficult to discern fact from factoid and truth from belief, not only in news reports but on bylines of those reports and the media companies purported to be delivering those reports. To commemorate the "6 Fakest Fake News Stories of 2017," *Vanity Fair* published accounts of false news that ranged from First Lady Melania Trump having a body double to avoid appearing in public with President Donald Trump to a wide range of conspiracy theories.[4] Moreover, the story was filed in advance of President Trump's Fake News Awards criticizing *The New York Times* and network and cable news, along with other national media, for "unrelenting bias, unfair news coverage, and even downright fake news" that overwhelmingly depicted the president in a negative light.[5] Fake news is not news at all. As early as a decade ago, Geneva Overholser noted the demoralization of mainstream media and the moral implications for U.S. democracy. She was especially concerned about the diminishment of international and national news, with fewer reporters at the state legislative level, resulting in "questions not asked (or not pushed tenaciously), investigations not done, young reporters not mentored because veterans have taken buyouts, and on and on."

A moral convergence across platforms can help correct that outcome. This should motivate you to act in your own and your company's best interests. "The thrill of today's ever-richer and more diverse media landscape is that it can lift us out of this woe-is-me landscape into a world where anything is possible," Overholser says. Teens with digital tools can become entrepreneurs. A zealous person can make police-department information easily accessible to countless citizens. Opportunities are boundless, she says. "We can restore vigor to a woebegone media world, that it might better fulfill its ethical obligations."

MAKE PLATFORMS TRUTHFUL AGAIN

There are many pathways to truth. The goal of journalist and practitioner is to perceive the world as it actually exists without allowing basic influences to color perception. Although processes may differ, all traditional or digital media platforms rely on an unassailable fact base. This is apparent when we view objectivity (or "impartiality," if you prefer that term) as a process rather than as an outcome. But there is another concept related to truth across media platforms, and that is whether the audience is perceived geographically (as found on a map) or attitudinally (as found in lifestyle statistics).

Newspapers, local and network broadcast stations and many online news sites often report to a general, or eclectic audience; consequently, their stories or segments must disseminate information the public needs to know. They must do so factually and impartially. Moreover, the factual assertions in those documents must be put into context, as one jigsaw piece must fit into another piece of the mosaic. When facts are reported out of context, they can seem as forced as incompatible puzzle pieces. Ideally, a reader, viewer or listener should be able to verify facts without finding errors, inventions or omissions in reports. A person may be quoted accurately, but that person also may be fabricating, exaggerating or justifying. The most ethical journalism fact-checks the veracity of all quotations, and when discrepancies are found, informs the source and follows up, assembling more information. Facts and images in proper context document for the audience reliable depictions about people, places, issues, situations, motivations, incidents and/or events. When a report lacks sufficient facts and images, the audience may question the truth of news, the motives of the journalist and the credibility of the outlet. Because each newspaper, broadcast or online outlet may cover the same assignment through the same impartial process, stories, segments and posts should vary *only by degrees*. The best report will contain the most information and clearest picture. Certainly, newspapers may be able to delve into topics with more depth than radio or television, but without sound and sight. Radio and television may be able to provide more data appealing to the ear and eye than online journalism, but without links providing more depth or streaming audio and video enhancing that dimension. Ideally, the only limitations will be those that the medium imposes, and in our inter-connected and engaged digital world, lines separating one medium from the next are blurring. But ethical standards are not. Reporters may deliver the news with style, flair or zeal; but the focus on facts ensures that any person of any sex, age group, social class, race or religion, in good or poor health, with or without disability or military or police record, will not feel overlooked, condescended to or otherwise excluded from coverage.

Magazine journalism, advertising and public relations and their digital media equivalents (such as vendor, public service, political and webzine sites) take a different and more subjective route. Their goal is to cover the world as it actually exists *for targeted groups of people*. Employees of magazines and advertising and public relations agencies usually inform a select or narrow audience known as a niche or public; consequently, their stories or campaigns must do two things: disseminate data that targeted groups want or should know and to do so personally and selectively. A magazine writer or practitioner initially must comprehend all of the facts about a person, place, issue, situation, motivation, incident and/or event. This is accomplished in the research phase of an article or ad/PR campaign. From the outset, the writer or practitioner also must understand how a person of any sex, age group, social class, race or religion, in good or poor health, with or without disability or military or police record, will feel about the story or campaign. The platform may target a segment of society but others inevitably will be exposed to the message, especially in digital environments. Assertions in those stories or campaigns can present one side of a truth but that slant still may not intentionally or unintentionally belittle, condescend to or otherwise offend segments of the geographic population.

Some of the most targeted magazine stories and campaigns have been spiked when that situation occurs. A city-guide insert in the student newspaper, the *Iowa State Daily*—prepared on the occasion of the National Special Olympics—bore the unfortunate headline "Ames for Dummies," alluding to the John Wiley popular book series for the college-age demographic.[6] The insert had to be pulled from the newsstands. Nike had to pull an advertising campaign for a trail shoe that purportedly could prevent spinal accidents that could rend users into "a drooling, misshapen non-extreme-trail-running husk" of their former selves, "forced to roam the earth in a motorized wheelchair. ..."[7] The campaign insulted the disabled, and Nike had to apologize. Public relations campaigns can be disastrous, too, when research is insufficient initially. After spending millions of dollars researching a brand name for the merger of two energy companies, to be called "Enteron," writes journalist Kurt Eichenwald, nobody bothered to look up the term in the dictionary: *Enteron*, he writes, was also a word "for the digestive tube running from the mouth to the anus. Given that one of 'Enteron's' major products was natural gas, the choice of names made the new company a laughingstock. 'Enteron' quickly became 'Enron' (now defunct)."[8]

When a magazine writer or practitioner bases an article or a campaign on an insufficient foundation of fact, these types of problems arise—often not because of any ethical shortcoming. Rather, the emphasis on demographics of the target group (age, marital status, income, etc.) and psychographics (hobbies, purchases, affiliations, etc.) becomes overly myopic, as if no one else will be exposed to the imagery or content. As a practical matter, it behooves everyone across platforms to remember that traditional and digital media are immensely powerful and reach segments beyond the targeted group. Here's the thing: In a mobile online environment, gaffes in one platform cross over easily to other platforms. For instance, when the "Ames for Dummies" insert appeared, the blogosphere reported the gaffe worldwide, prompting a wire service and other media to further distribute the story, given the occasion of the National Special Olympics. The student newspaper in a follow-up editorial titled, "Generation Gap Creates Confusion," acknowledged that the Dummies faux pas occurred because the brand meaning wielded more influence than the dictionary meaning. As this and countless other examples illustrate across platforms, journalists and practitioners alike must be aware of and sensitive to the spectra of demographics and lifestyles of *all groups* that may have access to potentially embarrassing or offensive content. This is yet another commonality between the journalist covering a geographic area and the writer or practitioner targeting a niche or public. As we will learn in upcoming chapters, situations that appear to be "unethical" often have little to do with motives and more to do with generational, cultural and other influences along with a lack of continuous learning.

Increasingly in the digital environment, this is the case. Students working for a campus newspaper are still learning their trade, often from mistakes. Professionals, however, lack that excuse. As public relations practitioner Linda DiJohn notes, "A client's worst nightmare is not the enterprising, sharp reporter who gets the story; it's the weak reporter working for a lousy editor or producer who doesn't bother to get it right."

Reporters have to determine and adjust for personal influences and biases that affect how they perceive the world so that assignments mirror reality as closely as possible. That is their primary objective. However, the task of writers and practitioners is a bit more complex. They also must determine and adjust for personal influences and biases to perceive the world the same way *as their targeted reader, consumer, public or client does*. Just like the reporter, writers and practitioners have to seek out information or other viewpoints via research, interviews or consultations to gain a clearer perspective about an assignment or a campaign. They must acknowledge diverse viewpoints so as not to exclude or offend others, inviting criticism and undermining a campaign. Only then can they depict narrow *slices* or *slants* of reality embraced by their target audience and publics.

From a broader perspective, other commonalities exist between journalist and practitioner. Journalism is judged on the fact-base of its product, as discussed earlier. However, because each magazine or agency targets a different niche or public, its objectives often vary. Each will have a different slant on the same truth involving a person, place, issue, situation, motivation, incident and/or event. But when the slants of each magazine or campaign are considered *collectively*, across the social spectra in a land enjoying free press and free speech, once again, the truths should vary *only by degrees*. For every alcohol or tobacco campaign, there exists an anti-alcohol or anti-tobacco counterpart. For every fast food or gambling campaign, there exists a wellness or rehabilitation campaign, and so on. Digital media have multiplied this effect with blogs, book sites and social networks. Moreover, in the course of a career across media platforms, news journalist, magazine writer and practitioner usually wind up covering rainbows of truths associated with myriad geographic areas or targeted niches and publics.

COMMIT TO TRUTH NOW, NOT LATER

It is never too late to commit to the truth as a journalist or practitioner. But it is better to commit to truth while preparing for an internship or job in media than resolving to do better after being fired for bias, fabrication or any number of other ethical missteps to be covered in this text. According to Deanna Sands, long-time managing editor for *The Omaha World-Herald*, the biggest challenge in training the next generation of journalists and practitioners "is instilling passion (for truth) in them. There are too many who lack the time to learn, who lack the skill and who lack the will." They not only need to have a commitment to the truth, Sands says, but also need to be able to research issues and document fact. This involves persistence, and that requires passion to pursue a story or create a campaign based on a foundation of fact at the appropriate juncture in the platform's process.

Journalists should be sensitive to the subjective truths of sources while still maintaining their time-honored role of "obligation" to tell the best factual truth. International public affairs reporter Teresa Krug has worked with some of the world's biggest news outlets, including Al Jazeera English, CBS, Associated Press, *The Guardian*, *Die Zeit*, *The Washington Post* and others. As such, she had to be sensitive to the subjective truths of sources in her global travels. At home, school and work, she followed "the ethical golden rule of listening to your conscience." But the search for truth, especially in diverse cultures, requires you to understand sources "who hold opposing and conflicting positions on an issue or story. Who is right? Are they both right?" Krug has come to believe that truths of sources can be subjective—

> not necessarily false. People experience situations differently, and we form our narratives and truths based upon our own experiences and previous exposures. But it should never take away from the obligation to tell the truth. Ask more questions, ask for supporting documents, be skeptical—even when your gut reaction is to believe everything someone tells you. You'll discover your own bias in the process, and you'll get closer to the truth.

Ziva Branstetter, senior editor for *Reveal* from The Center for Investigative Reporting, who serves on the board of Investigative Reporters and Editors, has practical advice when documenting truth. "Truth in journalism," she says, "is rarely in any one place. You have to triangulate—people lead you to documents and documents lead you to other people and so on. It's like peeling an onion." Branstetter believes journalists should adopt a standard practice of including "a truth box," a fact file containing all the evidence that a reporter has collected for a story or investigation. Title the file, *How do we know it's true?* The file would contain links to raw audio and video of key interviews (except off-the-record conversations) and PDF copies of every document mentioned in the news report in addition to explanation of data methodology, sources, Freedom of Information requests, etc. Then, if the story is likely to be challenged, the reporter can host an online "Ask Me Anything" session to which the public is invited to pose questions about how the news report came to be.

Such transparency is a component of truth in media. And the advice also serves public relations, especially for information officers covering crises or disputing false reporting. Truth and its documentation apply across platforms.

Freelance writer Allison Engel, former political speechwriter and government staff member, notes that journalists and practitioners often change careers. "In my career," Engel says, "I have been a newspaper reporter, magazine editor, news service editor, book author, public relations spokesperson, freelance writer for magazines and newspapers, television producer, visiting professor at a university, and political speechwriter." She recalls her first newspaper job. "When I left that to work for a consumer magazine, I vividly remember my city editor saying that it was a shame that I was leaving journalism. Many on newspaper staffs think they have a lock on the profession, and don't consider non-fiction writing for books or magazines in the same league." As far as truth is concerned, she emphasizes, it is in the same league of verifiable fact.

The notion that factual truth only applies to journalism can be found to this day in the news media and even in a few ethics books. In 1995, when an early edition of *Living Media Ethics* first appeared, the idea of moral principles across platforms distinguished the text from others in the genre. It foresaw the coming technological convergence and hence did not differentiate between "Public Relations Ethics" or "Advertising Ethics" and "Newsroom Ethics." As Peggy H. Cunningham writes in *The Advertising Business: Operations, Creativity, Media Planning, Integrated Communications,*

> Although ethical issues are implicit in most advertising decisions, few advertising textbooks mention the topic. The few texts that do contain some reference to ethical issues usually restrict their discussion to laws regulating advertising or to the codes of ethics governing advertising practice. Although good ethics takes compliance with the law as the base or minimal level of any ethical decision, ethical concerns go far beyond mere compliance with the law.[9]

Living Media Ethics makes this point about advertising, journalism and public relations throughout the text, noting that ethical issues in one field usually are similar in principle to other communication fields.

One commonality involves self-regulation around core principles such as truth, integrity and responsibility. As Margaret Duffy and Esther Thorson write in *Persuasion Ethics Today*,

> Advertising has long been criticized for being intrusive and ubiquitous, invading privacy, using sexual appeals and stereotypes to sell, and targeting vulnerable audiences. While some of these charges are certainly accurate, firms and industry associations make strong efforts to regulate themselves and give members tools for ethical decision making.[10]

Duffy and Thorson also note how conscience plays a role in public relations, as it does in other communication fields, involving "predicting potential problems, anticipating threats to the organization, minimizing surprises, resolving any issues that do arise, and preventing crises."[11]

Pulitzer Prize winner Joe Mahr, an investigative reporter for *The Chicago Tribune*, finds the approach of ethics across platforms refreshing. "As a print journalist, it is easy to get into the false mindset that we have a corner on media ethics" while PR or advertising practitioners are "shills for whoever signs their paychecks. But that mindset, of course, is way too arrogant and simplistic, and—as our customers demand new, better, and streamlined ways of getting their information—we could all benefit from understanding the ethical baselines we collectively should and must follow."

KNOW STANDARDS ACROSS MEDIA

Living Media Ethics argues that moral standards apply across platforms. Those who dispute that idea typically focus on *circumstances* and *settings* but not on *motives* and *values*. Even in top journalism schools, the misperception exists. Professionals hired from industry often are asked to teach as if each class was a newsroom or boardroom. At first blush, this may seem like a good approach for graduates to hit the ground running; however, they only have learned the conventional standards that apply in their own industry. News graduates do not understand public relations ethics, and PR grads do not understand advertising practices, and vice versa. Each platform, then, not only is uninformed about how one industry's ethics affect another's in the global media environment, none can apply philosophy or history to the situation to help resolve or even at times *understand* crises.

This phenomenon is at the heart of a 2017 study published in the *Journal of Media Ethics*. Marlene S. Neill noted how many public relations graduates were not getting ethical training on the job, prompting her to look at what they had learned about ethics during college. While ethics may have been infused throughout the PR curriculum, the best option for the workplace involves a stand-alone ethics class that covers all manner of media. Her study showed when ethics is offered as a stand-alone course, other codes of ethics beyond those of the Public Relations

Society of America are covered, along with philosophical theories, decision-making models, the effect of organizational culture and values, and global ethical perspectives.[12]

Several media ethics books still in print segment ethics according to platforms and typically end up elevating print and broadcast news over public relations and advertising. Consider that for a moment. Isn't it true that a reporter who plagiarizes a story is quite similar morally to a marketer who pilfers media-buying research? Newsrooms differ from agencies, to be sure, as do the assignments of reporters and marketers; but the motives that afflict ethically deficient employees—taking shortcuts, say, for personal or professional reward—causes them to yield to *temptation*, because they lacked the counteracting value of *honesty* in their work ethic. *Living Media Ethics* relies on interviews and case studies to document commonalities in sound decision-making under the following unifying theory: *While circumstances of ethical issues may vary, the moral processes addressing them are usually the same.*

Living Media Ethics hopes to provide that moral lens. In dealing with standards and values across media platforms, the intent here not only is to identify core principles that apply to legacy and digital media but also to illustrate how moral principles endure in static or interactive media environments.

To fully appreciate this, we might consider recent media history. Between 1995 and 2005, the specter of "new media convergence" confused the best ethical minds because standards and practices in one media, such as newspapers, no longer sufficed if those print journalists were shooting video and blogging. Advertising began to go digital, too, with local merchants creating their own websites and gradually seeing they could tout their own products and services without necessarily buying space in newspapers and magazines and airtime in television and radio. Those broadcast outlets also had websites, and suddenly those journalists were being asked to put down their cameras and microphones and start writing, blogging and interacting on social media. Public relations practitioners were being asked to create campaigns using print, magazine, video, internet and social media, too. As you can see, moral boxes of any one medium no longer apply because the practitioner, competitor and target audience are all multitasking across the same platforms. In 2003, in one of the first books on moral convergence, Anne Dunn wrote this in *Remote Control: New Media, New Ethics*:

> Technological change of a kind by now familiar, change that can be subsumed under the title of "digital convergence," has fragmented advertising's traditional markets, right down to the single consumer. Advertisers cannot assume people will be assembled in the same place, in front of one of four or five TV channels from around six o'clock each evening, positioned to receive a mass advertising message.[13]

Dunn, at the time, was speaking about "traditional markets" as identified by legacy media whose audience and clientele not only were defined by platform but also by population.

In much of the last century, when mass communication reached its height, the audience in the United States and much of Europe was generally homogeneous. That is no longer the case. According to data trends compiled by the Pew Research Center, the United States will not have an ethnic majority by the year 2055. The percentage of Caucasians is predicted to fall to about 46 percent, down from more than 80 percent in 1955.[14] The Center also reported steep declines in two-parent households and a sharp increase of women in the workforce, with more than 40 percent of mothers as primary breadwinner as of 2011. These demographic changes began to affect media content during the height of the transition to internet and multiple platforms. Advertisers no longer had well-defined target audiences "as small or as specific as we may have had in a different era when the market was primarily Caucasian," says Connie Frazier, executive vice president at the American Advertising Federation. "Now we have multiculturalism." The easily defined consumer market in the 1960s, for instance, now includes a mix of Caucasian, African American, Hispanic and Asian, Frazier says, requiring the journalists and practitioners to think more critically and inclusively about its ethical obligations toward audience.

Carolyn Kitch, a former editor for *Good Housekeeping* and now journalism educator at Temple University, noted years ago that legacy media would struggle initially to adapt to changing demographics. In a 2005 interview, she stated that mainstream media was losing a "sense of who the audiences are" as well as thinking critically about how to identify a diverse public. Worse, the digital newsroom at first kept reporters glued to their workstations rather than interacting interpersonally in their changing communities. That technological tendency may be more mobile in today's digital climate, but journalists and practitioners in community or on assignment are apt to be looking at smartphones rather than people.

Stephen Berry, Pulitzer Prize-winning investigative reporter and former journalism professor at the University of Iowa, remembers covering politics in Greensboro, North Carolina. Sometimes he would wander up the halls of City Hall "and pop into a Parks and Recreation meeting or a Housing Commission meeting" to see who was there, "and out of that came some of my early investigative stories. You have to be on the beat so that when sources see your face they remember your name." That holds true especially today when too many journalists and practitioners rely on email and text rather than on face-to-face meetings, which build strong interpersonal relationships. Building networks is vital in journalism, advertising and public relations. Trust is built on such ethical values as honesty, credibility, responsibility, fairness, compassion and discretion— topics to be addressed in upcoming chapters—which also transcend media platforms.

MORAL LITERACY ENHANCES CREDIBILITY

The distinguished ethicist, Clifford G. Christians, believes

> the challenge for media practitioners is the moral life as a whole: no harm to innocents, truth-telling, reparations for wrong actions, beneficence, gratitude, honoring contacts, human dignity. Moral literacy understands moral behavior in interactive terms, with reporters, advertising executives, script writers and producers and public relations practitioners operating in the same arena as citizen themselves.[15]

Living Media Ethics is grounded in that statement by Christians. "Understanding moral behavior in interactive terms" is the only way that media across platforms can maintain credibility with audience and clientele, especially when we are apt to communicate electronically rather than interpersonally. Each technological invention has displaced journalists and practitioners from the communities and clients that they are obligated to serve. As mass media gravitate more toward technology and away geographically from constituents, we might remember the following maxim by eminent journalist Hodding Carter III, former chief executive officer of the Knight Foundation: "The public is not an outsider. The public is the point of the enterprise."[16]

At the heart of moral convergence are two aspects of ethics:

- **Conscience:** An intuitive knowledge of *right and wrong*, involving how we choose to live among and view others in a diverse community. By developing this sixth sense through analysis of motives, choices and consequences, we will know intuitively what to do and avoid and when and how to act under the pressure of daily deadlines and assignments.
- **Consciousness:** A sense of *awareness*, involving how our interactions affect or influence others and ourselves in diverse community. By expanding our awareness, we can analyze outcomes of past actions and foresee consequences of potential ones before taking them, minimizing harm to others.

While consciousness is generally acknowledged to exist, philosophers like John Searle affirm that it does and matters enormously in deciphering our actions and intentions. "Consciousness is sometimes said to be hard to define," Searle admits, but nevertheless plays a key role in our states of being, a "feeling or sentience or awareness" of our world and our place in it.[17] If consciousness is difficult to define, so too is the conscience and its relationship to the human condition. Contemporary philosophy routinely includes conscience under the same umbrella of awareness as consciousness, sometimes even using the terms synonymously without associating them with dual aspects of the human condition. As you will learn throughout the text, we are creatures of duality with consciousness and conscience working conflictedly or harmoniously when dealing with issues involving morality.[18]

At the heart of this text is a full understanding of the ethical concept of conscience. Martin van Creveld, professor emeritus at the Hebrew University of Jerusalem, notes the Latin term for science is *conscientia*, or "knowledge with oneself," that provides a glimpse into a deeper self that very well may be a unifying trait of our species, compelling us to behave in certain ways deemed to be moral. When we opt for evil, rather than rightness, the conscience "makes us experience guilt, remorse and regret. It keeps us awake at night, gnaws at us and gives us no rest. Unless the act has been repented and/or atoned for, it can result in severe psychological problems."[19]

Earlier editions of this text advised readers to feel or intuit morality, especially that gnawing feeling, so that they can live up to the standards of the conscience, primarily by interpreting its sensations when we do or fail to do the right thing. Sir Richard Rustom Kharsedji Sorabji, emeritus professor of philosophy at King's College London, has written that 19th-century philosophers dubbed conscience as a feeling that can cause a painful sensation when we violate our own or social norms. "Conscience is *motivating* because it is a *value* belief about what was or would be wrong for oneself," he writes. "It can therefore cause both sentiments of approval or disapproval and painful or comforting sensations."[20] Paul Strohm, humanities professor at Columbia University, echoes that sentiment, believing the language of the conscience is "its capacity to cajole, to wound, to mark or stain ... harassing the bad and upholding the good, and visiting pain, terror, pallor, and trepidation upon those who ignore its strictures."[21]

One of the best general descriptions of conscience appears in Timothy Sandefur's *The Conscience of the Constitution*, in which he states:

> Whether we imagine it as a still, small voice, or Jiminy Cricket from Disney's *Pinocchio*, conscience is a quality within us that seems to stand outside our more mundane thoughts to guide our actions. It lies at the boundary between is and ought: it understands reasons and it gives reasons. It is the hallmark of a reliable person—or nation.[22]

The observation that conscience "understands reasons" is another way of stating that it communicates with consciousness, or awareness of our actions. The conscience, as we shall learn, is a powerful individual tool not only in learning to live our ethics but as a general guide for social reform. Frederick Douglass, the 19th-century icon of such reform as abolitionist, orator and statesman, discusses the collective conscience of society in another outstanding citation of this allusive concept:

> Conscience is, to the individual soul, and to society, what the law of gravitation is to the universe. It holds society together; it is the basis of all trust and confidence; it is the pillar of all moral rectitude. Without

it, suspicion would take the place of trust; vice would be more than a match for virtue; men would prey upon each other, like the wild beasts of the desert; and earth would become a *hell*.[23]

The great theologian, Dietrich Bonhoeffer, writes eloquently in his book, *Ethics*, about the power of the conscience. Bonhoeffer, who was hanged by the Nazis shortly before the end of World War II, acted on his conscience in opposing Adolph Hitler's oppressive regime. He believed that the true conscience holds integrity higher than any other value. That is why, Bonhoeffer says, ethical people do not act against their consciences. "Conscience," he writes,

> comes from a depth which lies beyond a man's own will and his own reason and it makes itself heard as the call of human existence to unity with itself. Conscience comes as an indictment of the loss of this unity and as a warning against the loss of one's self. Primarily it is a particular mode of being. It protests against a doing which imperils the unity of this being with itself.[24]

When one lives ethics, as Bonhoeffer did, a person develops a continuing dialogue with the conscience. That is an interactivity that truly matters in our pursuit of moral convergence in this book. The conscience informs us on social and political matters of a grand and tragic scale, as it did in Bonhoeffer's life; but conscience also informs us on a much smaller scale every day at the workplace. It interacts with us, as does consciousness—the voice we typically hear in our heads. Conscience speaks more quietly as intuitive feeling. "What does my conscience say?" write authors Charles Warner and Joseph Buchman in *Media Selling: Broadcast, Cable, Print, and Interactive*.

> Salespeople should ask themselves, "How would I feel if what I am doing appeared in the *Wall Street Journal* or the *New York Times*?" ... A company's and a salesperson's most valuable assets are their reputations and their relationships with their customers. Reputations and relationships are built by consistently doing ethics checks on the way they do business, by taking a long-term view and not doing anything that would put them in jeopardy, even 100 years from today.[25]

Again in this citation, much like the one from Bonhoeffer, we see the focus on integrity and interactive dialogue with the conscience—even in examples as divergent as ones grounded in theology and business.

Each chapter in the book pivots on conscience and consciousness, portals of emotional and rational intelligence through which we learn to feel values rather than merely explicate them. That defines moral literacy. If we take time to analyze how temptation or manipulation feels physically, for example, we will intuit similar scenarios on the job without overly assessing situations or rationalizing decisions. We can act on the spot, in a blink, as it were. This ability is described at length in Malcolm Gladwell's *Blink: The Power of Thinking Without Thinking*. Gladwell discusses the "adaptive unconscious," which he calls our *internal* computer and which processes information rapidly so that we can function as human beings in complex scenarios. This would include ethical decision-making at the workplace. Gladwell writes,

> The only way that human beings could ever have survived as a species for as long as we have is that we've developed another kind of decision making apparatus that's capable of making very quick judgments based on very little information.[26]

Consider how we assess people and issues instantaneously during our everyday routines. We avoid sales pitches that sound too good to be true and people who sound too solicitous to be genuine. We scoff at emails offering us a share of million-dollar inheritances and question strangers at an office party who ask us about our astrological signs. We get gut feelings and seem to act on instinct. But often, even when we do not realize it consciously, we are merely responding to past experience when we signed a deceptive contract or encountered a bad contact. When confronted with similar instances in dissimilar circumstances, our emotional stimuli flood the conscience. We may wonder why we feel constriction rather than relief while purchasing expensive cameras online at huge discounts, following prescribed low-bid guidelines at work. But the twinge in the gut is worth heeding, for it might cause us to focus on the lack of a security certificate on the website URL that asks for credit card information. That is the lesson of *Blink*. Granted, some feelings and snap judgments are false, misleading or even biased. Gladwell's book addresses these phenomena, too, and those are associated with bias and exclusion, indicating that the conscience is incommunicado with consciousness. The point is, journalists and practitioners must internalize their ethics or risk lapses on the job and be held accountable for their actions.

Jessie Opoien, political reporter for the *Capital Times* in Madison, Wisconsin, relies on her conscience in everyday decision-making. "One of the most basic rules I have always applied to my job, whether it's a question of a potential conflict of interest or whether I should tweet a particular sentiment, is this: If you're wondering whether you should do it, you probably shouldn't," she says. "Whether you call it a gut feeling or your conscience, in my experience, it's rarely wrong. If I'm invited to an event that could create an appearance of conflict of interest, and I find myself wondering about it—I don't go. If I have an idea for a funny tweet but I wonder if it crosses an ethical line—I don't tweet it."

A basic tenet of ethical decision-making is listening to the conscience and developing a strong value system to affirm it. That is also the opinion of Howard Buford, founder of the New York City advertising agency,

Prime Access, and currently CEO of Quorum Consulting. Buford states: "It's important to have a pre-thought-out or internalized system of values, basically because of the deadlines and pressure involved in day-to-day business." Those daily demands require us to act quickly and ethically. Employees rarely commit ethical lapses when the conscience works harmoniously with consciousness, providing us with useful information upon which we can foresee outcomes and act accordingly. In this sense, living one's ethics is about your development as a person as much as a journalist or practitioner. As educator and writer Christina Hoff Sommers observes,

> Once the student becomes engaged with the problem of what kind of person to be, and how to *become* that kind of person, the problems of ethics become concrete and practical and, for many a student, moral development is thereafter looked on as a natural and even inescapable undertaking.[27]

Hers is an example of how one "lives ethics," a glimpse into concepts that upcoming chapters will probe in depth. Journalists and practitioners who embrace professional values also are able to:

- **Distinguish between good and bad**, outcomes over which we have little control, versus right and wrong, choices over which we have much control.
- **Intuit ethical principles** to guide us in complex situations, knowing that those principles not only apply across platforms but also across cultures.
- **Foresee short-term vs. long-term consequences** before making choices.
- **Accept responsibilities for their choices**, no matter if the outcome is good or bad.
- **See the world as it actually is** rather than through personal filters of self-interest, ego or fear.
- **Develop conscience and consciousness** so that they work as effortlessly as hand–eye coordination, informing each other so we make ethical choices.
- **Be sensitive to others' viewpoints** and their own emotions so that they can learn from others and become more aware of motives, including their own.
- **Apply only as much power as needed** to resolve a challenge without creating greater problems or harm to innocent others.

In sum, *Living Media Ethics* helps build an ethical foundation based on mindfulness in diverse community and then tests and enhances that foundation. The work encourages readers to explore and analyze their own values and that of the various media, with the ultimate objective of aligning personal values with those of an organization, so that readers can practice their work ethic with commitment and zeal in a supportive environment. This is an inclusive book because media ethics are not defined by diploma, job title or platform but by work ethic and personal standards. In today's fast-paced competitive world, we can assume that rivals for media jobs will have impressive portfolios. But they may not possess qualities that will help them keep *and* enjoy their jobs: strong professional values.

"MEDIA LITERACY: MOTIVE VS. MOTIVATION"
Personal Journal Exercise
PART I

Media literacy relies on reliable sources of information, deep reading and additional research. This exercise invites you to explore news sites with a focus on concepts that dominate news and human-interest coverage: "motive" and "motivation."

"Motive," defined, involves *a reason for doing, thinking or communicating something*. Motives are difficult to discern in others because we can only speculate about their state of mind. Sometimes even our own motives are allusive. The term "motivation" or its verb "motivate" often are synonymous with "motive," as in: "What motivates a person to say, think or communication something?" However, the term "motivation" and its verb forms also have another meaning, defined by the online *Business Dictionary*:

> Internal and external factors that stimulate desire and energy in people to be continually interested and committed to a job, role or subject, or to make an effort to attain a goal. Motivation results from the interaction of both conscious and unconscious factors such as the (1) intensity of desire or need, (2) incentive or reward value of the goal, and (3) expectations of the individual and of his or her peers. These factors are the reasons one has for behaving a certain way. An example is a student that spends extra time studying for a test because he or she wants a better grade in the class.[28]

Detecting "motive" and "motivation" is part of media literacy. Both involve ethical concepts. "Motive" often is associated with truth, falsehood, manipulation, temptation, bias and other tenets driving the news. Sometimes motives are easy to discern. For instance, sources cited in political news may affirm party affiliation, or loyalty, even in the wake of malfeasance. Conversely, many human-interest stories, or profiles, focus on people "motivated" to achieve—often against all odds—in sports, business, education, fine arts or medical sciences. Those motivations may be uplifting, involving work ethic, generosity, integrity, faith, responsibility, mentors or justice. The goal again is to read deeply.

Exercise

1. Visit your favorite site for news and choose three major headline stories that occurred in the past month. You'll be searching for "motive."
2. Note the headline, author, date, publication/website and write a paragraph of background concerning the content of the story.
3. Identify by name and title, if appropriate, the main source(s) in the story and select a quotation or two that may indicate a motive.

Example

News Article: "Mark Zuckerberg disavows controversial Facebook memo," by Ivana Kottasová, March 30, 2018, CNN, http://money.cnn.com/2018/03/30/technology/facebook-zuckerberg-ugly-memo/index.html.

Background: Facebook CEO Mark Zuckerberg renounces a memo distributed internally by senior company executive Andrew Bosworth who argued in 2016 that growth was more important than users being harmed by content on social media. Excerpt from memo: "Maybe it costs a life by exposing someone to bullies. Maybe someone dies in a terrorist attack coordinated on our tools. And still we connect people."

Sources Cited in Story:
Mark Zuckerberg: "This was one that most people at Facebook including myself disagreed with strongly. We've never believed the ends justify the means. We recognize that connecting people isn't enough by itself."
Andrew Bosworth: "The purpose of this post, like many others I have written internally, was to bring to the surface issues I felt deserved more discussion with the broader company. Having a debate around hard topics like these is a critical part of our process."

Suspected Motive, Zuckerberg: Damage control, especially since Facebook at the time was under pressure for a security breach via Cambridge Analytica whose data was used in the 2016 presidential campaign.

Suspected Motive, Bosworth: Justification, or an excuse for his statement to mitigate the impact on him personally within the company.

Now do the same exercise with human-interest profile stories.

1. Visit reputable online sites for human-interest or feature stories and choose three major headline stories that occurred in the past month. You'll be searching for "motivation."
2. Note the headline, author, date, publication/website and write a paragraph of background concerning the content of the story.
3. Identify by name and title, if appropriate, the main source(s) in the story and select a quotation or two that may indicate a motive.

Example

Profile: "NHL stunner: A 36-year-old accountant who has never played pro stars in Blackhawks win" by Allyson Chiu, *The Washington Post*, March 30, 2018. www.washingtonpost.com/news/morning-mix/wp/2018/03/30/nhl-stunner-a-36-year-old-accountant-whos-never-played-pro-stars-in-blackhawks-win/

Background: Scott Foster, Blackhawks' emergency goalie and accountant who never played in the NHL, is called into action against the Winnipeg Jets, stopping seven shots on goal.

Source Cited in Profile:
Scott Foster: "Who would have thought? You just keep grinding away in men's league, and eventually you get your shot."

Suspected Motivation: Work ethic.

Take care to use the above format in your news and profile outlines because you will hand those in to your instructor or group leader for the "Communal Journal Exercise."

PART II

Exercise

1. Expand on your suspicions about "motive" and "motivation" by researching your topics and sources, trying for at least three other accounts of the same news item, source or profile chosen in Part I. List the links for those other versions and note any affirmations or discrepancies from facts in your summarized articles. Other accounts may change your opinion about "motive" or "motivation." That is perfectly fine. Perhaps you harbor a bias for or against a source or topic. Once again, just acknowledge that. If you believe a particular news site has a bias, note that as well. You may find that additional research alters your initial viewpoint entirely. That is all right, too.

2. After researching your items, create a 500-word journal entry or blog post or a short podcast or multimedia presentation about media literacy based on your findings. Whenever possible, emphasize "motive" and "motivation" as constructs of media ethics as noted earlier in this chapter.

Communal Journal Exercise

1. If you are the instructor or discussion leader, collect news and feature summaries (Part I exercise earlier) from the class or group members. Analyze what was said about motive and motivation in each account. Do you agree with observations? Why? Why not? Be a role model for media literacy by citing additional sources or

facts to affirm or challenge observations. The lesson here is to test suspicions about "motive" and "motivation" via research and to expound on any ethical tenets associated with observations.

2. After the research phase, schedule a class or group discussion. By now members of the class or group will have done more research in Part II of the "Personal Journal Exercise." Without naming the person who handed in the summary assignments, show how your research and deep reading enhanced literacy with a focus on media ethics. Ask the class or group to add to the discussion about what they learned concerning "motive," "motivation," deep reading and research.

NOTES

1 Sam Amico, "Workplace Ethics and Behavior," *Houston Chronicle*, February 1, 2018, http://smallbusiness.chron.com/workplace-ethics-behavior-5239.html

2 Matthew Jenkin, "Millennials Want to Work for Employers Committed to Values and Ethics," *The Guardian*, May 5, 2015, www.theguardian.com/sustainable-business/2015/may/05/millennials-employment-employers-values-ethics-jobs

3 Stephen J.A. Ward, "Digital Media Ethics," Center for Journalism Ethics, no date, https://ethics.journalism.wisc.edu/resources/digital-media-ethics/

4 Maya Kosoff, "The 6 Fakest Fake News Stories of 2017," *Vanity Fair*, January 17, 2017, www.vanityfair.com/news/2018/01/the-6-fakest-fake-news-stories-of-2017

5 See "The Highly-Anticipated 2017 Fake News Awards," Team GOP Media, January 17, 2018, https://gop.com/the-highly-anticipated-2017-fake-news-awards/

6 Lisa Rossi, "ISU to Remove Papers with 'Dummies' Headline," *Des Moines Register*, June 30, 2006, www.dmregister.com/apps/pbcs.dll/article?AID=/20060630/NEWS/60630017/1001

7 For text of advertisement, see "The Lowest Moments in Advertising," *Adweek*, June 9, 2003, www.adweek.com/aw/magazine/article_display.jsp?vnu_content_id=1909165. For Nike apology, see "Nike Rescinds Advertisement, Apologizes to Disabled People" by Anne Grimes, *The Wall Street Journal*, October 26, 2000, www.ucp.org/ucp_generaldoc.cfm/1/9/10438/10438-10438/1067

8 Kurt Eichenwald, *Conspiracy of Fools: A True Story* (New York: Broadway Books, 2005), 33–34.

9 Peggy H. Cunningham, "Ethics of Advertising: Oxymoron or Good Business Practice?" in *The Advertising Business: Operations, Creativity, Media Planning, Integrated Communications*, ed. John Philip Jones (Thousand Oaks, Calif.: Sage, 1999), 500.

10 Margaret Duffy and Esther Thorson, *Persuasion Ethics Today* (New York: Routledge, 2016), 44.

11 Ibid., 49–50.

12 Malene S. Neill, "Ethics Education in Public Relations: Differences Between Stand-Alone Ethics Courses and an Integrated Approach," *Journal of Media Ethics*, 2017, Vol. 32, No. 2, 118–31.

13 Anne Dunn, "Ethics Impossible? Advertising and the Infomercial," in *Remote Control: New Media, New Ethics*, eds. Catharine Lumby and Elspeth Probyn (Cambridge: Cambridge University Press, 2003), 137.

14 D'Vera Cohn and Andrea Caumont, "10 Demographic Trends that are Shaping the U.S. and World," Pew Research Center, March 31, 2016, www.pewresearch.org/fact-tank/2016/03/31/10-demographic-trends-that-are-shaping-the-u-s-and-the-world/

15 Clifford G. Christians, "The Media and Moral Literacy," *Ethical Space: The International Journal of Communication Ethics*, Vol. 1, No. 1, 2003, 18.

16 Hodding Carter III, Ohio University speech, May 3, 2002.

17 John R. Searle, *Seeing Things as They Are: A Theory of Perception* (New York: Oxford University Press, 2015), 46.

18 Michael Bugeja won the Clifford G. Christians Award for research in media ethics twice, in 2005 for *Interpersonal Divide: The Search for Community in a Technological Age* and in 2008 for the previous edition of *Living Media Ethics*.

19 Martin van Creveld, *Conscience: A Biography* (London: Reaktion Books, 2015), 7.

20 Richard Sorabji, *Moral Conscience Through the Ages* (Chicago, Ill.: University of Chicago Press, 2014), 217.

21 Paul Strohm, *Conscience: A Very Short Introduction* (New York: Oxford University Press, 2011), 7.

22 Timothy Sandefur, *The Conscience of the Constitution: The Declaration of Independence and the Right to Liberty* (Washington, D.C.: Cato Institute, 2015), 157.

23 Frederick Douglass, "Slavery and the Slave Power," speech, December 1, 1850, Douglass Papers, ser. I, 2: 255–56.

24 Dietrich Bonhoeffer, *Ethics* (New York: Touchstone, 1995), 238.

25 Charles Warner and Joseph Buchman, *Media Selling: Broadcast, Cable, Print, and Interactive* (Ames, Iowa: Iowa State Press, 2004), 37.

26 Malcolm Gladwell, *Blink: The Power of Thinking Without Thinking* (New York: Little, Brown; 2005), 11–12.

27 Christina Hoff Sommers, "Teaching the Virtues," *The Chicago Tribune Magazine* reprint, September 12, 1993, 16.

28 "Motivation," Business Dictionary, no date, www.businessdictionary.com/definition/motivation.html.

PART I

Building Your Ethical Base

In the next three chapters you will identify basic influences affecting your perception and values. You will become better acquainted with the conscience and consciousness and how they work at odds or harmoniously with each other as part of the human condition. You will acknowledge who has influenced your perception so that you can adjust your viewpoint to make independent, ethical choices. In doing so you will also deepen your knowledge of right and wrong, taking more responsibility for your actions. You will analyze various types of "truths"—facts to archetypes— and encounter ethical principles that apply across media platforms. Each chapter contains information from journalists, practitioners and media scholars, sharpening your awareness and deepening your intuition, laying the foundation for a solid value system.

CHAPTER 2

Influence: Who Shaped Your Values?

DEVELOP ETHICAL VALUES

The word "value" is neutral not moral. A person's values constitute the mosaic of how a person chooses to conduct his or her affairs in community with others. For instance, greed (i.e. the pursuit of money at the expense of others) can influence behavior. So can honesty. Loyalty is a neutral value; you can swear it to a violent gang or to a life partner. *Ethical* values, however, are somewhat different. Sometimes they are called "principles" because they apply across many, if not all, cultures. For instance, truth, responsibility and fairness might be considered universal principles. There is some philosophical debate, to be sure, about whether universal principles exist. John Locke (1632–1704), the Englishman otherwise known as America's philosopher, questioned the limits of human understanding, especially the universality of principles etched on the human psyche, and made a strong case, appropriate for his time, on the power of reason. Other philosophers also questioned the existence of universal principles, especially ones associated with truth. There is the "subjective truth" of romanticism, "scientific truth" of positivism, "progressive truth" of modernism, and "relative truths" of post-modernism, and so forth. Nonetheless, some philosophers, including Immanuel Kant (1724 1804), based their life's work on the universality of principles. To argue whether such principles exist is an exercise in rhetoric, which *Living Media Ethics* aspires to avoid by keeping the focus on moral convergence across platforms. Thus, if you disagree with the term "principle," substitute the term "ethical value" so that you can distinguish neutral values like "loyalty" from moral ones like "responsibility."

Ethical values are personal as well as universal and so are associated in part with our intuitive emotions, or conscience, and our external awareness, or consciousness. As we will discover throughout the text, these dual aspects of the human condition seem at odds with each other philosophically. Consciousness tells us we come into the world alone and leave it alone. Conscience tells us what is in me is in you. You can interpret both messages in a spiritual or evolutionary manner, making the case that humanity embraces religion in the name of deities or social cooperation in the name of natural selection. That is not the point here, of course. This is: Sometimes we favor conscience over consciousness or vice versa and feel out of balance. Individuals who rely only on consciousness often lack empathy, a topic to be covered later in this book. They tend to overlook how their actions affect others. Individuals who rely solely on conscience without regard to consciousness often enable others at their own expense. Most of us, however, vacillate between those two polarities without realizing the empowerment of harmonizing them, the goal of *Living Media Ethics* and the key to personal and professional success.

When conscience informs consciousness, and vice versa, we feel whole, balanced, able to deal effectively with any challenge. Consciousness gives us a glimpse into the short-, middle- and long-term consequences of our actions before we take them. Conscience assesses the impact of actions on others so that we develop a sixth sense of right and wrong when new encounters arise. Both can work in tandem rather than independently and help us counter pressure from outside forces, such as "competition" or "profit margin." Outside forces are neither moral nor immoral; they simply exist as a natural part of the world or the workplace. What counts is how we respond to them. For example, there is nothing unethical about competition or profit—especially in media and communication disciplines; competition challenges us to perform at our peak and profit can give us a reason to invest time and energy in our work. But participation in competition and pursuit of profit can undermine other aspects of our lives at home, school and work and cause unintended conflicts. We will encounter myriad examples of that in the chapters ahead. Thus, the focus of *Living Media Ethics* is on the *pressure* that outside forces exert on our inner lives, tempting us to take ethical shortcuts or resist them, undermining or enhancing our values.

SHORTCUTS COMPROMISE ETHICS

The pressures on us and our values, personal and professional, have increased substantially in the digital age since the mid-1990s, when technology first began to permeate our homes, schools and workplaces. Now, in an age of data analytics and augmented and artificial reality, with smartphones accessing and producing all manner of media at all hours anywhere on the globe, that pressure has intensified. Never before in media history have communication devices been as powerful, portable and seductive.[1] Accordingly, lines between home, school and work have blurred to such extent that relationships in all of those places compete for our time and attention, causing added stress that often undermines workplace goals and priorities.

The last edition of *Living Media Ethics* cited magazine editor Jill Andre-sky Fraser, author of *White-Collar Sweatshop: The Deterioration of Work and Its Rewards in Corporate America*, who wrote this in 2001:

> The overwork, stress, and insecurity of today's workplaces has been exacerbated, not relieved, by the proliferation of high-tech equipment— laptop computers, cell phones, electronic desk calendars, beepers, portable fax machines, Palm Pilots, and more—that help people try to keep up with growing workloads while also making it impossible for them to fully escape their jobs and relax. New technologies, meanwhile, facilitate intrusive efforts by employers to monitor everything from their staffers' comings and goings to computerized keystrokes and mouse tapes, e-mails sent and received, and personal productivity on a weekly, daily, or even hour-by-hour basis.[2]

Fraser's observation years ago has been exacerbated by the ubiquitous algorithms of data analytics, monitoring every keystroke and emotion of workers in high-tech environments. According to a 2017 BBC report, "Advances in technology and a hunger for data have now created a market for devices that can measure workers' movements, fitness and even sleep – all in the name of productivity," deploying such devices that track "everything from movements and interactions around the office, to lengths of conversations, and even voice tone."[3] No doubt these invasive technologies cause stress during working, waking and even non-waking hours; but the biggest stressor for modern-day employees is the fear of losing jobs to machines. That fear alone can compromise values, prompting us to take ethical shortcuts. A recent workplace report found that 52 percent of U.S. employees suffer from stress, with six of ten feeling stressed all or most of the time, with the highest levels attributed to Millennials who fear "losing their jobs to new technology or artificial intelligence (43 percent)."[4]

The blurring of interpersonal boundaries, the added workload and the competing relationships—including ones now from machines as well as from people—have combined to cause stress, or internally felt pressure. That is why more than ever moral shortcuts like cheating or lying seem so attractive in the short term. They can fulfill our ambitions quicker, helping us arrive at a destination (meeting a deadline, say) or attain a goal (plagiarizing to complete an assignment) while others struggle to play by the rules or obey the laws. One study indicates that Millennials, in particular, are prone to knowingly violating ethics, often because they do not want to disappoint their supervisors. The study, done by the insurance company Aflac, showed that one in four employees were asked to perform unethically with 47 percent of Millennials in that group most prone to compromise values.[5] When we take ethical shortcuts, circumventing our personal and/or professional standards, we might experience an immediate sense of relief. However, in a little while, we will feel a build-up of another type of pressure as we shore up lies to cover our tracks or otherwise deceive people about our deeds. Pressure impacts conscience, triggering consciousness to go into overdrive to cover our deceptive tracks. The more out of sync we feel, the greater the consequences of our actions on our psyche and others.

It bears repeating: *Ethical shortcuts compromise values.* They make us less honest or fair to others than we really are inside or want to be—precisely why living an immoral life is complicated and self-defeating. First, we start hiding aspects of our true selves, and soon we start hiding evidence of our actions. Because our actions and interactions occur in physical as well as virtual environments, it is difficult to keep our lies and ethical transgressions from being discovered by others. If we persist, our values metamorphose from fairness to falsehood or from honesty to deceit, allowing outside forces—those daily pressures exacerbated by technology—to dominate or control our lives. In the long run, as you might imagine, a journalist or practitioner who takes ethical shortcuts encounters more pressure and expends more energy at greater risk than his or her ethical counterpart. Problem is, you might not be able to imagine this *without a value system.*

ETHICS CAN BE TAUGHT

When it comes to ethics, especially on social media, the tendency is to pass judgment about the actions of others, focusing on topical issues, such as presidential politics, climate change or adequate health care. While those are important in case studies and analyses, too often we divide up sides— pro and con—and argue according to our pre-existing beliefs instead of investigating the facts and values *behind* such beliefs. Who or what shaped them, for example? Even when social debates engage us, such as political positions on pro-life vs. pro-choice, usually nobody changes his or her stance. Why? *Living Media Ethics* explores such questions, putting the focus on you so that you examine your existing beliefs as impartially as possible. "Ethics requires us to go beyond our own personal point of view to a standpoint like that of the impartial spectator who takes a universal point of view," writes ethicist Peter Singer who adds:

> Given this conception of ethics, "Why should I act morally?" is a question that may properly be asked by anyone wondering whether to act only on grounds that would be acceptable from this universal point of view. It is, after all, possible to act—and some people do act—without thinking of anything except one's own interests. The question asks for reasons for going beyond this personal basis of action and acting only on judgments one is prepared to prescribe universally.[6]

Singer's concept of universality involves an observation and a challenge: Why should people develop values not exclusively associated with their own self interests? The observation seems to be that such a singular focus does not stand the test of time in community with others or the situations that we may encounter collectively throughout our lifetimes. Rules in society as well as in education, industry, science, arts, humanities, health and public service emphasize the well-being of the communal entity—not the individual. Blatant self-interest will be called out and, in many cases, prohibited. Okay then: Is it possible to develop broader, communal values that remain uncompromisingly strong no matter how much pressure a person is under to violate them? That challenge may seem difficult, if not impossible, to achieve or even conceive, because the question assumes we know what is and is not universally prescriptible in any given situation.

Do you believe, as some philosophers do, that only people who learned morality at home or from reliable mentors at an early age are capable of discerning values that apply across lifestyles and cultures?

This argument was deliberated in the late 1980s when educators began to question whether ethics could be taught at all. In an article condensed from *The New York Times* and reprinted later in *Reader's Digest*, showcasing its popularity, Michael Levin stated: "Moral behavior is the product of training, not reflection. As Aristotle stressed thousands of years ago, you get a good adult by habituating a good child to doing the right thing."[7] In sum, Levin believed that you learn ethics at home, not in class, because by then it might be too late.

This is a powerful but ultimately spurious argument. Let's focus on an ideal physical world where stable parents or caregivers educated and reared their children morally so that they would lead ethical lives. In this ideal world, no other adult dared to mistreat those children or violate their trust so that they could fully embrace their family values. We use the word "family" not in the conventional two-parent sense but as the place members feel they *belong*, adding even more trust to the experience. In this happy world, these children would grow to adulthood without experiencing personal tragedies like disease, accidents, poverty, unemployment, natural disasters or violence. They enjoyed good health and health care along with unconditional love. In this controlled, hypothetical environment, we can rest assured that these children would apply sound values and contribute to our nation's moral fiber. And indeed, thousands, if not millions, are fortunate to have been reared in relatively safe, wholesome environs. But many more millions, if not hundreds of millions, have not. What about *them*? Are they doomed to lead unethical lives?

Now let's take this theoretical argument a step further to illustrate why it is possible to teach ethics. Assume for the moment that an ideal world exists in which young adults since childhood have been habituated to do the right thing and so enjoy trust and security in their everyday dealings at school, home and work. Is there anything that can happen at any one of those places that can turn trust into distrust and a sense of security into one of apprehension? Again, speaking hypothetically, to make a point about the teaching of ethics, envision that moral person who trusts others and feels secure ... *falling victim to a random act of violence.* Can trust evaporate suddenly and require years of rebuilding for the person who had learned family values from ideal caregivers? Can a sense of security turn into fear of others? If you have answered yes, then ponder this: Doesn't it follow if we can lose our values by the cruel actions of other people, then we can also regain most if not all of our values through helpful actions of different people? *Yes.*

To be sure, in many cases the severity of violence can result in years of rehabilitation, especially if people suffer post-traumatic stress. National calamities such as the September 11 terrorist attacks in addition to wars in Afghanistan and Iraq have provided opportunities for dramatic advances in psychological and medical therapies, according to the American Psychological Association.[8] We mention this not to debate whether people suffering from severe PTSD can regain their previous lives. The point is: *We do not discard people by believing they are beyond hope.* That is a prime example of communal ethics. By our kind or helpful actions, rebuilding trust, we empathize with the afflicted as individuals and often as a society, with media being an integral part of society. In doing so, we model a collective type of unconditional love expressed through uncompromising values. Finally, don't trust and well-being have to be rebuilt dozens if not hundreds of times for everyone in the course of a lifetime because the human condition requires it, especially when we are the targets of immoral, unfair or deceptive acts? The answer, again, is *yes.* Ethics not only can be taught but must be relearned repeatedly over time. That is why you must *live* as well as learn ethics.

REVISIT "FAMILY VALUES"

People are complex creations. Some of our most revered cultural role models such as Benjamin Franklin—known for his ethical maxims in *Poor Richard's Almanac* and other writings—were reared in what we now would label troubled homes. Franklin, a teenage runaway, was one of 17 children and beaten regularly by his older printer brother James. Who, if anyone, taught young Ben ethics? Certainly not his family alone, although the Franklins were known for their outspokenness and diligence. As a child, Franklin excelled at Boston Latin School, preparing him to attend Harvard; but his father Josiah changed his mind about sending his son to college. At the top of his class, Benjamin could have secured financial support to attend this revered school. Worse, when Franklin showed an interest in poetry, his father ridiculed his performances, telling him that poets were beggars. And in spite of or because of such hardships, Franklin kept learning and writing. As an adult, he developed character and character education for an entire nation, founding the University of Pennsylvania and penning some of America's most poetic ethical maxims, including:

- *A penny saved is a penny earned.*
- *Early to bed, early to rise makes a man healthy, wealthy, and wise.*
- *Honesty is the best policy.*
- *Great haste makes great waste.*
- *The door to wisdom is never shut.*
- *A man wrapped up in himself makes a very small bundle.*
- *Well done is better than well said.*
- *Three may keep a secret, if two of them are dead.*
- *There was never a good war, or a bad peace.*
- *Any society that would give up a little liberty to gain a little security will deserve neither and lose both.*

No doubt Franklin was influenced by his family values, but he also nurtured his own through life education and interactions with others in community. In fact, civic involvement became the centerpiece of his moral compass as he helped found public libraries, hospitals, postal services and fire departments. His experiments kept houses warm with stoves and buildings safe with lightning rods. He became one of America's first diplomats. Throughout his long life, he continued to raise his conscience, especially on the issue of abolition. His record on slavery, that abominable aspect of American history, is checkered, to be sure. He owned two slaves as personal servants. In later life, however, Franklin became the president of a Quaker abolition group and one of his last pieces of legislation in 1790 petitioned the Congress to abolish slavery. He argued that humanity is "formed by the same Almighty Being, alike objects of his care, and equally designed for the enjoyment of happiness," adding that Congress had a duty "to secure the blessings of liberty to the People of the United States and this should be done without distinction of color."[9] Ideally, Franklin should have come to that realization sooner. Nonetheless, the record also shows that he lived his ethics regardless of age and continued to keep an open mind—one that harmonized consciousness with conscience.

As you can see, the whole issue of family values is provocative if one believes that parents alone are the sole moral providers. As in Franklin's day, other relatives may contribute along with educators, coaches, clergy, friends, acquaintances, neighbors, coworkers, employers—anyone with whom we have contact.

For the moment, we should contemplate the history of that ethical term, "family values." In 1992, many voters misinterpreted then Vice President Dan Quayle when he spoke about the importance of "family values" in a speech in San Francisco to the Commonwealth Club. The issue of "family values" was deemed safe at the time. A *New York Times*/CBS poll was indicating only 1 percent of the voters considered this a "crucial" concern.[10] (Some 15 years later, a Gallup poll showed that some 75 percent of respondents thought family values was extremely important or very important.[11]) The spike in interest may have been triggered when Quayle, acting on advice from a speechwriter, questioned the morals of a fictive celebrity broadcaster—Murphy Brown—played by actor Candice Bergen in a CBS situation comedy by the same name. Scriptwriters for the show had prepared a plot over several segments so that Murphy Brown, single professional woman, would have a baby. Babies attract viewers and increase ratings, scriptwriters knew, as documented historically in television with such TV shows as *I Love Lucy*, *The Flintstones* and *Bewitched!*. But this particular baby would soon attract a different kind of attention.

Back in San Francisco, Quayle was speaking about such issues as social responsibility and personal integrity. He noted that children need discipline and love and bemoaned the breakdown of the American family. Then he added: "It doesn't help matters when prime-time TV has Murphy Brown—a character who supposedly epitomizes today's intelligent, highly paid professional woman—mocking the importance of fathers by bearing a child alone and calling it just another 'lifestyle choice.'"[12]

Quayle's speech became one of the most quoted in 1992 political campaigns. For more than a year the issue consumed U.S. voters. Lance Morrow, writing for *Time*, was one of the first journalists to acknowledge then how mass media influences social debate. In an article titled "But Seriously, Folks," Morrow asserted,

> This is national theater: surreal, spontaneous, mixing off-hours pop culture with high political meanings, public behavior with private conscience, making history up with tabloids and television personalities like Oprah Winfrey. The trivial gets aggrandized, the biggest themes cheapened. America degenerates into a TV comedy—and yet Americans end up thinking in new ways about some larger matters. The little television screen, the bright and flat and often moronic medium of these spectacles, works in strange disproportions of cause and effect.[13]

Three weeks later Candice Bergen was on the cover of *Time*, wearing a political button that proclaimed: "Murphy Brown for President." Riding the publicity wave, the producers of *Murphy Brown* scheduled a one-hour premiere episode in which the fictive broadcaster would rebut Quayle's speech. The show attracted 44 million viewers. The advertising trade magazine *ADWEEK* noted that Quayle had helped make an ordinary show the most expensive slot on television. Public affairs spokespersons for Saturn and Reebok International issued releases stating that they supported their sponsorship of *Murphy Brown*. Representatives of the telephone company Sprint, for which Bergen was a spokesperson, seemingly had no ethical problem with a fictive TV character taking on the Vice President of the United States. Within a few months, the term "Murphy Brown" no longer applied to a situation comedy on CBS but to a social situation.

In a column in *Money*, titled "What's a 'Murphy Brown' like me supposed to do?," writer Marlys Harris gave investment advice for single mothers.[14] About a year after the controversy over family values began, *Newsweek* published an article titled "Daughters of Murphy Brown," noting the "most rapid rise in single motherhood is among educated, professional women."[15] In a word, "Murphy Brown" had become a fleeting term in the lexicon of pop culture.

There are several ethical lessons to note at this point:

- **How the media influences public debate**, stirring a topic in which viewers had little (1 percent) interest into a premiere TV show that attracted roughly one-fifth of the entire population at the time.
- **How all communication platforms become involved in aspects of such debates**, from the Quayle speechwriter who suggested the idea to the *Murphy Brown* sponsors and spokespersons who rebutted it, from the newspapers and networks that covered the debate to the talk shows and magazines that popularized it.
- **How "Murphy Brown" became a term with a distinct definition**, illustrating the flexibility and power of English language.
- **How ethical debate concerned the definition of "family" but not "values,"** providing participants with enough distance to judge someone else rather than themselves.

Indeed, Quayle's comment seemed to imply that only traditional male-female/ two-parent families were capable of transferring values to children. Opponents were right to press him on this point. They seemed to be asking the Vice President: "What about children of single, divorced, deceased or gay/lesbian parents? What about children who are reared in extended families of other cultures in which grandparents, say, have a particularly influential role? What about social conditions like unemployment that contribute to the breakup of marriages? Do these children lack families or values or both?"

To this day, the topic of "family values" is powerful and controversial, influenced in media history by a fictive TV show *about* a TV show. Sadly, some people still define the wrong word in a two-word phrase: "*family* values." By debating what constitutes a "family," we can voice our ardent, astute or angry opinions and judge others without looking inward at the values bestowed by our own families, no matter the make-up, culture, race, lifestyle or social class. As noted earlier, *Living Media Ethics* defines "family" as the place where one feels she or he belongs.

There is another important lesson in the history of "family values," and that is, how language can get in the way of informed debate, influencing agendas for better or worse. That is why we must be careful to use language as precisely as possible, a topic to be explored in more depth later in this chapter. By heeding the power of language, we can set the parameters for ethical debate. Otherwise we may not listen to other viewpoints, arguing with closed minds. Journalists and practitioners who know the impact of precise language, empowered by an open mind—such as Benjamin Franklin strove to nurture throughout his life—will report to or target audience with greater insight.

LEARN A FEW PHILOSOPHICAL TENETS

Open minds usually find common ground and so often act on behalf of the "common good"—an essential ethical concept. According to ethicist Clifford G. Christians, the common good has "a core meaning that the welfare of all citizens, rather than that of factions or special interests, should be served impartially."[16] Christians states that the meaning of common good is moral rather than empirical and so cannot be explicated by an opinion poll or understood by voting patterns. Moreover, he adds, the future of public journalism, in particular, not only requires an open mindset and concept of the common good, but also demands that "we can articulate it, justify it philosophically, establish its logic and rationale."[17] Such is also the goal of *Living Media Ethics*, which posits that the common good can be expressed across media platforms as a core principle. Otherwise the use of powerful communication technology can do massive harm intentionally or unintentionally.

We can better understand the common good by reviewing a few basic philosophical approaches upon which *Living Media Ethics* is based: teleology (a focus on outcomes) and its kin, utilitarianism (a focus on happiness), in addition to aspects of deontology (or a focus on duty). Because the aim of this book is to identify ethical values that apply across platforms, it is only natural that the approach here would harmonize elements of all these approaches and then some. As previously stated, this text will not focus solely on philosophical concepts but will analyze situations in context with historical and political tenets, too, as having roles in shaping current practices in advertising, journalism and public relations. However, a brief discussion of these philosophical tenets might prove useful for you to associate your values within a larger context.

People who embrace a teleological or utilitarian approach to ethics avoid acts that cause others pain by foreseeing consequences of their thoughts, words and deeds. As such, the best actions are ones that result in the best consequences for the most people.[18] Some take this to mean that people must hone consciousness so that they can perceive as accurately as is humanly possible the range of possible outcomes from any one action. Many ethicists believe that codes help such people ascertain consequences with greater clarity so that they can articulate ethics and achieve moral goals. Consequently, teleology focuses on *positive* outcomes. Utilitarianism—as the root of the term suggests—has *utility*, or practical application.

John Stuart Mill, the famous 19th-century British philosopher, wrote eloquently about "the principle of Utility":

> The creed which accepts as the foundation of morals, Utility, or the Greatest Happiness Principle, holds that actions are right in proportion as they tend to promote happiness, wrong as they tend to produce the reverse of happiness. By happiness is intended pleasure, and the absence of pain; by unhappiness, pain, and the privation of pleasure. To give a clear view of the moral standard set up by the theory, much more requires to be said; in particular, what things it includes in the ideas of pain and pleasure; and to what extent this is left an open question. But these supplementary explanations do not affect the theory of life on which this theory of morality is grounded—namely, that pleasure, and freedom from pain, are the only things desirable as ends; and that all desirable things (which are as numerous in the utilitarian as in any other scheme) are desirable either for the pleasure inherent in themselves, or as means to the promotion of pleasure and the prevention of pain.[19]

As the authors of *Media Ethics: Cases and Moral Reasoning* observe, utilitarianism guides ethical choices by asking us to envision as conscientiously as possible the consequences of our various options. "We would ask how much benefit and how much harm would result in the lives of everyone affected, including ourselves."[20] Once we envision those consequences through consciousness, aware of how our actions might play out, we must rely on conscience and make a moral choice to act in a manner that minimizes harm to others and ourselves. This also shows how consciousness and conscience work in tandem with each other concerning choices. To act without awareness, causing harm to others and then feeling guilty about outcomes, is as unacceptable as consciously choosing a course of action and not caring that it may harm others.

Consider this: On a Midwestern campus "party school," some students served alcohol to minors and then felt pangs of conscience when those minors were hospitalized with alcohol poisoning. However, at a college forum in which this was discussed, other students said they felt no remorse if underage drinkers were harmed because partying took priority. We may sympathize with students who felt guilt, but their actions caused as much harm as those who felt little remorse. The guilty group heeded consciousness too late and the remorseless group ignored conscience. True, the guilty group, now aware, may think twice in the future before serving minors alcohol, but that would be of little value to those hospitalized victims of alcohol poisoning. One mistake of this magnitude is all it takes to sidetrack one's life morally and legally.

While it is vital to foresee consequences, a drawback of both teleology and utilitarianism is the emphasis on outcomes. Life at times is simply too random and complex to foresee the range of likely results from a course of action, even ones meant to elicit happiness or security. What about philosophical happiness? Is the pursuit thereof an inalienable right, as essential to well-being as liberty and life, all of which are cited in the U.S. Declaration of Independence? This is where deontology, whose chief proponent—the 18th-century philosopher Immanuel Kant—picks up the debate. Kant believed that our actions should not focus on pursuit of any goal based solely on outcomes, no matter how happy the results for the greatest number of people, because those people have intrinsic worth as moral agents, or ends in themselves. If we take the binge drinking example, students who felt guilty about harm to others had a duty to treat minors with respect and students who felt no remorse while partying had a duty to think of others rather than themselves. In sum, being aware of others' well-being is a simple act of consciousness and serving minors as role models rather than as bartenders is a simple act of conscience.

Out of this paradigm arose deontological ethics, with the Greek root "deon" meaning "duty" as opposed to teleological ethics whose Greek root means "results" or outcomes. Certain actions are right or wrong regardless of the consequences. That is the ultimate test of moral law. In explaining this, ethicist James Rachels cites Kant's "categorical imperative," or supreme command, "from which all our duties and obligations are derived," guiding people to act in ways that are commonly acceptable and never as a means toward an end.[21] Elaborating on this process in a step-by-step manner, ethicist Valerie Alia states that duty must meet three basic provisions, the first being "good will," or the intent to perform dutifully; the second, making a commitment toward moral behavior; and the third, practicing the categorical imperative "required of everyone: duties are universal."[22]

Deontology asks us to be both aware of such truths and to intuit them conscientiously. Universal principles such as responsibility and fairness apply to all of us in both our personal and professional lives. We are obligated to have one set of values at home and at work, in real community or in cyberspace. The notion of universality may be controversial in our secular age. Granted, millions of people have diverse cultural values. For instance, the three great religions of Christianity, Judaism and Islam all have flash points in the Middle East and practice different forms of worship. But all also believe in a power greater than themselves, and in that imperative, we might find common ground for the common good. Many current-day media ethicists—chief among them, Clifford G. Christians—remind us repeatedly that higher truths exist and that we intuit those truths not only by heightening our powers of reason but also by deepening our conscience so that both inform us to choose right and avoid evil. "To violate one's conscience—no matter how feeble and uninformed—brings about feelings of guilt," Christians and co-authors write in *Media Ethics: Cases and Moral Reasoning*. "Through the conscience, moral law is imbedded in the texture of human nature."[23]

Because of that, we not only are able to intuit higher truths but also are able to explain how to apply those truths to practical situations in everyday media environments. Applied ethics has an ancient history in the four cardinal virtues of justice, wisdom, courage and moderation, which we inherit from Plato, with moderation as a touchstone for virtuous living, which we inherit from Aristotle (also known as "Aristotle's Mean"). Through moderation, or temperance, we can negotiate conflicts of interest between two or more parties, find common ground or compromise, and otherwise achieve balance and fairness—two fundamental concepts of modern-day mass communication.

By no means was Aristotle alone in intuiting higher moral truths. Finding common ground was developed in China more than a century earlier in Confucius' "Golden Mean," which emphasized the golden rule, doing unto others what you would have them do unto you. Confucius believed that "reciprocity" was the highest principle of conduct: *Do not do to others what you do not want them to do to you* (Analects 15.23). Similar truths also can be found in Hinduism, Islam and Buddhism and appeal to conscience and consciousness, constructs of the human condition. A rudimentary knowledge of these concepts is useful at this point, however, to illustrate why philosophical approaches are being converged in this text.

Conscience and consciousness are metaphysical, or beyond scientific measurement. Nevertheless, they determine as much as our genome whether we will lead fulfilling and productive lives or empty, painful ones. Philosophers from Plato to the current day have debated the essence of conscience and consciousness for centuries because those aspects of human existence influence the well-being of nations as well as individuals. Although philosophers use different terminologies or advance deontological, utilitarian or teleological theories, apart from the other, a blending of all yields a harmonious alternative.

The conscience demands:

- *That we love and are loved by others.*
- *That we have meaningful relationships with others.*
- *That we contribute to community.*

This affirms in some part the deontological perspective, noting the intrinsic, universal worth of each individual and emphasizing duty in our contributions to society.

Consciousness demands:

- *That we see the world as it actually is rather than how we would like it to be.*
- *That we foresee the impact of our actions before taking them.*
- *That we assess consequences of past actions to make informed choices in the future.*

This affirms in some part the teleological perspective, asking us to sharpen our vision so that we can ascertain the range of outcomes before taking action. And if we do, we might ensure greater happiness in some part, in effect, affirming certain aspects of the utilitarian perspective. In the process, it might be argued in a text about moral convergence, that we may better understand the consequences of our actions from all perspectives, strengthening relationships and enhancing social contributions—with a sense of duty to ourselves and others. Factor this: If moral convergence exists, we cannot ascribe to one philosophical school of thought, especially as we explore technological convergence in mass media.

Harmonizing these philosophical approaches helps us intuit right and wrong (aspects of conscience) and foresee outcomes of our thoughts, words and deeds (aspects of consciousness), determining what will yield "the best consequences for the welfare of good over evil."[24] Rather than identifying your philosophical position, as more teleological, utilitarian or deontological, *Living Media Ethics* will simplify the process in a manner than harmonizes philosophical approaches. Repeatedly in this text, we will focus on consciousness and conscience working in tandem with each other. That subsumes all philosophical approaches, enhancing values because it fosters the requisite critical thinking mandatory in any media profession.

This is not a unique approach. As others have noted, the 20th-century philosopher William David Ross advanced the idea that ethical values compete for our attention depending on circumstances and on how we perceive "duty." In this Ross differs from both Kant and Mill who saw only one path to the oracle.[25] And the theoretical field of "metaethics" further blends approaches by asking us to make concrete the meaning of abstract terms such as justice or fairness so that we can articulate them in our codes and apply them in our lives.[26] Complicating matters is how we can translate these approaches in the modern workplace so that we can influence policy and disseminate information ethically.[27] Doing so again may require a blend of several philosophical strategies supported by concrete applications to complex problems, especially in an age of data science, when we must deal with audiences in real and cyberspace, complicated further by a blend of those two environments via augmented and virtual reality (in addition to wearable and biologically embedded technologies). In simple terms, the goal of understanding various philosophical approaches is not to program your moral agendas, but to make you aware of the influences that have programmed them for you already and to provide you with ways to make choices more conscious and conscientious. As the 19th-century philosopher Arthur Schopenhauer maintained, we all have free will; the issue is, who has determined that will?

Before you will be able to build a value system, you have to answer that basic question.

KNOW RIGHT FROM WRONG

So far, we have defined values and their importance across media platforms in addition to philosophical precepts associated with ethics. But we have said little about the concepts of right and wrong, upon which the very definition of ethics is based. According to *The Random House Dictionary of the English Language*, ethics deals with "values relating to human conduct, with respect to the rightness or wrongness of certain actions ... and the motives and ends of such actions."[28] Authors Edward Spence and Brett Van Heekeren, in their text *Advertising Ethics*, note, "Ethics can simply be defined as a set of prescriptive rules, principles, values, and virtues of character that inform and guide *interpersonal* and *intrapersonal* conduct: that is, the conduct of people toward each other and the conduct of people toward themselves."[29] These concepts were developed in almost all ancient civilizations, beginning with Babylonian laws and Hebrew Ten Commandments and including Indian writings of the Vedas and Chinese virtues of the Tao. Western culture is heavily influenced by the ancient Greece, which gave us the word ethics, derived from *ethos* (or "customs"). It was the great thinker Socrates who said, "The unexamined life is not worth living."

The unexamined professional life is not worth much, either. The concepts of right and wrong help us examine our lives at the workplace as surely as they do our lives at home and school. With regard to media and communication, employees must be aware that an action or deed *is* right or wrong in the first place. They intuit this from the conscience. Then they must make a conscious decision to do the right or wrong thing. Finally, they need to ascertain what influence, if any, caused them to make that choice. A cursory knowledge of teleological or deontological ethics might imply that we can discern moral outcomes or higher truths with a relatively high degree of accuracy. However, our perception and intuition are influenced for better or worse by the lifestyles that we lead, the families that we have, the communities in which we live, the cultures in which we are reared, the faiths that we embrace, the experiences that we endure or enjoy, the media and technology that we consume or create, and even the cuisine and drink that we prefer. A basic objective of *Living Media Ethics* is to make you aware of these influences and the filters through which you experience the world. The more aware we become, the more independent our choices, increasingly allowing us to take responsibility for our actions.

Let's begin by analyzing "intention." Marketing expert and business professor Peggy H. Cunningham states that intention is a core concept of the ethics process. "For actions to be considered ethical, the decision maker must intend no harm to the parties affected by the decision."[30] Cunningham also observes that the medium influences our concept of intentions. "Because advertising is so pervasive—almost environmental in nature—ethical advertisers must consider intended and possible unintended consequences of their activity."[31] Thus, it is one ethical issue to consider intention in the framing of a questionable advertisement and another to foresee the unintended outcomes of that ad. For instance, a few years ago *The Los Angeles Times* ran print and television ads that featured "a group of bikini-clad women posed opposite Muslim women draped head to toe in traditional chadors,"[32] a loose and usually black robe. The intention of the ads was to connect seemingly diverse groups to the newspaper as part of a U.S. $15 million campaign for new subscribers. But the unintended consequences included angering women, Muslims and other groups who found the images stereotypical and offensive, triggering a petition signed by 200 members of the *Times* editorial staff who demanded that the ads be withdrawn. In this case, the newspaper not only had to deal with intended vs. unintended consequences but also the negative impact on audience and morale of its very own staff. A misguided intention to embrace diversity did little to counteract the effects of this ill-advised advertisement.

You have probably heard the phrase: *Ignorance is no excuse when breaking the law.* Sometimes ignorance is an excuse in ethics when dealing with intended vs. unintended consequences and the influence on both. Case in point: If a shopper believes that posters of a famous band on display in a music store are free samples and takes one from that store, he or she still can be prosecuted for shoplifting. The shopper may argue his or her mistaken intentions in a court of law and the judge can determine the punishment. But if the shopper truly made an honest mistake, then the matter is one of faulty judgment rather than ethics. Now let's remove legal ramifications from this situation. If a journalism intern borrows a poster of a band from the radio station where she works, to prepare for an interview with musicians, this is not a serious breach of ethics, until someone informs the intern that taking posters out of the station is against company policy. No exceptions. So informed, the intern in the future must make *a conscious choice*. If the intern decides to take another poster home and lies to a supervisor about doing so, the person is committing an ethical violation—two actually—corporate breach and lying about it. But the intern may have been influenced to make that choice because of a family motto: *Stealing is okay as long as you don't get caught!*

Michael Kent Curtis, an attorney and professor in constitutional and public law at Wake Forest University, notes that before we can understand our own intentions, let alone influences, we must grasp the difference between law and ethics. "First," he says in an interview, "there is the question of what the law requires. For instance, with the First Amendment you can publish things that are false so long as you are not reckless and still can be shielded from a libel action. But it wouldn't follow that it is right to be negligent or careless. The law is sort of a minimum ethical standard." The danger, according to Curtis, is that minimum standards sometimes are viewed as maximum standards. Thus, we often hear the excuse, when ethics are challenged by others, that a person's actions were "entirely legal." The best way to distinguish what is legal from what is ethical, Curtis says, is to acknowledge that ethics deals with *what is right* and law deals with *what you have a right to do*. "You have a right to do all sorts of things," he adds. "You have a right to use racist speech, but it is not right to engage in racist speech."

At this juncture, ignorance of right vs. wrong or intended vs. unintended consequences, is immaterial. You may or may not know standards of every case study or media topic presented in this book. In the recent past, a magazine writer accustomed to working with illustrators may not have realized that altering documentary photographs is considered an ethical breach in photojournalism. The photojournalist might not have realized that lack of quotations to indicate previously published material in an article could be deemed plagiarism in magazine journalism, even if the material contains a proper attribution. And so on through the various media platforms. Before those platforms converged in digital and mobile devices, a journalist or practitioner could get by simply by knowing the standards of his or her platform but still would likely have to learn other standards during the course of a communications career, in as much as media employees often acquire different jobs. Now, with communicators working across platforms, knowledge of various standards and practices is more important than ever. The goal of this book is to expose you to, discuss the rights and wrongs of, and analyze the values associated with each platform as well as analyzing what standards apply across them. Moreover, when you become familiar with these standards and practices, you no longer can claim ignorance. Our consciousness will have been informed, and your choices will be largely independent, as long as you can identify and free yourself as much as possible from filters of influence. Then the more interesting aspect of ethics begins, with chapters on falsehood, temptation, manipulation and bias in the second of three sections in *Living Media Ethics*. (The last section on fairness, power and value systems will enhance your moral base.)

When you know the specific rights and wrongs of a certain issue, and can act according to your conscience, you are making a voluntary choice for which you will be held accountable. According to the late Ben Blackstock, former director of the Oklahoma Press Association, "It's not oversimplifying the matter to claim that ethics is doing something or deciding not to do something for a payoff or other consideration." Blackstock, interviewed in 2008, used to represent dozens of Oklahoma newspapers and so had to know journalism ethics to address the many right-wrong inquiries his office fielded regularly from reporters and editors. He also lobbied for their newspapers at the state capitol in Oklahoma City and had to rely on his character and reputation when dealing with legislators. When a person chooses to do wrong, Blackstock said, he or she should feel "a stab of conscience"—a phrase that has become cliché because it is so true. If you do not feel that stab, Blackstock maintained, this says something about the erosion of values. To stress this point, Blackstock would tell a Native American story: "An elder spoke about conscience. He said, 'A conscience is a sharp stone someplace inside that has very sharp points and edges. When a person does something wrong it turns and hurts. But if the person keeps doing it long enough it will turn back and forth until it's smooth. Then it doesn't hurt anymore.'" Blackstock added: "May your stone stay sharp. May it continue to hurt."

REMEMBER WHO MOLDED YOUR MORALS

Although we may make conscious ethical choices, as indicated earlier, other factors often influence them. Determining the various influences is complex and consumes much of this chapter and parts of others. For now, we will briefly consider these basic influences: familial, experiential, generational and cultural along with ones associated with social mores.

Familial

We already have discussed this influence with regard to family values. Families also pass along to children a work ethic, worldview and/or mottoes that play a big role in influencing our actions. Steve Mores, president and co-publisher of Tribune Newspapers in Harlan, Iowa, credits his father Leo Mores, an award-winning community journalist and publisher of the *Harlan Tribune*, as his main influence. "He would review stories and advertising practices at home and the consequences of those stories or ads with our Mom and as we grew older, we became part of the discussion. It was a foregone conclusion that I would be a journalist," Steve Mores recalls, adding: "I've told my kids the same thing I was told by my father about our position in the community. If we ever did anything wrong, we probably would be put at the top of the list for everyone to see. No one would pull any strings for us." Mores and his siblings were reared knowing that they needed to be model citizens in the small town of Harlan, population 5,183. The work ethic of the Mores family also was shaped by a motto posted in the advertising department: *What you did for them yesterday was forgotten last night. You have to win them all over again tomorrow.* "That's probably true in life now, too," Mores says. "Society is not as forgiving as it once was."

Shirley Staples Carter, journalism professor and former administrator at South Carolina's School of Journalism and Mass Communication, says her parents taught her that knowledge and opportunity require responsibility, as in the old Chinese saying: *To know and not to do is, in fact, not to know.* She became curious about all aspects of life, leading to a career in journalism and journalism education. "Curiosity," she notes, "may be thought of as the need, thirst or desire for knowledge. As educators and professionals in journalism, advertising and public relations, broadcasting and visual communications, we are curious by nature. We poke, we probe, we prod, we explore, we exhort, we demand, we afflict and comfort, we agitate, we persuade, we motivate, we inform, and sometimes we apologize."

Curiosity is a great motto for those in mass communication. It prods you to continue learning about ethics. "We transmit knowledge through traditional and new media," Carter says. Curiosity helps us be innovative and creative, "and we adapt. We embrace the special entitlement we receive in the First Amendment and defend others' rights to free speech, to a point." Curiosity also inspired Carter to assess fairness in a democracy, especially in higher education, which is "not immune to society's decades long conflicts and debates over social justice, racial and gender inequalities." Our role as communicators, she adds, calls on us to be strategic thinkers, especially when investigating injustice and inequality, and to work with all sides "to ameliorate conflict and foster awareness, build bridges of understanding, and mutual trust and respect."

In 2007, Carter received the Charles E. Scripps Award for Journalism Administrator of the Year, becoming the first black and first female recipient. She was honored for her ethical leadership, which she credits in part to her faith. "My father was a Baptist minister and so the golden rule—*Do unto others as you would have them do unto you*—formed my moral compass, along with faith, hope and charity. My parents also instilled in me early on the belief that knowledge has power, and that education is the key to overcoming racial prejudice and being viewed as a disadvantaged member of society. That was a powerful message for me as a GRITS—girl raised in the South—during the height of the civil rights movement and it piqued my curiosity to seek a world different from the images I saw on television of people who looked like me being attacked by policemen with hoses and dogs, beaten and arrested as protestors, and defiant politicians standing in school house doors. I asked my parents, 'Why?' and because of my faith, I believed in a better place and time."

Public Relations practitioner Angela Krile, owner of Krile Communications, was influenced by her grandmother from which she learned these principles:

- "If Grandma wouldn't approve of it, then it's probably the wrong thing to do."
- "Live like you're on TV or like someone you deeply admire is watching you. You never know when someone is watching you, so you must assume that someone always is and act accordingly."
- "Don't try to hide something or cover up a mistake."
- "Check your gut. If it doesn't feel right deep down in the pit of your stomach, then you just shouldn't do it. Period. It's just that simple."

Familial mottoes vary. Some are basically true or prudent like those of Steve Mores, Shirley Staples Carter and Angela Krile. And some are basically false, especially ones that stereotype race, social class, lifestyle, sexual preference or religious predilection. Some mottoes fall in-between—part true/part false—but are adopted by children nonetheless and cause problems in adulthood. Such was the case with Barbara Neikirk, who worked as a community development manager for a telephone company. "I was reared with the belief that anyone older than me knows more than me," she recalls. "'Respect your elders' was a frequently repeated rule in my family" when children addressed anyone over the age of 30. A motto such as *Respect your elders* depends on the morality of the elder in question. Some mottoes are downright false or inhibiting. One journalism student in Athens, Ohio, shared a motto that was afflicting his work ethic. Whenever he experienced a success—such as winning a writing competition or securing an internship—he would remember his father stating, "Even a blind squirrel finds an acorn now and then." That's a debilitating motto which, if not addressed morally, can afflict one's conscience and impair one's consciousness for a lifetime.

Experiential

Experience is such a strong influence on values that it is addressed in every chapter in this book, especially in the one on truth and later in this section on "trigger words." Because many life-altering occurrences are associated with the family, it is easy to confuse how parents, caretakers or guardians, say, influenced values and how experiences with them did. Experiences, of course, can happen with or without people. They can happen with your mother or with Mother Nature or with both. What you encounter in your life influences how you perceive the world and that, as we shall learn, colors your values. The most effective way to begin then is to assess what experience, if any, prompted you to pursue a career as a communicator.

Gail Taylor, former investigative reporter for *The Morgantown (W.V.) Dominion Post*, who now writes, teaches and freelances, lives and works according to this motto: *Without truth, there is no integrity.* "Although I am paraphrasing that quote, I wish that I had said the words first because they sum up my personal philosophy—a philosophy shaped by my parents. I was born in the late 1960s to parents who, along with thousands of other Americans from all faiths and ethnic backgrounds, fought for civil rights. I was nine months old when my parents and I lived in Washington, D.C. My dad tells me that he took me to the rooftop of the apartment building where we lived so I could see the city afire. People were rioting because Dr. Martin Luther King had been murdered."

Shortly after that experience, Taylor's family moved to Illinois where they lived in college towns. She would discuss current events with parents and professors. "Early on, I got the sense that if smart people read newspapers, then newspapers must be written by equally smart people. It wasn't until much later in my life, really not until I became a journalist, that I realized that people don't read newspapers to become smart so much as to become informed. And that often, they take what journalists write with a grain of salt."

It's interesting to analyze the combination of influences that led Taylor to a career in investigative journalism. The one experience with her father on the apartment rooftop watching the nation's capital aflame in the aftermath of the King murder probably was etched in her conscience, although we will never know. Surely, she was told the anecdote by her father, another powerful influence. The interaction with scholars who visited the family was a function of experience, too, as was all the reading of newspapers, magazines and books that went on in her household. It's not surprising that Gail Taylor believed a newspaper career was related somehow to her intellect. If you read her testimonial closely, however, you can see that even her powerful experiences with regard to print journalism did not hold up entirely when she began working for *The Dominion Post*. Readers purchase newspapers for information, not for self-improvement; moreover, she realized, they don't often believe the information that they consume in the newspaper.

Generational

Each generation comes with its own set of experiences shaped in part by history, economy, weather patterns, technology and war (to name a few). These situations and events combine to create generational filters through which people born in a specific era tend to view the world. For instance, only a few years separated the Roaring Twenties era—known for its prosperity and capriciousness—from the Great Depression era, known for its hardships and determination. Similarly, your own generation has its own set of experiences in store for you. Later, when you are a working journalist or practitioner, your values influenced by generation may clash with those of the emerging generation.

That was Gail Taylor's experience, and it shapes how she views media, particularly news, in the current digital environment. Ethical journalism is harder to practice today, she says, than it was when she worked as an investigative reporter in the early 1990s. "At least back then, the nation's press, and the public in general seemed capable of dealing with complexity." Today, she says, we are fixated on our mobile and digital devices. "We are a nation that is used to getting our information fed to us on the silver spoon of our own choosing.

"There are simply so many options available to us when it comes to finding news, or other information, that there is no incentive to have to try to understand anything," she adds. "Should anything be too eloquent, too multi-syllabic, or simply too deep, it is, with the flick of a switch, turned off, tuned out, or scanned by. I am reminded of this almost daily as an instructor of English composition classes at a Midwestern state university where plain-speech, blue jeans and T-shirts, and Vera Bradley handbags (quilted, cotton, and colorful), dominate the senses. However, it should also be noted that thrown into this mix of modern-day Americana are students who bring other tastes—Louis Vuitton, faux and real, the gold jewelry and frosted hair, denim-and-parka chic of urban hip-hop culture. Add to this, my students' overwhelming penchant for texting, and you have, to my eyes, a complex culture where sub-cultures predominate." In response, Taylor believes, the news media are trying to determine "just how much detail the public can handle before we all simply turn off."

Cultural

This is the catch-all category that includes predominant beliefs within segments of society like entertainment, sports, education, arts and sciences, and ethnic races, regions and religions. Influences and examples from these segments are too lengthy to cite now and are covered in other chapters (particularly ones on manipulation and bias).

Technology or the mechanisms of media—from printing press to smartphones—not only are responsible for generational influences but also cultural ones. "The global mass media are agents of acculturation: not neutral purveyors of information, but creators and shapers of culture,"[33] writes ethicist Clifford Christians. "From this perspective, media technologies are not tools or products *per se* but cultural practices. Technology is a distinct cultural enterprise in which humans form and transform natural reality aided by tools and processes for practical ends. The contemporary media are cultural institutions."[34]

One of the most cultural of such institutions is CNN's International Desk. Eli Flournoy, former senior director of CNN's International Newsource and now an international media consultant, says he thought about ethics every day while working at CNN. Often, he had to deal with overseas affiliates and so had to be sensitive to how CNN presented news about other countries. "Criticism about underreporting and misreporting on The Third World is of particular interest to me," he adds. Often viewers, let alone media critics, realize the many obstacles in commercial television news that influence ethics. "The greatest come from financial considerations: the concern for ratings, the need to attract advertising and cut costs, for instance. This often clouds the ability to make ethical decisions. Some stories don't get covered because it's just too expensive. Why cover Rwanda and not Angola? Less expensive? More interest? Easier access? There is usually a combination of factors but the battle between covering stories (especially international) and covering costs is a daily one."

Social Mores

As noted earlier, a person perceives the world through familial, experiential, generational and cultural filters. If you could assess these influences for every person in the United States and somehow tally and condense them, you would end up with another important element: *mores* (pronounced *mor'-ez* from the Latin, meaning "morals"). Mores, or "social mores" as they usually are called, are beliefs—specific rights and wrongs—that a society or group accepts unquestioningly *at a certain point in time*. The best way to analyze mores is to page through advertisements in old magazines. All such ads contain conventionally held attitudes, which we will investigate here. Generally, the closer the date to the current time, the less obvious the social more. For instance, advertisements in hundreds of magazines depict smiling women in various stages of pregnancy in public settings such as beaches, parks or malls, with family members or acquaintances looking lovingly at them and the products being sold. Other advertisements about teen pregnancy are less inviting, warning about consequences or advocating for abstinence, condoms or some other issue. And then there is the political aspect for those intensely for or against government funding for Planned Parenthood, a non-profit organization that provides reproductive health care including information about abortion—an argument that is beyond the scope of *Living Media Ethics* and yet another example of how pro-and-con case studies do little to change opinions, especially in texts like this one. Pregnancy, as depicted in advertising and news stories, embodies social mores. That is the focus here.

To test public attitudes about pregnancy, Rene, a broadcasting major at Ohio University, spent an afternoon impersonating an expectant mother. "I took my summer jumper, which is very baggy, and put that on over a pair of shorts I had stuffed with padding to make me look pregnant," she recalls. "My rules were simple: I wasn't allowed to reveal the fact that I wasn't pregnant to people I knew unless they asked. I knew this might start some rumors about me, but that was okay because I knew I would have my figure back the next day." Then she strolled down the main street in her college town. "I normally cross the street without regard to approaching cars because pedestrians have the right of way. Drivers don't usually recognize this fact and beep and yell profanities at me if I hold them up." On this day, however, a driver beeped, stopped and "started to yell, but then saw my stomach, and said, 'Oh, I'm sorry.'" As Rene continued to walk, people were mostly indifferent. "An older man smiled and tipped his hat," she says. But Rene encountered different reactions on campus. Some students who knew but hadn't seen her in a while seemed shocked. In the newsroom where she worked, classmates openly stared but avoided asking her if she was pregnant. One complimented her dress. Rene began patting her stomach until her coworkers openly began wondering about "my new weight gain." Rene confronted them, wondering why "they just didn't ask me about it, and they said they didn't want to be rude. I thought it was rude that they stared at me and didn't ask." Finally, she concluded the experience showed that "people might be nicer to young pregnant women because they think you're married and expect you to have children, but when you're unwed and in school people are shocked or embarrassed."

Rene identified two mores associated with pregnancy. Fifty years earlier, if she did the same experiment, would the social attitudes have been the same? A century earlier? What about a decade from now?

Beliefs change over time. In the 1950s, for example, cigarette smoking was considered "sophisticated" and a symbol of progress. An "L&M" ad in the late 1950s states: "Live modern! smoke modern!" At the onset of the feminist movement in the 1960s, Leo Burnett Advertising Agency introduced a campaign juxtaposing fake sepia-toned illustrations of oppressed women of the 1900s alongside colorful modern counterparts liberated by Virginia Slims brand cigarettes.

In the 1990s it was considered "dumb" and a symbol of bad health habits, replete with Surgeon General's warnings. In the first decade of the 2000s, cigarette companies were targeted in the truth® campaign, which reported these results:

- *Seventy-five percent of all 12 to 17-year-olds in the nation—21 million—can accurately describe one or more of the truth® ads.*
- *Nearly 90 percent of youths aged 12 to 17–25 million—said the ad they saw was convincing.*
- *Eighty-five percent—24 million—said the ad gave them good reasons not to smoke.*[35]

Currently, the truth® campaign has a new concept associated, to some degree, on social mores: "Let's be the generation to finish it!"[36] The organization states that only 6 percent of teens still smoke and asserts that "finishing the job will come down to you" spreading the word and enlisting friends. On the organization's website (www.thetruth.com/about-truth), these values are emphasized:

- **We don't hate. We instigate.** We're not here to criticize your choices, or tell you not to smoke. We're here to arm everyone—smokers and non-smokers—with tools to make change.
- **Exposing big tobacco.** We've always been about exposing big tobacco's lies and manipulation. And while they keep adapting their tactics, we keep it real.
- **Gaming not shaming.** This isn't about throwing stones at smokers. It's about finding and turbo-charging new fun ways to do what no generation has ever done before—end smoking.

This campaign is fraught with language associated with social mores, but because they are embraced by many in the current day, you might not easily spot them. For example, the phrase—"not here to criticize your *choices*"—is carefully worded; in past generations, the goal precisely was to criticize "choices"—a word that many now associate with proactive, positive actions. The phrase—"we keep it real"—dates back to the early 2000s when celebrities flaunted extravagant lifestyles that few ever could experience in "real" or actual life, according to the Urban Dictionary.[37] The word "shaming" is rooted in the current day, too, associated with mocking or bullying individuals on social media according to a perceived short-coming or physical/lifestyle attribute. Maybe some future society will not recognize the phrase "turbo-charging," associated with internal combustion engines.

Identifying social mores can be complicated, because usually they are associated with newsworthy topics and/or other time considerations. You can assess the mores of the past only by understanding the influences of a specific era. It's more difficult to assess developing mores as events transpire in your own era. For instance, in the 1960s Volkswagen ran a magazine ad that asked, "Do you have the right type of wife for it?"[38] with copy indicating that a woman's place was in the home taking care of children. That's offensive today. But it may be more difficult for you to see the social influence regarding this 1990s Volvo slogan emphasizing safety concerns: "Where would you rather sit. Behind the front end or in it?"[39] The social more here, as in the earlier tobacco examples, seems to imply that we can circumvent health problems (even death) by being smart consumers. Of course, that notion doesn't take into account the role of genetics (who is more prone to contract certain diseases) and psychographics (who is more prone to have certain car accidents). You can bet that insurance companies know all about these statistics, explaining why applicants must provide information from medical and traffic records. How about a top car for Millennials in 2017, the Honda Civic, that features a woman rock climber scaling a mountain without safety gear to find the car at the summit with the slogan, "Who knows? You might just end up somewhere new!"[40] Compare the role of a woman with the earlier VW ad and ponder the social more being promoted in this 2017 ad. Even more difficult to discern are *future* mores because the events that will shape and define them have yet to happen and may only be predicted with imprecision. The lesson here is elusive: What society believes is good today may be deemed bad tomorrow. Finally, what society believes is right and moral or wrong and immoral today may still be so tomorrow—for a completely contradictory reason.

HISTORY MATTERS MORE THAN YOU THINK

Ethics becomes even more complex when we assess the influence of history. There are important reasons to include a brief historical section to an ethics book. The historian's motto—*We study history so as not to repeat the mistakes of the past*—may be one of those part true/part false maxims. Some historians believe this is wishful thinking in as much as our accumulated knowledge over time would help us avoid the tragedies of war, poverty, injustice and immorality in general.[41] Another historical maxim, that history repeats itself, again may be part true/part false. Historical repetitions are never exact because of the complexities of the human experience, but they may seem to flow in patterns due to the same ethical mistakes being made repeatedly since time immemorial. Ethics and historical events are intricately linked as are ethics and political philosophy.

Historian Steven Kreis, creator of web-based History Guide www.historyguide.org, studied political philosophy at Boston University as an undergraduate. He became interested in such philosophers as Plato, Hobbes, Locke and Mill and soon discovered that

> my lack of understanding of history, i.e. the actual historical context in which these writers conceived and executed their theoretical work, made my understanding of their philosophy one-sided. Sure, I knew what they had to say about liberty, or the proletariat, or monarchy or the franchise. But what was the historical environment that gave rise to their ideas?[42]

This is precisely the approach and question of *Living Media Ethics*, which posits that politics combining with philosophy—in addition to the prevailing familial, experiential, generational and cultural influences of leaders such as Benjamin Franklin, Thomas Jefferson, Alexander Hamilton, James Madison and John Jay—shaped current media values as much if not more than the philosophers said to have influenced their thinking. Several other political and/or newsworthy U.S. figures, including Abraham Lincoln, Frederick Douglass, Woodrow Wilson, Susan B. Anthony, Henry Ford, Franklin D. Roosevelt, Eleanor Roosevelt, Martin Luther King, Malcolm X, John F. Kennedy, Rosa Parks, Ronald Reagan, Bill Gates and countless others, also contributed to this effect. Certainly, ones cited here do not represent a comprehensive list, but they all in some ways create, enhance and/or contradict Constitutional freedoms—sometimes, all at once. Moreover, there is precedent in breaking from conventional ethics books that focus exclusively on philosophy as the shaper of media values, especially in as much as mobile media and augmented reality are blending content and blurring boundaries as fundamental as the definition of what is a journalist in a global digital environment. As Barbie Zelizer observes in her essay, "Definitions of Journalism":

> As journalism has come to be thought of as a profession, an industry, a phenomenon, and a culture, definitions have emerged that reflect various concerns and goals. Journalists, journalism educators, and journalism scholars all take different pathways in thinking productively about the subject, and the effort to define journalism consequences goes in various directions.[43]

As such, *Living Media Ethics* is taking a different pathway not only in arguing for a moral convergence to accompany the technological one but also in viewing philosophy through the political and historical filters of its day.

Doing so we can discern more clearly why modern-day journalism developed core principles to be shared in the next chapter.

Certainly, many of the Constitutional framers of the United States believed fervently, politically and philosophically in the concepts of anti-authoritarian John Locke (1632–1704) who promoted reason over both bloodline and entitlement and inspired generations to embrace not happiness or duty but the rights of survival, or natural law: life, liberty, health and property.[44] Keep in mind, however, that Locke's generation was greatly influenced by more tolerant religious values emanating from the Reformation, of which the monk-professor Martin Luther (1483–1546) was chief architect. Luther, who advanced the concept of "freiheit," or liberty, in his tract "On the Freedom of the Christian People," eventually undermined papal authority. His notion of liberty was associated with religion, but it also led to notions about individual and personal liberties realized philosophically during the Enlightenment.[45] They influence our thinking theologically and politically to this day. Luther's motto in his essay on liberty articulated the dualities of the human condition, an early precursor to Locke's survival motif: *A Christian man is the freest lord of all, and subject to none, a Christian man is the most dutiful servant of all, and subject to everyone.* Luther is a controversial figure in that he could not reconcile conflicting maxims in the Old and New Testament, such as "eye for an eye and tooth for a tooth" (Exodus 21:24) and "If anyone slaps you on the right cheek, turn to them the other cheek also" (Matthew 5, 38–39). That conflict may have led to anti-Semitism.[46] Theologians also note, however, that Luther also intuited some enduring truths through the conscience. A century later, Locke questioned those same truths through consciousness. In time this influenced the distinctly U.S. value of separation of church and state.

But Luther's contribution cannot be overlooked. In journalism history we pay far too much attention to Johannes Gutenberg (1398–1468) because he printed a run of bibles on his movable type press. He also printed indulgence coupons for the Catholic Church—junk mail of the 15th century—in the form of certificates with blank spaces for names, which could be added after payment to clergy to pray for the sins of souls in purgatory between hell and heaven. Gutenberg did not invent movable type in 1451 or 1452; that honor goes to the Chinese cloth merchant Bi Sheng in the 11th century. But as early as 1452, Gutenberg was printing indulgences at the request of German cardinal Nicolaus Cusanus,[47] a practice that eventually led Luther a generation later to nail his famous 95 theses on the Castle Church door in Wittenberg, Germany, on October 31, 1517, and which eventually sparked the Reformation. Although Luther is still known as an activist and reformer, he influenced U.S. media values through John Locke more than is commonly noted in the historical annals. Consider this: Luther proved that truth is greater than authority 218 years before German émigré John Peter Zenger's acquittal on charges of seditious libel for criticizing the royal governor in the *New York Weekly Journal*, a historical incident to be covered later in this section.

Nonetheless, John Locke's contribution was to alter Luther's ruminations on liberty by disassociating it from religion. This is reflected in two of our charter documents, the Declaration of Independence in 1776 and the Constitution in 1787. Harvey C. Mansfield, a professor of government at Harvard University, calls Locke "America's philosopher" and notes:

> To Locke, or to Locke's contemporary audience, virtue seemed to be always in the company of religion; and favored by this association, virtue seemed to have the upper hand over liberty. Locke's task was to promote liberty, giving it priority over virtue, while not destroying virtue of denying religion.[48]

Locke, an economics writer as well as philosopher, also associated concepts of survival and natural law with the marketplace. This concept also finds roots in ancient Greece. As Robert Schmuhl, a professor of American Studies, and Robert G. Picard, a professor of economics, note,

> The concept of the marketplace originates in the agora, the place of congregation, in ancient Greece. The agora, typified by the heart of ancient Athens, was simultaneously the locus of commercial, political, administrative, social, religious, and cultural activity, and citizens freely participated in the range of activities.[49]

Activities of the agora influenced the Roman forum, especially in the time of the great orator Marcus Tullius Cicero (105–43 B.C.), who saw philosophy's role "as the means to more effective political action."[50] Others, including founders of the United States, often maintained the same viewpoint, embracing natural law because it furthered political means at a time when Colonists resented the 1765 Stamp Act, which taxed Americans without representation. The act essentially required payment of a tax on any printed document, including bills of sale, inventories, wills and legal filings, which affected attorneys and plantation owners in particular. Even more infuriating were taxes that printers had to absorb, especially printers who also happened to be publishers of newspapers and almanacs. Here are representative clauses of the Act:

> And for and upon every paper, commonly called a pamphlet, and upon every news paper, containing publick news, intelligence, or occurrences, which shall be printed, dispersed, and made publick, within any of the said colonies and plantations, and for and upon such advertisements as are herein after mentioned, the respective duties following (that is to say). ... For every pamphlet and paper being larger than one whole sheet, and not exceeding six sheets in octavo, or in a lesser page, or not exceeding twelve sheets in quarto, or twenty sheets in folio, which shall be so printed, a duty after the rate of one shilling for every sheet of any

kind of paper which shall be contained in one printed copy thereof. For every advertisement to be contained in any gazette, news paper, or other paper, or any pamphlet which shall be so printed, a duty of two shillings. ... And for every almanack or calendar written or printed within the said colonies and plantations, to serve for several years, duties to the same amount respectively shall be paid for every such year.[51]

Among those who protested the Stamp Act, as you might imagine, was printer Benjamin Franklin who published the November 7, 1765 edition of the *Pennsylvania Gazette* without date, number, masthead or imprint, publicizing "the impact of royal policies on colonial freedom."[52] Franklin's motive, of course, not only was the impact of the Stamp Act on colonial freedom but also on his pocketbook. And while the natural law of anti-authoritarian John Locke might have provided the intellectual frame through which Franklin's motives might be filtered, the result was Cicero-like in effect, using philosophy as a means toward an economic end. In a word, economics and politics are seamlessly woven into philosophy influencing media practices, present and past.

Framers of U.S. charter documents were influenced by the Enlightenment, which spans from the 17th through 19th centuries. Fact, rather than rhetoric, and reason rather than royalty, became the touchstones of truth and the search thereof in science, philosophy and politics. Scientists embraced the experimental method, which included observation, objectivity and replicability—requiring proof of rather than proclamations about discoveries. Philosophers in particular began testing and rebutting conventional wisdom, incorporating into their paradigms the role of perception and communication, often acting as collaborator in advancing scientific truth over rhetorical argument. These social and intellectual shifts inevitably affected how language was used, especially in communication and later in mass communication.[53] Because the Enlightenment pivoted on fact and provable truth, individual freedoms, inalienable human rights, the role of education and the importance of information all combined to influence journalism.

It can be argued that the concept of an adversarial news media—such as one might witness at any televised White House briefing or presidential press conference—dates back to Benjamin Franklin as journalist rather than as scientist. He spoke out zealously in his publications and letters that people should not be governed according to rank and privilege of feudal lord or monarch but on their own merits, a concept that led to his work ethic of merit, discussed later in this chapter, and the rising middle class through virtues of frugality, industry, diligence and responsibility. "He was cheeky in his writings and rebellious in his manner,"[54] writes biographer Walter Isaacson. Long before the signers of the Declaration of Independence even realized that independence was what they inevitably would seek, Franklin as journalist understood that the diffusion of information was essential if the Colonies were to unite. Increasingly through his press and franchises of his press, Franklin was forging a national identity based on unity, a key principle of journalism reflected in such organizations as UNITY, which represents the Asian American Journalism Association, the National Association of Hispanic Journalists, the National Lesbian and Gay Journalists Association, National Association of Black Journalists and the Native American Journalists Association. The concept of unity as embraced today in journalism and communication alludes to the motto of the United States before the United States was conceived and even before seven of the signers of the Constitution, including Alexander Hamilton (1757–1804), were even born: *Join, or Die.* That slogan appeared as one of the first political cartoons to be published in the United States, showing the Colonies as a snake snipped into segments. Franklin published the cartoon in the May 9, 1754 edition of the *Pennsylvania Gazette.* That year, in his Albany Plan, he also proposed a federal infrastructure for America in which individual states would share power with a national government. He was ahead of his time in part because he used the power of the press—rather than philosophy—to achieve political ends.

Thomas Jefferson rather than Benjamin Franklin is often seen as journalism's advocate. In part this is due to Jefferson's comment that he preferred newspapers without government rather than government without newspapers. Typically, that statement is published out of context. Jefferson qualified that remark in a January 16, 1787 letter to Edward Carrington:

I am persuaded myself that the good sense of the people will always be found to be the best army. They may be led astray for a moment, but will soon correct themselves. The people are the only censors of their governors; and even their errors will tend to keep these to the true principles of their institution. To punish these errors too severely would be to suppress the only safeguard of the public liberty. The way to prevent these irregular interpositions of the people, is to give them full information of their affairs through the channel of the public papers, and to contrive that those papers should penetrate the whole mass of the people. The basis of our governments being the opinion of the people, the very first object should be to keep that right; and were it left to me to decide whether we should have a government without newspapers, or newspapers without a government, I should not hesitate a moment to prefer the latter. But I should mean that every man should receive those papers, and be capable of reading them.[55]

Jefferson, like Franklin, was a citizen of the Enlightenment. He believed that a free press must combine with public education to inform citizens so that they could make intelligent choices in the voting booth. That notion alludes to the Enlightenment precept that fact-based truth eventually rises to the top so that an educated electorate can discern which candidates for public office would abuse political power and which would share it with the people. John Jay, first chief justice of the U.S. Supreme Court, upheld that Jeffersonian ideal. "I consider knowledge to be the soul of a republic," Jay wrote in 1785, noting that citizens needed information and enlightenment to protect their rights. "Education is the way to do this, and nothing should be left undone to afford all ranks of people the means of obtaining a proper degree of it at a cheap and easy rate."[56] Taken together, Jefferson and Jay imply that free speech is meaningless without education. And, in turn, education is meaningless without free speech. You can't have one without the other.

This, too, reverberates today. Terry Anderson, former Middle East bureau chief for the Associated Press, held hostage in Lebanon for seven years, observes, "If government is able to limit information then they are taking away from us a major part of freedom of speech. I can say anything I want to say, but if I do not know what I am talking about and lack the information to find out, then what good is talking?" In this quotation, Anderson echoes a Jeffersonian political idea articulated in the Declaration of Independence, which blends Enlightenment philosophy with clearly defined legal arguments directed at the British monarchy. According to attorney and biographer R.B. Bernstein, in framing his principles of democracy Jefferson relied on Locke's natural rights of human beings to

> lay the ground for involving the right of revolution against a tyrant, which was the stated purpose of the Declaration. Jefferson also hoped to state the values by which Americans would govern themselves. Thus, the Declaration looks backward, as the last word in the American argument with Britain, and forward, as a statement of the principles of American experiments in government.[57]

Bernstein also notes that Jefferson was the first in Colonial America to advocate for a fully developed public education system to bolster his belief that an educated and informed citizenry would be an effective foil against political tyrants. "The root of his Bill for the More General Diffusion of Knowledge was his belief that citizens who hoped to govern themselves had to be educated."[58]

The irony of this, of course, is that neither the inalienable rights of Locke nor the eloquence of the Declaration addressed whether American Indians, African Americans and immigrants were entitled to liberty and education so generally and publicly diffused. Jefferson, icon of the Enlightenment in America, and one of the most gifted political writers of his day, essentially was using philosophy like Cicero as a means for political ends. He was a slave owner who believed that blacks could not be trusted with freedom, and though he purportedly hoped to end slavery, feared that race riots would result because of resentment among his peers and their freed slaves.[59]

John Jay, to a lesser degree, suffered from the same malady. While he advocated passionately for the educational principles of his era, "religion, morality, virtue and prudence,"[60] he could not fathom why one of his slaves named Abby would run away from the family's rented home in Paris. Abby, captured and imprisoned, was told that she could return if she "behaved"; however, for reasons that Jay could not grasp, she rejected the offer because she was happier behind bars than performing her usual slave tasks. Jay again was confused, believing Abby's stance went against common sense, and hoped that "sobriety, solitude and want of employ-ment will render her temper more obedient to reason."[61] Abby became ill in prison and died shortly thereafter. According to biographer Walter Stahr, Jay might have been moved by Abby's death to arrange for the con-ditional release of another slave named Benoit.[62] Seemingly using philos-ophy to ease his conscience, Jay prepared a legal agreement that alluded to Enlightenment philosophy: *The children of men are by nature equally free, and cannot without injustice be either reduced to or held in slavery.* However, Jay also reasoned that it was proper for Benoit to be freed but only after he served long enough to reimburse what money Jay had spent on his slave. Writes Stahr, "Like Jay's attitudes towards slavery, the document is contradictory: it recognized the injustice of slavery in general, but also required Benoit to serve Jay for another three years."[63] This represents yet another example—and many more can be added from the U.S. historical record—documenting the contradiction of inalienable rights drawn from philosophy and disenfranchisement drawn from politics that has plagued the United States since its founding. *This is the result of using philosophy as a means to a political end.* The contradiction exists to this day as access to education remains a fundamentally political rather than moral issue associated more with economics rather than ethics. At various periods in media history, journalism has argued for and against the status quo. That debate continues today.

Many Enlightenment ideals incorporated in U.S. charter documents were genuinely felt and frequently also practiced. These core principles, or ethics of government, found their way into the Constitution in the form of the Bill of Rights, or first ten Amendments. Jefferson saw these rights as a means through which citizens could evaluate the actions of their elected officials.[64] Madison, who drafted the rights, wanted another check on the balance of power between the government branches and states. The First Amendment in the Bill of Rights did that perhaps more than the other nine, clearly stating what legislators can and cannot do: *Congress shall make no law respecting an establishment of religion, or prohibiting the free exercise thereof; or abridging the freedom of speech, or of the press; or the right of the people peaceably to assemble, and to petition the government for a redress of grievances.* The people's "first right" actually was five: freedom of or from religion, free speech, free press, assembly and petition. These, of course, are core principles of media professionals and their ethics to be explored in more depth later in *Living Media Ethics.* From a historical perspective, however, Madison's notion of "balance" and "check on powers of government" also are core principles that define news media, in particular, in holding elected officials accountable. That is why journalism is sometimes referred to as "The Fourth Estate," checking the power of the executive, judicial and legislative branches of government.

Some founders, including Alexander Hamilton, opposed these rights as unnecessary and potentially harmful to the operations of government. Others were concerned that these rights gave too much freedom to the people and prophesied continual protests and demonstrations. Madison had an eloquent answer to this as well:

> There are again two methods of removing the causes of faction: the one, by destroying the liberty which is essential to its existence; the other, by giving to every citizen the same opinions, the same passions, and the same interests.
>
> It could never be more truly said than of the first remedy, that it was worse than the disease. Liberty is to faction what air is to fire, an aliment without which it instantly expires. But it could not be less folly to abolish liberty, which is essential to political life, because it nourishes faction, than it would be to wish the annihilation of air, which is essential to animal life, because it imparts to fire its destructive agency.[65]

Jack N. Rakove, in his book *James Madison and the Creation of the American Republic*, believes that the Bill of Rights symbolized Madison's greatest achievement. His legacy influenced journalism more than that of any other founder, especially in the area of majority power and minority rights. "In both cases, his grasp of what was at stake was both modern and forward-looking, anticipating issues that would vex American politics henceforth,"[66] Rakove writes. The watchdog media's motto—*comfort the afflicted and afflict the comfortable*[67]—finds its historical influence in Madison's check on the powerful to ensure that the minority was heard. The motto often is misinterpreted because of changing social mores. As the Project for Excellence in Journalism notes,

> [T]he notion that the press is there to afflict the comfortable and comfort the afflicted misconstrues the meaning of the watchdog and gives it a liberal or progressive cast. ... As history showed us, it more properly means watching over the powerful few in society on behalf of the many to guard against tyranny.[68]

Madison stands behind this influence.

It is important to acknowledge that the Bill of Rights, especially the First Amendment, not only enlisted and entrusted the participation of the people as a foil to federal government; those rights were based on the notion that truth supersedes authority in a land that enjoys liberty. As mentioned earlier, this emanates from the 1735 seditious libel trial of John Peter Zenger, printer-journalist and contemporary of Benjamin Franklin. Zenger and others criticized the royal Governor William Cosby in the *New York Weekly Journal*, which Zenger published. Imprisoned, he won acquittal through the efforts of a famous lawyer, Andrew Hamilton (1676–1741), no relation to Alexander Hamilton, who argued, "It is pretty clear that in New York a man may make very free with his God, but he must take special care what he says of his Governor."[69]

Finally, the "other" more revered Hamilton, Alexander, also an attorney and resident of New York, whose portrait graces the U.S. $10 bill to commemorate his service as Secretary of the Treasury, founded the *New York Post*, still in publication today. Like Zenger before him, Hamilton used his newspaper "to hurl invectives" at those in office, in his day, the administration of President Thomas Jefferson and Vice President Aaron Burr[70] (Hamilton's feud with Burr culminated in the infamous duel between the two that claimed Hamilton's life.) As attorney, Hamilton promoted the ethic of truth superseding authority in the February 1804 appeal trial of *People v. Croswell*, a New York Federalist publisher convicted of libel. Hamilton tried to win a new trial by arguing that governmental tyranny eroded basic liberties. Truth was the anecdote without which the people were doomed to remain ignorant of government action against them. Hamilton told the judge, "I never did think the truth was a crime, for my soul has ever abhorred the thought that a free man dared not speak the truth."[71] Biographer Willard Sterne Randall notes that Hamilton lost the requested appeal for his client, "but his words had such a profound effect on the legislators who heard them that day that, in the next year's session of the New York Assembly, they enacted into law the principle of truth as a defense."[72]

From this brief and admittedly condensed section on historical and political influences, you can discern some common themes. Although the times, social mores and technology may change, these seven principles have endured in the United States as part of moral convergence:

1. **Equality:** *Every person has a right to life, liberty and the pursuit of happiness.*
2. **Inclusivity:** *Our national identity is incorporated in our name, the* **United** *States.*
3. **Work Ethic:** *Reason and merit prevail over bloodline and entitlement.*
4. **Honesty:** *Truth supersedes authority.*
5. **Access:** *Education ensures free speech in a republic.*
6. **Tolerance:** *The majority may rule, but the minority must be heard.*
7. **Accountability:** *Journalism is the watchdog over government.*

The great journalist and educator Ben H. Bagdikian puts these precepts into perspective. "From its birth," he writes, "the United States' most sacred principle has been government by the consent of the governed."[73]

Journalist and author Davis Merritt furthers that argument by stating that a free press is essential to a functioning democracy and vice versa:

> The synergy of those two ideas is important because a free society cannot determine its course—that is, self-determination does not exist—without three things: shared relevant information; an agora (that is, a place or mechanism where the implications of that information can be discussed); and shared values (at a minimum, a belief in personal liberty itself).[74]

Media critic Jay Rosen notes that journalists and practitioners frame and narrate our common history. Rosen asks us to engage the public "in the give-and-take of political dialogue," so that we "make participants out of spectators, and illuminate the promise of public life."[75]

LANGUAGE SHAPES PERCEPTION, TOO

The meanings of words change with the times and, in doing so, absorb social mores along with cultural and other influences. According to Clifford G. Christians, words are symbols and, as such, communication is the connective tissue in building cultures and communities. "Words," he writes, "derive their meaning from the interpretive, historical context humans themselves supply."[76] This is especially evident today because technology adds to that effect, transforming communication, not only in how messages are sent but also in how they are deciphered, often in abbreviations accompanied by memes and emojis. Historian Theodore Roszak observes that alterations in meanings of words have occurred throughout history, especially in the areas of science and technology. Specialists often take a commonly understood word from the public vocabulary and corrupt it with an esoteric definition, causing confusion to the point that we "may forget what the original word meant."[77] Roszak cites as a case in point the meaning of "information," which used to be *fact*-based term—a fact that few technologists recall anymore, perceiving information merely as quantifiable data.

Take a moment to evaluate how technology has changed the meanings of dozens of everyday terms that once depicted physical place and people. "Communities" referred to neighborhoods. A "cloud" rained on communities and now functions as digital storage space. "Property" used to mean land, not a characteristic of HTML. "Icon" used to mean a celebrity and "platform," where they entertained; now it is a clickable design on a computer running Windows®. "Windows" used to be what people looked out of. "Engagement" happened with a marriage proposal but now measures digital interaction. "Traffic" used to be what happened at rush hour and now tallies visitors to websites. "Bridge" used to be a metal structure over a river and now means a data connection device that forwards "packets" between "networks." "Conversion" used to happen when people switched religions; now it means the transformation from potential to actual online customer. "Application" used to mean what you filled out for a job and now is a mobile phone software. *Browser* used to be a person who shopped, *surfer* a person who rode the ocean, *domains* and *half-duplexes* where people lived, *hub* where they gathered, *patch* where they grew vegetables, *shell* what they found on the beach, *skin* what got burned on that beach, *TWAIN* what they read on that beach, *wave* what they watched there, and *memory* what they recalled about these places and activities.

The influence of language affects all platforms, especially public relations, because practitioners often must use language to resolve crises involving community and communication. In the essay "The Role and Ethics of Community Building for Consumer Products and Services," authors Dean Kruckeberg and Kenneth Starck write, "The meaning of 'community' has been devalued, defaced, disfigured—mugged, if you will—to the point that the word, itself, has been rendered almost useless."[78] Kruckeberg and Starck believe that the highest calling of public relations today is to help resolve the loss of a sense of community in the contemporary world. They note that the word not only has been usurped by technologists but also by journalists who write about the "international community," "Islamic community," "broader community," "financial community" and "community of scholars." Increasingly, they maintain, commercialism alters the interpersonal meaning of words, undermining the preciseness and power of language and with it, the practice of public relations. "New means of communication and transportation have destroyed the sense of geographic community that had existed earlier among proximate people."[79]

Language influences perception. Nowhere is this more evident than in advertising. Practitioners know that slogans contain key words—"The *Real* Thing" or "The *King* of Beers"—geared to give the product brand identity, attracting consumers. But advertisers also realize that words change with social mores. Since the 1900s, synonyms for the operative word "real" in the Coca-Cola slogan have included this abbreviated list: *absolute, actual, all-out, authentic, bona fide, de facto, downright, factual, flat-out, genuine, honest, incarnate, indubitable, intrinsic, irrefutable, legitimate, natural, original, positive, solid, sound, substantial, substantive, tangible, true, true-blue, undeniable, undoubted, unquestionable, unadulterated, valid, veritable.* If you plugged "true-blue" into Coke's slogan now, as in "Coke, the true-blue thing," it would depict "a colorful beverage" rather than "a genuine one." If you substituted "natural," it might be conceived as "containing no artificial ingredients." Some slang terms for "real" such as the 1980s term "bitchin'" would make no sense at all, consigned to the linguistic junk heap with words like "swell" or "groovy." To see how Coca-Cola has dealt with the changing meaning of operative words, consider the following abbreviated timeline of official slogans since 1886,[80] which began with the obvious "Drink Coca-Cola" and henceforth alluded to operative words "real" or "thing."

- **1942:** *The only thing like Coca-Cola is Coca-Cola itself.*
- **1956:** *Coca-Cola ... makes good things taste better.*
- **1963:** *Things go better with Coke.*
- **1970:** *It's the real thing.*
- **1971:** *I'd like to buy the world a Coke. It's the real thing.*
- **1985:** *America's real choice (Coca-Cola Classic).*
- **1990:** *You can't beat the real thing (Coca-Cola Classic).*
- **2003:** *Coca-Cola ... Real.*
- **2005:** *Make it Real.*

Advertisements playing off of those and other slogans also used or alluded to official slogans: *Real satisfaction in every glass* (1911), *Demand the genuine—refuse substitutes* (1912), *Demand the genuine by full name* (1914), *Thirst and taste for Coca-Cola are the same thing* (1926), and *Make it a real meal* (1959).

As some of the slogans and advertisements above indicate, concerning use of such terms as "genuine" or "real," Coca-Cola has been in competition with Pepsi since the start of the 20th century. In the 1980s and early 1990s, the so-called Cola Wars were waged when Pepsi began doing blind taste tests that showed people preferring Pepsi over Coke. In 1985 Coca-Cola sweetened its recipe to compete with the sugary Pepsi in a product campaign for "New Coke." This has gone down as one of the biggest marketing blunders of all time, not only because Coke changed the recipe but also competed with itself and a century of slogans promoting its brand as the real [not Pepsi] thing. Now the product and the slogan seemed artificial. Worse, the company did not practice effective brand management by sharply delineating one product from another but substituted the new thing for the real one. This only prompted people to hoard the real thing, and organizations such as Old Cola Drinkers of America were born to preserve it. The company yielded and re-introduced the real thing with Coke *Classic*, another operative word that required monitoring for alterations in meaning caused by social mores or other influences. The word "classic" was associated with such terms as "oldies but goodies" (music) and antique automobiles. In 2009, with "new" Coke no longer on shelves, the company dropped "classic" from its brand.

Coca-Cola learned valuable lessons about the power of branding from this experience, including the prospect that losses in market share at the time might not have been associated with the taste of Pepsi but with the superior competence of Pepsi marketers in brand advertising. Thirty years after the "New" Coke fiasco, a company spokesperson put the entire matter into ethical perspective, stating:

> [W]e introduced New Coke with no shortage of hype and fanfare. And it did succeed in shaking up the market. But not in the way it was intended. When we look back, this was the pivotal moment when we learned that fiercely loyal consumers—not the Company—own Coca-Cola and all

of our brands. It is a lesson that we take seriously and one that becomes clearer and more obvious with each passing anniversary.[81]

Another ethical lesson involves how far marketers should go in distinguishing how one product is superior to another similar product, as might be found in colas, toothpaste and beer. Often companies rely on slogans to influence consumers, with copy writers consciously appealing to people's psyches rather than taste buds. Advertisers, in particular, have to be wary about "word baggage," or the alteration of meanings caused by social mores and other influences. A word like "king," in "The King of Beers," once may have connoted "tops" as in the Baby Boomer generation childhood game "King of the Hill." In the 1990s this particular Budweiser slogan no longer seemed to appeal to younger consumers who considered the word "king" too aggressive or arrogant, associating the product with their parents' and grandparents' generations. Nonetheless, Anheuser-Busch had invested millions in establishing its trademark and filed a notice of opposition in 2015 when a California company, "She Beverage," attempted to trademark its beer "Queen of Beer." (Anheuser-Busch had defended its trademark successfully when another company tried to brand its beverage, "Queen of Beers.")[82]

Advertisers spend billions of dollars each year, researching new products and their slogans, according to Cassandra Reese, former manager of consolidated brand purchases for Kraft USA. "One time at Kraft USA a slogan used over 40 years—'Good Food, Good Food Ideas'—was challenged by the new marketing managers." The phrase "good food" rang "apple pie and mom," says Reese, "and that was not what the younger generation was responding to. Conversely, if moms used the product, the slogan implied that it must not be for *my* generation, younger consumers might think." Reese says advertisers test words and align slogans with products using scientific research, consumer panels, taste-test kitchens, focus groups, and telephone and electronic surveys. "Sometimes research will lead marketers to a word if a product is really 'whiter' or 'fluffier.' Then advertisers can say, 'Our brand is *whiter*' or 'Our brand is *fluffier*.' You would give those words to your copywriters and then they would have to test those words in a slogan."

Words, especially proper nouns, also can affect us personally and therefore influence us, coloring how we view the world. These are so-called "trigger" words because they usually trigger a reaction inside us and, consequently, cause us to lose perspective often when we most need it (when someone pushes an emotional button or when we respond favorably to a stranger or source, thinking we know them or share values, simply because they have used a certain word). Trigger words also reflect social mores. As noted, words are symbols that play on our perception, or how we view the world and others in it. Journalists in particular view the world as witnesses for society. As such, they must guard against being influenced by words manipulating perception. Depending on a person's values and experiences, these "trigger" words spark positive or negative emotions inside us. Journalists can lose perspective when a source intentionally or unintentionally uses a trigger word. Also, because of the media's power, words that journalists use in print, broadcast or online trigger emotions in the mass audience and so shape social mores.

You have heard these potent words thousands of times via mass media and probably have an opinion or a feeling about several common ones such as "Jesus," "God," "Satan," "Hitler," "CIA," "KKK," "FBI," "Dr. Martin Luther King," "Barbie," "Clinton," "Bush" or "Trump." These opinions and feelings are associated with social mores and/or basic influences. Depending on your awareness, these words can spark reactions—arguing instead of listening, for instance—or cloud perception: believing someone is a friend or an enemy based on his or her use of one of these words. Proper nouns signifying specific people, places or things often are associated with history, religion, community, media and cultural change (social mores). Each person may have a personal reaction to lowercase words based on experience rather than news. For example, if someone said his or her trigger word was "abortion," others may make an assumption that violates privacy. That would not be the case if the person said, "Roe v. Wade," the landmark 1973 Supreme Court decision on the issue. **WARNING: It is vital to make that distinction and protect privacy as we explore trigger words later in this chapter.**

The matter before us now is how media is a primary driver of social mores. For more than 20 years, the author of *Living Media Ethics* conducted a study with each media ethics class (enrollment 80–100) at Ohio University and Iowa State University, surveying students on proper nouns that evoked a pleasant or unpleasant emotion. The exercise was to show media influence on agendas. Here is a sampling from specific classes with italicized words associated with media coverage.[83]

- **1995:** 1. Jesus, 2. Satan, 3. *Hillary*, 4. Nazi, 5. KKK, 6. *UFO*, 7. *Newt*, 8. Roe v. Wade, 9. Elvis, 10. *CIA*
- **1998:** 1. KKK, 2. Hitler, 3. Friday, 4. *Challenger*, 5. Martin Luther King, 6. Roe v. Wade, 7. Christmas, 8. *Jane*, 9. *Saddam*, 10. Budweiser
- **2000:** 1. God, 2. KKK, 3. AIDS, 4. Nazi, 5. *Y2K*, 6. *Columbine*, 7. Roe v. Wade, 8. First Amendment, 9. *Internet*, 10. Affirmative Action
- **2003:** 1. Ohio University, 2. KKK, 3. Holocaust, 4. Jesus, 5. AIDS, 6. *Iraq*, 7. *George W. Bush* AND Pro-Life (tie), 8. Satan, 9. Wal-Mart, 10. *Taliban*
- **2006:** 1. *Sept. 11 and George W. Bush* (tie), 3. *Iraq*, 4. Jesus, 5. South Dakota, 6. *New Orleans*, 7. *Dick Cheney* and Adolf Hitler (tie), 9. AIDS, 10. *Al Qaeda*

- **2013**: 1. Holocaust, 2. KKK, 3. God, 4. Hawkeyes, 5. Pro-Choice, 6. *Al Qaeda*, 7. Bible, 8. Pro-Life and *Syria* (tie), 10. *Obama* (tie)
- **2015**: 1. *9/11*, 2. Hawkeyes, 3. *Trump*, 4. Hoiberg, 5. *America*, 6. *Kim Davis*, 7. New York, 8. *Syria*, 9. Jayhawks, 10. Taco Bell

Analyzing this list, you can easily spot proper nouns associated with place or specific culture, as in Hawkeyes (ISU's rival University of Iowa). Many of the terms are associated with history and religion. You may want to research italicized words in the above list that you do not immediately associate with news coverage. In 1995, for example, Republican House Speaker Newt Gingrich—a rising star at the time—was *Time Magazine*'s "Man of the Year." In 1998, the magazine *Jane* targeted young women who disliked how traditional women's magazines depicted or addressed women. Although you may have heard of Columbine, referring to a 1999 high school shooting massacre, you may not immediately recognize Y2K, or the millennium bug that was supposed to shut down computers at the start of the year 2000 (the metric "K" represents "thousand"; aka "Year 2000" or Y2K.) In 2006, the city of New Orleans was recovering from one of the most devastating hurricanes on record, *Katrina*, which caused $108 billion in damage and claimed the lives of 1,833 people. In 2013, President Obama was just re-elected and in 2015, President Trump began his successful run for the White House. You might not immediately recognize Kim Davis, a Kentucky county clerk who refused to issue marriage licenses to same-sex couples, thereby attracting national media attention by defying a court order that she do so.

If you cover news, or work as a practitioner on advertising or public relations campaigns, your reaction to certain trigger words (upper and lowercase) can affect your job performance. Learning to adjust for personal filters also can help you fulfill the responsibilities of reporting. John Lenger, the former Sunday editor of *The Post-Star* in Glens Falls, N.Y., recalls an incident with a reporter that did both. "Police had told her that teenagers were conducting Satanic rituals that included animal sacrifices," Lenger says. "She had an interview with a police informant who said he had witnessed a sacrifice, and an interview with the anti-Satanist leader of a Christian group. The reporter told me she was ready to go with a three-part series." Lenger asked her to balance the story by talking to Satanists, but the reporter refused. "She was morally opposed to giving such people any outlet for their message," Lenger says, but ultimately took his advice and interviewed the high priest of the largest organized Satanic church in the country. "That interview made her story. And that story won her awards and made her a star. Playing devil's advocate was not just the ethical thing to do," Lenger adds, using a pun to make a point. "It was also the smart thing to do" because it provided information to the community.

In that case, the reporter was responding to a trigger word, "Satan," that somehow was associated with her basic influences. But she adjusted for that and wrote an informative article. This happens often in the news business because reporters cover hundreds if not thousands of topics in the course of their careers. Someone, sometime, will use a trigger word that appeals to or angers the reporter in the course of an interview. Print and online journalists may be able to hide their immediate reactions from the audience, because of the nature of their platforms; not so radio and television reporters. In some sense, because of ubiquitous mobile phone videos, everyone at the scene is on display. As such, responding to a trigger word personally rather than professionally, in the course of an interview, is unsound in any media profession. Imagine advertisers and PR practitioners forgetting etiquette during pitches to prospective clients. That can lose an account. But there are more ominous scenarios. What about conscious attempts by others, from sources to prospective clients, who intentionally try to manipulate reporters and practitioners by using trigger words? Because so much information is online and immediately accessible, from blogs to social networks to search engines, manipulation of media is becoming more common—so much so, in fact, that the 2016 presidential election was influenced to some degree by fake news. Manipulation will be covered extensively in an upcoming chapter, as will propaganda; but it is useful to know at this point how trigger words can impact outcomes when used as means toward an end.

SHARPEN INSIGHT AND ATTAIN BALANCE

Perception, or how one interprets the outside world, is perhaps the most important element in any journalism job. Perception is also key in developing objectivity, defined as: *Viewing things, people and events as they actually exist without filtering them through basic influences or accepting or rejecting them without question because of social mores.* Or, simply: "Objectivity is seeing the world as it is, not how you wish it were."[84] Objectivity, by the way, applies to all media platforms—not just print, electronic news and photojournalism. You'll read more about that in the chapter on truth, which explores objectivity as a communication process. True, reporters, writers and photographers try to perceive the outside world as it exists to cover it accurately. But advertisers and public relations practitioners also must target audience and consumers with a keen, objective eye to determine the need for or effectiveness of a product or campaign. They also must evaluate dispassionately such aspects of an account as brand identity, copywriting, product or statistical research, market distribution and, at times, crisis management. Thus, to report to or target an audience effectively, *all* journalists and practitioners across platforms have to identify and adjust for influences and social mores cited in earlier sections. Only then will perception improve and with it, objectivity.

Too often, print and broadcast journalists believe objectivity means getting two sides of the story and giving them equal play. If so, they contend, a story is "balanced." That formula may work in legislative or election coverage—interviewing supporters and opponents of a bill in Congress or candidates of all parties in a campaign; but it falls short on other, more common types of assignments. A news reporter must clear his or her mind of influences and mores and try to perceive a situation as it exists, highlighting the most important aspects of a story in the lead, broadcast summary or cutline. Otherwise objectivity becomes a tone of voice—words that sound dispassionate but miss the mark, the newspeg and the truth.

Tom Knudson, reporter for the *Sacramento Bee* and winner of two Pulitzer Prizes, is known for his in-depth balanced investigative coverage, especially on environmental issues.[85] He credits his mentors, including such professors as Bill Kunerth, who taught at his alma mater, Iowa State University, with instilling in him the need for research to adjust for influences on his perception of the world. Kunerth, interviewed in 2005, remembered Knudson as "a natural" information gatherer, interviewer and writer. "He actually enjoys doing the research that too many journalists avoid, even though it is the key to successful investigative reporting. Whenever I'd discuss public records in class, most students' eyes would glaze over," Kunerth recalled. "Tom's would brighten."

Knudson says that most of the investigations and projects he is involved in are controversial to begin with, so he has to be sure to get perspectives from all sides of an issue. That requires extensive analysis, on-site travel and lengthy interviews. The more complex the topic, the more research is required for balance. "It's not my job to decide who's right or wrong," Knudson says, "but to report the issue as clearly as I can. That means double-checking, even triple-checking, everything, quoting people accurately, in context and by name and trying to give readers a sense of the larger drama behind the story. Ethics," he adds, "means being fair to individuals involved in the story and the reporting process. Too often, we in the press give short-shrift to complex issues because of time and financial constraints, and sometimes both. This serves no one well."

Tracey Noe, corporate communications executive at CVS Health, began her career not in public relations but in magazine journalism as an intern at *National Geographic* magazine. Since then, she has worked in PR for both multinational companies and global non-profits, leading a variety of disciplines including media relations, investor communications, brand marketing, crisis management, executive speechwriting, employee communications, and philanthropy—an indication of the scope of duties in the current digital milieu. Not only must Noe understand issues associated with her myriad responsibilities but also core principles of journalism. Like Tom Knudson, Noe believes that controversial issues are complex and often encompass many viewpoints. "As children, we were taught that there are two sides to every story," she says. "Journalists, however, must understand that human events arise from myriad, inter-connected forces—and that two sides are rarely sufficient to fully explain the consequences of a given action. The 'he said, she said' or 'point/counterpoint' style of reporting can be a tempting shortcut—but it fails to provide readers the breadth of information they deserve." In that respect, research is essential, Noe states, especially in reporting on science and medical issues. "For example, news reports attribute the growing obesity epidemic among U.S. children to a wide range of factors—from the popularity of video games and high-fat diets to the decline of public school physical education programs. But an issue of this magnitude deserves much more thorough analysis than a hackneyed quote from a concerned physician, followed by a boilerplate call for greater regulation from a public official. Responsible journalists understand that reversing the troubling trend of childhood obesity will require broad collaboration among both the public and private sectors—and that this kind of collaboration may take decades to evolve.

"Fair, accurate reporting also requires journalists to work closely with industry spokespeople—including (heaven forbid!) public relations professionals, who all too frequently are caricatured as shills or villains in newsroom banter," Noe adds. "Talented PR people offer well-researched, insightful perspectives on the issues of the day, and we often can help reporters develop fresh angles on evergreen topics. We share reporters' commitment to educating and enlightening the public—especially when consumers need to take action on emerging health and safety issues such as product recalls. Our code of ethics substantially parallels the code that guides journalists."

Deanna Sands, former managing editor of *The Omaha World-Herald*, believes that reporters have a moral obligation to do research. Otherwise they parrot the mores of the day. "We seldom explain what we really mean and then leave people to their own interpretation," she says. Balance is more than citing both sides of an issue. The world doesn't work that way, she says, especially when the topic involves controversial issues in science, society and technology.

In the end, balance means documenting and challenging all sides and viewpoints and providing additional data so that readers can put a story into proper context. The more fact and documentation, the better your audience will be able to see what you have seen, hear what you have heard, feel what you have felt, and experience what you did on assignment. Public relations practitioners will be able to represent clients' interests with more credibility if they research issues with the same vigor as news journalists. Advertisers will use precise words empowered by engaging visuals to showcase products and services, distinguishing them from competitors. However, to achieve that caliber of expertise, journalist and practitioner must be able to identify their own influences and adjust their perception so that they intuit the world without bias or error, as we will learn in the upcoming chapter on truth, the cornerstone of personal and professional ethics.

"DEPROGRAMMING YOUR INFLUENCES"

Personal Journal Exercise

1. Make a list of mottoes, phrases or sentences that a parent or relative repeated often enough to have become family lore. Include in your list any phrase or sentence that a friend, coworker, superior, teacher, mentor or other person has said often enough for you to remember and record. Try for at least ten, and do not identify the person who passed along the motto. Analyze each motto as objectively as possible and ascertain whether you think it is true, part true/part false, or false. Example: "*Respect your elders.* Part true/part false. (Depends on the elder.)" **Note:** *Do not put your name on this list, as you will hand it in as a printout or digital file to the instructor or group leader for the "Communal Journal Exercise."*

2. Analyze the advertisements in at least five print or online magazines which, you believe, reflect some kind of social more in the slogan, brand name, photograph, illustration or copy. Make a screenshot and printout of the advertisement (or photocopy it) and then use text to write a brief statement identifying any operative word(s) in the slogan, brand or copy or symbolism in the photograph or illustration indicating a specific social more: "Women should be concerned about their appearance" or "Men should drive rugged trucks." Create a 500-word journal entry or blog post or a short podcast or multimedia presentation discussing each of these messages and how it might influence the beliefs or behaviors of certain people or groups.

3. Make a list of ten proper nouns that trigger reactions, feelings or opinions (pleasant or unpleasant) within you. **Note:** *Do not put your name on this list, as you will hand it in as a printout or digital file to the instructor or group leader for the "Communal Journal Exercise."* Without violating your own or another person's privacy, analyze your own list concerning why the specific word causes you to respond in a certain way. Which words on your list were influenced by social mores? Which seem influenced by family or personal experience? Which seem influenced by media, history, culture, pop culture and/or politics? Write a paragraph in your personal journal about each influence and then state how you will adjust for it as a journalist or practitioner. **Note:** *You may also want to compile a list of lowercase personal trigger words for your own edification. Do not share those lists with others but contemplate what you learned about the power of words from these personal assignments. If you opt to write or blog about this, do not violate your own or anyone else's privacy or reputation.*

Communal Journal Exercise

1. Devise a confidential way to collect printouts of anonymous lists of mottoes, phrases or sentences from the class or group members' first "Personal Journal Exercise" earlier. (If you wish to collect these digitally, use an anonymous drop box.) Make a master list from all who turned in the assignment. Distribute the list via email or printout. As class instructor or group discussion leader, your role is to lead a discussion by reading those mottoes and asking the class or group if they agree with assessments concerning whether each motto is true, part true/part false, or false.

2. Devise a confidential way to collect printouts of lists of proper-noun trigger words from the third "Personal Journal Exercise." (If you wish to collect these digitally, use an anonymous drop box.) Make an alphabetical master list from all who turned in the assignment. Distribute the list via email with instructions to select and send back to you ten terms from the master list that also might qualify as a personal trigger word. Rank order responses, listing the top ten *collective* choices and distribute that list to the class or group. Base a discussion on how news media might have influenced the rank-ordered top-ten list and how some items may be associated with social mores, so that in a few years, people might forget what the specific term actually was about.

3. **Optional:** *Keep doing this with each new class or group and over time, you, too, will have a list of words that indicate news framing and social mores influenced by media.*

NOTES

1 Carolyn Marvin and Philip Meyer, "What Kind of Journalism Does the Public Need?," in *The Press*, eds. Geneva Overholser and Kathleen Hall Jamieson (New York: Oxford, 2005), 400.

2 Jill Andresky Fraser, *White-Collar Sweatshop: The Deterioration of Work and Its Rewards in Corporate America* (New York: Norton, 2001), 10.

3 Ryan Derousseau, "The Tech that Tracks Your Movements at Work," BBC, June 14, 2017, www.bbc.com/capital/story/20170613-the-tech-that-tracks-your-movements-at-work

4 Helen Leggatt, "Biggest Stressor in U.S. Workplace is Fear of Losing Job to AI, Tech," *Biz Report*, June 7, 2017, www.bizreport.com/2017/06/biggest-stressor-in-us-workplace-is-fear-of-losing-jobs-to-a.html

5 Brittany Jones-Cooper, "Millennials Are Most Likely to Behave Unethically at Work, Survey Finds," Yahoo Finance, October 25, 2017, www.aol.com/article/finance/2017/10/25/millennials-are-most-likely-to-behave-unethically-at-work-survey-finds/23256092/

6 Peter Singer, *Practical Ethics*, 2nd ed. (Cambridge: Cambridge University Press, 1993), 317.

7 Michael Levin, "Ethics Courses: Useless," *The New York Times*, November 25, 1989, Sec. A, 23.

8 Tory DeAngelis, "PTSD Treatments Grow in Evidence, Effectiveness," *Monitor on Psychology*, January 2008, Vol. 39, No. 1, 40.

9 Benjamin Franklin (as president of the Pennsylvania Society), "Petition from the Pennsylvania Society for the Abolition of Slavery," February 3, 1790, www.ushistory.org/documents/antislavery.htm

10 Barbara Lippert, "Dream Sequence: Dan Quayle's Family Values Fail to Motivate Apathetic Voters," *ADWEEK Eastern Edition*, September 21, 1992, 41.

11 See Joseph Carroll, "Public: 'Family Values' Important to Presidential Vote," Gallup, December 26, 2007, www.gallup.com/poll/103375/public-family-values-important-presidential-vote.aspx

12 Lance Morrow, "But Seriously, Folks," *Time*, June 1, 1992, 29.

13 Ibid., 29.

14 Marlys Harris, "What's a 'Murphy Brown' Like Me Supposed to Do?," *Money*, November 1992, 191.

15 Michele Ingrassia, "Daughters of Murphy Brown," *Newsweek*, August 2, 1993, 58.

16 Clifford G. Christians, "The Common Good as First Principle," in *The Idea of Public Journalism*, ed. Theodore L. Glasser (New York: The Guilford Press, 1999), 68.

17 Ibid., 67.

18 See "The Best Action is the One with the Best Consequences" by John Hospers in *Computers, Ethics, and Society*, eds. M. David Erman and Michele S. Shauf (New York: Oxford University Press, 2003), 3–11.

19 John Stuart Mill, Utilitarianism, "What Utilitarianism Is," 1863, www.utilitarianism.com/mill2.htm

20 Clifford G. Christians, Mark Fackler, Kim B. Rotzoll, Kathy Brittain McKee, *Media Ethics: Cases and Moral Reasoning*, 6th ed. (New York: Longman, 2001), 64.

21 See "The Best Action is the One in Accord with Universal Rules" by James Rachels in *Computers, Ethics, and Society*, 12–16.

22 Valerie Alia, *Media Ethics and Social Change* (New York: Routledge, 2004), 16.

23 Christians, Fackler, Rotzoll, McKee, 16.

24 Ibid.

25 See Philip Patterson and Lee Wilkins, *Media Ethics: Issues and Cases*, 5th ed. (New York: McGraw-Hill, 2005), 12.

26 Johan Retief, *Media Ethics: An Introduction to Responsible Journalism* (Cape Town: Oxford University Press, 2002), 7.

27 Christians, Fackler, Rotzoll, McKee, 64.

28 *Random House Dictionary of the English Language*, 2nd ed., unabridged, 665.

29 Edward Spence and Brett Van Heekeren, *Advertising Ethics* (Upper Saddle River, N.J.: Pearson, 2005), 2.

30 Peggy H. Cunningham, "Ethics of Advertising: Oxymoron or Good Business Practice?," in *The Advertising Business: Operations, Creativity, Media Planning, Integrated Communications*, ed. John Philip Jones (Thousand Oaks, Calif.:, Sage, 1999), 501.

31 Ibid.

32 Frank Swertlow, "Pulled Ads Called the Latest Gaffe from L.A. Times," *Los Angeles Business Journal*, April 24, 2000, www.findarticles.com/p/articles/mi_m5072/is_17_22/ai_61894510

33 Clifford G. Christians, "The Media and Moral Literacy," *Ethical Space: The International Journal of Communication Ethics*, Vol. 1, No. 1, 2003, 13.

34 Ibid.

35 See "The truth® campaign" at www.protectthetruth.org/truthcampaign.htm

36 See www.thetruth.com/about-truth

37 See www.urbandictionary.com/define.php?term=Keep%20it%20real

38 See myethicsclass.files.wordpress.com/2012/08/vw_influence1.jpg

39 See www.etsy.com/listing/461793292/volvo-station-wagon-original-1990

40 See www.youtube.com/watch?v=uiUXLWQH2U4

41 Steven Kreis, "Why Study History," in *The History Guide: A Student's Guide to the Study of History*, www.historyguide.org/guide/study.html

42 Ibid.

43 Barbie Zelizer, "Definitions of Journalism," in *The Press*, eds. Geneva Overholser and Kathleen Hall Jamieson (New York: Oxford, 2005), 66.

44 See "John Locke: Human Nature and God's Purposes," 3.2, *Stanford Encyclopedia of Philosophy*, plato.stanford.edu/entries/locke/

45 See Washington State University's educational website, *World Civilizations*, "Martin Luther," www.wsu.edu/~dee/REFORM/LUTHER.HTM. At that site you can also find a link leading to a translation of Luther's essay on freedom.

46 For more information on this topic, see Eric W. Gritsch, "Was Luther Anti-Semitic?," *Christianity Today*, Issue 39, 1993, www.christianitytoday.com/history/issues/issue-39/

47 See the Gutenberg entry "Indulgences" in the online British Library at www.bl.uk/treasures/gutenberg/indulgences.html

48 Harvey C. Mansfield, "Liberty and Virtue in the American Founding," in *Never a Matter of Indifference: Sustaining Virtue in a Free Republic*, ed. Peter Berkowitz (Stanford, Calif.: Hoover Institution Press, 2003), 4.

49 Robert Schmuhl and Robert G. Picard, "The Marketplace of Ideas," in *The Press*, eds. Geneva Overholser and Kathleen Hall Jamieson (New York: Oxford, 2005), 141.

50 See "Cicero," *The Internet Encyclopedia of Philosophy*, www.iep.utm.edu/c/cicero.htm

51 Several online sites reprint the Stamp Act in its entirety, including this one maintained by Steven Thomas at Georgia Tech Research Institute: ahp.gatech.edu/stamp_act_bp_1765.html

52 Mary Bellis, "Benjamin Franklin was a Statesman and Inventor," *About Business & Finance*, inventors.about.com/od/fstartinventions/a/Frank lin.htm

53 Patricia Bizzell and Bruce Herzberg, *The Rhetorical Tradition: Readings from Classical Times to the Present* (New York: St. Martins, 1990), 637.

54 Walter Isaacson, *Ben Franklin: An American Life* (New York: Simon and Schuster Paperbacks, 2004), 295.

55 "Excerpts from the Correspondence of Thomas Jefferson," Letter to Edward Carrington, January 16, 1787, from www.cooperativeindivid ualism.org/jefferson_d_01.html#D10

56 "Common Good," John Jay, in a letter to Benjamin Rush, Michigan Council for Social Studies, www.michcouncilss.org/resources/WORDS_ TO_LIVE_BY.pdf

57 R.B. Bernstein, *Thomas Jefferson* (New York: Oxford, 2003), 33.

58 Ibid., 39.

59 Ibid., 40.

60 Walter Stahr, *John Jay: Founding Father* (New York: Hambledon and London, 2005), 186.

61 Ibid., 190.

62 Ibid., 193.

63 Ibid., 193.

64 Ibid., 72.

65 James Madison, *The Federalist 10*, "The Utility of the Union as a Safeguard Against Domestic Faction and Insurrection," November 22, 1787, www.constitution.org/fed/federa10.htm

66 Jack N. Rakove, *James Madison and the Creation of the American Republic*, 2nd ed. (New York: Longman, 2002), 224.

67 The phrase "The business of a newspaper is to comfort the afflicted and afflict the comfortable" comes from Mark Twain's friend and fellow journalist, the muckraker Finley Peter Dunne, and is derived from the following passage: *"Th newspaper does ivrything f'r us. It runs th' polis foorce an' th' banks, commands th' milishy, controls th' ligislachure, baptizes th' young, marries th' foolish, comforts th' afflicted, afflicts th' comfortable, buries th' dead an' roasts thim aftherward."* Dunne, in the first syndicated column in the United States, "Mr. Dooley," spoke in an Irish accent and satirized the politics of the late 19th century. Read his writings at onlinebooks. library.upenn.edu/webbin/gutbook/author?name=Dunne%2C%20 Finley%20Peter%2C%201867-1936

68 "The Watchdog Misunderstood," Project for Excellence in Journalism, no date, www.journalism.org/resources/tools/reporting/watchdog/mis undestood.asp

69 "Andrew Hamilton, Statement at Trial of John Peter Zenger, 1735," in *A Patriot's Handbook: Songs, Poems, Stories, and Speeches Celebrating the Land We Love*, ed. Caroline Kennedy (New York: Hyperion, 2003), 229.

70 Willard Sterne Randall, *Alexander Hamilton: A Life* (New York: Perennial, 2003), 423.

71 Ibid.

72 Ibid.

73 Ben H. Bagdikian, *The New Media Monopoly* (Boston, Mass.: Beacon Press, 2004), 2.

74 Davis Merritt, *Knightfall: Knight Ridder and How the Erosion of Newspaper Journalism is Putting Democracy at Risk* (New York: AMACOM, 2005), 17.

75 Jay Rosen, *Getting the Connections Right: Public Journalism and the Troubles in the Press* (New York: The Twentieth Century Fund Press, 1996), 5.

76 Clifford G. Christians, "The Media and Moral Literacy," 14.

77 Theodore Roszak, *The Cult of Information* (Berkeley, Calif.: University of California Press, 1994), 13.

78 Dean Kruckeberg and Kenneth Starck, "The Role and Ethics of Community Building for Consumer Products and Services," in *Handbook of Product Placement in the Mass Media: New Strategies in Marketing Theory, Practice, Trends, and Ethics*, ed. Mary-Lou Galician (Binghamton, N.Y.: Haworth, 2004), 134. Note: In the citation above the authors quote and revise their own work in *Public Relations and Community: A Reconstructed Theory* (New York, Praeger, 1988).

79 Kruckeberg and Starck, 134.

80 See the official website press kit citing official slogans at www2.coca-cola.com/presscenter/presskit_120_slogans.html

81 Rachid Haoues, "30 Years Ago Today, Coca-Cola Made its Worst Mistake," CBS News, April 23, 2015, www.cbsnews.com/news/30-years-ago-today-coca-cola-new-coke-failure/

82 For more in the Anheuser-Busch trademark disputes, see "'King of Beers' Duking it Out with 'Queen of Beer'" by Lisa Brown, *St. Louis Post-Dispatch*, August 20, 2015, www.stltoday.com/business/local/king-of-beers-duking-it-out-with-queen-of-beer/article_2a11cdc3-41eb-53 7e-a488-b347df437100.html

83 For an expanded list, see: myethicsclass.files.wordpress.com/2012/09/trigger-words_2015.pdf

84 Brent Cunningham, "Re-thinking Objectivity," *Columbia Journalism Review*, July/August 2003, archives.cjr.org/feature/rethinking_objectivity.php

85 Tom Knudson's article, "State of Denial," analyzing California's consumption patterns, received the Reuters-World Conservation Union

award for excellence in environmental reporting. The article, available online at www.sacbee.com/static/live/news/projects/denial/, carries this introduction summarizing content and indicates the extent of research required to do the series: "California's environmental legacy of conserving resources at home is on a collision course with its habit of consuming them in record quantities from abroad. And often the losers are impoverished citizens and communities—and spectacular ecosystems—in remote parts of the globe, where money speaks louder than the land."

CHAPTER 3

Responsibility: Take or Forsake It

RIGHT AND WRONG DIFFER FROM GOOD AND BAD

The influential 1947 Hutchins Commission report noted the "first link in the chain of responsibility" demands "that the media should be accurate. They should not lie."[1] Before we can embrace truth, we have to understand responsibility as a principle associated with both conscience and consciousness and shaped, in part, through mottoes, mentors and role models and the values by which we choose to live our ethics. In the previous chapter, we said the conscience is an inner voice that helps distinguish right from wrong and consciousness, an inner knowing that helps foresee how our actions affect others. They must work in tandem for conscience to be unencumbered and consciousness to be keen. We also noted the influence on our perception of family mottoes such as *Treat everyone equally* or *Pick your enemies as carefully as you pick your friends*. We said that some of these mottoes were mostly true, such as "Know thyself" (Socrates); others such as *Respect your elders*, only part true; and some false such as *Stealing is okay as long as you don't get caught!* When it comes to ethics, there is another motto passed down by recent generations that is at best only part true: *If it feels good, do it!* Variations of the motto can be found in popular songs, company slogans and advertisements. That motto often is irresponsible. It suggests that we should sate our appetites rather than live our ethics. Because it confuses outcomes with actions, or means with ends, and is widely believed to be true, no other saying has done more harm to values in particular and ethics in general than this one.

The motto muddles concepts of right and wrong with outcomes of good and bad. It throws our ethical compass off course. The fact is that doing the right thing can feel good or bad. Just like doing the wrong thing can feel good or bad. The terms often are used interchangeably but have distinct definitions. Right and wrong are *choices* over which an individual has much control. Good and bad are *outcomes* over which an individual has little, if any, control. Right and wrong are functions of *your* behavior. Good and bad are functions of *events* that affect others and that you may help set into motion by your behavior. Concepts of right and wrong are *internal*. Concepts of good and bad are *external*. The more that people follow the motto—*If it feels good, do it!*—the more they are controlled by outside forces, succumbing to ethical shortcuts that may ease pressures temporarily but that eventually complicate our own and others' lives.

A person who lives by the concepts of right and wrong learns to accept *consequences*. This is essential if we hope to lead ethical lives. Accepting consequences is a two-step process: a person reflects on the possible moral outcomes of an action before deciding to take it. Depending on the issue at hand, a person asks such questions as: "Will I be able to live with such a decision? How will it affect others? Could it bring harm to them or me? What is the worst-case scenario? Is the decision legal? Untruthful? Manipulative? Deceitful? Biased? Unfair? Indiscreet? Unprofessional?" Keep in mind that an ethical person, at one point or another in his or her development, may have seriously considered these and other moral questions. After a time, though, they do not go down the above checklist based on every decision; the mere practice of it fine-tunes the conscience so that they learn to trust and intuit responses. Then the person decides to make, postpone or reject the decision, assuming responsibility for that choice— *regardless of whether the outcome happens to be good or bad*.

How does a journalist or practitioner take time to "reflect" on right and wrong actions when many of them on the job must be made in a split second covering a story or interacting with a client or meeting a deadline? That's the *value* of a value system. It helps you assess situations quickly by putting you in touch with gut feelings (conscience) and sharpening perception (consciousness) so you can react responsibly. According to H.M. Schulweis in *Conscience: The Duty to Obey and the Duty to Disobey*, our perception of the world must be as close to reality as possible or else we risk dysfunction.[2] Moreover, he adds, "Values are also important for the evolution of consciousness" because they give meaning to experience.[3] As such, the more conscience informs consciousness, and vice versa, the sharper your moral constitution—otherwise known as your *character*— will become over time. "Time" is a factor when living your ethics. The conscience takes you back in time so that you can access how you felt in similar situations. It operates in the past, primarily because it is nurtured "by parents, teachers, religion, and the collective conscience of a community," according to Harvard Medical School psychiatrist John J. Ratey.[4] Consciousness takes you forward in time so that you can predict consequences with increasing accuracy. Schulweis notes, "As we gain more attention and consciousness we can better evaluate actions and consequences and be less impulsive than our current selves."[5] Thus informed, you can better intuit in the moment what actions you can take or decisions you should make.

Unethical journalists and practitioners lack a value system. Concepts of right and wrong are not priorities; self-interest or promotion take precedence in the supposed cut-throat world of instantaneous mass communication. Because of this, such a person believes that assessing each situation takes too much time and does nothing to alleviate immediate pressures. So, the person follows the concepts of good and bad: *If it feels good, do it; if it feels bad, don't.* Depending on the situation at hand, the unethical communicator asks such questions as: "How will I profit from such a decision? How will it affect me? What is the best-case scenario? Will my action go undetected? If it is detected, what steps can I take, lies can I fake, or excuses can I make to blame someone else or escape punishment?" The less you listen to your conscience, the muter its voice will become over time. The less you hone your consciousness, the more myopic its vision will become over time. Poorly informed, you may make snap judgments that continuously have to be modified or shored up to suit the ever-changing circumstances reflecting the complexity of the world and the diversity of the people in it. Instead of learning from the past and accepting future consequences, the unethical person becomes increasingly skilled at *justifying* his or her actions.

"JUSTIFICATION" IS JUST AN EXCUSE

The word "justification," like "motivation," has two meanings. As we learned in the first journal exercise in Chapter 1, motivation can mean "motive" or the *reason* for doing, acting or communicating something. "Motivation" or its verb "motivate" can appeal to the conscience, serving as a catalyst or inspiration. One can feel "justified" or vindicated in his or her choices or behaviors. Another more common meaning associated with ethics is an "excuse" for making wrong choices or behaving immorally.

Compare two systems of behavior. The concept of justification, or excuse-making in context of this discussion, is aligned with concepts of good and bad. The unethical journalist or practitioner has keen interest in outcomes and only passing interest in value systems and professional standards. Conversely, accepting consequences is aligned with right and wrong. The ethical employee has passing interest in outcomes and keen interest in actions being right or wrong, honoring his or her value system along with professional standards. And while it is true that living ethics on occasion may cause you to lose a plush job, assignment or account or even friendships at the workplace, those who interact with you will come to trust your word because they can rely on it. The unethical employee who uses other people for personal gain on occasion may win that plush job, assignment or account, but in doing so, risks complaints, lawsuits and even imprisonment as happens routinely at all echelons of business. The goal of living ethics is to serve the public and constituents to the best of your ability and then return home to a good night's sleep on the pillow of an unencumbered conscience. In sum, ethical people accept responsibility and consequences, grounding their decisions in values and standards. Unethical people shun responsibility and consequences, grounding decisions in excuses and justifications.

Examine the basics of irresponsibility or deflecting blame. The news media as a whole often are accused of negativity, overemphasizing only the bad in society while overlooking the good. Editors and reporters often use the excuse of "blaming the messenger." According to journalist James Fallows,

> [T]he press claims no responsibility for the world that it displays. Accuse a publication of left-wing bias, and its editors will reply that they are often accused of being right-wing, too—or of being pro-black, or anti-black, or pro-business, or nuttily pro-environment, or of being biased in every other conceivable way. If people are complaining from all sides, the editors reason, it must mean that they've got the balance just about right. Say that coverage is shallow or sensationalistic, and reporters will reply that they are already serving up more extensive, thoughtful news analysis than a lazy public will bother to read. If they don't feature crime and gore in the paper, they'll lose their audience to competitors that do.[6]

Fallows' example is directed at several news platforms, including newspapers and electronic media. But individual journalists and practitioners make excuses, too, and these also fall into predictable patterns.

Charles Warner, Goldenson Chair Emeritus at the University of Missouri School of Journalism, notes that there are four common reasons for unethical behavior. People tend to heed authority and so claim that they were just following orders from superiors. They use that justification to excuse unethical actions. People also yield to peer and social pressures, justifying actions on the claim that "everyone does it."[7] Warner also believes that unethical behavior happens in the absence of clear policies, practices and codes, allowing people to say that no one had informed them—yet another common justification. He states that some corporate cultures encourage employees to "wink" at codes or mission statements, enabling wrongdoers to claim, "No one will know; I won't get caught."[8]

Philosopher Sissela Bok believes that the purpose of an excuse is to mitigate or remove entirely any blame that can be attributed to a person's actions. Excuses attempt to accomplish this in three ways, she states, by implying that a fault is not really one, or if it is, the agent of that action was not responsible for it. "And finally, it can suggest that, though there has been a fault, and though the agent is responsible, he is not really to blame because he has good reasons to do as he did."[9]

That third strategy is associated with the concept of justification, which Bok sees as a more intricate process, defending an action by associating it with a standard and directing your reasoning toward a specific audience: "to God, or a court of law, or one's peers, or one's own conscience."[10] The 2016 presidential campaign was fraught with stereotypically offensive missteps followed by lame justifications. Democratic candidate Hillary Clinton told those attending an LGBTQ fundraiser "you can put half of Trump supporters into what I call the basket of deplorables," claiming they were racist, sexist, homophobic, xenophobic, Islamophobic, "you name it."[11] While she apologized for the statement, she justified it by claiming she should have said "some" rather than "half." The issue here is that "some" can apply to anyone in any group. When a 2005 video of Republican candidate Donald Trump emerged, with audio of vulgar predatory terms about kissing and groping women, he claimed, "when you're a star, they let you do it," only to justify those remarks during the campaign as "locker-room banter."[12] At issue here was the justification that all males in locker rooms speak so malignantly. They decidedly do not. With a little online research about the "worst moments of the 2016 presidential campaign," you can find many more examples from all candidates and their surrogates across media platforms. Many such examples will have one thing in common from an ethical perspective: Deflecting responsibility rather than accepting consequences for a decision, action or statement, and trying to cast blame on others to effect a good outcome from a wrong choice.

Ethicist Lou Hodges writes that a journalist or practitioner who gives an accounting of his or her actions or decisions also "seeks to explain what he did and why, by offering justification for his choices between what to do and what to avoid doing."[13] As you can see, Hodges' view of justification is similar to that of Sissela Bok's in that an explanation for a person's actions is directed at reasonable people—readers, viewers, sponsors and constituents. Reasonable people, however, share one quality: *They expect people to take responsibility for their actions.* When mistakes are made, they expect sincere, full apologies free of justifications whose intent may be to absolve the employee and/or corporation from liability rather than resolve the matter at hand. In analyzing justification, Bok uses the term "God." When companies seek absolution rather than resolution, "justification" becomes pejorative, losing its Biblical appeal as an "act of God" that should be "free from guilt or penalty"[14] to an attempt at "vindication" or "defense." Or, in current media lingo, to "spin" and make excuses. Hodges further distinguishes accountability from the principle of responsibility. "Responsibility," he writes, "has to do with defining proper conduct, accountability with compelling it."[15]

When viewed from this perspective, journalists and practitioners have a responsibility to be truthful when disseminating information to their audience and clientele, and when that information is inaccurate or misleading, accountability compels them to set the record straight by making a full, transparent disclosure.

BE ACCOUNTABLE FOR BEHAVIOR

Responsibility has many facets. In addition to justification, the concept of accountability also comes into play in mass communication. Simply, it means an employee's willingness to accept consequences for words, actions or behaviors and to be held accountable for doing that by the publics being served. Employees not only have a responsibility to adhere to value systems, but also to audiences and clientele, stockholders and other constituents, not to mention colleagues and supervisors. In an essay titled, "Ethics of Advertising: Oxymoron or Good Business Practice?" Peggy H. Cunningham notes how relationships with and obligations to others often complicate the notion of responsibility, which she believes is at the heart of moral decision-making. People are complex enough, she observes, but diverse people working in companies with distinct cultures become even more complex when all these relationships are considered. "Individual advertising practitioners have numerous obligations: the duty to comply with the law, the responsibility of helping their firms make a profit, the duty to serve their clients well, the obligation to treat suppliers fairly, responsibilities to their employees, obligations to the people toward whom their promotions are directed, duties to society in general, and obligations to themselves,"[16] Cunningham explains. She notes that ethical dilemmas arise when these varying obligations conflict, "when more than one group of stakeholders must be served, and when personal values are opposed to business needs."[17]

Initially these may sound like justifications. Cunningham, however, is quick to associate them with accountability which, she says, is the second most important ethical consideration after responsibility.[18] Practitioners must remember that they are accountable to all of these constituents and so must be conscious of their core relationships and obligations when creating, designing or executing campaigns. In a word, assessing consequences *beforehand* not only safeguards relationships and clarifies obligations; it also ensures a substantive level of responsibility.

Unethical journalists and practitioners not only avoid responsibility but see no value in accountability. Frankly, they reason, that could feel bad. If a certain outcome is bad to begin with—a supervisor questioning an anonymous quotation in a news story or PR release, say—such a journalist or practitioner might think: "Why make it feel worse by admitting the quote is a fabrication? Better to justify my actions to myself by saying the deadline was inhumane to begin with and the supervisor who suspects the infraction, an ogre; better to justify my actions to my boss by claiming the fabrication was not a fabrication at all. After all, the editor has no real way of checking. And if the quote is challenged by readers or sources, then tomorrow I'll just have to invent some other scenario."

It *does* feel bad to miss a deadline or be beaten by a competitor. It feels worse to tell that to a supervisor. The ethical employee knows this but makes a decision to admit defeat and vows to try harder next time, which is all any individual can do; thus, he or she accepts consequences: The boss might become angry. So what? People become angry all the time and often for good reasons. The ethical journalist accepts that situation, too, and attempts to work out a solution—learning better time-management skills or agreeing to a progress plan that will determine his or her future with the company. These consequences might feel bad in the short term but are *liberating* choices in the long term. First, they are choices over which the employee has control: learning new skills or improving performance. Second, they indicate to the supervisor that the employee realizes the values of hard work, determination and honor. Third, no matter how supervisors may respond, the more an employee practices this ethical tenet, the more she or he will enhance experience and expertise.

ACCOUNTABILITY MEANS HAVING TO SAY YOU'RE SORRY

Accountability applies to all levels of the work force, from public relations and advertising interns to celebrity news anchors and agency heads. As we will see more in depth in the chapter on fairness, it is standard practice to correct factual errors and apologize quickly in print, online and broadcast platforms. Conscientious journalists and practitioners typically focus on where corrections and apologies should be placed in a publication or website or conveyed during a broadcast or media conference. Such admissions also should be timely and prominent. In *Journalism Ethics*, for instance, Philip Seib and Kathy Fitzpatrick state that "corrections should be made as soon as the error is discovered" and "presented in the way most likely to offset whatever damage was done by the error."[19]

Accountability requires a full, transparent accounting, acknowledging mistakes. The more a news outlet "justifies" rather than apologizes for a mistake, the more likely that company rather than the error will become the focus of a follow-up news story. There are many failed examples in recent media history. One such case happened on September 8, 2004 and involved former CBS News anchor Dan Rather in a "60 Minutes Wednesday" segment focusing on memos said to have been written by George W. Bush's commanding officer during the former president's Air National Guard service in Texas. The memos' formatting, typeface and other characteristics suggested that they were composed with Microsoft Word® rather than on a 1970s-era typewriter. As for the type font at the center of the controversy and the possibility that Bush's commander, Lt. Col. Jerry Killian, was using a sophisticated typewriter capable of Microsoft-like formatting, "60 Minutes" chose, simply, to stand by its report rather than recheck its story. In fact, CBS News issued this statement soon after questions arose about the segment:

> The documents are backed up not only by independent handwriting and forensic document experts but by sources familiar with their content. ... Contrary to some rumors, no internal investigation is under

way at CBS News nor is one planned. We have complete confidence in our reporting and will continue to pursue the story.[20]

This only intensified the debate about the memos' authenticity. At a minimum, CBS News should have reassured its critics that it would look into allegations about the segment, especially questions raised on the internet about the document being created in Microsoft Word®. That suggested media manipulation and a hoax—topics to be covered in the chapter on manipulation. Instead, CBS News stated "with absolute certainty" that the memos could have been produced on typewriters available in the 1970s.[21]

Bloggers and traditional media scrutinized these justifications until an investigation was launched, ultimately resulting in the firing of Mary Mapes, the story's producer; Josh Howard, executive producer of "60 Minutes Wednesday"; Howard's associate, Mary Murphy; and CBS News Senior Vice President Betsy West.

Rather, who would retire shortly thereafter as CBS network news anchor, escaped disciplinary consequences and issued this apology:

> Last week, amid increasing questions about the authenticity of documents used in support of a "60 Minutes Wednesday" story about President Bush's time in the Texas Air National Guard, CBS News vowed to re-examine the documents in question—and their source—vigorously. And we promised that we would let the American public know what this examination turned up, whatever the outcome.
>
> Now, after extensive additional interviews, I no longer have the confidence in these documents that would allow us to continue vouching for them journalistically. ... We made a mistake in judgment, and for that I am sorry. It was an error that was made, however, in good faith and in the spirit of trying to carry on a CBS News tradition of investigative reporting without fear or favoritism.
>
> Please know that nothing is more important to us than people's trust in our ability and our commitment to report fairly and truthfully.[22]

As an apology correcting the record, this is not bad. There remains a smidgeon of justification in the sentence—"It was an error that was made, however, in good faith and in the spirit of trying to carry on a CBS News tradition of investigative reporting without fear or favoritism." Ethically, this justification is easy to refute. To begin with, the sentence contains "trigger" words and phrases—language so loaded with cultural and personal meaning that it detracts from the issue at hand—namely, "good faith," "in the spirit," "tradition," "investigative reporting," "fear" and "favoritism." Fearless, spirited investigative journalism done in good faith that shows no favoritism happens, coincidentally, to be based on fact. When a factual report questioned by audience is not rechecked, it may be associated more with arrogance than tradition. The justification line might have read:

Initially we believed that the error was made in the CBS tradition of fearless, objective investigative reporting; however, in hindsight, we acknowledge those news values rely on fact rather than presumption thereof. In the end our own reluctance to check facts may have seemed arrogant, especially because it undermined people's trust in our ability and our commitment to report fairly and truthfully.

Accountability is difficult when journalists and practitioners trust their sources and clients who turn out to be deceptive or manipulative. This becomes more complicated when we try to balance accountability with our own deeply held beliefs. In 2014, *Rolling Stone* published a story titled "A Rape on Campus," which depicted a gang sexual assault at a University of Virginia fraternity house, contending, in part, that the University failed to respond appropriately in handling the situation. *The Washington Post* and other news outlets began to fact-check the story, perhaps to match it and follow up on the allegations for their own print and online outlets. They discovered inconsistencies, forcing *Rolling Stone* to issue a statement about the story, admitting discrepancies in the rape account as told by a survivor named Jackie:

> The fraternity has issued a formal statement denying the assault and asserting that there was no "date function or formal event" on the night in question. Jackie herself is now unsure if the man she says lured her into the room where the rape occurred, identified in the story as "Drew," was a Phi Psi brother. According to *The Washington Post*, "Drew" actually belongs to a different fraternity and when contacted by the paper, he denied knowing Jackie.[23]

The Washington Post followed up with more discrepancies, but *Rolling Stone* justified its coverage by pointing to a standard of withholding names of rape complainants and being sensitive to the horrors of sexual assault:

> We published the article with the firm belief that it was accurate. Given all of these reports, however, we have come to the conclusion that we were mistaken in honoring Jackie's request to not contact the alleged assaulters to get their account. In trying to be sensitive to the unfair shame and humiliation many women feel after a sexual assault, we made a judgment—the kind of judgment reporters and editors make every day. We should have not made this agreement with Jackie and we should have worked harder to convince her that the truth would have been better served by getting the other side of the story. These mistakes are on *Rolling Stone*, not on Jackie. We apologize to anyone who was affected by the story and we will continue to investigate the events of that evening.[24]

Ethically, a journalist can be sensitive in reporting sexual assault and still be accountable to the audience. Accountability in this case required the reporter, Sabrina Rubin Erdely, to get both sides of the story. She should not have agreed to disregard sources who might have been able to affirm Jackie's account. To make matters worse, *Rolling Stone*'s initial explanation was published before its purported facts were thoroughly investigated and verified by its own staff. Instead, news reporters from other companies continued to find holes in the assault story until the magazine was forced to retract the article. Later, a report by the Columbia Graduate School of Journalism, which *Rolling Stone* commissioned, confirmed that the magazine failed to honor routine journalistic practices in verifying specific details of the reported assault. Ultimately, *Rolling Stone* was successfully sued for libel. Erdely, who lost her job, said this about the ordeal:

> This experience has been devastating to me, both professionally and personally. Never in my 20-plus years as a reporter have I had a story or a source fall apart on me after publication. After feeling so sure about the Article, and believing so strongly that it would help spur change on college campuses, losing faith in the credibility of one of my major sources post-publication took me entirely by surprise. I was stunned and shaken by the experience, and remain so to this day.[25]

In sum, publications should refrain from justifying a questionable action until all the facts are known and, once those facts are known, the outlet is accountable to the audience and should make a full, transparent disclosure. *The Washington Post*, in analyzing the *Rolling Stone* debacle, stated, "Awful journalism can either be exposed by editors before publication or by competitors after publication."[26]

One more observation about the *Rolling Stone* story in case you plan on a career in public relations or advertising and believe the previous passage does not affect you. Teresa A. Sullivan, president of the University of Virginia, had to conduct her own internal investigation after the initial story was published to ascertain the veracity of the allegations. Public information specialists then had to deal with media about the story as well as campus demonstrations and other inquiries by legal counsel. If you sold advertising during this troublesome time at *Rolling Stone*, you also had to deal with the fallout when working with clients during crisis management at your publication. At every level, in every platform, fact is a vital component of accountability.

Trust is a key component in public relations and advertising, too. Trust is at stake and at the heart of crisis management. Consider a historic case of justification that involved the computer chip maker, Intel, and which occurred in 1994. The case is summarized below from an enlightening article authored by Cindy Williams, titled "Intel's Pentium Chip Crisis: An Ethical Analysis."[27] Williams analyzes the case from a philosophical perspective. This analysis again refers to the concept of justification. Here are key components of the corporate crisis that led to a full-page apology in *The Wall Street Journal* and other media:

1. A mathematics professor working on a project using five computers noted that the answer from one computer differed from the other four. The one had a Pentium chip.
2. The professor notified other scientists on the internet. Their Pentium computers also reproduced the error.
3. After a publication reported the professor's findings, Intel acknowledged that it knew about the problem. But it would not notify customers, the company said, because a normal spreadsheet user would encounter the error once in every 27,000 years.
4. Soon the mass media were reporting the problem, prompting Intel to create policy whereby unhappy consumers could call the company, which would decide whether they really needed replacement chips.
5. Then IBM announced that it was stopping shipment on computers using the chip because it discovered that the typical spreadsheet user would run into the problem not every 27,000 years but every 24 days.

Intel held meetings to rethink its conditional return policy and decided, in its own and customers' interests, to replace the chip because it was the ethical thing to do. Here is the company's published full-page apology:

To owners of Pentium™ processor-based computers and the PC community:
We at Intel wish to sincerely apologize for our handling of the recently publicized Pentium processor flaw.
The Intel Inside® symbol means that your computer has a microprocessor second to none in quality and performance. Thousands of Intel employees work very hard to ensure that this is true. But no microprocessor is ever perfect.
What Intel continues to believe is technically an extremely minor problem has taken on a life of its own. Although Intel firmly stands behind the quality of the current version of the Pentium processor, we recognize that many users have concerns.
We wish to resolve these concerns.
Intel will exchange the current version of the Pentium processor for an updated version, in which this floating-point divide flaw is corrected, for any owner who requests it, free of charge anytime during the life their computer.[28]

Passages associated with justification again are easily identified and refuted. As in the Dan Rather apology, trigger words such as "second to none," "quality" and "performance"—especially in association with Intel's work ethic—all rely on fact, in this case mathematical. Moreover, "extremely minor" mathematical problems can cause extremely major catastrophes, especially when errors are incorporated and applied to projects associated with medicine, engineering and other sciences whose foundations are math-based.
A complete apology by Intel, rather than a conditional replacement policy—only to be followed by an unconditional one—would have spared

that company embarrassment and loss of credibility. In corporate culture, loss of credibility means loss of profit. Too often CEOs forget that correlation. From an ethical perspective, in news, crisis management or even one's personal life, the accountability lesson is the same: Apologize for errors, correct the record as soon as possible in a prominent setting, and present apology and correction in such a way as to offset any damage. Otherwise, the damage will be to the journalist, practitioner and company.

SEEK ROLE MODELS AND MENTORS

Ethical journalists and practitioners usually have role models and mentors who guide them in the course of their careers. Too often, however, we embrace icons and idols and know little about them, apart from their celebrity or nefarious status. True, they may have extraordinary talents and, in that respect, can inspire us. Or they may be so notorious that we fear them or covet their power or mystique.

We need to define these terms to understand their influence on our ethics:

- A **role model** is someone whose values and/or work ethic we admire. We need not have a personal or professional relationship with that person.
- A **mentor** is someone whose values and/or work ethic we embrace. However, that person is or was an active participant in our personal or professional lives.
- An **icon** is someone whose image and status are so well known because of their talents or triumphs that we identify them by first or last name or even initials, such as Madonna (Louise Ciccone), Cher (Cherilyn Sarkisian), Beyoncé (Giselle Knowles-Carter), Jay Z (Shawn Corey Carter), Lady Diana (Spencer) and Lady Gaga (Stefani Joanne Angelina Germanotta).
- An **idol** is someone who commands our attention for a short while because of intense media coverage about something they did or experienced. Their status is as fleeting as the coverage. We identify them by news monikers such as BTK Strangler (serial killer Dennis Rader), D.B. (hijacker Cooper), Runaway Bride (Jennifer Wilbanks), O'Reilly (news host Bill O'Reilly), O.J. (Orenthal James "O.J." Simpson) or Stormy (adult film actress Stephanie Clifford associated with a Donald Trump scandal).

> **Note:** *Personalities can be both icon and idol. For instance, O'Reilly was an iconic star on the Fox News channel until his fall from grace concerning allegations of sexual harassment; O.J. Simpson was an icon on the football field and later a media idol because of his implication in the murder of spouse Nicole Brown Simpson.*

Later in this chapter we will learn more about the influence of role models and mentors. At this point, we want to probe the meanings icon and idol because of their influence on our own and our audience's values and belief systems. We often confuse a renowned celebrity (icon) with the symbol of a false god (idol). *The Random House Dictionary of the English Language* defines *icon* as "a picture, image, or other representation" or "some sacred personage, as Christ or a saint or angel," and *idol* as "a mere image or semblance of something, visible but without substance, as a phantom."[29] Journalists and practitioners help create icons—mere images or brands—that dominate coverage over an extended period. We also help glorify idols—visible, but without substance—who occupy our interest intensely and then disappear from media view. Audiences and publics cannot get to know the typical personality, athlete or actor *three dimensionally* in time, space and person. Instead, the media give them phantoms on a flat screen. As we probe responsibility in this chapter, we should also acknowledge some fundamental facts: All platforms help create icons and idols; you undoubtedly will do that, too, as journalist or practitioner. Thus, you should know what is enduring and edifying in content creation from what is fleeting and detrimental to you, your audience or clientele.

Journalists and practitioners often are accused of elevating celebrities and news sources to icon and idol status and then knocking them down when the opportunity arises. Consider the case of short-lived media idol Jennifer Wilbanks who disappeared from her Duluth, Georgia, home on April 26, 2005 and was initially feared kidnapped and slain. Her disappearance occurred in the wake of the highly publicized cases of Laci Peterson and Lori Hacking, young women murdered by their husbands. Wilbanks eventually turned up in Albuquerque, New Mexico, claiming that she had been abducted and assaulted by a Hispanic man (racial stereotyping here) and white woman. In reality, her disappearance was a hoax to avoid her scheduled April 30 wedding to John Mason. But her escapade would dominate the news for months, propelling her to idol status as viewers, readers and listeners sought tantalizing tidbits about her would-be bridal escapade. The ethical situation is how media across platforms provided those tidbits at the expense of other news. Doing so they were not accountable to audience seeking legitimate news.

The day after Wilbanks was reported missing *The Washington Post* reported that the number of serious terrorist attacks rose from a previous record of 175 in 2003 to 655 in 2004. The newspaper reported that terrorist "incidents in Iraq also dramatically increased, from 22 attacks to 198, or nine times the previous year's total."[30] The article also disclosed that the State Department had begun withholding statistics on terrorist attacks from its congressionally mandated annual report. Rather than learn about the complexities of a deadly school seizure in Russia or violence in Kashmir, most of us learned that missing Wilbanks had planned a wedding with a 600-person guest list and 14 bridesmaids and groomsmen. Those reports were funneled through internet, blogs, emails, cell phone alerts, podcasts and social media. In other words, what was once "media overkill"—nauseatingly repetitive reports, such as the "runaway bride" story (now forgotten)—increased in intensity through the technology that occupies our time, 24/7. That is why the making of icons and idols is more prominent today than in the past when we heard sensationalized news a few times per day in local newspapers or on network television. Now we have *media* overkill in continuous cable news coverage with talking heads discussing the same news story over a period of days or weeks. *Tech* overkill via mobile devices ever at our disposal adds dozens of variations of that same story in every physical location at any hour.

Marilyn Greenwald, professor at the E.W. Scripps School of Journalism, Ohio University, says, "Wilbanks is the classic example of someone who became famous for being famous, someone who was literally created by the media. She is not really a newsmaker. Her story fits few if any classic definitions of news." Tech overkill triggered an expanded "media feeding frenzy" around the runaway bride, idolizing Wilbanks. "Few people will remember who she is."

James Fallows, national correspondent for *The Atlantic*, echoes that sentiment, writing that journalists must make a choice to entertain or engage the public:

> If they want to entertain, they will keep doing what they have done for the last generation. Concentrating on conflict and spectacle, building up celebrities and tearing them down, presenting a crisis or issue with the volume turned all the way up, only to drop that issue and turn to the next emergency. ... They will view their berths as opportunities for personal aggrandizement and enrichment, trading on the power of their celebrity. And while they do these things, they will be constantly more hated and constantly less useful to the public whose attention they are trying to attract. In the long run, real celebrities—singers, quarterbacks, movie stars—will crowd them off the stage. Public life will become more sour and embittered, and American democracy will be even less successful in addressing the nation's economic, social, and moral concerns.[31]

For the record, Fallows wrote this in 1997. His words are prescient more than two decades later.

The emphasis on entertainment has so saturated society that sometimes it occurs unintentionally in legitimate news stories. Case in point: Early in his career the iconic basketball star Michael Jordan endorsed athletic footwear to generate publicity about the rightness of athletic achievement, hoping to influence young people to work hard at what they love, contributing to community. In response, many adopted Jordan's work ethic as their own. In that respect, he was a role model. Others worshipped him to the point that Jordan became both icon and idol. Like most with that dual distinction, he also came to be known by one name: "Mike."

Several youths ignored his role-model aspirations, robbing teens wearing the Jordan sneakers. They didn't want to "Be like Mike," a nifty advertising slogan: They wanted to *be* Mike. They wanted those shoes.

Several sports magazines reported this in the late 1980s. *Sports Illustrated* even reprinted an article, "Your Sneakers or Your Life," in May 1990, about Michael Jordan feeling distraught about his role-modeling efforts. He had delivered the right message at the right time to the right target audience; however, Jordan could not control how that message was being received. First of all, the medium—television commercials—promoted footwear, not guidance. Jordan may have wanted the message to be about personal values; instead, it was about branding. His sneakers rather than his work ethic had become the message. Moreover, if readers subscribed to *SI* around this time, they received as a free premium, or gift, a "sneaker phone," more evidence that media feed our idol worship without their or our even knowing it.

A popular Nike advertisement at the time featured basketball star Charles Barkley scowling at the camera and proclaiming, "I am not a role model." The spot was controversial because, as Jeff Jensen writes in *Advertising Age*, "marketers have traditionally used sports figures as celebrity endorsers, presenting them as super-achieving, larger-than-life figures worthy of admiration, emulation and respect."[32] But at the core of the Barkley spot was a significant truth: *He is not a role model.* He was a gifted athlete. However, many of his fans did not admire, emulate or respect his values. (Barkley obviously had important ones, or else he never would have met the challenges of the National Basketball Association.) But these fans, even ones who aspired to play in the NBA, overlooked the values that propelled Barkley into the pro league—determination, courage and discipline. Instead they coveted his wealth and fame. In sum, they wanted to *become* Charles Barkley. They *idolized* him.

We may desire the status of icons or the possessions of idols and even pattern our wardrobe or lifestyles after them, buying their products and adopting their mannerisms. And yet, in the end, we will not be them or own their belongings. We may even idolize broadcast anchors and media moguls, believing that their standing in journalism and communication is inspiring. Perhaps. But there is self-deception even in this, for we may never be Anderson Cooper or Megyn Kelly or possess Ted Turner's wealth or Bill Gates' empire. However, we can research their achievements and learn from them by switching the focus from fame and fortune to work ethic and values. If we do enough research about their lives, they can even serve as role models who have knowledge, advice or methods that we can apply to our own lives or careers to achieve long-term success. Because role models teach us about determination, discretion, discipline and other intangibles, their values exist apart from the person or the person's possessions. He or she may fall from favor, and though we may express regret, the values—if genuine—should continue to serve us.

RECOGNIZE RESPONSIBILITIES

Journalists and practitioners operate within a press theory called "social responsibility." Other press theories include "libertarian," "authoritarian" and "communist" and are described along with social responsibility in the watershed text *Four Theories of the Press* by Fred S. Siebert, Theodore Peterson and Wilbur Schramm. In recent years, these theories have been challenged with the demise of the Soviet Union, the emphasis on profit by media conglomerates, and the advent of mobile digital media and worldwide communication technologies. Some argue for a unifying theory of media based on the marketplace—both of commerce and ideas—acknowledging that diverse cultures will require time to adapt to this Western imperative.[33] Others argue that the blogosphere, in particular, still can be best understood by these four theories, especially in holding traditional media accountable via the tenets of social responsibility.[34] In any case, social responsibility remains the most ethical media theory in that it is based more than the others on a moral principle rather than on a political premise. Authoritarian and communist press theories may be best understood as part of political communication and media history. In the *Four Theories of the Press*, the authors delineate similarities and differences between libertarian and social responsibility theories, which have made the greatest impact on U.S. journalism. They note that the functions of media under social responsibility and libertarian theory are essentially the same, involving:

> (1) servicing the political system by providing information, discussion, and debate on public affairs; (2) enlightening the public so as to make it capable of self-government; (3) safeguarding the rights of the individual by serving as a watchdog against government; (4) servicing the economic system, primarily by bringing together the buyers and sellers of goods and services through the medium of advertising; (5) providing entertainment; (6) maintaining its own financial self-sufficiency so as to be free from the pressures of special interests.[35]

Further, the authors note:

The social responsibility theory in general accepts those six functions. But it reflects a dissatisfaction with the interpretation of those functions by some media owners and operators and with the way in which the press has carried them out. Social responsibility theory accepts the role of the press in serving the political system, in enlightening the public, in safeguarding the liberties of the individual; but it represents the opinion that the press has been deficient in performing those tasks. It accepts the role of the press in servicing the economic system, but it would not have this task take precedence over such other functions as promoting the democratic processes or enlightening the public. It accepts the role of the press in furnishing entertainment but with the proviso that the entertainment be "good" entertainment. It accepts the need for the press as an institution to remain financially self-supporting, but if necessary it would exempt certain individual media from having to earn their way in the market place.[36]

Judy Phair, president of PhairAdvantage Communications, embraces social responsibility in public relations. One of her early mentors was Patrick Jackson, considered the founder of behavioral public relations, establishing a consulting firm based on that concept in 1956. "He was a genuine change agent," Phair says. "In fact, when he became president of PRSA in 1979, he was among the first leaders to go outside of corporate New York to find out the challenges that faced public relations professionals around the country, and how the Society could best serve them." Phair was impressed by his insistence that an organization exists only by public consent. "That concept has had a profound impact on my philosophy, and career," she says. "To me, it means that public relations can, and should, have a significant social benefit, bringing people in touch with their leaders so that they can have an impact on those leaders." All branches of public relations must accept that tenet of social responsibility. "Relationships are the currency of what we do, and those relationships must be based in a trust that incorporates integrity, dependability, and competence." In that sense, the overriding ethic of social responsibility is *respect for the public*. That relates to advertising, journalism and public relations.

Ethicist Louis Alvin Day notes that respect emanates out of the ancient Greek value of civility whose root word alludes to "civilization," or community, and by extension, audience. Civility and respect are rule-based so that individuals can interact more effectively with others. According to Day,

> When projected against the tapestry of the various media enterprises, we can see the necessity for some consensus on rules of conduct that enhance the media's public credibility and esteem. If one examines closely the industry codes, for example, fundamental to all of them is respect for the reader, listener, or viewer.[37]

There also is commitment to these principles:

1. A sense of responsibility to consumers, community concerns, and society.
2. Decency, honesty, and truth.
3. Avoidance of misrepresentation and deception.
4. A sense of fair competition.
5. The protection and promotion of the reputation of the advertising industry.[38]

Most principles in this chapter are associated with social responsibility. So are tenets from codes of ethics across platforms. Here is a sampling from association codes representing several media:

[C]oncern and respect for the public's natural-law right to freedom in searching for the truth and the right to be informed truthfully and completely about public events and the world in which we live.[39]— The National Press Photographers Association

[P]ublic enlightenment is the forerunner of justice and the foundation of democracy. Ethical journalism strives to ensure the free exchange of information that is accurate, fair and thorough. An ethical journalist acts with integrity.[40]—The Society of Professional Journalists, "Preamble"

Professional electronic journalists should operate as trustees of the public, seek the truth, report it fairly and with integrity and independence, and stand accountable for their actions.[41]—The Radio-Television Digital Directors Association, "Preamble"

We serve the public interest by acting as responsible advocates for those we represent. We provide a voice in the marketplace of ideas, facts, and viewpoints to aid informed public debate.[42]—Public Relations Society of America professional values

Advertising shall tell the truth, and shall reveal significant facts, the omission of which would mislead the public.[43]—The Advertising Principles of American Business, adopted by the American Advertising Federation Board of Directors

Ethical bloggers treat sources and subjects as human beings deserving of respect.[44]—The Online News Association

It is important to acknowledge that although the various media serve segments of society in different ways across platforms, they all aspire to do so responsibly, emphasizing the public interest or the public's right to know or to be informed in a truthful manner. Equally as important are the individual journalists and practitioners who aspire to live up to these standards, being accountable to the public and thereby earning its trust.

RESPONSIBILITY CREATES TRUST

Betsy Carter believes that audience sets standards of trust and responsibility in magazine journalism. Over the years she has worried that the industry is forgetting this concept in its pursuit of increasing profits. Carter, a contributing editor for *O, The Oprah Magazine*, has served as editor at *Esquire, Newsweek* and *Harper's Bazaar*. She is familiar with a wide range of magazines and their readers. "If you look at magazines now, she says, "you see that so much is being done for the money, for the advertising. It's a big mistake to think that your readers won't notice that you're not doing a magazine for them. It's all a matter of trust. That's what a magazine has with its readers—an intuitive connection. If you break that, if you allow something to come between that, then, what do you have?"

Carter emphasized trust and respect for the audience as founding editor of *New York Woman*. She worked closely with her staff in the newsroom, fostering trust interpersonally and advocating respect for her readers. She acknowledges that this has become more complex at the digital workplace, with editorial staff scattered across the country in different offices or at home, disseminating information electronically as well as in print. Nevertheless, Carter believes judicious use of technology can also effect positive change, too. "Different kinds of technology call for different kinds of skills," she says, "with the TV people here and the online people there, and the art director in one state and the editor in another. But with technology you can communicate to all more easily, bringing everyone up to speed at once on an issue or topic. Still," she adds, "there has be a sense of mutual respect and confidence in one another in such an environment. As an editor, my business was to know everyone and to speak with everyone so that we would have a common language even if using e-mail or telephones. It's not as easy as it was with face-to-face communication in a small group. But now it's important to bring everyone together from time to time, and to know everyone's face and name."

"As journalists, we all have a joint responsibility to create trust," says John Kaplan, Pulitzer Prize-winning photographer and journalism professor at the University of Florida. Kaplan is concerned about the tabloid media undermining the theory of social responsibility. "Sometimes what gets reported as a lead story on the networks originated from tabloid sources," he observes. "The media of lower credibility are wagging the tail of the supposedly more ethical (mainstream) media because of competitive pressures." Kaplan thinks that news is blurring increasingly with entertainment, a long-standing ethical concern. "What's presented to the public as news in whatever medium it happens to be is becoming more and more a facet of entertainment." Kaplan believes that the news media has a responsibility to set a high ethical standard for society. "Then," he concludes, "the public will rise to that standard and expect high quality coverage."

Nonetheless, as we have seen in the 2016 presidential election, a proliferation of "fake news" appealing to viewers' political convictions flooded the internet and social media. This has damaged the trust that audience once invested in their preferred media. Colleen McCain Nelson, a Pulitzer Prize-winning editorial writer, notes, "Just within the last couple of years we've seen this proliferation of outlets emerge that are basically created to deceive and to put out information masquerading as an actual news story that is completely fiction."[45] Some of this fake news is based on generating clicks for advertising, and others are advancing an agenda. The result, she says, is confusion "about what is actually a fact."[46]

White House adviser Kellyanne Conway, justifying the administration's claim of Donald Trump's largest inauguration attendance ever—despite photographic evidence to the contrary—used the term "alternative facts." It did not go over well, despite her attempts to clarify that dubious concept. She explained her term as providing different facts to document the same truthful information. "Two plus two is four," she said. "Three plus one is four. Partly cloudy, partly sunny. Glass half full, glass half empty. Those are alternative facts."[47] Her definition assumes that all the facts of an event or issue lead to the same conclusion, or answer. Hers does not account for missing facts or ones that do not lead to the same result. Two plus *something* (not disclosed) does not equal four. It invites the viewer to supply the missing information. And when viewers do that, they tend to supply their deeply held convictions or beliefs, without regard to facts withheld from them. Worse, often stakeholders in a news report supply false or misleading information for missing facts in an account. This phenomenon erodes the very nature of social responsibility and libertarian theory. Journalists and practitioners cannot serve the political system by fostering public debate based on incomplete records or misleading facts. Neither can the media enlighten the public so that it is capable of self-government if that government provides alternative facts promoted by fake news outlets that share the same political philosophy. When that happens, media do not serve as watchdog over government but an untrusted source of information, undermining the role of accountable journalism in a republic.

SOME THINGS ARE ALMOST ALWAYS TRUE

In seeking principles that apply to all platforms, we encounter philosophy again, this time in how notions of right and wrong vary and, as a result, define differently our duties as journalists and practitioners. Two such philosophies are moral relativism and moral absolutism. In between those polarities lie situational ethics. According to ethicist Louis Alvin Day, a relativist believes that one person's notion of right and wrong usually differs from another's because value systems exist apart from any universals, even when people make moral decisions in similar circumstances. "In other words," Day explains, "moral agents determine what is right or wrong from their own point of view but will not judge the adequacy of others' ethical judgments."[48]

Philosopher Christina Hoff Sommers believes that some principles are always right and others always wrong. As such, she asserts, universals exist, and we should be aware of them. Then there is moral situationalism, a philosophical compromise, which holds that "certain moral principles, such as telling the truth," may exist as a general rule, but also can be violated on a case-by-case basis.[49]

For generations, the news media in particular have embraced situationalism to their detriment—not only because the philosophy implies lack of moral commitment—but also because the public regularly questions the particulars of professional practice when journalists deceive sources or use unnamed ones, violating privacy (and sometimes, the law) to scoop competitors. As ethicist and former broadcaster Sandra H. Dickson has observed, "The pattern of criticisms of the press over the decades underscores the problems caused by the absence of universal ethical standards. Situation ethics, or 'adhocracies,' are an insufficient moral compass to guide a fast-paced, technologically-driven, bottom-line oriented industry."[50] Dickson suggests that journalists and practitioners revisit Aristotle's "moral mean" for guidance in difficult circumstances.

Aristotle (384–322 B.C.) believed that a person could make sound moral decisions by choosing a middle ground, or "golden" mean, between two extremes. For instance, the middle ground between timidity and hubris might be modesty or between cowardice and recklessness might be courage. Louis Alvin Day relates this to professional practice, stating that concepts such as balance and fairness often represent golden means between two extremes. As modern-day examples, he uses the banning of advertisements for tobacco products in broadcasting and the mandating of warning labels on cigarette packages. This, he believes, represents the mean "between the extreme of outlawing tobacco altogether and the other extreme of doing nothing to counteract the harmful effects of the product."[51]

Sociologist and author Manuel Castells, whose books include *The Power of Identity* and *The Internet Galaxy*, in a 2006 speech in Dresden, Germany, spoke about the millions of blogs worldwide that doubles every six months in an explosion of "I" mass media across cultures. After his talk to the International Communication Association, he was asked: "For centuries in Occidental culture there has been a philosophical debate, entirely conjectural, that universal principles exist or do not exist. We now have some empirical evidence to answer this question. Given the expanse of the blogosphere across cultures, are there any philosophical patterns that qualify now as universal, from Jeremy Bentham's happiness principle to Immanuel Kant's duty principle to John Locke's natural law?"[52] After some reflection, Castells answered affirmatively: "The longing for freedom."

As such, freedom may be a moral absolute, as well as its implied components of equality and respect for the rights of others. Abraham Lincoln embraced this tenet in his Gettysburg Address when he reminded the audience that the United States was "conceived in liberty and dedicated to the proposition that all men are created equal." Yet Lincoln was careful in his address to call equality a "proposition" rather than a given,[53] which positioned him in the "moral mean" between violent anti-slavery activists and pro-slavery activists in the South who rejected any notion of equality for non-whites. Lincoln ironically is known as a universal icon of equality because his Emancipation Proclamation, actually a military document, and other measures helped abolish slavery. However, he was a utilitarian who as president put his faith in logic and reason, or consciousness, above the universals of conscience. Equality, then, was a *proposition*, writes Lincoln biographer Allen C. Guelzo, "like one of the Euclidean theorems he had worked his way through in the 1850s, to be demonstrated and defended by reason rather than accepted as the voice of an instinctive common moral sense."[54] While it is true that Lincoln remains one of the most moral presidents of the United States, in that he ultimately earned for others their birthright of self-evident truths, including liberty, his iconic status requires us to put his contributions into context via the facts of his life. Equality was neither sacred nor universal, he reasoned, else, the South would have intuited that. Therefore, he appealed to reason, stating,

> My paramount object in this struggle *is* to save the Union, and is *not* either to save or to destroy slavery. If I could save the Union without freeing *any* slave I would do it, and if I could save it by freeing *all* the slaves I would do it; and if I could save it by freeing some and leaving others alone I would also do that.[55]

For this he was chastised by many, including Horace Greeley, publisher of *The New York Tribune*, who believed Lincoln lacked moral resolve because he could not intuit equality as a sacred principle.

Ethicist Clifford G. Christians identifies a universal principle in the sacredness of life itself. "The rationale for human action is reverence for life on earth, respect for the organic realm in which human civilization is situated."[56] Christians affirms that principle empirically in his study of ethical foundations in 13 countries on five continents, noting that "the veneration of human life is consistently affirmed as bonding us universally into an organic whole."[57] The late ethicist Claude-Jean Bertrand indirectly endorsed that finding, adding "If a single value exists on which all humans can agree (except a few fanatics), it is the survival of the species, the fate of the planet. That concern should move all of us, whatever our ideology."[58] Bertrand also acknowledged that some traditional values, which many consider absolute, such as equality for women or universal suffrage, are not found in other cultures that may condemn the West's consumerism and selfishness. "Moreover," he stated, "each culture has specific features, quite independent of its stage of economic development: thus, female nudity offends in Saudi Arabia and in the U.S., whereas in Europe it has become a normal part of the seaside landscape and of advertising."[59] Therefore, we must be sensitive to cultural norms when identifying universals across platforms.

Some philosophers and ethicists, including the author of *Living Media Ethics*, believe that certain truths, called moral absolutes, apply to almost everyone across cultures. In other words, these are true almost all of the time. Philosophers in any country or continent generally will agree with that assertion. Philosopher Christina Hoff Sommers states that "students may easily lose sight of the fact that some things are clearly right and some are clearly wrong, that some ethical truths are not subject to serious debate."[60]

To illustrate that, she lists these truths as moral absolutes:

1. *It is wrong to mistreat a child.*
2. *It is wrong to humiliate someone.*
3. *It is wrong to torment an animal.*
4. *It is wrong to think only of yourself.*
5. *It is wrong to steal, to lie, to break promises.*
6. *It is right to be considerate and respectful of others.*
7. *It is right to be charitable and generous.*

Sommers adds,

I am aware that not everyone will agree that all of these are plain moral facts. But teachers of ethics are free to give their own list or to pare mine down. In teaching ethics, one thing should be made central and prominent: Right and wrong do exist. This should be laid down as uncontroversial lest one leave an altogether false impression that *everything* is up for grabs.[61]

Philosophers who believe in the sanctity of life might add to her list these other absolutes:

1. *It is wrong to prejudge others based on physical or racial features.*
2. *It is wrong to treat human beings like objects or property.*

In addition to these, there are also civic absolutes associated with U.S. history and culture. According to the Johnson Foundation, "There are some values, rooted in national experience, even defined in the Constitution, that Americans share. These 'constitutional' values have evolved into a set of civic virtues":[62]

1. *Respect for the individual and commitment to equal opportunity.*
2. *The belief that our common interests exceed our individual differences.*
3. *Concern for those who come after us.*
4. *Support for the freedoms enunciated in the Bill of Rights, including freedom of religion, of the press, of speech, and of the right to assemble.*
5. *The belief that individual rights and privileges are to be exercised responsibly.*
6. *The conviction that no one is above the law.*
7. *Respect for the views of others.*

Compare these with the philosophically based political principles of the United States, cited in the previous chapter on influence:

1. **Equality:** *Every person has a right to life, liberty and the pursuit of happiness.*
2. **Inclusivity:** *Our national identity is incorporated in our name, the **United** States.*
3. **Work Ethic:** *Reason and merit prevail over bloodline and entitlement.*

4. **Honesty:** *Truth supersedes authority.*
5. **Access:** *Education ensures free speech in a republic.*
6. **Tolerance:** *The majority may rule, but the minority must be heard.*
7. **Accountability:** *Journalism is the watchdog of government.*

All of the above principles speak to responsibility. They guide us as individuals or as a collective thereof. Many of these principles as enumerated by Manuel Castells, Christina Hoff Sommers, Clifford G. Christians and ethicists at the Johnson Foundation (individuals of diverse backgrounds and political beliefs) can be linked to media practice across platforms. For instance, it is wrong to steal, to lie and to break promises—*especially for journalists and practitioners*; it is wrong to prejudge others based on physical or racial features—*especially for journalists and practitioners*; it is right, *especially for journalists and practitioners*, to believe that individual rights and privileges are to be exercised responsibly; and it is right, *especially for journalists and practitioners*, to believe that the majority may rule, but the minority must be heard. The more you analyze these principles, the more you can see how inclusive they actually are, demanding that we serve society responsibly.

"WHAT ARE YOUR MORAL ABSOLUTES?"

Personal Journal Exercise

1. Study the lists of ethical values that appear throughout this chapter, including responsibility, credibility and trust. Which ones appeal especially to you or, conversely, are missing in the text and should have been addressed? Make your own list of "wrong" and "right" items that *you* feel are moral absolutes—deeply held beliefs that are part of your value system but may be missing from those universal ones that Christina Hoff Sommers noted earlier, such as: "It is wrong to mistreat a child, to humiliate someone, etc.; it is right to keep promises, to be charitable, etc." **Note:** *Do not put your name on this list, as you will hand it in as a printout or anonymous file to the instructor or group leader for the "Communal Journal Exercise."*
2. Identify someone on campus who you believe is a moral person, role model or mentor, and ask him or her to make a similar list of moral absolutes. Compare your list with this person's and note any similarities or differences. Note these in your journal for use later in this exercise.
3. Arrange an interview with a practicing journalist (any platform) or practitioner (advertising or public relations) and ask him or her before you arrive to make a list of courageous acts that he or she has done during the course of his or her career. Has the person ever questioned the ethics of a superior, for instance? Has the person ever challenged authority? Quit a job? Refused an assignment?

During the interview, ask the person whether his or her sense of right and wrong was involved in the incident.

4. Review your journal notes about moral absolutes from No. 1 and No. 2 above. How, if at all, have these exercises enlightened you? What truths have come to light after your interview with a journalist or practitioner about his or her courageous acts. With permission from the journalist or practitioner, create a 500-word journal entry or blog post or a brief podcast or multimedia presentation— incorporating content from previous notes—in a profile of the person, emphasizing in particular what motivates him or her ethically.

Communal Journal Exercise

Collect lists from the first "Personal Journal Exercise" about moral absolutes, devising a manner that protects confidentiality, such as a mailbox for printouts, or a drop box that bestows anonymity. Make a master list of absolutes from class or group members who turned in the assignment. Distribute that master list via email or printout. As the instructor or discussion leader, read those collective absolutes, one by one, and ask the class or group whether they agree with the assessment that the particular item is almost always true. **Optional:** *Without violating your own or another person's privacy, ask the class or group to base a 500-word journal or blog entry or short podcast or multimedia presentation based on observations from the discussion.*

NOTES

1. *A Free and Responsible Press*, The Commission on Freedom of the Press, Robert M. Hutchins, Chairman (Chicago, Ill.: University of Chicago Press, 1947), 21.
2. H.M. Schulweis, *Conscience: The Duty to Obey and the Duty to Disobey* (Woodstock, VT: Jewish Lights Pub, 2008), 53.
3. Ibid., 142.
4. John Ratey, *A User's Guide to the Brain: Perception, Attention and the Four Theaters of the Brain* (New York: Vintage Books, 2002), 55.
5. Schulweis, 146.
6. James Fallows, *Breaking the News: How the Media Undermine American Democracy* (New York: Vintage Books, 1997), 5.
7. Charles Warner, "Sales Ethics," in *Media Selling: Broadcast, Cable, Print, and Interactive*, 3rd ed., eds. Charles Warner and Joseph Buchman (Ames, Iowa: Iowa State Press, 2004), 30.
8. Ibid.
9. Sissela Bok, *Lying: Moral Choice in Public and Private Life* (New York: Vintage Books, 1999), 74.
10. Ibid., 91.

11 Dan Merica and Sophie Tatum, "Clinton Expresses Regret for Saying 'Half' of Trump Supporters are 'Deplorables,'" CNN, September 12, 2016, www.cnn.com/2016/09/09/politics/hillary-clinton-donald-trump-bas ket-of-deplorables/index.html

12 David A. Fahrenthold, "Trump Recorded Having Extremely Lewd Conversation About Women in 2005," *The Washington Post*, October 8, 2016, https://www.washingtonpost.com/politics/trump-recorded-hav ing-extremely-lewd-conversation-about-women-in-2005/2016/10/ 07/3b9ce776-8cb4-11e6-bf8a-3d26847eeed4_story.html?utm_term=. c586fcd4a162

13 "Accountability in Journalism" in "Accountability in the Professions: Accountability in Journalism," by Lisa H. Newton, Louis Hodges, and Susan Keith, *Journal of Mass Media Ethics*, Vol. 19, Nos. 3–4, 2004, 173.

14 *Random House Dictionary of the English Language*, 2nd edition, unabridged, 1040.

15 Newton, Hodges and Keith, 173.

16 Peggy H. Cunningham, "Ethics of Advertising: Oxymoron or Good Business Practice?," in *The Advertising Business: Operations, Creativity, Media Planning, Integrated Communications*, ed. John Philip Jones (Thousand Oaks, Calif.: Sage, 1999), 501.

17 Ibid.

18 Ibid., 499–513.

19 Philip Seib and Kathy Fitzpatrick, *Journalism Ethics* (Fort Worth, Texas: Harcourt Brace, 1997), 114–15.

20 "Officer's Widow Questions Bush Guard Memos," ABC News, September 10, 2004, http://abcnews.go.com/Politics/Vote2004/story?id= 123461&page=3

21 "Authenticity of New Bush Military Papers Questioned," by The Associated Press, *USA Today*, September 9, 2004, www.usatoday.com/news/ politicselections/nation/president/2004-09-10-bush-guard_x.htm

22 "Dan Rather Statement on Memos," CBS News, September 20, 2004, www.cbsnews.com/stories/2004/09/20/politics/main644546.shtml

23 See "A Note to Our Readers," *Rolling Stone*, December 5, 2014, www. rollingstone.com/culture/news/a-note-to-our-readers-20141205

24 Ibid.

25 T. Rees Shapiro and Emma Brown, "Rolling Stone Settles with Former U-Va. Dean in Defamation Case," *The Washington Post*, April 11, 2016, www.washingtonpost.com/local/education/rolling-stone-settles-with-u-va-dean-in-defamation-case/2017/04/11/5a564532-1f02-11e7-be2a-3a1fb24d4671_story.html?utm_term=.9a713fa666eb

26 Erik Wemple, "The Full Demise of Rolling Stone's Rape Story," *The Washington Post*, December 11, 2014, www.washingtonpost.com/blogs/ erik-wemple/wp/2014/12/11/the-full-demise-of-rolling-stones-rape-story/?utm_term=.4458d5f1ee7b

27 "Intel's Pentium Chip Crisis: An Ethical Analysis," by Cindy Williams, *IEEE Transactions on Professional Communication*, Vol. 40, No. 1, March 1997, 13–19.

28 As cited in "Intel's Pentium Chip Crisis: An Ethical Analysis."

29 *Random House Dictionary of the English Language*, 2nd ed., unabridged, 949 and 951.

30 "U.S. Figures Show Sharp Rise in Terrorism," by Susan B. Glasser, *The Washington Post*, April 27, 2005, A01.

31 James Fallows, *Breaking the News: How the Media Undermine American Democracy* (New York: Vintage Books, 1997), 267.

32 Jeff Jensen, "Bad Role Model Can Make Good Ad," *Advertising Age*, September, 27 1993, 10.

33 See "Modernization and Media in the Arab World," by Gregory Mendel Selber and Salma I. Ghanem, *Global Media Journal*, Vol. 3, No. 5, http://lass.calumet.purdue.edu/cca/gmj/fa04/gmj-fa04-selber-ghanem.htm

34 See "CBS, Dan Rather and the Blogosphere: An Anatomy of a Crisis," by Terry A. Hinch and Laurence A. Jarvik, *Proceedings 2005*, Association of Business Communication, www.businesscommunication.org/conventions/Proceedings/2005/PDFs/18ABCEurope05.pdf

35 Fred Siebert, Theodore Petersen and Wilbur Schramm, *Four Theories of the Press* (Urbana: Univ. of Illinois, 1974), 74.

36 Ibid.

37 Louis Alvin Day, *Ethics in Media Communications: Cases & Controversies* (Belmont, Calif.: Wadsworth/Thomson Learning, 2003), 12.

38 Edward Spence and Brett Van Heekeren, *Advertising Ethics* (Upper Saddle River, N.J.: Pearson, 2005), 26.

39 See the National Press Photographers Association code of ethics at www.asne.org/ideas/codes/nppa.htm. Note: Associations often adapt their online codes but usually only reword their standards of responsibility.

40 See the Society of Professional Journalists code of ethics at www.spj.org/ethicscode.asp

41 See the Radio-Television Digital Directors Association code of ethics at www.rtnda.org/ethics/coe.shtml

42 See the Public Relations Society of America code of ethics at http://prsa.org/_About/ethics/values.asp?ident=eth4

43 See the American Advertising Federation ethics and principles at www.aaf.org/about/principles.html

44 See the Online News Association bloggers' code of ethics at www.cyberjournalist.net/news/000215.php

45 Bill Burton, "Journalist Colleen Nelson on the Rise of #FakeNews," WFPL News, July 18, 2017, https://wfpl.org/journalist-colleen-nelson-on-the-rise-of-fakenews/

46 Ibid.

47 Brooke Seipel, "Conway Seeks to Define 'Alternative Facts,'" *The Hill*, March 18, 2017, http://thehill.com/blogs/blog-briefing-room/news/324 621-conway-defines-alternative-facts-additional-facts-and

48 Day, 59.

49 Ibid.

50 Sandra H. Dickson, "The 'Golden Mean' in Journalism," *Journal of Mass Media Ethics*, 1988, Vol. 3, 33–37.

51 Day, 56.

52 *Living Media Ethics* author Michael Bugeja attended Manuel Castells' June 19, 2006 speech to open the 56th annual International Communication Conference in Dresden, Germany, and asked the question following Castells' speech.

53 See Allen C. Guelzo, *Abraham Lincoln: Redeemer President* (Grand Rapids, Mich.: William B. Eerdmans, 2003), 371.

54 Ibid.

55 "The American Presidency: Lincoln, Abraham," response to Horace Greeley, August 22, 1862, *Encyclopedia Britannica*, available from www. britannica.com/presidents/article-8729

56 Clifford G. Christians, "The Sacredness of Life," *Media Development*, Vol. 2, 1998, 3.

57 Ibid.

58 Claude-Jean Bertrand, *Media Ethics & Accountability Systems* (New Brunswick, N.J.: Transaction Publishers, 2000), 29.

59 Ibid, 30.

60 Christina Hoff Sommers, "Teaching the Virtues," *The Chicago Tribune Magazine* reprint, 12 September 1993, 16.

61 Sommers, 16.

62 *An American Imperative: Higher Expectations for Higher Education*, multiple authors (Racine, Wis.: The Johnson Foundation, 1993), 14.

CHAPTER 4

Truth: Levels, Shades and Hues

BE A FONT OF TRUTH

To embrace truth and be a font thereof as a journalist or practitioner, you must acquaint yourself with its philosophical meanings. Truth as a universal principle is debatable, the notion that some things are factual and others, false; but not in *Living Media Ethics*. When one adjusts for cultural and other influences, including social mores, the various levels and shades of truth become clearer and decipherable. Ethicist Clifford G. Christians makes a case for two kinds of truth from the Hebrew: *emeth*, meaning "genuine" or "authentic," and from the Greek *aletheia*, meaning "open" or "disclosed." As such, *emeth* relates to consciousness, what we can verify as real, and *aletheia* relates to the conscience, what we intuit or confide as meaningful. Christians traces the various shades of those terms historically and linguistically across cultures and historical figures, noting, for instance, that truth "is one of the three highest values in Latin American communication" and "eventually wins over force" for spiritual leader Mahatma Gandhi.[1] "The fundamental norm of Arab-Islamic communication is truthfulness," Christians states. "In Hinduism, truth is the highest dharma and the source of all other virtues. In the powerful wheel imagery of the Buddhist tradition, truth is the immoveable axle. For Jesus, we live the truth, and the truth will set us free. Zen meditation seeks truth in experience."[2]

Truth is the universal cornerstone of trustworthy value systems. Some philosophers would challenge that, asserting that truth and the process to attain it, "objectivity," are relative. This is as much a rhetorical as a journalistic debate, although post-modernists would disagree with that assessment, embracing relativism as a "fact of life." Theirs is a view shared by many sociologists, humanists, legal scholars and other social critics.[3] Other philosophers disagree. "Have we not learned a thing or two over the past several thousand years of civilization?" asks philosopher Christina Hoff Sommers. "Why should we be the first society in history that finds itself hamstrung in the vital task of passing along its moral tradition to the next generation?"[4]

Philosophers may differ about the universality of truth, but almost all would concur with the idea that truth is complex, containing myriad shades and hues, from the verifiable to divine. They also would agree that our ability to articulate those levels using the inexactness of language often is limited or impossible. And yet, the truths of consciousness must be apparent, a tapestry of fact to be deciphered, assembled and replicated. Science is founded on this notion. It rejects rhetoric. That is why scientists frequently criticize journalists who seek balance by reporting two sides of a controversial research topic such as intelligent design or cold fusion. Scientists say that findings or discoveries can or cannot be proved, can or cannot be replicated. Otherwise, they simply don't know. There is only *one side* to this story: proof, lack of proof or no answer as of yet. The most eloquent rhetoricians may claim the sun rotates around the earth, as happened in the time of condemned astronomer Galileo Galilei (1564–1642), but the fact that planets rotate around the sun is not debatable. It is, simply, a fact. It is true. While it is also true that people are subjective, perceiving the world through their personal filters, people have been known to see things exactly the same way when the stakes are high enough. In that sense, objectivity exists.

Case in point: Convicted murderers C. Michael Anderson and Peter Hochstein escaped from their Omaha, Nebraska, cell in 1978 with another inmate, Dan Sheppard. Their purported method of escape was to hone perception. Each time the jailer opened their cell with a key, they drew its perceived dimensions. When the drawings aligned, they made the key in metal shop. It worked.[5] They were impartial enough to see an object exactly as it really was. As educator and journalist David Mindich tells us, objectivity as a goal may not be attainable, but impartiality or non-partisanship is possible when we are so motivated.[6]

Subjectivity exists. That is a fact, too. Objectivity may be impossible to attain. That also is a fact. As ethicist John C. Merrill reminds us, facts are based on meanings of words communicating those facts and that variable must be factored into any debate about objectivity. Merrill notes that *epistemology*, or the science of knowledge, and *semantics*, the study of meaning, have a symbiotic bond. Knowledge is impossible without meaning, he writes, and meaning is both complex and relative. Without meaning, we lack knowledge, and vice versa.

> If journalists want to impart truth, they must be concerned with both epistemology and semantics. They must get the real facts, the real story, and as much of the story as possible. They must then present these facts in a meaningful context that approximates the event in reality.[7]

Merrill emphasizes that when journalists speak about objectivity, they are really talking about "effort and degree."[8]

OBJECTIVITY IS A PROCESS

Objectivity is not a synonym for truth but the process through which we seek to attain it. That process applies across media platforms. Objectivity came into public consciousness early in the 20th century after World War I. Because of the propaganda of the era, people sought verifiable truth rather than political rhetoric. "An understanding developed that facts were subject to interpretation and that interpretation was always subjective," writes journalist Jeremy Iggers, noting that the great writer Walter Lipmann was an early advocate of "objectivism," or the application of the scientific method to journalism.[9] Truth may not be completely attainable, the people understood, and objectivity may be theoretically impossible, but *some* semblance of reality had to be possible. They demanded it. Because people also happened to be the audience, many newspapers, wire services, magazines and radio stations complied. They tried to report impartially by assembling a tapestry of fact through which a mirror of the world reflected.

To put this issue into perspective, let's use a metaphor, which Aristotle said represents the highest, most truthful language, to illustrate why a substantive measure of truth is attainable. Imagine a jigsaw puzzle depicting the solar system. Now imagine a competition in which puzzlers do not know what the mosaic depicts but have three hours to piece the puzzle together. The goal of this competition, however, is not to complete the puzzle but just enough of it to discern what it portrays. This hypothetic puzzle is extraordinarily complex with 10,000 pieces—each one representing a fact, with "truth" symbolized by the completed mosaic. Some individuals may possess the skill to piece together only 50 or so pieces of that puzzle in the allotted period. They cannot see any depiction, or truth, at all from their modest assemblies. Others may be able to piece together only 100, 250 or 500 pieces so that the depiction of the solar system is very incomplete. The person who fit 100 pieces may believe the depiction is an oil slick. The person who fit 250 pieces may believe it is not an oil slick but an asphalt highway. The person who fit 500 pieces may believe the puzzle depicts fireflies at night. These are subjective renderings. However, the person who worked diligently and quickly on that puzzle, assembling 1,000 pieces before attaining his or her skill level, may behold the incomplete puzzle accurately enough to perceive a representation of the solar system. As this metaphor shows, truth may not be completely attainable. We may see no truth at all or misinterpret subjectively what we perceive. But journalists and practitioners who assemble enough facts can attain truth by degrees to envision a reliable depiction of the world. According to Sissela Bok in *Lying: Moral Choice in Public and Private Life*, "The fact that the 'whole truth' can never be reached in its entirety" should not hinder us in the pursuit of truth-telling.[10]

To be sure, we may possess different values based on influences cited in Chapter 2. What is virtuous for one individual may be less so for another. But just as it is a cop-out to claim that truth does not exist, surrendering morally when confronted with complex situations, it is equally defeatist to argue that ethical values are relative and should not be embraced or endorsed. That attitude is intellectually lazy. Eventually it can lead to disrespect of or disinterest in ethics altogether. In a global media environment, it behooves journalists and practitioners to recognize that cultural and other values may vary. That reflects the diversity of the human experience. However, it also behooves us to recognize that some moral values transcend cultures and define the human experience.

You can take a secular or a spiritual approach to this truth. You can say that humans are social creatures, like wolves, and that the origin of our ethics is one of inter-dependence, with its value represented by the group's being more vital than the individual—ensuring the survival of the community.[11] Many biologists, chief among them Matt Ridley, have documented this through consciousness. Or you can claim, as many theologians do, that humans intuit the universal principle of conscience: *What is inside me is also inside you.* Further, you can claim that the seemingly conflicting biological and theological precepts are both true, defining the human condition, with consciousness stating that we come into the world alone and leave it alone and with the conscience stating that we are spiritual beings having a physical experience. But in each instance, from the secular to the theological to the agnostic, universal truths exist. Moreover, after analyzing the principles and moral absolutes in the previous chapter, you should conceive yet another, practical, undeniable truism: *We live and work in community with others.* We must adopt the values of the common good or democracy or due process or corporate codes to be in good standing as a person, student, citizen or an employee.

Little in life is truly relative. Our values may be relative, the meanings of words may be relative, and our beliefs may be relative, too. But as a practical matter, we must make choices to follow laws, codes or cultures of a given community to be a part of that community. Of course, we may rebel against or change those norms or find different communities or cultures. But we still will have to adapt or adopt. To do otherwise, a person would have to be entirely self-sufficient, relying on no one for anything. As the 17th-century author John Donne wrote, "No man is an island, entire of itself; every man is a piece of the continent, a part of the main."

TRUTH IS SUBJECT TO PROOF

Because communication is a social science whose methods are fact-based and verifiable, truth is subject to proof. Proof is more laborious than belief. It is one thing for a reporter to believe that a politician is corrupt and another to prove that in an investigative piece. It is one thing for an advertiser to *believe* there is a need for a product and another to prove that *true* via marketing studies. It is one thing for a public relations practitioner to believe that he or she can represent a client better than a competitor and another to document that in a business meeting. Too often, however, we assume that only journalism must be impartial or objective, a stance that has led to elitism in communication schools, elevating news editorial above advertising and public relations. For instance, the authors of an advertising text ask what role, if any, truth plays in that profession. They note that advertising is rhetorical because its goal is to persuade, not to prove, often using disparate or incongruent imagery to achieve its ends. "In those cases," they write, "the ads are not intended as true representations of reality or as narratives that correspond to the truth, but rather as rhetorical and metaphorical evocations that are designed to appeal to the consumers' emotions and aspirations for the purpose of creating positive and alluring images for the products in the minds of the consumers."[12] In articulating their case, the authors argue that exaggeration through a metaphor differs from puffery whose purpose is to deceive through factual misinformation or unsubstantiated claims. Puffery in advertising lacks free speech protection and is not only unethical but illegal, overseen by the Federal Trade Commission.[13] Advertising and, to a degree, public relations seemingly operate on different standards from news journalism.

They don't.

An advertising or a public relations campaign can be just as objective (or subjective) as an investigative news story. By viewing objectivity as a process, rather than associating it merely with news, we can embrace another standard across platforms. How can that be, especially when advertisers openly state that persuasion rather than truth-telling is the norm? How can that be when the practice of public relations reportedly represents one view of the truth, the client's, and overlooks or devalues other verifiable views? The answer is simple: Objectivity in news as opposed to advertising and public relations simply happens at a different stage of the process.

News Process

The news process starts with an idea and ends with a published or electronic report. Simple enough. But the beginning of the process usually is more subjective than the end. For instance, a reporter might investigate fraud or a public official on mostly objective grounds—public records, say—or on completely subjective grounds: suspicion about agenda, say. Of course, unethical journalists target officials because of political concerns or even self-interest. Whatever the case, the front-end of the process typically involves a reporter's individual perception. That is only half the story. The initial stages of the news process are usually subjective when ideas target motives of sources—business or political rivals, for instance— mean-mouthing the competition. Most reporters also feel obliged to fact-check (if not report) gossip and rumor that come into the newsroom as "anonymous tips."

Reporters understand the subjectivity involved in conceiving an investigative story. Seasoned journalists are unconcerned because they trust editorial procedures, knowing standards of objectivity will kick in as the process progresses from idea to a fact-checkable article. If not, the editor spikes the story (or should). That's why the back-end of the process is supposed to be as failsafe as possible. Reporters and editors put the focus there to avoid editorializing or libel; otherwise, thousands of dollars may be lost in litigation and their credibility, damaged.

Melanie Rigney, former *Ad Age* managing editor and *Writer's Digest* editor—applauds standard-bearers of objectivity. Rather than questioning public relations and advertising, however, she maintains that we ought to re-emphasize the back-end of the news process in light of staff cuts in newsrooms—an ethical concern associated with profit rather than proof. "It's not uncommon these days even at medium-size publications for just one person other than the writer to read the story and ask the hard, objective questions before it's published," Rigney says.

In 2017, employees at *The New York Times* staged a walkout after management announced a plan to end the publication's stand-alone copy desk. The *Times'* rival *Washington Post* reported,

> For those in the business of words, copy editors are considered the 'safety nets,' the meticulous proofreaders who catch everything from spelling mistakes to major factual errors. And in the era of 'fake news,' averting error is more important than ever.[14]

Because print outlets have trimmed copyediting jobs, it is more important than ever for journalists to be as accurate as possible via fact and objectivity than ever before. Fewer gatekeepers at the back-end of the process (depicted below) harm the credibility of the news industry.

Objectivity Arrow

Front-end  **Back-end**

Process is increasingly objective via research, interviews, editing

Unethical Arrow

Front-end  **Back-end**

Process lapses into editorializing without sufficient gatekeeping

Diagram 4.1 News process

As the above depiction shows, successful reporters increasingly become more objective as the news process nears completion, following the facts like bloodhounds tracking the truth. However, when objectivity is not enhanced through the editorial process, a news story can fail, resulting in editorializing, inserting opinionated content (now often called "analysis") into news masquerading as impartial. In the beginning, though, reporters place a premium on the subjective proboscis.

Advertising/Public Relations Process

In public relations and advertising, the process usually begins with a high degree of objectivity. Practitioners must gather sufficient data and/or market research to analyze a situation, identify publics or markets, develop strategies or target channels of communication—newspapers to digital media. "It's absolutely necessary to begin the PR process objectively," says Bojinka Bishop, former director of public affairs for the American Water Works Association and a named professor of public relations at Ohio University. According to Bishop, the PR process begins by thoroughly researching three fundamental components of any situation: the client, organization, product, service, or issue; the publics involved; and the necessary media to reach those publics. "Only then can you begin to be subjective or creative in developing communication strategies and tactics to connect the players in positive ways," she adds.

Objectivity is especially critical during crisis management. Bishop points to high-profile crises involving product tampering of Johnson & Johnson Tylenol in 1982 and a product-tampering hoax at Pepsi in 1993, noting "strong proof of truth and positive actions are necessary to repair damage and that hiding facts and using 'spin' never solve a crisis of confidence."

Concerning objectivity, the advertising process is similar to the public relations process. One way to illustrate that is to compare a news headline with a campaign slogan. When headlines are composed, the news process is all but finished. Slogans, on the other hand, usually come early in the advertising paradigm because an entire marketing strategy might rest on a single operative word.

Cassandra Reese, former advertising executive at Kraft Foods, described the objective process in Chapter 2 on the influence of language, noting that advertisers must test words and align slogans with products using scientific research, consumer panels, taste-test kitchens, focus groups and telephone surveys. Jan Slater, an advertising professor at the University of Illinois, notes the advertising process "obviously entails objectivity that stems from understanding the consumer's wants, needs and desires and then determining how Crest, a Big Mac, Diet Coke or Tide can meet those wants, needs and desires." After all, Slater observes, the foundation of all brand strategy is repeat purchase and that has to be based on objective data and information. "The greatest advertising control is from the consumer. If advertisers lie, exaggerate benefits and make promises the brand cannot keep, the consumer will not purchase the brand again."

In general, a practitioner's or a client's subjective opinion—about the salability of a new toothpaste or the feasibility of a political strategy—has to be tested impartially before funds are spent on a campaign. Because so much money is at stake, not to mention the prospect of repeat business, an agency has to evaluate the need for a product or the viability of a candidate before launching a campaign. As the process continues, however, facts can get in the way of publicity. So strategy is important in promoting one brand or candidate over an otherwise worthy rival. That's when the process begins to get more subjective.

According to Bojinka Bishop, "The challenge in public relations is always to create balance between the real and the hoped for." The "real" is emphasized in the beginning of the process via standard avenues of objectivity (i.e. fact-gathering, expert interviews, field and library research, etc.). "Without knowing what's real," Bishop says, "you might send a computer story to the city editor or promote the benefits of holistic medicine to surgeons. You can't afford *not* to examine all facts objectively." When initial phases are too subjective, campaigns fail, just as news stories do, only at a different point in the process. In sum, practitioners have to trust the *front-end* of the objectivity process to achieve subjective goals, from positioning a candidate for office to a new product in the marketplace. Here's a depiction:

Objectivity Arrow

Front-end  **Back-end**

Process must be objective initially in a well-targeted campaign

Unethical Arrow

Front-end  **Back-end**

Process becomes deceptive without initial front-end objectivity

Diagram 4.2 Ad/PR process

Because the arrows of objectivity and ethics point in different directions, we tend to elevate news above other platforms merely because the final stage of journalism is objective and disseminated to the public whereas the beginning stage of advertising/public relations, also objective, is hidden from public view. The initial subjective motives of journalism associated with newsworthiness are hidden. However, the effectiveness of advertising or public relations campaigns relies on the initial, fact-based data. The end product—a commercial or political campaign, say—may seem rhetorical or subjective because the initial objectivity helps to target the message or slogan. But truth in each instance and platform is founded in fact-gathering to see the world as it actually is, rather than as we wish that it were. Thus, we can make these assertions about the objectivity process:

- *Processes for the journalist vs. the practitioner are inherently opposite, which explains why a successful public relations campaign combines objectivity and strategy to nullify a news story with a weak fact-base.*
- *It also explains why voters choose one candidate depicted in advertisements over another endorsed in editorials by the news media.*
- *Conversely, a well-documented news story nullifies a PR release grounded in spin as well as an advertisement with a weak fact-base, advocating for a candidate or cause.*

TRUTH SHOULD BE TRANSPARENT

Journalists should strive for *full disclosure* in a news report, segment, image, video or online post, including all available facts and providing an impartial and as complete a truth as possible. When they do, truth shines through like light through a glass pane, transparent, for all to see. They should avoid *partial disclosure*, omitting facts and details that might bias an assignment or cast it in an improper light or context. When this happens, truth is slanted, "opaque" or cloudy, filtering the truth. Likewise, practitioners not only must research campaigns as fully as journalists before launching them; they also require full disclosure from the clients whom they represent. Motives must be shared as transparently as possible. Otherwise practitioners may base campaigns on *partial disclosure*, inviting complaints or crisis management because they failed to account for all of the facts and details up front about a product, issue or promotion.

Mara Bovsun worked as a public relations executive in a highly competitive market, which sometimes put more emphasis on pleasing the client than on disseminating the truth. That culture concerned her to the extent that she found herself responding routinely with "no problem" to her clients' questionable demands, donning what she calls "the publicist's smile." Bovsun urges practitioners to avoid actions "that will kill or cripple your career. Lie to the press, for example, and you'll end up having a bad reputation, no media outlets and no income. Don't participate in an event that shows bad taste, faulty judgment or insensitivity. Don't allow clients to twist your arm by using that time-honored tactic: 'Do you want to keep our business?' All you will end up with is humiliation, a shoulder splint and a client who is trying to skip on paying the bill. Another good tip: Make sure that you and your clients agree on what you will and won't do at the outset. Get it in writing, in a contract. A client who will not consider such a contract is no doubt up to no good, and you should run. After a few years in the business, you'll be able to distinguish honorable clients who want you to communicate a message (yes, they do exist) from those who want to hide behind you while they do some dirty work."

Sue Porter, former vice president of the Scripps Howard Foundation, recalls an incident years ago involving partial disclosure in the newsroom. The editor of a daily Cincinnati newspaper assigned a major feature story about northern Kentucky and southern Ohio business and political leaders competing to develop industrial complexes on their respective sides of the Ohio River. "The assignment was given to me with a distinct slant: expose the Kentuckians' unethical dealings," Porter recalls. "After months of research, I told my editor that I couldn't give him exactly what he wanted. We debated my findings. I was told to use information that supported the premise. I did that but not without presenting information that also disputed those facts."

Porter said the lengthy story was returned to her for revision 16 times. "'Change a verb here,' the editor told me. 'Drop a paragraph there.' Slowly my editor, the surgeon, was crafting the story *he* wanted and I was sick about it." Porter reached her limit. "'This is it. No byline, please,' I declared as I placed the story on his desk for the seventeenth time." She told the editor if he wanted any more revisions or reporting on the story that "someone else will have to do it." Years later, Porter still remembers the anger on her editor's face as he rewrote her story, which was published without a byline. "It was a long time before I got another 'big story,'" she says. After her editor retired, she invited him to lunch to discuss the matter. "He said he was determined to give his boss what he wanted, and that he really didn't feel he was compromising reality by presenting only a portion of the facts." Porter adds, "In his mind, the end justified the means. Telling the story his way was a higher calling."

Full disclosure in advertising, journalism and public relations is linked to the ethical tenet of transparency, or the ability to do one's job literally in the open, without concern about what others may discover about your background, credentials, methods, affiliations and even personal life. Transparency is a byproduct of a free press and the social responsibility theory of the media. It presumes commitments to *equality, inclusivity, work ethic, honesty, access, tolerance* and *accountability*, based once again on principles derived from U.S. history as cited earlier in *Living Media Ethics*. Practitioners across platforms and the professional organizations that represent them have endorsed these seven principles directly or indirectly. They form a pact grounded in trustworthiness with audience and constituents. Trustworthiness is achieved "through works that are compatible with the best professional standards," write Carolyn Marvin and Philip Meyer who advocate that media professionals "acquire new information-retrieving and interpreting skills" and submit themselves to a "ruthless self-imposed transparency."[15]

Lack of transparency sometimes is a fact of life in Armed Forces communication. Disclosures during military conflicts can trigger casualties in the field. Public affairs divisions, part of information public relations, also are tasked with providing journalists with truthful accounts of battles. In 1997, a civil war broke out in Europe between Kosovo and Serbia. The Serbs launched a campaign of "ethnic cleansing," or genocide, to kill Albanian Muslims in Kosovo. In 1998, the U.S. and NATO forces were sent to the war zone to stop the genocide. Communication specialist Lindsey Borg served in the Air Force during that war, later rising to the rank of colonel. "The terms 'alternative facts' and 'fake news' may be new, but the challenges faced by professional communicators are certainly not," he says in an interview. During the Kosovo campaign, Borg saw the effects of misinformation overwhelm his media relations staff. On a typical day, NATO air operations over Kosovo gave Serbia the opportunity to spread false reports of allied aircraft being shot down. "These claims, made to media outlets, generated waves of calls from reporters seeking confirmation or correction," he notes. "The simple process of finding out the truth was complicated by the timing of aircraft returning and the reluctance to share too much publicly about the operations for fear of giving valuable intelligence to the Serbs for the days ahead."

The Serbian misinformation continued, directly affecting NATO communication. "We had no time to tell about the campaign's objectives or its progress because we were consumed with finding the truth to answer reporters' questions," Borg says. "The misinformation also took valuable time from the operators and commanders as they worked to find the operational information we needed—time that could have been spent planning or conducting the next set of operations to end the genocide in Kosovo." As a result, his public affairs unit was given greater access to operational and classified information to verify any claims. The Kosovo experience directly led to the military embedding reporters in 2003 during the Operation Iraqi Freedom campaign. During that conflict, the military embraced "eye-witness transparency," or full disclosure, because reporters rode or flew with troops. "Embedding reporters with our combat forces enabled us to counter enemy misinformation and propaganda in real time because the reporters saw reality firsthand. These developments resulted in truthful, timely communication in the most challenging of circumstances."

Borg, current director of integrated communications for Raytheon Intelligence, Information and Services business, upholds truth in his civilian career, especially in a competitive environment. "It would be easy to misrepresent our capabilities or to seed misinformation about a competitor. However, truth—and the high value placed on it—is the guidepost that helps to ensure a fundamental line is not crossed. In the long run, crossing that line wouldn't be an advantage, instead it would tarnish our brand reputation and undercut our competitive edge. Telling the truth is one of life's first lessons and, in the communications business, it's still paramount."

MAKE APPROPRIATE DISCLOSURES

In any discussion of truth, we encounter another ethical concept that applies across media platforms: *appropriate and inappropriate disclosure.* So far you have been read about the virtues of truth in this chapter. We noted its importance in media professions and introduced journalists and practitioners who embraced truth as a value, defining the ethics of full and partial disclosure. But disclosing the whole truth or all facts to the *wrong* audience or to the right one on the wrong *occasion* can be just as unethical as lying. This relates to the concepts of appropriate and inappropriate disclosure:

- **Appropriate disclosure:** Providing facts, details or data that the intended audience needs or perceives to need within the established boundaries of privacy and taste associated with individual media platforms.
- **Inappropriate disclosure:** Providing facts, details or data that the intended audience needs or perceives to need *in addition to other details or data that violate privacy or are inherently distasteful.*

Appropriate and inappropriate disclosures are especially important in public relations. The news industry and public relations have a special relationship dating back to "PR founder" Ivy Ledbetter Lee who began his career as a newspaper reporter in New York City from 1899 to 1903. Thereafter he began representing coal miners and later the Pennsylvania Railroad Company and other powerful clients, improving their image in the news and adding another dimension: supplying information to reporters about companies and their special interests or projects. In his day, Lee was known for candor and openness when dealing with media; but he also emphasized partial disclosure with particularly persuasive flare.

"Sometimes he presented only facts and arguments that favored his clients," according to Hugh Culbertson, educator and public relations researcher. That was Lee's right, Culbertson argues, noting, "Critics sometimes accuse him of going to great lengths to suppress or deny opponents a fair hearing." This second practice, however, is subject to ethical debate, Culbertson states. It is one thing for a practitioner representing a petroleum company to decide which facts to release and which to withhold about a tanker leaking oil after colliding with a reef. But it is another thing for the practitioner to suppress information by providing fabricated rebuttals or inaccurate data or to mislead reporters or send them on false trails. As Culbertson puts it, "Perhaps a practitioner need not 'shout from the house tops' that his or her client got drunk and did embarrassing things. But he or she has no ethical right to prevent that story from being told."

There are two major consequences related to suppressing information or misleading the news media. If a cover-up becomes known, the practitioner will cause immeasurable embarrassment to the client. He or she will compound the original problem and undermine the client's image or special interests. Worse, the practitioner will lose credibility so that the media and public will question those facts that *do* support the client.

Credibility is a priority in public relations. Linda DiJohn cites two reasons for public relations practitioners to tell the truth: "First of all, it's the right thing to do. Once you've lost your credibility, it's extremely difficult to get it back. Second, telling the truth is easier. No worrying about remembering what you've said and to whom." Telling the truth appeals to pragmatists, DiJohn says. "My personal and professional style is to tell the truth and tell it quickly. I counsel clients to do the same, particularly in a crisis. My most frustrating and rewarding work has been in counseling clients through a crisis—frustrating when they won't take the leap of faith and rewarding when they tough it out and do the right thing."

Jean Cochran, news consultant and former anchor for National Public Radio's "Morning Edition," recommends discussing issues of disclosure with colleagues in the newsroom. Together they can make decisions on what facts and components should be aired in a news report. In describing how that process worked at NPR, she notes, "A producer pulls in reports and actualities (interview segments), organizing the sound to be used in each newscast. But then the newscaster decides where it will be placed and what else to write to make up the five full minutes." At 3 a.m., Cochran would scour the news wires to search for relevant stories and then discuss them with then cohost Carl Kasell, deciding how best to represent a report for fairness and balance. They would "try to exercise some good taste, remembering that people are eating their Corn Flakes while listening to 'Morning Edition.'"

"Perhaps as I decide what is 'not appropriate,' I belie some personal bias," she admits. "But another way to put it is, we each bring our own set of sensibilities to the job and we should use them. So many factors enter in during the decision-making process. The questions we ask ourselves include: *Who cares? Should we care, and if so, why? Is there another side to this story?* And sometimes, *How on earth can I tell this entire story fairly in less than a minute?*" When it came to issues of appropriate and inappropriate disclosure, Cochran's motto guided her. "You don't check your 'humanity' at the door when you come to work. Quite the opposite, I believe you must apply it."

EXERCISE GOOD JUDGMENT

In our analysis of full, partial, appropriate and inappropriate disclosure, we encountered journalists and practitioners who opted to act conservatively or boldly in response to moral conundrums. Some of those situations can be intense, especially in broadcasting or online and photojournalism, because of graphic visuals. An online journalist may be privy to all available facts relating to a murder but does not necessarily need to disseminate ones that the audience might find distasteful—images and particulars from the coroner's report, say—or that might violate someone's privacy: images of grief by family members identifying the body.

Figure 4.1 "Grieving Family": Photograph by Morris L. Manning, reprinted with permission.

As a student journalist, Morris L. Manning had to make that decision in documenting a drowning at a lake. Of the numerous photos that he shot that day, Manning says that the one reprinted in *Living Media Ethics* stands out as most representative of the grief felt by the family and friends of 17-year-old Michael Noel-Russell who drowned on June 12, 2005. It was published in the *Iowa State Daily* and distributed by The Associated Press. "Although I did shoot images of the anxious moments while divers were searching the waters for the boy and the horror of the mother when she identified his body, I thought some of them to be too personal for publication. For example, the photos of the mother identifying the boy actually showed portions of his body. I did not want to sensationalize the tragedy by intruding too far into the personal lives of the survivors." Nonetheless, Manning acknowledges, the published and disseminated photo showed "the tremendous grief and profound agony of this event," including "the image of a friend's disbelief, the mother and friends holding one another, and the patient police officer." Those newsworthiness elements were key in Manning's decision to distribute the photograph.

Judgment calls are a part of every photo shoot. Some are easy, and some more complex. But they span the spectrum of documentary, portraiture and illustration, the major genres of visual communication, which we will analyze further in the next chapter. "When photographers discuss ethics, we are usually concerned with questions dealing with the appropriateness of taking or printing particular photos," says Dennis Chamberlin, who shared in the 1983 Pulitzer Prize awarded to the *Fort Wayne News-Sentinel* editorial staff for flood coverage. His photos helped document the devastation of that event in Indiana. A flood is public. But other photographs can be personal. Judgment calls come into play when news images might be viewed as an intrusion into a person's privacy, Chamberlin states, noting that taking a photo is inherently an intrusive act. "The important thing to remember," he adds, "is that every situation is different and that you have to make decisions regarding how to balance journalistic values against any potential harm that the photographs might cause."

Chamberlin, who has shot for such publications as *National Geographic*, *The New York Times Magazine* and *Time*, also was a former staff photographer at the *Denver Post*. He shares commentary and photographs here that required him to make judgment calls balancing truth with intrusion.

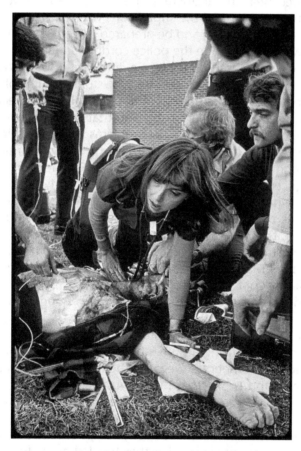

Figure 4.2 "Flight Nurse": Photograph by Dennis Chamberlin, reprinted with permission.

Dennis Chamberlin's Commentary

As a photojournalist I have always tried to be aware of the environment in which I am working, and to respect the people whom I am portraying. Sometimes this sensitivity toward the subject needs to be weighed against the news value of the story and this is what can lead to mistakes, or at least questionable decisions when it comes time to publish. The image titled "Flight Nurse" is one such image. At the time I made the photograph I had been photographing the flight crews at a Denver hospital for more than six weeks and was looking for a lead image that would capture the mixture of chaos and stress that I saw in the world where these people worked. One afternoon we were sent to the scene of a suicide that took place in the middle of the afternoon in a city park. The situation was tragic—the victim had a hole in his back, from the shotgun blast, the size of a football and he had most likely bled to death before we arrived. Normally a member of the press would not be allowed near the accident scene, but since I was a member of the helicopter crew (one of the stipulations was that I had to complete some basic medical training and be prepared to perform CPR, etc.) I was allowed to work freely inside the police cordoned area.

The story was focused on the nurse, and I tried to avoid identifying the victim and when it came time to edit the story a couple of weeks later the editor and I agreed that this photograph should be the lead. We both felt that the man was not identifiable and that the story-telling value of the image outweighed any potential problems with publishing it.

A few days after the story ran I received a letter from the family of this man along with the threat of a lawsuit. The newspaper's lawyers were not concerned and no lawsuit ever evolved. My editor seemed to feel that this vindicated our decision to publish the image but I still have doubts. I think that part of the problem is that we had written the captions in a style that identified time and place, and therefore any person who knew this man would have immediately known who it was on the ground. Would I make the same decision to run the photograph today? I would definitely not write a caption that was so specific in identifying the situation. I do not feel that the details added enough to warrant their inclusion.

Another news situation that photojournalists often deal with is photographing funerals. A strong argument can be made for the newsworthiness of some, but sometimes we cross the line of appropriateness. The funeral photograph is one that I feel is justified because it was part of a story that was in the national headlines. A military transport plane crashed off the eastern coast of Canada, killing all the troops on board. These soldiers had survived a particularly rough tour of duty in the Middle East and were tragically killed as they headed home for the holidays. Two of the soldiers were from Denver and we covered both funerals.

Figure 4.3 "Marine Funeral": Photograph by Dennis Chamberlin, reprinted with permission.

There was a large group of media at each cemetery, and everybody respected the rights of the grieving families. I remained at a distance from the ceremony.

I felt self-conscious and chose to observe the proceedings through a long telephoto lens that I braced against a tree to hold it steady. The ceremony ended, and I had nothing worth publishing until the family headed back to the limousine and the grandmother broke down and began to wail. I was still quite a distance, but from my position behind the tree I had a direct view of the family. I remained against the tree and shot three frames. A photographer from the competing paper later berated me for being so insensitive to the family. He told me that he was a Vietnam veteran and claimed to not have made any frames of the situation out of respect for the family. His admonishment did not bother me, and while I did not physically intrude upon the family I still feel that the "photographic intrusion" made possible by the telephoto lens did not cross the boundary of decency.

Sometimes when people are feeling passionate they forget where they are. This young couple on the bench were caught in a moment when they obviously had strong feelings for each other. What the viewer doesn't see in this photograph is that several bystanders, mostly elderly, were gawking in disbelief. I felt a bit like a voyeur when I looked through the camera but snapped the shutter and quickly looked away to give them a bit more privacy. Years later when this photo was shown in an exhibit I met a woman who was a friend of the young lady and it turns

Figure 4.4 "Couple Kissing": Photograph by Dennis Chamberlin, reprinted with permission.

Figure 4.5 "Magdalena": Photograph by Dennis Chamberlin, reprinted with permission.

out she was embarrassed to have been photographed at such a moment. When it was originally published I thought that the couple was not particularly identifiable but that was not the case because several of the girl's friends saw the photo and named her right away. The question remains: What privacy are people entitled to in public locations?

Portraiture is a situation where ethics are less likely to creep into the equation. Perhaps this is because the subject is aware of being photographed and often times is happy for the attention and promise of being famous for a day. Sometimes, however, this is not the case and the photographer is told "I hate to be photographed" by the subject. This was the situation in which I found myself with the Polish artist Magdalena Abakanowicz. I had assumed that she was exaggerating and continued to photograph her in a variety of situations in her Warsaw studio. After a few hours it became clear that she was distressed and she held her face in her hands for several minutes. I suggested that we quit for the day and she readily agreed.

Later that night I had dinner at her home and I learned that she truly did not like to pose for photographs. We talked about many subjects that evening and the next morning when I again appeared at her studio I was very conscious of how I worked. Instead of working like a photographer obsessed with documenting every angle I was an interested observer who occasionally made a snapshot. I think some of the better images came from this second day but, more importantly, I know it was much less painful for her.

The photo of Lanier in his game room is one that illustrates how important context is when portraying a person or situation. The photograph, in my mind, does not fairly present Lanier as a person. When I think about him the first things that come to mind is his intelligence

Figure 4.6 "Lanier": Photograph by Dennis Chamberlin, reprinted with permission.

and dry sense of humor. This photograph does not even attempt to show these aspects of the man but the image was made to show a situation rather than the person. As long as the photo is used to illustrate the idea of technology taking over our homes I feel comfortable with the image. If it were to be used as an attempt to depict him only as a person I would have deep misgivings.

SATIRE IS TRUTH EVERYONE KNOWS BUT WON'T ADMIT

In any discussion about truth, it would be inappropriate to exclude satire. In his book *Satire: A Critical Reintroduction*, Dustin H. Griffin states,

> Satirists can provoke by challenging received opinion; they can also provoke by holding up to scrutiny our idealized images of ourselves—forcing us to admit that such images are forever out of reach, unavailable to us, or even the last things we would really want to attain.[16]

Further, he writes, "The satirist's 'truth' has sometimes proved to be extraordinarily persuasive," literally changing history.[17] These observations are of critical importance when understanding satire as an ethical construct. An idealized image of self is what celebrities, politicians and companies often try to convey, creating a fiction or untruth. Satire exposes that, and in doing so, overwrites the hype with an image more closely grounded in truth.

Satire is found in every platform, from columns and cartoons in newspapers and magazines, to radio and television talk and entertainment shows, to advertisements and public service announcements. Most journalists think that satire is humorous, but it doesn't have to be. The two key ingredients are "truth" and "unreliability" (commonly known as a "double message"). The best satire exposes the 1 percent of truth that society refuses to heed or acknowledge but nevertheless exists. Poor attempts at satire merely parrot conventional truths or contain no discernable truth whatsoever. Without truth, satire lapses into *sarcasm*—achieving humor at the expense of another person or group. Without unreliability, satire lapses into *vulgarity*—communicating distasteful or offensive ideas. **Be forewarned:** *These considerations make satire particularly difficult to execute because sarcasm and vulgarity almost always are unethical across media platforms.*

The touchstone for modern day satire is "A Modest Proposal," composed in 1729 by Irish-born writer Jonathan Swift. In that piece, Swift attacked English landlords exploiting the Irish. Instead of using an angry tone of voice, he used an upper-class legislative voice as one might find in the House of Lords, resolving to end Irish overpopulation and famine and improve the economy via cannibalism.

Titles are particularly important in satire because they usually convey irony and enhance the double message. Swift's "A *Modest* Proposal" does that nicely because the proposal is anything but modest. Moreover, Swift added this subtitle: "For Preventing the Children of Poor People in Ireland from Being a Burden to Their Parents or Country, and for Making Them Beneficial to the Public." The subtitle prepares the reader to anticipate a helpful solution:

> It is a melancholy object to those who walk though this great town or travel in the country, when they see the streets, the roads, and cabin doors, crowded with beggars of the female sex, followed by three, four, or six children, all in rags and importuning every passenger for an alms. These mothers, instead of being able to work for their honest liveli-hood, are forced to employ all their time in strolling to beg sustenance for their helpless infants: who as they grow up either turn thieves for want of work or leave their dear native country.

The reader soon realizes the solution is satiric:

> I have been assured by a very knowing American of my acquaintance in London that a young healthy child well nursed is at a year old a most delicious, nourishing, and wholesome food, whether stewed, roasted, baked, or boiled; and I make no doubt that it will equally serve in a fricassee or a ragout. ... I grant this food will be somewhat dear, and therefore very proper for landlords, who, as they have already devoured most of the parents, seem to have the best title to the children.
>
> Infants' flesh will be in season throughout the year, but more plen-tiful in March, and a little before and after; for we are told ... that fish being a prolific diet, there are more children born in Roman Catholic countries about nine months after Lent than at any other season; there-fore, reckoning a year after Lent, the markets will be more glutted than usual, because the number of popish infants is at least three to one in this kingdom: and therefore it will have one other collateral advantage, by lessening the number of papists among us.

As you can see, Swift's satire was not humorous. But it does contain a grain of truth and unreliability grounded in a title that enhances both components. At the time, the English ruling class was doing little to end Irish famine and hardship. The attack was not sarcastic but true, expos-ing the 1 percent that the British monarchy refused to acknowledge. The double message becomes painfully obvious, too—otherwise the idea of cannibalizing children would be vulgar.

Swift's satire and standards still hold up today. As he knew, satire has great power to make us see what we don't want to see. But it is risky, too. If done poorly, without a grain of truth and a *clear* double message, attempts at satire wound or offend the audience because they come off as sarcasm or vulgarity and usually make a point at the expense of innocent parties. Consider how adoptive children and adults might have felt when reading a Valentine's Day card published by American Greeting Cards in

1997. The card depicted a cat on the front saying, "Sis, even if you were adopted, I'd still love you," and on the inside, continued:

> not that you are, of course. At least I don't think so. But, come to think of it, you don't really look like Mom or Dad. Gee, maybe you should get a DNA test or something. Oh, well, don't worry about it. We all love you, even if your real parents don't. Happy Valentine's Day![18]

A company spokesperson justified the card's content, stating, "It was intended to be off-the-wall, totally ridiculous humor. The copy was never meant to be taken literally. It refers to the classic sibling rivalry issue." A spokesperson for the Greeting Card Association in Washington also justified the content, stating, "I think different age groups have different humor that attracts them, and it's really hard to have cards out there that appeal to everyone." Despite these justifications, American Greeting Cards apologized and discontinued the card, costing the company $10,000.

Justifications aside, the satire comes off as sarcasm because the grain of truth, sibling rivalry, hardly qualifies as the grain of truth that society refuses to heed or acknowledge. Although the card's copy is unreliable, it makes points at the expense of innocent others, in this case, adoptees. One adoptee, who spotted the card on American Greetings internet site, was quoted as saying, "Valentine's Day is a day for love. It's not a day to play cruel, hateful jokes." The attempt at satire might have been more effective if its opening line— "Sis, even if you were adopted, I'd still love you"—were changed to: "Sis, even if you were switched *in the delivery room*, I'd still love you." That still would have conveyed the unreliable operative message about sibling rivalry, but not at the expense of innocent others. The card's text would have to be slightly altered, too:

> not that you were, of course. At least I don't think so. But, come to think of it, you don't really look like Mom or Dad. Gee, maybe you should get a DNA test or something. Or check the police log for any shenanigans at the hospital that day. Oh, well, don't worry about it. We all love you, even if you're not actually related to us. Happy Valentine's Day![19]

These ethical tenets apply especially to editorial cartoons. "My feeling is that the best cartoons reveal some aspect of the truth and at the same time convey a message," says Jim Borgman, Pulitzer Prize-winning syndicated cartoonist. "Sometimes we lose our way when we are doing five or six cartoons a week. Often as a cartoonist you are trying to be a humorous illustrator of world news, which is what our profession suffers from most right now. At your best, you're trying to reveal something new, state and stir up opinions, provoke debate—unpeel the onions—all those things. And it's wonderful when one can break out of the woods and remember that that's what the point of all this is."

The point of unpeeling the onions—exposing that 1 percent of truth— is a risky business which, at any time, can be misread by others. According to Borgman, "It is critical in doing editorial cartoons to be sure that friendly fire is kept to a minimum. We need to clearly identify the targets of our outrage." He acknowledges that in any editorial cartoon the subtlety and double meanings invite "the possibility of misreading, particularly by readers who don't have sensitivity to the visual vocabulary of the art form. I hear complaints from time to time on aspects of a cartoon that were not intended to be part of my message. Often, I can only shrug. I manipulate my tools as best I can to deliver a message with a nuanced tone and attitude, keeping innocent bystanders as far as I can from the focal point of my criticism."

Satire uses irony to expose or attack human vices like greed or vanity, says Henry Payne, award-winning editorial cartoonist for the *Detroit News*. "The key word here is 'expose,'" Payne says. "Like an inquisitive police investigator, the serious satirist will find his opponent's flaw and hang him with it. But if the satirist is only a jealous adversary, he will substitute spite for proper investigation, leaving his own methods vulnerable to exposure." Payne adds, "It is not enough, then, for the satirist to be a skilled marksman. He must first do the necessary legwork to ensure he has the right mark."

Satire is found in advertising and public relations, too. One of the most famous and long-running series of satirical ads and promotions featured the drum-playing, shade-and-sandal wearing Energizer Bunny®. The company's website (www.energizer.com/energizer-bunny) chronicles the history of the rabbit animation dating back to its 1989 debut. Many of the parodies satirize advertising itself, with one famous parody, "Sitagin Hemorrhoid Remedy," featuring a cowboy on a horse needing that fictional ointment, with the Energizer Bunny® interrupting that segment with its hallmark march across and beyond the screen. Then the slogan, which has become part of American slang: "*It keeps going, and going, and going ...*"

In summing up the components of ethical satire, whether you attempt to create it or want to analyze the topic further, keep in mind that the best examples begin with a double entendre title and state their case in an unreliable voice, expose the 1 percent of truth that people realize but rarely admit, and do not make their points at the expense of innocent others. When these components come together across media platforms, truth prevails whether we want to admit that truth or not. That's what makes satire so powerful.

TRUTH CAN BE MYTHIC, TOO

Higher truths are known as archetypes (from the Greek *archetypos* or "beginning pattern"). The word usually is associated with the doctrines of psychologist Carl Jung who wrote about "the collective unconscious" or the passing along of myths—symbols, stories, images—from generation to generation. For our purposes, we'll define archetype as *universal truth* across cultures and platforms. Whether these ideas are "higher" or even "true" is unimportant. You may disagree with or rebut them. However, as a journalist, you must be aware that people around the world view these truths with similar respect as if, indeed, they *have* been passed along generation to generation.

In his groundbreaking book *The Hero With a Thousand Faces* mythologist Joseph Campbell describes the prototype—or "monomyth"—upon which cultures around the world have based values or beliefs:

> A hero ventures forth from the world of common day into a region of supernatural wonder: fabulous forces are there encountered and a decisive victory is won: the hero comes back from this mysterious adventure with the power to bestow boons on his fellow man.[20]

With variations, most societies have a story in their cultural canon that features:

- A hero being identified and providing new hope, as spring does after winter.
- The hero having special powers, celebrated in summer.
- The hero falling from favor, symbolized by autumn and approaching death.
- The hero being defeated or executed, ending hope, as in winter.
- The hero being resurrected with new power, inspiring higher hopes.
- The cycle beginning again.

Don't confuse the word "myth" with the word "lie," as when someone tells you—"Oh, that's just a 'myth.'" As the works of Joseph Campbell document, myth is a higher truth on which many moral values are actually based. The monomyth, incidentally, does not only pertain to ancient religious narratives but also to modern pop-cultural ones, as in comic books concerning the death and resurrection of Superman in the early 1990s and of other fictional characters, such as E.T., the extraterrestrial, in the 1982 film of that name by Steven Spielberg.

The monomyth is based on a pattern like the seasons. Cultures also articulate higher truths on a totem or stepladder or "Great Chain of Being":

Deity—Supreme Power
Angels—Supernatural Beings
Mortals—Humans
Animals—Non-human Lifeforms
Vegetation—Tree and Plant Life
Minerals—Rocks, Gems, Earth

Reading this list you may be tempted again to think about ancient religious stories as found in American, Native American, European, Middle

Eastern, African or Asian holy books. Instead, let's analyze the Great Chain of Being in *The Wizard of Oz*, a 1900 children's story by L. Frank Baum. The book was popularized in a 1939 movie starring Judy Garland and has come to represent American values about the importance of family and home:

Deity—Wizard
Angels—Good and Bad Witches
Mortals—Munchkins, Dorothy
Animals—The Lion, Flying Monkeys, Toto
Vegetation—The Straw Man, Talking Apple Trees, Poppies
Minerals—The Tin Man, Emerald City, Yellow Brick Road, Ruby Slippers

The Wizard of Oz is a powerful story because it not only incorporates a Great Chain but also is based on the monomyth:

> *Dorothy ventures forth from the world of common day in Kansas into a region of supernatural wonder: Oz. The munchkins believe she is their messiah and celebrate her. Dorothy follows the yellow brick road to meet a great spiritual leader. On her journey she encounters fabulous forces—talking straw, lion and tin men along with good and bad witches—and wins a decisive victory over the Wicked Witch who wants the ruby slippers. When Dorothy realizes the power of those slippers, she returns from this mysterious adventure bestowing boons on Munchkins in Oz and love on her family and fellow Kansans.*

The higher truth of The *Wizard of Oz* is not that the so-called wizard is a hoaxster but that Dorothy only needed to click her heels three times and say "home" to tap the power within her conscience. *That, alas, is the archetype.*

Universal truths are not only found in religious or literary works. These works have great impact because they are tapping something inside *you*. The following monomyth may sound familiar:

> *In spring a boy or girl blossoms into adulthood. In summer he or she celebrates and ventures forth from the world of common day into a region of supernatural wonder: first love. Fabulous forces are there encountered and the hero or heroine wins a mate. The mate betrays him or her in the fall, and the hero or heroine suffers a kind of death. Life is cold and still. Then spring returns, and the hero or heroine resurrects, wiser now with new power or maturity as the cycle begins again.*

Life is a great teacher of truth. It requires that we live our ethics. Life challenges us with situations that require us to rely on *epiphanies* and *peak experiences*. Let's define these terms:

- **Epiphany:** A time when your *mind* seems at one with the universe. You understand an important truth that bestows meaning in your life. For instance, you realize the significance of circumstances or events that led to your parents' or your divorce; a friend or relative's death; a successful or unsuccessful relationship; or your own mortality, talents, shortcomings and opportunities.

- **Peak Experience:** A time when your *body* seems at one with the universe. The feeling is routinely encountered during sex or winning a race, scoring the winning point in a game, surviving a dangerous accident or close call, or giving birth. But a peak moment also may come when you master a difficult song on an instrument so that your fingers convey emotions or when you command a powerful machine like a plane so that your body seems to have wings.

Undoubtedly you have experienced several epiphanies or peak moments in your life. Inside you exists a storehouse of truth upon which you can analyze your current values or even build a new system. Epiphanies and peak experiences usually occur during or following high points, low points and turning points in your life. It is important to note that not only you but members of your audience have experienced these highs, lows and turning points. Although society is diverse and cultures vary, the experience of the human species when viewed in this light can be remarkably similar around the globe. Highs are associated with births as well as with successful personal, familial and professional relationships or achievements; journeys and travel-related encounters; and academic, athletic, scientific or artistic successes. Lows are associated with deaths, injuries and disease; with unsuccessful personal, familial and professional relationships or achievements; homesickness during journeys; and academic, athletic, scientific or artistic failures. Turning points also occur after both highs and lows, typically associated with journeys, accidents, diseases or reversals (failures that became successes and vice versa). Or they can happen when an individual is exposed to a cultural, natural or other awe-inspiring event.

Knowledge of higher truths enhances media practice across platforms. Journalists and practitioners can evaluate their own highs, lows and turning points to analyze filters on perception as covered in the chapter on influence. You can also determine whether you accepted consequences associated with each high, low or turning point, as you learned to do in the chapter on responsibility. Finally, you can ascertain the truth-based lesson that you learned from each experience. These are your "truths" and the foundation of your current value system. Moreover, the best journalism and most effective advertising or public relations often are based on similar epiphanies or peak experiences meant to motivate, inspire or spark others to action. Understanding truths associated with these pivotal human moments also provides insight into other vital communication topics that involve trust, manipulation, cowardice, fear, courage and authority and other ethical abstractions. In upcoming chapters, you will learn about these concepts from a concrete perspective and how they relate and can be applied to journalism and professional practice. Thus far we have noted influences that may affect your perception and identified dozens of concepts associated responsibility and truth. Now you should be able to build a solid foundation on which to base a value system.

Living Media Ethics will test and enhance that base.

"YOUR HIGHS, LOWS AND TURNING POINTS"

Personal Journal Exercise

1. Make a list of your highs, lows and turning points in life. (Try for at least ten.) State each item simply with a word or phrase and do not put your name on it, as you will be turning this in anonymously to the class instructor or group leader.

Example: 1. (*Turning Point*: Disease); 2. (*Low*: Death of Relative); 3. (*High*: Travel Abroad); 4. (*Turning Point*: Internship); 5. (*High*: New Love); 6. (*Low*: Divorce); 7. (*Turning Point*: Step Parents); 8. (*High*: Birth of Sibling); 9. (*Low*: Car Accident); 10. (*High*: Won Scholarship)

2. Make a copy of that list of highs, lows and turning points. Next to each item on that list—with a minimum of ten—write a 50- to 100-word statement about a peak experience or epiphany associated with that incident (or write a statement about your lack of a peak experience or epiphany, i.e. an incident with which you are still coming to terms). Do not turn in this assignment with your name as it might inappropriately disclose information that violates your or others' privacy. The goal here is to awaken your deepest held truths.

Example: *Turning Point. Cancer. Someone I care about was diagnosed with skin cancer. I took her to some of her treatments.* **Epiphany:** *I should stop worrying about small hassles in my life and set some priorities.*

3. Write another 50- to 100-word statement pertaining to each item on your list of highs, lows and turning points, determining whether the experience has influenced your perception and whether you have accepted the consequences thereof. Once again, do not turn in this assignment as it might inappropriately disclose information that violates your or others' privacy.

Example: *The person who had skin cancer recovered fully. I tend to think that people can overcome the ravages of disease if they catch it in time and seek treatment. Of course, with the specter of diseases such as AIDS, I realize that the turning point above may have overinfluenced me in this regard. As for consequences, I will have to adjust for this bias by not blaming individuals who become ill but by informing them about symptoms and treatments.*

4. Under each item write a short statement articulating the lesson you learned from the experience.

    Example: *Lesson: Live life to the full because it is short and precious.*

5. Look over your responses to 2–4 above. Do not disclose the specific highs, lows and turning points but do compose a 500-word journal entry or blog post or short podcast or multimedia presentation explaining what emotions, epiphanies and peak experiences might have been awakened by doing the exercise. **Note:** *In formulating your responses, keep in mind the concepts of appropriate or inappropriate disclosures. Do not violate your own or anyone else's privacy or reputation. If you find the exercise too emotionally challenging to complete, **do not do so**. To compensate, write a 500-word commentary on what, if anything, the exercise taught you about truth.*

Communal Journal Exercise

1. Collect the highs, lows and turning points from members of the class or group, as explained in No. 1 of the "Personal Journal Exercise." Be sure to collect printouts or devise a confidential way for class or group members to send their lists to you, such as an anonymous drop box. Make a master list of highs, lows and turning points from those who turned in the assignment. In other words, code items from the class or group lists under general headings (disease, romance, travel, death, etc.) to show similarities of collective highs, lows and turning points. Distribute that list to the class or group for an upcoming discussion.

2. Make your own list of highs, lows and turning points as described in No. 1 of the "Personal Journal Exercise."

3. Go to the master list of items and see how many items listed there are the same or similar to the ones on your list. The goal may be to use the master list to represent your own personal list. If that happens, it shows universality of the human condition.

4. In the class or group discussion, explain how you felt doing the exercise and what, if anything, reinforced lessons about truth. Moderate a discussion emphasizing the human condition and noting how truth permeates our existence as perceived by the conscience and consciousness.

NOTES

1 Clifford G. Christians, "Truth in a Technological Age," 2004 Leo Hindery Media Ethics and Values Annual Lecture, November 9, 2004, Emerson College, Boston, Mass., 7.

2 Ibid.

---

3 Judith Lichtenberg, "Objectivity in Reporting," in *The Concise Encyclopedia of Ethics in Politics and the Media*, ed. Ruth Chadwick (San Diego, Calif.: Academic Press, 2001), 127.

4 Christina Hoff Sommers, "Teaching the Virtues," *The Chicago Tribune Magazine* reprint, September 12, 1993, 18.

5 *Living Media Ethics* author Michael Bugeja covered the jail break for United Press International. The inmates stole an airplane and almost made it to Canada before being recaptured again. Bugeja's account about the prison escape appears on the front page of June 14, 1978 edition of *The Chicago Tribune*.

6 David T.Z. Mindich, *Just the Facts: How "Objectivity" Came to Define American Journalism* (New York: New York University Press, 1998), 41.

7 John C. Merrill, *Journalism Ethics: Philosophical Foundations for News Media* (Boston, Mass.: Bedford/St. Martin's, 1997), 117–18.

8 Ibid., 119.

9 Jeremy Iggers, *Good News, Bad News: Journalism Ethics and the Public Interest* (Boulder, Colo.: Westview Press, 1999), 62.

10 Sissela Bok, *Lying: Moral Choice in Public and Private Life* (New York: Vintage Books, 1999), 13.

11 Matt Ridley, *The Origins of Virtue: Human Instincts and the Evolution of Cooperation* (New York: Penguin, 1996), 6.

12 Edward Spence and Brett Van Heekeren, *Advertising Ethics* (Upper Saddle River, N.J.: Pearson, 2005), 41.

13 Jay B. Wright, "The Supreme Court of the United States and First Amendment Protection of Advertising," in *The Advertising Business: Operations, Creativity, Media Planning, Integrated Communications*, ed. John Philip Jones, (Thousand Oaks, Calif.: Sage Publications, 1999), 488.

14 Samantha Schmidt, "Why hundreds of New York Times employees staged a walkout," *The Washington Post*, June 30, 2017, www.washingtonpost.com/news/morning-mix/wp/2017/06/30/the-new-york-times-is-eliminating-its-copy-editing-desk-so-hundreds-of-employees-walked-out/?utm_term=.e4c4e7285cae

15 Carolyn Marvin and Philip Meyer, "What Kind of Journalism Does the Public Need?," in *The Press*, eds. Geneva Overholser and Kathleen Hall Jamieson (New York: Oxford, 2005), 402. Note: In this essay Marvin and Meyer refer specifically to news journalists, but their tenets of transparency apply to practitioners as well.

16 Dustin H, Griffin, *Satire: A Critical Reintroduction* (Lexington, KY: Univ. Press of Kentucky, 1995), 60.

17 Ibid., 128.

18 Content of card and spokesperson quotations that follow are taken from an Associated Press story published on February 13, 1997 in *The (Elyria, Ohio) Chronicle-Telegram* under the heading, "No love lost on Valentine card, American Greetings pulls card with adoption theme punchline," E2.

19 Content of card and spokesperson quotations that follow are taken from an Associated Press story published on February 13, 1997 in *The (Elyria, Ohio) Chronicle-Telegram* under the heading, "No love lost on Valentine card, American Greetings pulls card with adoption theme punchline," E2.

20 Joseph Campbell, *The Hero With a Thousand Faces* (Princeton, N.J.: Univ. of Princeton, 1973), 30.

PART II

Testing Your Ethical Base

In this section, you will read about ethical concepts associated with false-hood, manipulation, temptation and bias, confronting situations to test your value system. You will study several types of falsehoods, from seem-ingly innocent white lies in everyday dealings to global ones in govern-ment propaganda. You will be able to identify and defuse different types of hoaxes whose goal is to program media with perpetrators targeting your deeply held biases, fears, desires and convictions. You will encoun-ter monetary and non-monetary conflicts of interest that challenge you to harmonize consciousness and conscience to make prudent choices at the workplace. You will deal with consequences of racism and stereotypes that afflict media across platforms. Each chapter contains advice from and interviews with journalists, scholars and practitioners. Their views may challenge your awareness and deepen your intuition, empowering your ethical values. All chapters contain personal and communal journal exer-cises to drive home key concepts.

CHAPTER 5

Falsehood: Lie at Your Own Risk

LIES UNDERMINE TRUST

Aristotle believed that we are most human when we listen to the conscience and strive to lead a moral life. Liars, he believed, are ultimately unhappy because dishonesty undermines awareness and erodes trust. Moreover, according to K. DeLapp and J. Henkel in *Lying and Truthfulness*,

> [T]he virtuously honest person will reliably be able to resist the temptation to lie even when the truth would be too painful or the deception too sweet. For this reason, it is also conceptually impossible on Aristotle's account to be too honest.[1]

Aristotle's observations about truth and falsehood hold today. Journalists and practitioners gain their audience's and clientele's trust by conducting truthful business and lose credibility when they lie or exaggerate, obscuring awareness so that reports or campaigns risk failure on that basis alone. That's the golden rule that pertains to the communications workplace. Falsehood entails risk.

Don Ranly, professor emeritus at the Missouri School of Journalism, has worked across print and electronic platforms, conducting journalism seminars for press associations, corporations, associations. He knows the media business. He also knows that lies, half-truths, exaggerations and omissions are facts of life across platforms. "You're going to be asked to do things," he warns, "things that go against your ethical values. The moral choice is if you allow it."

Ranly recalls incidents involving students who compromised or embraced their values in stressful situations. Some obeyed employers and acted against their conscience or, conversely, set moral boundaries on what they would and would not do. For instance, on her first day on the job, one of Ranly's magazine students was instructed to write letters to the editor—*to her own publication.* "She did it," Ranly said, "and she told me she did it." She did more, too. That same student analyzed an article that appeared in another magazine and changed the name of the town and the streets so that it appeared to readers that hers was a local story. "Her editor asked her to plagiarize. He told her, 'Let's just *localize* it!'" Plagiarism, covered in depth later in the text, also is a lie.

Lies can be visual. "I had a photographer at a big magazine publishing company who was told to go out and take pictures of grandparents taking children to pick strawberries," Ranly says. "The editor said, 'Go to the market and buy little pails filled to the top with strawberries so we have good pictures.'" Unlike his magazine student, the photographer refused to obey her editor. When she returned to the newsroom with terrific pictures of people picking strawberries, her editor asked, "How did you get people to pose like that?" She responded, "I just took pictures." That's how visual truth is done. Life needs no embellishment.

Truth is more powerful than fiction. That is why we say that a newspaper story "has a ring of truth" or that a photograph "is worth 1,000 words," clichés based on fact. The sad truth, according to Ranly, is that students often fail to realize that they can draw their ethical boundaries, making a commitment to report truth and shun falsehood. "I knew a young man years ago who went to work at a great advertising agency, J. Walter Thomson, and he was an exceedingly bright guy. He told that agency, I will work for you if I never have to work for tobacco or alcohol clients. And they hired him. I think people can say, 'I will work for you but not do this.'"

The first step in resisting falsehood is to know in advance what you will or won't do in the name of a paycheck. We'll learn more about that in the upcoming chapter on temptation, which discusses conflicts of interest. What are your moral boundaries? As you recall, in the previous chapter we discussed moral absolutes from a universal perspective, such as it is wrong to lie or steal and it is right to be generous. Every journalist and practitioner should know his or her *individual* moral absolutes, especially when it comes to spreading lies.

Actually, all of us live in a climate of lies. We tell them. Our sources and clients tell them to us and each other. In *The Ethics of the Lie*, Jean-Michel Rabaté, reports that we "lie quite often, four to six times a day on average, as statisticians and psychologists agree with some variations; at the same time, we *do* hate liars, and even more detest being lied to—quite often we experience lies from close friends or family as a radical betrayal of trust or love."[2] Nevertheless, he adds, "we don't want other people to do to us what we do to them."[3] Every lie has a motive. For instance, some interns and new employees lie because they are ambitious. They want to succeed as journalists or practitioners and so agree to whatever their supervisors ask. That is why philosopher Sissela Bok warns people to take care in choosing our ambitions, "for in our later years, we may achieve them."[4]

Ambitious people often use falsehood to achieve ends. Studies show that much of the public distrusts advertising, news and public relations because people believe that journalists and practitioners are too ambitious, thinking more about themselves or their ratings rather than their audience and clientele. According to the Gallup organization,

Americans' trust and confidence in the mass media 'to report the news fully, accurately and fairly' has dropped to its lowest level in Gallup polling history, with 32% saying they have a great deal or fair amount of trust in the media.[5]

(In 1997, that percentage was 55 percent.) Moreover, with the proliferation of digital and mobile media and the rise in multitasking, with people looking at screens nearly 11 hours a day,[6] falsehood may be seamlessly woven into the fabric of contemporary society. However, Bok warns about making that assumption. Perhaps the online and traditional media may be lying more or merely focusing more on lies, scams and cover-ups. Bok is wary about how researchers measure "ongoing practices of lying, given the proportion of lies that are never uncovered, the shady regions of half-truths, self-deception, and hypocrisy, and the motives for those most embroiled in lies to undercut all efforts to probe their attitudes."[7] Bok implies that falsehood comes in many shades and hues but unlike truth; liars are anything but transparent, covering up and shoring lies and thereby complicating any analysis. When you do that, you'll pay the price.

LIES HAVE CONSEQUENCES

Of all platforms, advertising must be wary about stretching the truth in the name of persuasion until it lapses into falsehood. They must ensure that product claims are fact-based and unassailable. After all, advertising generates most of the revenue underwriting media platforms, from print to the blogosphere and beyond. Charles Warner, a strategy consultant and author of *Media Selling: Broadcast, Cable, Print, and Interactive,* states, "If salespeople lie, cheat, gouge, or over-promise and under-deliver in order to make short-term numbers, they jeopardize revenue far into the future."[8] That's a consequence of falsehood. Warner adds that lies hurt business because customers inform others about untruths, "especially your competitors and the press. The press loves stories about corporate bullies, liars, and cheaters."[9]

Ethical practices build trust, day after day. In the previous chapter, we noted that truth is the cornerstone of an ethical value system. Falsehood corrodes that foundation. We also observed that objectivity may be impossible theoretically, but we can develop conscience and consciousness sufficiently to perceive a reasonable semblance of reality. You cannot attain that if you lie routinely to yourself or others. No value system, however strong, can filter out falsehood all of the time. The goal of living ethics is to be cognizant of the consequences of falsehood so that you can make a conscious choice to go with or against your conscience. The more a person tells lies, the less aware he or she becomes of consequences because attention shifts from seeing the world as it actually is to shoring up the original lie, a habit that many scholars have documented, including philosopher

Bok,[10] and one that you can test for yourself in the journal exercise at the end of this chapter. Finally, it is one thing for a non-journalist or non-practitioner to lie, and quite another for a media professional to perpetuate lies using powerful communication technologies, because the impact multiplies like a virus—literally and figuratively—across platforms.

Media professionals have other reasons to commit to truth. Not only do they require strong value systems to navigate complex moral decisions; they also need to perceive when their sources, clients or constituents are making false claims in everyday scenarios and transactions including interviews, requests for proposals, product reviews, contract negotiations and strategic planning. "Nothing in the media business spreads faster than a hot rumor,"[11] writes *The Washington Post*'s Howard Kurtz in his book, *Media Circus*. Although he is discussing the blurred line between gossip and news, his observation that "our moral compass is increasingly erratic" once again applies across platforms.

The power of the lie has increased multifold in the past 30 years. Communication has advanced from magnetic tape, three networks and antennas to CDs, DVDs, 3-D, desktops, laptops, smartphones, cable and satellite offerings, podcasts and internet reaching billions of people worldwide through blogs, social networks, texting, digital personal assistants and other devices, including mobile wearable and even embedded technologies. Falsehoods not only are disseminated and multiplied through these platforms; they also metamorphose into urban legends, undermining integrity and credibility. Some ethicists make the argument that our social conscience is being dulled by the proliferation of media lies so that the typical person no longer can distinguish between truth and falsehood. The consequences of that are extreme, as a 2018 study affirmed in the journal *Science*, which reported that falsehoods on Twitter spread more rapidly than truth.[12] Researchers at the Massachusetts Institute of Technology's Media Lab reportedly analyzed 126,000 rumors on Twitter in a 10-year span resulting in some 3 million tweets from multiple accounts. Rumors were meticulously fact-checked. According to *Slate*, which also reported results of the study, "On average, it took true claims about six times as long as false claims to reach 1,500 people, with false political claims traveling even faster than false claims about other topics, such as science, business, and natural disasters."[13]

We saw this phenomenon escalate during the 2016 presidential election and beyond in an era of so-called "fake news" and "alternative facts." These reports blend seamlessly with instantaneous social media and digital ads that data-mine our devices, especially smartphones, and then vend our searches, likes, dislikes, emails, texts and other data to offer us products through applications that entertain, mislead or inform us every hour of the day. How, if at all, does that influence our notion of truth?

Consider this opinion of scholar and writer Hayden Carruth who writes:

Constantly we are told that this or that commercial product or service, or even this or that candidate for office, is "better," when we know it cannot be true. ... Children today are taught, in lessons compounded every five minutes, that untruth may be uttered with impunity, even with approval. Lying has become a way of life, very nearly now *the* way of life, in our society. The average adult American of average intelligence and average education believes almost nothing communicated to him in language, and the disbelief has become so ingrained that he or she does not even notice it.[14]

Take a moment to analyze that statement. Do you believe it to be true, partly true or false? Now factor this: Carruth published the above citation in 1981 when the media world consisted mostly of magnetic tape, three networks and antennas. If we acknowledge that the technology explosion of the mid- to late 1990s to the present day has also increased our exposure to media, evidenced by previously cited reports about our spending most of our waking hours looking at screens, then we have to put the profusion of lies into sharper focus. Not only are we exposed to more falsehoods during a typical digital day, journalists and practitioners also may be desensitized to the "ring of truth" because media consumption has become a substantial part of our own work day and leisure activity. More than ever, then, we have to understand the concepts and consequences of falsehood.

DETECT THE MANY TYPES OF LIES

Just as there are many types of truths, facts to archetypes, there are several types of lies:

- **White lies:** Untrue statements about seemingly minor topics usually told to flatter or spare the liar or another person or group of persons, pain, embarrassment or some other uncomfortable feeling.
- **Half-truths:** Statements that contain a mix of falsehoods and truths meant to mislead the listener or provide the liar with an escape-route, if challenged.
- **Exaggeration:** To inflate out of proportion a small truth, not for the social good—as satire intends—but to make an employee's job or assignment easier or to embellish a person's reputation or accomplishments.
- **Falsehoods:** Complete lies or fabrications masquerading as truth.[15]

Each type of lie has its own set of consequences, depending on three factors: the liar, the lie in question and the person(s) it deceives or affects. In her book *Lying: Moral Choice in Public and Private Life*, Sissela Bok states: "[M]ost lies *do* have negative consequences for liars, dupes, all those affected, and for the social trust. And when liars evaluate these consequences, they are peculiarly likely to be biased; their calculations frequently go astray."[16] As Bok notes in her book, a person who tells or condones "white lies" usually believes they are harmless. However, because liars usually fail to foresee consequences, their views about white lies often are flawed. Nonetheless, many people condone white lies, deeming them "well-intended" or "compassionate." If, for example, a friend who relies on you for homework puts you on the spot one day and asks—"Do you think I am lazy?"— you might feel tempted to respond: "Not at all." But friendship should be based on truth. Thus, if you are uncomfortable with that question, you can respond: "What I think doesn't matter, what you think *does*" or "I don't like to answer questions like that" or "I wish you wouldn't rely on me to help with homework." Or some other prudent, discrete or truthful reply. Some people would justify telling a white lie in this instance because they believe that truthful comments could hurt the friend's feelings. But there are consequences for that, too.

Hugh Culbertson, public relations researcher and Ohio University professor emeritus, says, "If our friends come to realize that we have complimented them insincerely, they may put little stock in future compliments. As a result, the compliments may lose their meaning. And friendships may even be endangered." Bok agrees that the cumulative effect of telling so-called harmless lies is not so harmless after all. Our intention may be harmless, she notes, but we usually cannot control outcomes. And if we tell minor lies, the habit alone can lead to more serious ones. "The aggregate harm from a large number of marginally harmful instances may, therefore, be highly undesirable in the end—for liars, those deceived, and honesty and trust more generally,"[17] she writes, adding that we often tell such lies to flatter, cheer up and show gratitude for unwanted gifts.

The ethics of gift-giving illustrate the consequences of and alternatives to the white lie. Fact is, giving and receiving gifts can be driven by motive as easily as by generosity. Some gifts, such as flowers, are symbols of love, friendship or forgiveness, and accepting bouquets conveys to the gift-giver that a relationship can be pursued or restored. Rejecting them sends another message. Some gifts are suggestive, so much so that it can be embarrassing to open them in front of others at a birthday party or other celebration. Consider the gift of lingerie or video discs on weight loss. Some gifts are self-serving. If you collect coins or antiques, don't give them to others unless they, too, are collectors. If you are a "James Bond" movie buff, don't give your partner the ultimate 007 Blu-ray collection that you wanted but didn't receive on your birthday. Gifts not only are symbols but often associated with symbolic holidays or occasions such as a retirement or an anniversary. For example, your household may need a new vacuum cleaner, but you might not want to give it on Valentine's Day. As you can see, there are ethics to giving and receiving gifts because gifts, like words, sounds and images, communicate motive, symbol, occasion and perception. When you give gifts at the workplace, these factors intensify, which is why there are rules concerning junkets, freebies and bribes to be covered in a later chapter on conflicts of interest. A gag gift symbolizing or suggesting sexual practices can be so inappropriate at an office party as to be actionable.

When gifts are mentioned, ethicists often look to the "rule of reciprocity," or obligation to repay for favors or occasions. The rule states that we should try to repay in value and kind what another person has given us as gift. As R.B. Cialdini writes in *Influence: The Psychology of Persuasion*, the rule can be exploited when one individual decides to make an unequal gift:

> Since [the] rule allows one person to choose the nature of the indebting first favor and the nature of the debt-cancelling return favor, we could easily be manipulated into an unfair exchange by those who might wish to exploit this rule.[18]

Some ethicists believe that minor falsehoods may be appropriate if the intent is to spare someone bad feelings—perhaps, say, an aunt who has given you an ugly necktie. On those occasions, they say, you may engage in the deceptive act of admiring the tie in front of Aunt Maude and then later storing it in a drawer. There may be fallout immediately or in the future from such a falsehood. You may not be able to admire the tie convincingly enough. Your voice tone and/or facial expression may reveal your true feelings for the tie to a family member. If you are a good actor, you may have to wear that tie or repeatedly proclaim your admiration for it at family functions. And if you give away the tie (otherwise known as "regifting") you partake in a particularly risky practice that can harm relationships permanently if the regifting becomes known. In the end, you don't have to lie to Aunt Maude about the tie but graciously thank her for thinking of you. In all genuine occasions, the maxim of "It's the thought that counts," counts. If you adopt the practice of telling white lies to assuage feelings of others, you'll tell those lies more frequently, both at home, school and work. That affects your reputation and credibility, particularly at your place of employment.

Like white lies, half-truths might seem innocent or occur in the most innocent-sounding stories. Writer Pam Noles recalls an incident that happened years ago when she was a newspaper reporter about a grocer decorating his yard for Halloween. "His display featured a black effigy hanging from the oak tree in his front yard. Next to the hanged man stood a figure in a white robe and a hood. A reporter was dispatched, collected quotations from the man about the mongrelization of America and the need for whites to be proud and ready to fight. That story was written, cleared by the bureau editor and sent up the chain. But it ran the next morning with all the racial overtones removed. An editor in the main office decided the racial angle had nothing to do with the story and would only upset people." Noles adds that sometimes reporters "can only tell part of the truth."

One would like to think that such a story today would elicit strong condemnation and that the editor would emphasize the racist symbolism of the display. In fact, you can do a search of "Racist Halloween Displays" and find stories that focus on that symbolism along with the impact on specific neighborhoods. On October 31, 2016, *The New York Daily News* ran a national story about a similar display in Florida concerning a man who hung dummies in what appeared like lynching.[19] Moreover, with the advent of mobile media, passersby can upload video to platforms like YouTube. So can news outlets, as was the case with CBS Los Angeles, which recorded a Halloween display featuring a Confederate flag and lynching.[20] While social mores might have changed since the incident described earlier, with an editor deleting race-based information, consider the long-term impact of such a half-truth on African Americans and, in this case, Pam Noles. "I entered journalism with the dream of gathering facts, and in the telling, exposing truth," she says. This example undermined her morale. She not only lost respect for this particular news outlet, she lost respect for her chosen profession, journalism.

Half-truths involve withholding essential information, providing a partial picture. Exaggeration involves inflating the truth, providing a substantively fictitious picture. When tempted to exaggerate one's experience or abilities, practitioners need to "come clean" and disclose the truth, says Grant Castle, former president of Castle Underwood agency in New York City. Castle has long warned against exaggeration at the workplace. He often advises advertising and public relations students to tell the truth on small and large matters alike. "It usually takes getting caught in an exaggeration or lie early in a career to cause sleepless nights and dysfunctional days. Hopefully it happens early enough in a career to be written off as 'youthful enthusiasm.'" Castle notes that the consequences of being caught in an exaggeration outweigh the immediate benefits. "You're going to be in the business a long time. Every new business meeting you have may not be a win, but you have the chance to impress people in the pitch who will remember you later on, perhaps after they have moved to another company. That's really how you get into pitches." Clients have long memories. "Making a 'cooked' presentation won't set you up well for the future," he adds.

Exaggeration also can bring down the most accomplished of journalists and practitioners. Case in point: In 2015, Brian Williams, NBC Nightly News anchor, was suspended after he exaggerated an account that he had referenced many times about being onboard a military helicopter that took enemy fire during the 2003 Iraq War. He lost his anchor seat and was demoted to a similar position at the smaller MSNBC outlet. In covering his return to the newsroom, *USA Today* recounted how veterans "who had been at the scene challenged Williams' claim on Facebook," with Williams finally recanting the account "after *Stars and Stripes* published a story about the online exchange."[21] Here again is an incident that had to be addressed because of exchanges on social media, holding Williams accountable, until the story was picked up by mainstream media. It is also important to note that upon being challenged, Williams did not immediately tell the complete truth in an apology that damaged his credibility and that of NBC. According to *The New York Times*, "In his apology, Mr. Williams said that he had been on a different helicopter, behind the one that had sustained fire, and that he had inadvertently 'conflated' the two."[22] Williams substituted the word "conflated" for "exaggerated," and that "explanation earned him not only widespread criticism on radio and TV talk shows, but widespread ridicule on Twitter, under the hashtag '#BrianWilliamsMisremembers.'"

Exaggerating achievements on resumes also can bring down beginners and veterans alike. A *New York Post* article lists five most common resume lies, which include falsifying or embellishing educational degrees, job duties, employment histories, achievements and titles. Writer Gregory Giangrande states, "With stiff competition for jobs, it might be tempting to include little white lies on your resume to help get your foot in the door."[23] He also reports that almost all companies now conduct background checks on job applicants, especially since the internet simplifies that process and can uncover facts that come back to haunt liars years later, as was the case with Notre Dame football coach George O'Leary who lied about playing varsity football as well as earning a master's degree.[24] Another high-profile case involved Bausch & Lomb CEO Ronald Zarrella who claimed to have earned an MBA from New York University's Business School. He did attend the school but did not graduate. When a corporate news release falsely stated that he had earned a degree, an online journalist reported the exaggeration, causing Bausch & Lomb stocks to decline by 3 percent.[25] Zarella reportedly responded: "Clearly it's my obligation to proofread such things carefully and ensure their accuracy."[26] It would seem by his response that the CEO was indirectly implicating the public affairs person who wrote the release. But the MBA reference also appeared on Zarella's biographies for at least ten years.[27]

Loss of reputation is perilous in public relations. "From the days of the printing press to our era of advanced, ever-changing technology, basic ethical principles have not changed," says Judy Phair, president of PhairAdvantage Communications. "Bad behavior leads to bad communication, which in turn leads to a lack of trust and loss in profits." Phair is especially wary about overuse of advanced technology, such as social media, which only magnify falsehoods of every stripe. "High-speed communication is often unfiltered, inaccurate and impersonal. It's a breeding ground for losing trust." Unfortunately, she says, some organizations and individuals ignore the consequences of the lie. "The fact is, communication based on misinformation and manipulation is not only wrong—it also doesn't work."

Public relations practitioners work on a continuing basis with the news media. Caught in any fabrication, they face dire consequences. Reporters who work with them no longer may trust basic information and suspect or reject every release instead of disseminating it on good faith. Reporters may feel they have to cover events themselves if they do not trust practitioners and may simply not make time for that in their schedules. Lisa Richwine, who worked for States News Service in Washington, D.C., now reports on science for Reuters. When working for States News, she often had to rely on press secretaries for information and story leads about Congress. Soon she began to question the credibility of staff workers "who issue statements from members of Congress with completely fabricated quotes." According to Richwine, "Often the lawmakers don't even see the words attributed to them." Result? Richwine interviews those politicians without trusting news releases about them, or occasionally decides not to do the story.

QUOTE-MAKING CAN BE UNTRUTHFUL

Public relations practitioners immerse themselves in campaigns. They have to know objectives of their clients or companies so intimately that they can write news releases that include, for lack of a better word, "invented" quotations. These are phrases or sentences that the client or chief operating officer or other executive never actually said verbatim, but that are attributed to him or her using direct quotation marks in releases or statements meant for public distribution. Often those quotations have been based on notes or conversations that the practitioner has had with clients and executives; however, in the strictest sense, the words usually are a composite of real and *made-up* statements. Hence, the term *quote-making*—so commonplace in public relations that professional practitioners reading concerns about it in *Living Media Ethics* might take offense; nonetheless, there are legal, ethical and educational problems with quote-making that do *not* apply across platforms and are, in fact, forbidden ethically in journalism and mass communication and, some might even argue, in advertising, whose testimonials should be real rather than created. Problems involving quote-making can be prevented and resolved through standard PR practice, preserving "the integrity of the communication process" and being "honest and accurate in all communications," pursuant to the Public Relations Society of America code of ethics.[28]

This is an ethics book, not a legal one. But practitioners should familiarize themselves with *Masson v. The New Yorker, Alfred A. Knopf, and Janet Malcolm.* The 1991 case, which reached the Supreme Court, concerns alleged altering of quotations by a magazine writer in a two-part 1983 essay in *The New Yorker.* This may seem far removed from the ethical issue at hand. It isn't. Because contents of a news release may appear across platforms in the converged environment, quote-making can be called into question, given the right set of circumstances. Consider the standard for direct quotations, set in the Malcolm case by Justice Anthony M. Kennedy:

In general, quotation marks around a passage indicate to the reader that the passage reproduces the speaker's words verbatim. They inform the reader that he or she is reading the statement of the speaker, not a paraphrase or other indirect interpretation by an author. By providing this information, quotations add authority to the statement and credibility to the author's work.[29]

The loophole, of course, is the phrase "in general." Reporters have been tampering with quotations ever since there have been news and notepads. Benjamin Franklin not only made up quotations but on one occasion, an entire newspaper, describing alleged gruesome details of British violence on Americans and enhancing the invention with fake advertisements about the sale of a house and a missing bay mare.[30] Increasingly in today's litigious society, however, editors—cautious because of the Malcolm case—believe that direct quotations must be verbatim or recast into indirect attributions.[31] Conversely, Justice Kennedy's phrase "in general" also has represented a problem for public relations. As Fraser P. Seitel writes in *The Practice of Public Relations*:

Like it or not, public relations people do indeed fabricate statements for their employers—it goes with the territory. And if such statements are approved by employers in advance, ethical questions are less pertinent. However, public relations people rarely announce or even acknowledge that they have authored such statements.[32]

This makes the topic difficult to discuss. Indeed, guidelines about quote-making are missing from the PRSA code, accessed in 2017. A key change in 2000 rewrote what used to be "code paragraph 4," which stated: "A member shall adhere to the highest standards of accuracy and truth ... giving credit for ideas and words borrowed from others." The guideline under "honesty" can be interpreted as allowing quote-making: "We adhere to the highest standards of accuracy and truth *in advancing the interests of those we represent and in communicating with the public* (emphasis added)."[33] PR interns and recent graduates may have impressive portfolios, solid recommendations and savvy technical and computer skills. They may understand the core tenets of the PRSA code, a model for other media platforms in its completeness and moral inspiration. Who, if anyone during college, has schooled students in the oxymoronic ethics of quote-making? Is there such a thing? Just as tellers of white lies experience a cumulative effect from that habit, eroding credibility, makers of quotations can easily lose respect for Supreme Court-mandate of "verbatim" use and so can easily misinterpret a file, account or objective; fabricate libelous or embarrassing quotations; or release an erroneous statement before in-house or client approval.

An apropos case study appears in the *Public Relations Review*. In "Lies, Deceptions, and Public Relations," Elaine E. Englehardt and DeAnn Evans discuss an invented quotation by a house organ writer for a hospital. The quotation served the hospital's interests—heralding its "charitable care account." The ethical problem, however, was two-fold: The patient, who delivered a premature-birth baby, happened to be a reporter and did not tap funds from the charity account; her insurance company paid the $130,004.99 bill. As Englehardt and Evans state,

> The writers of the house organ lied. The emotional story needed something to compel readers to donate, so a quote was added. It was a lie, one that hurt the parents, the hospital, the reputation of the house organ, and perhaps the charitable arm of the hospital.[34]

This case study is as much about respect for quotations as it is about falsehood. A beginner who knows the craft of quote-making without understanding its ethical ramifications can jeopardize an agency and put its accounts at risk in precisely this manner. To be sure, not all practitioners condone quote-making, even with a client's review and pre-approval. Dan Pinger, president of Dan Pinger Public Relations in Cincinnati, believes that PR writers should quote sources verbatim. "Inventing the quotes that you want and then getting someone to agree to them is wrong because the source might say something differently if asked directly," Pinger observes, "not necessarily the invented quote." Practitioners at his agency sit "face to face with a person to be quoted and take accurate notes. It's different if we are working together on a statement. Then we work together." Pinger says that he prefers accurate quote-*taking* to -*making* because credibility is his top priority. "A major concern in public relations is always credibility, and that comes from authenticity. A communication that is other than the real spoken word might not ring true. If it rings with authenticity," he says, "then it is credible."

John Paluszek, senior counsel at Ketchum, one of the world's leading public relations agencies, understands the risks involved in quote-making. He mentions that Larry Speakes, former Reagan press secretary and Merrill-Lynch executive, may have "lost his corporate job over this exact issue." In his 1988 book *Speaking Out*, Speakes disclosed that he fabricated statements and attributed them to Reagan at a Geneva conference—without the President's approval. At the time, the disclosure conflicted with Merrill-Lynch's "Tradition of Trust" campaign, and Speakes resigned soon after.

The anecdote is pertinent today. Values and mission statements are becoming increasingly popular at major agencies, and they are easily accessible online. Such documents can ensure sound business practices, enhance corporate philosophy and guide practitioners in crisis management. Again, quote-making often is omitted from those codes. Thus, novice practitioners often remain uninformed about proper procedures and learn them through mistakes, a potentially costly practice.

Although PR executives differ on the ethics of quote-making, all emphasize these components:

- Intimate knowledge of a client and an account.
- Accurate note-taking during sessions with clients to understand key objectives.
- Client review and pre-approval of direct quotations.

Concerning the latter, unforeseen situations can arise, requiring experienced practitioners with intimate knowledge of an account to draft quotes without prior approval from a client. "From a purely ethical point of view, and a practical standpoint, getting the statement as drafted approved either in toto, or as adjusted, is always the best route," Paluszek says.

To validate quote-making ethically, one has to consider components of speechwriting. There are some differences. Speechwriting is closer in nature to statement writing, in which a practitioner and client respond formally and publicly to an issue or incident. Most important, speeches will be reviewed and edited by the spokesperson. Eventually words attributed to him or her *will be said*. (That is why reporters worry about pre-publishing speech stories; if they do, they must monitor the speaker to determine if he or she improvised or perhaps omitted quoted words.) In sum, when Larry Speakes wrote a speech for Ronald Reagan, the media knew that the President would eventually say those words. But when it was learned that Speakes fabricated quotes without Reagan's review or pre-approval— even ones that echoed administrative policy—Speakes was condemned by reporters and practitioners alike.

Review and pre-approval are pivotal ethical elements in quote-making. The question then becomes, "Is getting prior approval in quote-making akin to prior approval in speechwriting?" After all, a client who reviews direct quotations is, in essence, *reading* them—aloud or silently. That may constitute an intellectual equivalent to actually reading words, as in a speech. There is little excuse anymore to skip the review and pre-approval process. Clients are available via mobile phone, text, email, fax and other digital venues. These days anyone can reach anybody in a matter of seconds, should the need arise.

"One important aspect of quote-making is that it is a much faster process now with technology," Ketchum's John Paluszek says. "But technology is still just a tool that is used after trust is developed between practitioner and client." Paluszek believes that trust is as much an interpersonal as well as technological factor in public relations. "A lot has to happen (interpersonally) before technology can be used efficiently to save time." A client has to be available for face-to-face meetings, he notes; however, that can be difficult to arrange because of schedules with so many people requesting "face time" with a VIP. "This function of PR is so very vital to the organization's success that the CEO, or whatever title he or she has, must value this, and it can happen face to face or in an executive committee environment or even in a broader context." Once an interpersonal relationship has been established, then digital access can save people time.

Paluszek's tenet applies across platforms. The news reporter who interviews sources face to face is as important as the practitioner in public relations or advertising who consults with a client. The same holds true for online and electronic journalism where the temptation may be greatest to allow the technology to establish the day's agenda. Let's conclude, then, by investigating other ethical practices involving quotations across platforms, using Supreme Court Justice Kennedy's "in general" observation to preface these guidelines:

- **Don't** "fabricate" quotations. Your job is to put your sources and clients on record—not to put words into their mouths. Take notes at meetings and interviews. If a source refuses or is unable to give you the quote that you need, request another session.
- **Don't** lift quotations from other stories. The internet makes it easy to locate sources with nifty things to say. If you use those quotations in your work but did not interview sources, reference the journalist or practitioner who did.
- **Don't** excerpt passages from online or print documents, including speeches, proceedings, testimonials and minutes of meetings, and reprint them as quotations, pretending newsmakers or clients said the excerpts to you in an interview. Cite the source of those passages accurately or interview newsmakers and clients anew.
- **Do** research sources and clients on the internet before interviewing them. Everything from resumes to public records is available online. Accessing those documents before interviews saves time and earns respect from your constituents because you did the necessary legwork.
- **Do** interviews face-to-face when possible. Good journalism and public relations writing rely on "sensory data," descriptive passages that appeal to the five senses or convey motion. You can't always convey that doing telephone or email interviews, which may suffice for a quick expert quotation or round-up but seldom for a campaign or an article.
- **Maybe** you can correct grammar and syntax. Purists will argue that you can't fix such common errors as wrong verb tense or idiom, noun-pronoun disagreement, or run-on sentences. When you get such quotes, purists believe, you should make them indirect. Realists believe you can make minor corrections that typically involve a word or two. Your goal is to quote sources, realists say, not embarrass them. Bottom line: If you change meaning when you change a word, you can't use a direct quotation.

How you quote sources reflects your standards, especially in an electronic age whose emphasis is on convenience rather than legwork. If you take shortcuts with quotations, you can lose more than assignments and accounts. You can lose your reputation.

PICTURES CAN LIE, TOO

People make photographs. Photographs lie in all the ways people do. With digital technology, a photographer can remove a distracting diploma in a dentist's office and convey the white lie of a blank wall for background. Or digitally remove a boy from the dentist's chair and place a girl there instead, conveying a half-truth as the dentist hovers over the wrong patient. Or fabricate the entire shot, asking the dentist to pretend she is pulling a tooth and the boy to pretend he is crying. "In the 1950s, because of slow film, newspaper photographers began setting up photographs the way magazine photojournalists were doing it, following the example of *LIFE* and other publications," says Terry Eiler, photojournalism professor emeritus with decades of experience shooting assignments for *National Geographic*.[35] "Some photographers back then made pictures that just were too good to be true. For example, I remember one of a parent chasing a bare-assed child down the hallway. The parent was just coming into focus in the right-hand corner and the kid was in the upper left corner turning down and right into a second hallway. The kid was multiple-strobe-lit (or flashed) and was turning to a cross-lit-strobe (or flash). It seemed set up the same way Norman Rockwell would set up a portrait. The kid actually may have done that, but this was a picture that *illustrated* the story rather than *documented* it." Therein is the deception. The picture suggests that the photographer spent the day observing the mother and child for a good shot when the photographer may simply have orchestrated the shot because the editor wanted to illustrate a story with a Rockwellian motif. "These types of pictures still exist and are set up to illustrate text or a theme," Eiler says.

"In photojournalism or news photography you have a sense of being part of immediacy," he adds. "You can still have the news-photography mentality. But photojournalism now is also portraiture and illustration. In fact, all of the visual tools of the magazine world have landed in the lap of the broad-based photojournalist." A documentary photograph captures a snippet of life whether news, sports or some other happening or event. It documents or presents a slice of reality or history. Portraiture is what the word implies, a portrait of an individual, who may or may not be cognizant that the photographer is taking a picture. Illustration has a fictive component, some visual or staged manipulation or enhancement, which accompanies text or digital material across platforms.

From an ethical standpoint, Eiler says, the major concern with illustration is not to pretend that it is a documentary photograph. "In an era gone by in American photojournalism there would always be these terrible pictures on the last day of school with kids busting through the doors and cheering," he states, "and these (photos) were as phony as a $3 bill. Illustrations should not pretend to be a real slice of life. So, the worst thing that illustration can be is 'documentary fiction'"—an oxymoron on par with "unbiased opinion" in television news.

"You can swing both directions ethically with portraiture," Eiler explains. The key is in the collaboration between the photographer and person photographed. A photo can be a candid documentary or illustrative portrait. In classic portraiture, the photographer seeks to reveal information about the person being photographed through elements of illustration. "For instance," Eiler says, "when I do a glamour portrait of someone, the (real-life) accuracy may be considerably reduced because I am trying to make the person the best, most glamorous depiction that I can." However, the documentary side of portraiture requires accuracy without those enhancements. "Ethically, then, there is a level of collaboration that we all have to agree on," Eiler adds.

Documentary photography has strict standards of accuracy. "The worst thing that can happen with documentary photography is a photographer adopting an illustration mindset," Eiler says, "a photographer saying, 'I can make this a better documentary image if I illustrate it.' Documentary images need to have that candid sense of accuracy—not a candid sense of truth, mind you. Your truth and my truth can be opposite. Accuracy is what counts." Eiler has a maxim for the ethic: *This is what I observed, not what I orchestrated.* "Of course," he adds, "there is the argument that the photographer being present on the scene changes the situation, and so does a reporter. But that is not the point. Documentary photojournalism is an observed and captured venture. Certainly, there are choices—the moment the photographer shoots, the lenses being used—they influence what is seen. But the bottom line is whether the photograph captures candidly what was observed."

CROSSING THE LINE IN PHOTOJOURNALISM

Figure 5.1 "Dandelion Boy": Photograph by Diane Bugeja, reprinted with permission.

The above picture was taken by photojournalist Diane Bugeja as a documentary photo. She followed the boy into an Iowa meadow and shot the picture. Ethically, she could use it as a portrait or as an illustration to accompany text. On the line below, there are three types of photographs: Documentary, Portraiture, Illustration. Documentary photos can move from left to right without an explanatory note. Portraiture is the fulcrum or center between documentary and illustration and contains elements of both. Illustration cannot move to the left and masquerade as a documentary without an explanatory note. Neither can illustration move to the left and masquerade as portraiture if it has been digitally altered without an explanatory note.

Documentary	Portraiture	Illustration

A documentary photo can move left to right on the line without an explanatory cutline. Portraiture is the fulcrum. It can either document or illustrate, depending on the shot. But an illustration cannot be used as a documentary unless editors carefully and clearly note it.

The Los Angeles Times has strict guidelines concerning photos that cross the line or may be perceived as crossing the line, moving from documentary to illustration. For example, in 1994 a photographer at that newspaper shot a documentary of a Los Angeles firefighter splashing his head with water from an in-ground swimming pool during a firestorm that consumed a luxury home behind him. *The LA Times* was planning to enter the shot for a Pulitzer Prize when the authenticity of the photograph was questioned. After an editor investigated rumors, the photographer was accused of fabricating the photograph, a charge that he denied; nonetheless, he was suspended without pay for one week. In an article about the suspension by Howard Kurtz, published in *The Washington Post*, the photographer said,

> I deny categorically asking or telling any fireman to pose for me in front of a pool. I may have been guilty of saying this would make a nice shot, but to the best of my recollection, I did not directly ask him to do that. ... I've been doing breaking news stories for years and years and I've never in my life set up a picture.[36]

The lesson in this case does not concern whether the photographer did or did not set up the shot. Neither does it concern whether he lied or told the truth about the circumstances surrounding the picture. The example merely shows the consequences that can accompany suspected set-ups. The photographer was in the process of being nominated for a Pulitzer Prize when the allegations arose. Instead of receiving the acclaim that comes with such an honor, he was disciplined. Moreover, *The LA Times* asked The Associated Press to notify its clients nationwide that the photograph should not be used again.

"Photojournalists take these issues very seriously," Terry Eiler says. Any student who knowingly sets up a shot and passes it off as a documentary can be suspended or expelled. He recalls an incident at Ohio University concerning a student covering a dancer, following him into the restroom. "The photographer staged a shot, asking the dancer to practice in the bathroom in front of the mirror. We found out it was a set-up. We could have thrown him out of school." But Eiler didn't because nobody had told the student that this was a visual lie. On another assignment, the student was overheard telling a railroad worker to walk past a train after a derailment. "When I asked him about it, he said, 'No, no. It happened. I just missed the frame.' I told the student, '*Stop right there,*'" Eiler recalls. Again, he didn't suspend the photographer because the student did not know that even this was unethical. "Thereafter that student took a real interest in ethics," Eiler says. "Twelve years later he won the Pulitzer Prize, is one of our prized graduates, and a leading voice about ethics in our profession."

That student was John Kaplan featured in *Living Media Ethics* as one of the most ethical photojournalists in the business. "In my case," Kaplan recalls, "I set up what I thought was an innocuous picture and I learned from that experience the consequences of that mistake. But I never knew it was a mistake because nobody taught me. I had learned about photojournalism from some very talented successful people. In those days, it was more acceptable to pose a picture. I actually was taught that if a situation isn't quite pleasing enough to help create it to make it so. Then I got to college and realized that this is a serious ethical problem." Kaplan says the derailment photo is a good case study for aspiring photojournalists. "Even though it doesn't seem like a serious crime, it might make people who witnessed me doing that question the credibility of any picture I would take. It was a hard lesson," he adds. "But I'm glad I learned it in college."

QUESTION EVERY LIE

Bob Woodward, *The Washington Post* reporter who helped break the Watergate scandal with Carl Bernstein, used anonymous sources. Both reporters set high ethical standards for investigative journalism. Their coverage of the break-in at the Democratic National Headquarters at the Watergate Hotel eventually led to the resignation of President Richard Nixon in 1974. The acclaimed movie *All the President's Men* showcases the dogged pursuit of that story through the anonymous source code-named "Deep Throat," one of the best-kept secrets in journalism. According to Woodward, keeping anonymous sources confidential is "an unbreakable contract unless somebody is dishonest with you. ... You have to make that pledge and that pledge doesn't have any ifs or speculation attached to it."[37] Woodward kept that pledge until Associate Director Mark Felt, the No. 2 official at the FBI during Watergate, revealed himself as "Deep Throat" in May 2005.

In Woodward's book about Felt, titled *The Secret Man: The Story of Watergate's Deep Throat*, the reporter discloses that years before Felt's admission, a friend of his and Bernstein, columnist Richard Cohen at *The Post*, told Woodward that he believed Felt was Deep Throat. Here is how Woodward describes an encounter between him and Cohen when Woodward was metropolitan editor with some supervisory authority over Cohen:

> At first I discouraged him from doing the column.
> He persisted. It was one of the great mysteries, he said. ...
> Deep Throat was my source, I said, and I have to protect him.
> Don't be ridiculous, after so many years? Cohen said. It had been eight years at that point.
> So I misled him, trying as best I could to steer him away from Felt without flat out denying it.
> Look, he said, he had heard from someone ... that at the top of my Deep Throat memos were the initials "M.F."—obviously Mark Felt, right?
> It's not him, I said, adopting the well-tested Watergate strategy that when all else fails, lie. I lied, and insisted to Cohen that he had it wrong. W—R—O—N—G! I spelled it out, I recall. A real, safe truth between friends, I indicated, suggesting that I was helping him from writing something monumentally stupid.
> Cohen didn't do the column.[38]

Woodward justified his lie by saying that he objected to journalists' trying to figure out confidential sources of other reporters; that if everyone tried to do this, there would be no such sources; and it was every reporter's job to protect such sources—"Even from other reporters."[39] Some would argue that Woodward had told an ethical, or "questionable lie."

Questionable lies are just that, *questionable*. Should the U.S. government lie to the news media and disseminate propaganda to save lives? Should a reporter ever lie to get a story if that story saves lives? These types of lies test value systems of otherwise moral people who tell them in the name of the national interest or the public's right to know. Some ethicists are absolutists when it comes to lying, believing, as did the 18th century philosopher Immanuel Kant, that any lie for any reason, however noble, is immoral and destroys a person's dignity.[40] Others, such as philosopher Sissela Bok, say in rare instances, which people seldom face, lying can be considered as ethical as self-defense. She analyzes a case study in which a ship captain in World War II is transporting fugitives from Nazi Germany. The Nazis stop the ship and ask if there are any fugitives on board. If the captain tells the truth, as Kant would have required, the fugitives could lose their lives. That latter reality would far outweigh the duty to speak truthfully. "In fact," Bok writes, "in times of such crisis, those who share Kant's opposition to lying clearly put innocent persons at the mercy of wrongdoers."[41] Bok, in essence, suggests that such lies are rare but can be told providing they contribute to an important moral goal that cannot be attained without lying.

Some government officials use that logic to justify propaganda. For instance, telling the truth to the media about the Allied invasion at Normandy in 1944 would have been disastrous because Germans would have learned about and prepared for the assault. But this historic incident is the exception, not the rule; as in personal life, nations seldom face such crises as the Allies did on "D-Day" so that lying can be considered a moral "self-defense."

Also, there exists the government specter of "disinformation," which ethicist John. C. Merrill defines as, "One kind of information dissemination that is in the twilight zone between intentional and unintentional propaganda."[42] He also notes that "journalism propaganda" concerns "those messages purposely designed to diminish the reliability, objectivity, balance, and thoroughness of journalism."[43] The concept of government officials practicing disinformation harkens the Russian word *dezinformatsiya*, which means disseminating fabricated or deceptive information for political gain. That policy was at work in the 2016 U.S. presidential election, not only in content disseminated as fake news on social media, but also through advertising of such content on Facebook.

In 2017, Facebook shared such advertisements with the Senate and House intelligence committees. According to a *New York Times* report, the company reported about 470 Russia-linked accounts—"in which fictional people posed as American activists"—which posted inflammatory messages on divisive issues, some of which attacked Hillary Clinton or praised Donald J. Trump.[44] The disclosure elicited an apology from the social media company, which vowed to "fight any attempt to interfere with elections or civic engagement on Facebook," resulting in these internal changes:

- **Making advertising more transparent:** We are building new tools that will allow you to see the ads a Facebook Page is running, including ads that aren't targeted to you directly.
- **Strengthening our ad policies and enforcement:** We are adding more than 1,000 people to our global ad review teams, requiring more thorough documentation from advertisers who want to run U.S. federal election-related ads, and expanding our policies around violence in ads.
- **Investing in security:** We will more than double the team working to prevent election interference on Facebook and develop new technologies dedicated to security and safety.
- **Expanding our partnerships with election commissions:** We are working with election commissions around the world to proactively communicate online risks we've identified.[45]

Disinformation is at the heart of undermining credibility in journalism. Chuck Raasch, chief Washington correspondent for the *Saint Louis Post-Dispatch*, says increasingly the role of journalists is to fact-check and correct the record of propagandists and liars. They are able "to infect communications bloodstreams" to such a degree that reporters are challenged, continuously, in their efforts to verify claims and disseminate truthful news. "I tell my non-journalist friends that the fakery and lies and propaganda and meanness they see on social media is not that new to those of us in the news business; it's the kind of stuff that gatekeeper editors kept out of their newspapers and off their broadcast before the age of the World Wide Web." This is why Raasch hates the term *fake news*. "Fake is a lie," he says. "News, done right, is the closest approximation to the truth of current events than any human, with our inherent biases and shortcomings, can bring forth. 'Fake news' commoditizes the truth—like 'I Can't Believe It's Not Butter!'" did to soy bread spread. News and fake news are not even remotely in the same galaxy."

Fake or fabricated news has been around ever since the invention of the printing press, which became the first mass communication technology in occidental culture, eventually creating a national newspaper platform. According to Tom Standage, deputy editor of *The Economist*,

> [S]earch engines and social media have blown apart newspapers' bundles of stories. Facebook shows an endless stream of items from all over the web. Click an interesting headline and you may end up on a fake-news site, set up by a political propagandist or a teenager in Macedonia to attract traffic and generate advertising revenue. Peddlers of fake stories have no reputation to maintain and no incentive to stay honest; they are only interested in the clicks.[46]

Standage cites fake news associated with the 2016 U.S. presidential election campaign, including false accounts that Republication candidate Donald Trump had been endorsed by the pope and Democratic candidate Hillary Clinton has sold arms to the Islamic State. Standage believes more fact-checking and media literacy may be able to mitigate the continuing presence of fake news. But he is not so sure, primarily because of an ethical precept: reputation. If purveyors of fake news are unconcerned about credibility, with a goal of spreading propaganda or affirming conspiracies, who can stop them?

Deceiving citizens of a democracy to protect democracy is contradictory, according to Sissela Bok, chiefly because those who advocate for deception are susceptible to bias and typically overestimate the benefits of the questionable lie.[47] Soon they are using disinformation to cover up past mistakes, practicing journalism propaganda to further their ambitions. However, Bok's analysis also applies in part to media professionals who lie to get stories, interviews, sound bites, photos, accounts, clients and freelance or other assignments. Journalists and practitioners who engage in half-truths and other falsehoods as means to an end also are susceptible to bias. They, too, can overestimate the likelihood that their efforts will benefit the public good and underestimate the negative ramifications on people whom they deceive in the name of that good.

Worse, media professionals can be as self-righteous as politicians and are just as quick to justify their behavior. Those who lie in the pursuit of truth usually are no better morally than politicians who deceive citizens to preserve democracy.

So-called "questionable" lies are rare. They happen once or twice in a typical media career. Usually there are other alternatives besides lying to resolve dilemmas involving vital moral goals. Problems arise, however, when media professionals cannot perceive alternatives because their perception has become skewed. Moreover, questionable lies come with consequences that can harm credibility. In the end, all lies test values. The common motto—"Truth will set you free"—underscores that notion and constitutes the intent of the First Amendment, the rights of which every media platform enjoys and must safeguard by renouncing falsehood.

"JUST HOW TRUTHFUL ARE YOU?"

Personal Journal Exercise

1. Keep a weekly journal of all the white lies, half-truths and falsehoods that you say or indicate to others. Without violating your own privacy or the privacy of others, or identifying anyone by name, summarize each one with a descriptive sentence—such as "Told my roommate I wasn't hungry; I was, but I didn't like the Taco pizza he ordered"—incident by incident, item by item. **Note:** *Do not put your name on this list but set a copy of it aside as you will hand that in for the "Communal Journal Exercise" later.*
2. Look at your list of lies compiled in the above assignment. Under each incident or item, briefly note the immediate, future or possible consequences of the lie.
3. Keep a weekly journal of all the white lies, half-truths and falsehoods that others say or indicate to you. Without violating your own or others' privacy or reputation, summarize them incident by incident, item by item. Under each incident or item, briefly note the immediate, future or possible consequences of the lie.
4. Keep a weekly journal of times when you wanted to tell a white lie, half-truth or falsehood ... but caught yourself and told the truth or declined to answer the question (doing so in a polite, discreet or otherwise appropriate way). Without violating your own or someone else's privacy or damaging anyone's reputation, briefly summarize these incidents and items and note the immediate, future or possible consequences of telling the truth.

5. Look over your notes from each of the above exercises. In a 500-word journal entry or blog post or brief podcast or multimedia presentation, note any conclusions you can make about each exercise and share what they indicate about how truthful you and others actually are.

Communal Journal Exercise

As instructor or group leader, devise an anonymous way to collect lists of lies from each individual who has done the first exercise in the "Personal Journal" assignment above. Printouts can be left in a mailbox and files in a confidential drop box. Code all the white lies, half-truths and falsehoods that each individual said or indicated to others and then compile a collective list of all the lies and reasons associated with the class or group. Without violating anyone's privacy, or using names, share the number of lies told in a week, the average number per person in the group, and some of the descriptions of particular lies for a discussion on possible consequences.

NOTES

1 K. DeLapp and J. Henkel, *Lying and Truthfulness* (Indianapolis, IN: Hackett Publishing Company, 2012), 53.
2 Jean-Michel Rabaté, *The Ethics of the Lie*, Suzanne Verderber, trans. (New York: Other Press, 2008), 348–49.
3 Rabaté, 349.
4 Sissela Bok, *Lying: Moral Choice in Public and Private Life* (New York: Vintage Books, 1999), xv.
5 Art Swift, Gallup, "Americans' Trust in Mass Media Sinks to New Low," September 14, 2016, www.gallup.com/poll/195542/americans-trust-mass-media-sinks-new-low.aspx
6 Rani Molla, "People Consumed More Media Than Ever Last Year—But Growth is Slowing," *Recode*, May 30, 2017; available from www.recode.net/2017/5/30/15712660/media-consumption-zenith-mobile-internet-tv
7 Bok, 1999, xvii.
8 Charles Warner, "Sales Ethics," in *Media Selling: Broadcast, Cable, Print, and Interactive*, 3rd edition, by Charles Warner and Joseph Buchman (Ames, Iowa: Iowa State Press, 2004), 29.
9 Ibid.
10 See Bok, 1978, 52. She notes that there are "risks to the liar himself of personal discomfort and loss of integrity, of a greater likelihood, however slight, of having to lie again to shore up the first lie; and of a somewhat diminished resistance to lying for causes he may wish to further in the future."

11 Howard Kurtz, *Media Circus: The Trouble with America's Newspapers* (New York: Times Books, 1994), 151.

12 Barbara R. Jasny, "Lies Spread Faster Than the Truth," *Science*, March 9, 2018, Vol. 359, No. 6380, 1114–115.

13 Will Oremus, "Lies Travel Faster Than Truth on Twitter—and Now We Know Who to Blame," *Slate*, March 9, 2018, https://slate.com/technology/2018/03/lies-travel-faster-than-truth-on-twitter-says-a-major-new-mit-study.html

14 Hayden Carruth, "Poetry in a Discouraging Time: A Symposium," *The Georgia Review*, Winter 1981, 739.

15 Errors of omission—suppressing or withholding facts to mislead the listener—can be a white lie, half-truth, exaggeration or falsehood, depending on the motive: sparing someone's feelings, providing the liar with an escape-route, or deceiving the listener.

16 Sissela Bok. *Lying: Moral Choice in Public and Private Life* (New York: Pantheon, 1978), 50.

17 Ibid., 60.

18 R.B. Cialdini, *Influence: The Psychology of Persuasion* (New York: Harper, 2007), 33–34.

19 Meera Jagannathan, "Florida Man's 'Halloween' Decorations Look a Lot Like Lynching," *New York Daily News*, October 31, 2016, www.nydailynews.com/news/national/florida-man-halloween-decorations-lot-lynching-article-1.2852375

20 Erica Nochlin, "Funny or Racist? Neighbors in Trabuco Canyon Neighborhood Debate Halloween Decorations," CBS2, October 30, 2016, https://www.youtube.com/watch?v=Gv0DfELQysE

21 Jiayue Huang, "Brian Williams Returns to the Airwaves," *USA Today*, September 22, 2015, www.usatoday.com/story/money/2015/09/22/brian-williams-nbc-return-msnbc/72625092/

22 Jonathan Mahler, Ravi Somaiya and Emily Steel, "With an Apology, Brian Williams Digs Himself Deeper in Copter Tale," *The New York Times*, February 5, 2015, www.nytimes.com/2015/02/06/business/brian-williamss-apology-over-iraq-account-is-challenged.html

23 Gregory Giangrande, "Resume Lies," *New York Post*, December 19, 2005, www.nypost.com/atwork/59086.htm

24 John Fountain and Edward Wong, "Notre Dame Coach Resigns After 5 Days and a Few Lies," *The New York Times*, December 15, 2001, www.nytimes.com/2001/12/15/sports/notre-dame-coach-resigns-after-5-days-and-a-few-lies.html

25 Greg Levine, "Faces in the News" *Forbes*, October 21, 2002, www.forbes.com/2002/10/21/1021facesam.html

26 Ibid.

27 "Bausch and Lomb CEO's Resume Falsified to Include Stern MBA," by Nicole Lynch, New York School of Business Opportunity, November 5, 2002, http://pages.stern.nyu.edu/~opportun/issues/2002-2003/issue05/

03_bausch.htm. Zarella later took more responsibility for the initial disclosure, stating, "I am fully responsible for the misrepresentation in my official biography, an error that has been repeated elsewhere."

28 The PRSA code does not mention quote-making. Its core values can be found under "Member Code of Ethics" at www.prsa.org. The cited values here are taken from "Free Flow of Information," http://prsa. org/_About/ethics/provisions.asp?ident=eth5

29 Masson v. New Yorker Magazine, Inc. (89–1799), 501 U.S. 496 (1991), www.law.cornell.edu/supct/html/89-1799.ZO.html

30 Walter Isaacson, *Benjamin Franklin: An American Life* (New York: Simon & Schuster Paperbacks, 2004), 401–02.

31 For an overview of the issue, see "Are Quotes Sacred?" in the September 1995 *American Journalism Review*. The article is available online at www. ajr.org/Article.asp?id=1340

32 Fraser P. Seitel, *The Practice of Public Relations* (Upper Saddle River, N.J.: Prentice Hall, 1995), 129.

33 "PRSA Member Statement of Professional Values," Honesty, no date, http://prsa.org/_About/ethics/values.asp?ident=eth4

34 Elaine E. Englehardt and DeAnn Evans, "Lies, Deceptions, and Public Relations," *Public Relations Review*, Fall 1994, 252.

35 Terry Eiler is well aware that *National Geographic* was one of the first magazines to be accused of visual lying by altering a photograph of the pyramids on a 1982 cover. According to Eiler, "[The] editors at *National Geographic* have taken years of grief because of their cover, which shows the pyramids closer together than they are in real life. The fact is that the editors had no cover shot for this particular issue, except for this horizontal one with the pyramids. Someone said he could solve that problem with a new tool (a Scitex), and a decision was made based on a design problem. The technology was new and it didn't occur to them that their publication stood for the accurate portrayal of geographical images, so they ran into trouble. Nonetheless, these editors are among the most ethical I know. They just were solving a technical problem at the time. The advent of computer editing of images has made us even more aware of ethical issues in photojournalism."

36 Howard Kurtz, "L.A. Times Gets Burned By Disaster Photograph," *The Washington Post*, 2 February 1994, Final Edition, Style, D1.

37 "Woodward and Bernstein Defend Anonymous Sources," by Sarah Abrams, *News from the Kennedy School*, December 5, 2005, www. ksg.harvard.edu/ksgnews/Features/news/120505_woodward_bern stein.htm

38 Bob Woodward, *The Secret Man: The Story of Watergate's Deep Throat* (New York: Simon & Schuster, 2005), 150.

39 Ibid.

40 See Immanuel Kant's "The Doctrine of Virtue," in *The Metaphysic Morals* (New York: Harper & Row, 1964), translated by Mary Gregor.

41 Bok, 1978, 40–41.

42 John C. Merrill, *Journalism Ethics: Philosophical Foundations for News Media* (Boston, Mass.: Bedford/St. Martin's, 1997), p. 133.

43 Ibid, p. 134.

44 Scott Shane and Mike Isaacs, "Facebook to Turn Over Russian-Linked Ads to Congress," *The New York Times*, September 21, 2017, www.nytimes.com/2017/09/21/technology/facebook-russian-ads.html

45 These and other actions taken by Facebook to combat disinformation can be found at www.facebook.com/help/1991443604424859

46 Tom Standage, "The True History of Fake News," *The Economist*, June/July 2017, www.1843magazine.com/technology/rewind/the-true-history-of-fake-news

47 Bok, 1978, 173.

CHAPTER 6

Manipulation: Feel It, Spot It, Bust It

REMEMBER HOW MANIPULATION FEELS

Manipulation, like temptation and betrayal, is accompanied by a physical sensation. There is no definitive scientific evidence that the conscience causes the pit in the stomach, tightening in the throat, and flush in the face; but everyone, at one time or another, has felt all three. There are theories. For instance, the James Lange theory—named after 19th-century psychologist William James and physiologist Carl Lange—aligns emotions with bodily reactions, such as tingle on the skin, muscle contractions and other physical reactions.[1] When it comes to manipulation, the physical feeling can be intense, especially a constriction in the gut, as if sucker punched there. We become aware that someone we had trusted and thought we clearly knew violated our confidence and saw *us* all too clearly—enough to manipulate and deceive us. We also can manipulate and deceive ourselves, stifling pangs of conscience and taking an action that we suspect may violate rules or even our own values. We'll learn more about temptation and conflicts of interest in the next chapter. As we focus on manipulation, the point is not to debate whether the conscience is informing our emotions or that it even exists, but to recognize rather than suppress our feelings in everyday situations at the workplace. Those feelings are generated by various forms of intimidation, including moral, physical and bodily coercion in addition to intimidation through threats, writes philosopher Allen W. Wood,

> But I take them all to be species of coercion in the sense that they limit, remove, or interfere with an agent's *freedom*. The freedom to make choices for yourself, rather than having them made for you, is what I take coercion to be most fundamentally about.[2]

Further, Wood adds,

> The worst thing about exploitation is that under most circumstances, it is shameful and reprehensible to make use of other people's vulnerabilities for your own ends, and it is degrading to have your abilities and resources, and especially to have you yourself, made use of in this way.[3]

In *Blink: The Power of Thinking Without Thinking*, Malcolm Gladwell uses the term "adaptive unconscious" rather than conscience. Some people use synonyms for conscience because of the religious overtones of that word. Another synonym is "unconscious." Use whatever term you prefer when you encounter references to conscience in *Living Media Ethics*, but don't let your consciousness manipulate you into thinking that human beings lack the capacity to intuit moral situations accurately and instantaneously. As Gladwell writes,

> The only way that human beings could ever have survived as a species for as long as we have is that we've developed another kind of decision making apparatus that's capable of making very quick judgments based on very little information.[4]

Living Media Ethics calls this a function of conscience because that term is associated with ethical decision-making.

In discussing the dual aspect of humanity, consciousness and conscience, philosopher Pedro Blas Gonzalez writes that the latter is the basic foundation for ethics. Conscience, he believes, is an internal system of checks and balances speaking to us intuitively about what is right and wrong. Further, he states, conscience is an integral part of personal identity. "We cannot readily disconnect our ethical behavior from conscience any more so than we can from personal identity," he writes, noting: "How some academic teachers of philosophy have made their claim to fame" by denying its existence "is tantamount to someone who claims not to speak a given language by communicating in it."[5]

This is why *Living Media Ethics* encourages you to experience feelings based on intuitive conscience when you find yourself in ethical or questionable life situations. Rather than acting on those feelings immediately, allow them to inform consciousness so that your rational mind is in sync with your moral intuition. The feeling is a signal, especially when it comes to manipulation. People are routinely manipulated into doing something that they know they shouldn't or in trusting someone who betrays that trust. When new, similar situations present themselves, conscience sends an alert. Consciousness then remembers past experiences and what we learned from them so that we can make sound moral decisions in the moment or immediate future. The more we heed the conscience, informing and thereby sharpening awareness, the more adept we will become in living our ethics.

MANIPULATORS VIOLATE CONSCIENCE

Another term associated with manipulation is "predictable behavior." The manipulator knows the biases, fears, desires and convictions of the person to be manipulated and so can rely on predictable behavior to set a plan into motion. The manipulator ciphers how an individual, company or even a country will react to a given scenario, making it part of a deceitful strategy. As such, manipulation represents more than a violation of privacy;

it is a violation of *conscience* subverting our most intimate sense of self. To demonstrate that, consider how some ethicists from the great 19th-century essayist Matthew Arnold to the 20th-century leadership author Stephen Covey define the self.[6] We have a worst, ordinary and best self. Our worst self succumbs to or even perpetuates manipulation; our ordinary self reacts predictably to manipulation; and our best self displays grace and forgiveness to manipulators and ourselves. We also have a public, private and secret self. We might mask our emotions in front of colleagues or constituents through our public self; share them with associates, relatives and partners through our private self; and discover or acknowledge intensely personal information about our motivations or biases through the secret self. That last revelation will prove key later in exposing manipulation.

Manipulators count on the predictability of the ordinary self to perpetuate their plots on the secret self. Moreover, there also exists a connection between manipulation and objectification, a harassment term involving the dehumanization of a person, making him or her inanimate so that another can perpetrate physical, sexual and mental violations against another. That is why, in the wake of real or perceived manipulation, a pit forms in the stomach, the throat constricts and the face flushes, as if to reinstate our humanity physically for all to see. Communications specialist Preston Ni, writing in *Psychology Today*, defines psychological manipulation as "the exercise of undue influence through mental distortion and emotional exploitation, with the intention to seize power, control, benefits and/or privileges at the victim's expense."[7] When we realize we have been manipulated, the emotions are intense.

There is a reason for this. Manipulators study us (or the media) to discern moral, physical, personal or professional weakness that they can exploit. They discern our patterns of behavior at home, school or work until they are able to predict with relative certainty how we will react under certain conditions, which they will set in motion. Over time, a manipulator understands that journalists and practitioners have multiple selves, a public one that they exhibit while in community with others, a private self that they share with loved ones and best friends, and a secret self, which they rarely divulge to anyone else, that acknowledges their deepest held biases, fears, desires and convictions. It is that secret self that manipulators analyze and exploit, and the emotional pain of that act is one we will remember long after the deception is exposed.

Psychologists say manipulation often involves:

- **Deception:** The manipulator hides his or her subversive intention and often displays behavior that is the exact opposite of the intention.
- **Strategy:** The manipulator analyzes vulnerabilities of the target victim to devise a plan to take advantage of him or her.
- **Remorselessness:** The manipulator premeditates the deception and strategy without pang of conscience to deter him or her from acting out on the victim.

Dr. George Simon, one of the leading experts on effects of manipulation, believes that perpetrators often have a "good read" on the character of their targets. "When a covert aggressor knows his or her 'opponent' inside out (i.e. knows their sensitivities, fears, insecurities, core beliefs, level of conscientiousness, etc.), a vast opportunity opens up for using that person's traits (often, their most socially desirable traits) against them in a covert war for dominance." Simon notes specific manipulation strategies, which include, lying, diverting attention, threats, evoking a guilty conscience, shaming, playing the victim, false accusation, seduction, charm, flattery, bandwagon (everyone is doing it) and giving little time to decide.[8]

All those strategies apply to media manipulation.

MANIPULATORS EXPLOIT MEDIA

Those who deceive journalists and practitioners rely on predictable behaviors of a media outlet (how staff operates under deadlines and what messages they routinely disseminate without substantial fact-checking). They study employees of agencies, organizations and news companies over time to discern any subjective bias, fears, desires and convictions. They have no remorse on how this will impact a person's career and his or her audience or clientele. Their goal is to expose and betray and then bask in the aftermath of deception.

The concept of "media manipulation" relies on probable reactions of a company, outlet or platform when presented with false information that their partialities readily embrace. Such manipulation is also interactive. People, organizations and even countries try to program media across platforms, causing journalists and practitioners to manipulate society intentionally or unintentionally through their reports and campaigns. In particular, the motive of "fake news," which became prevalent during the 2016 presidential campaign, was to manipulate consciousness by appealing to our base instincts and convictions about the world and candidates representing segments of that world. Fake news spoke to our fears with claims that many voters readily believed without checking facts, undermining democracy. In addressing that claim, *US News and World Report* noted that fake news was often devoid of fact or used half-truths with the intent of misleading viewers; "fake news is not a story or news report that you do not like."[9]

Chuck Raasch, chief Washington correspondent for the *Saint Louis Post-Dispatch*, contends on a regular basis with the latest version of fake news, associated with how some public relations practitioners have come to view their jobs, especially in government. In his job reporting political news from the nation's capital, he has to deal "with publicly paid press secretaries, communications officials, PR folks, and others who have no embedded ethic affirming the public's right to know and its place in a self-governing society," Raasch says. "This has been the biggest and most fundamental shift in communications and politics over my career, this shift from press secretaries as conduits between public servants and the people, through the press, to this construct that they are message shapers and boss protectors, first, with truth frequently a malleable commodity." This shift, which occurred over many years during several administrations, culminated in former Press Secretary Sean Spicer's claim that President Donald Trump's inauguration crowd size was the largest ever assembled. That assertion was "demonstrably false," Raasch says, "easily refutable by anyone with eyes, sans blinders." This is more than just Trump's style or manner of doing business, he adds: "It was a stark reminder of what can happen when PR capitulates to propaganda over fact. Unfortunately, for the republic, the business model has so rapidly shifted from journalism to the PR side of communications that we have not yet, fully comprehended its impact on the republic." As an example, Raasch states, "It is fundamentally dangerous for state capitals to be covered by fewer independent, probing, truth-seeking, investigative journalists than governors have on their personal communications payrolls. This is not to imply that every officeholder is a crook. But how do we know without an independent watchdog looking over them?"

Essentially, fake news falls under a long-standing concept: media manipulation. The most egregious example of that is the hoax. Hoaxes violate the secret life of journalists and practitioners, preying on their subjective biases, fears, desires and convictions. Such manipulation is a mortal iniquity across platforms. Deceived by a hoax, journalists or practitioners may never again perform as effectively or professionally. Deceived by the media, the audience, public or clientele may never again subscribe to, consume, underwrite or contract with the company in question. To guard against hoaxes and your own preconceptions, you have to analyze your secret self and acknowledge your fears, desires, biases and convictions that might invite manipulation. Hoaxsters, in particular, target those who claim to be fair, balanced and objective. Secretly, people are anything but. We're all subjective to a degree. However, journalists and practitioners must work at identifying our filters and overcoming our prejudices to be as objective as possible, as discussed in the previous chapter on truth.

According to Peter A. Hancock, in *Hoax Springs Eternal,* successful deceptions "must play more on people's intrinsic biases, which are stored in their long-term memory. Inherently biased individuals will tend to ignore even quite strong evidence of deception if the proposition strongly agrees with their own established perspective on the world."[10] Hancock makes a strong case that successful hoaxes rely on individuals or groups who desperately want to believe in the premeditated manipulation or falsehood. "Typically, a hoax will play upon widespread human failures, such as greed," he states.[11] A key element in the deception "must focus on most cherished beliefs."[12]

Carolyn Kitch, media professor at Temple University, encourages students "to think about what kinds of deceptions or distortions have the most serious consequences—in the short term and in the long term." Approaching media manipulation from this perspective, Kitch believes, produces surprising revelations. Students see how news media do short-term damage whereas advertising distortions, especially in political ads, can do "more long-term harm collectively. Certainly," she concludes, given the standard digital curriculum in schools of journalism and mass communication, educators must help students recognize the roles that manipulation and bias play across media platforms and in themselves. That also will help protect against hoaxes and other violations of the secret self.

The best protection, of course, is to acknowledge that each person has biases, fears, desires and convictions and that these differ from one person to the next. A person who identifies as conservative may actually have liberal or progressive views on some issues, and vice versa. The secret self is difficult to stereotype across diverse populations. The importance, then, is to acknowledge your own ethical weaknesses so that you can guard against being the victim or perpetrator of media manipulation. A first step is to learn the history and categories of hoaxes, which illustrate both the power of platforms and the motivations of people who use them for self-serving purposes.

HOAXES REWRITE HISTORY

Hoaxes (aka "fake news") have occurred throughout media history. A few have been so sophisticated and embraced that scientists and scholars have had to defuse them. These hoaxes include the forged diaries of Adolf Hitler, excerpts of which were published in 1983 in *Newsweek* and *The Sunday Times of London*, and the 500,000-year-old Piltdown man found with extinct animal fossils in England in 1912, confusing anthropologists and evolutionary theories up through 1953, a pivotal year for hoaxes, as we shall soon see. Scientific paper analysis exposed the Hitler hoax and fluoride tests exposed the Piltdown one.[13]

One of the greatest but unintentional hoaxes of all time occurred on the eve of All Saints Day, 1938, when Orson Welles broadcast his script of *The War of the Worlds*. The script was based on the 1898 novel by H.G. Wells, a journalist and freelance writer, depicting a cosmic event that shook the whole of England—

"A MESSAGE RECEIVED FROM MARS"
"Remarkable Story From Woking"

—a tabloid headline then as now. Welles, an actor who founded the Mercury Theater, set the script adaptation in "Grover's Mill," New Jersey, and broadcast it via the Columbia Broadcasting Company nationwide over 151 stations.

The adaptation contained disclaimers, noting the nature of the broadcast. Nonetheless panic ensued, precisely as it had in Wells' novel, with scholars heading out to find the Martians, members of religious congregations proclaiming Doomsday, and citizens offering their services to combat the threat.[14] One of the most telling articles about the broadcast was written by George M. Mahawinney of *The Philadelphia Inquirer* who is said to have composed the round-up story in one hour after being deluged with calls.[15] Here is his lead:

> Terror struck at the hearts of hundreds of thousands of persons in the length and breadth of the United States last night as crisp words of what they believed to be a news broadcast leaped from their radio sets, telling of catastrophe from the skies visited on this country.

The story goes on to quote several terrified motorists. One said: "All creation's busted loose, I'm getting out of Jersey." A teenage girl allegedly phoned the Princeton Press Club with an on-the-scene report: "You can't imagine the horror of it! It's hell!" A woman in a church screamed: "New York is destroyed; it's the end of the world. You might as well go home to die." By the time such messages reached Atlanta, Mahawinney reported, dozens of New Jerseyians were purported to have perished. Heart attacks were said to have occurred in Kansas City hospitals.

Orson Welles proved that mass media could spark mass hysteria. There is another important lesson about the hoax, however: *timing*. The broadcast happened on Halloween Eve, known as Mischief Night in New Jersey; moreover, the Germans were mobilizing against their enemies in Europe, threatening world war. Though written at the turn of the 20th century, Wells' *The War of the Worlds* contains prophetic images of holocaust and mass destruction, playing off public fears in 1938.

In July 1953, another hoax occurred in a large Southern city, according to Dan Lynch, managing editor of the Albany (N.Y.) *Times Union*.[16] He writes that three men entered a newsroom claiming to have run over an extra-terrestrial with their pick-up truck. They showed an editor the body of a small, red humanoid-looking creature. The newspaper ran a story—"Hairless critter killed, two escape"—and the men became celebrities. The creature, as it turned out, was a shaved, mutilated rhesus monkey. The men perpetuated the hoax because of a $50 bet that they could get their names on the front page of the newspaper.

Nonetheless, July 1953 is as important a date as October 1938. The Korean War was about to end in a stalemate, calling into question America's military dominance. Uncertainty reigned. Stalin, Soviet dictator responsible for mass executions in his country toward the end of his rule, had just died. Joseph McCarthy, U.S. senator, was making sensational accusations against alleged "Communist" Americans. On June 19, Julius and Ethel Rosenberg—alleged spies convicted on questionable evidence—were executed for selling nuclear secrets to the USSR. Everyone seemed suspect and fearful as the Cold War intensified. A UFO story coincided with the fear and uncertainty of 1953 as nicely as the Martian one did in 1938.

In 1994, UFO hoaxes had less impact on the populace. The publication of Budd Hopkins' *Missing Time* (Marek, 1981) and *Intruders* (Ballantine, 1987)—along with dozens of other UFO abduction books by other authors—already had flooded the bookstores, tabloids and talk-show circuits. An insect-eyed alien with a hairless, bulbous head had become an icon of pop culture, appearing in everything from credit card ads to beer commercials. In sum, E.T. had become one of us. But we feared another type of abduction related to 1990s' street crime and violence: carjacking.

In Union, South Carolina, a mother of two toddlers reported to police that a black man had carjacked her 1990 Mazda Protege, forced her from the vehicle and abducted her sons in the back seat. The report stunned the nation with as much impact as the Orson Welles' hoax and surpassed it as one of the greatest hoaxes of all time, given its length and the millions that it affected via modern mass media technology.[17] For nine days Susan Smith, 23, stuck to her story as police and citizens nationwide searched for 3-year-old Michael and 14-month-old Alexander. Smith gave tearful interview upon interview to network news and morning talk shows. Citizens prayed and searched for the boys as law officers mobilized across the country. When no evidence turned up to support Smith's story, detectives focused on her, searched her home, and found a letter from a boyfriend who said he was not ready for the responsibilities of fatherhood. Finally, Smith confessed. With her two boys strapped in the back seat, she had put her car into gear on a boat ramp and watched it plunge into a lake.

Smith's hoax also employed a racial element: the description of a black man in his late 20s to early 30s wearing a knit cap and a plaid jacket. In upcoming chapters you will read more about the news media's stereotyping of African Americans. At this point, the lesson relates to manipulation. Smith's invention was similar to that of Charles Stuart who shot his pregnant wife Carol in his car in Boston in 1989 and blamed it on an attack by a black man. (Stuart later took his life by jumping from a bridge.) Sadiki Kambom, director of the Black Community Information Center in Boston, commented on the racial element of both hoaxes in an Associated Press report distributed shortly after Smith's confession: "If you portray the black man as being the perpetrator, you have the chance to divert attention away from you who may be the guilty party."[18] The same AP report quotes Hester Booker of Union, S.C., who notes that during the nine-day ordeal, "The whites acted so different. They wouldn't speak, they'd look at you and then reach over and lock their doors. And all because that lady lied."

Susan Smith did more than lie. She told falsehoods to reporters who disseminated her hoax to millions around the world. Her story attracted so much attention because the audience believed that the lives of her two young sons were at stake. In 1993, it took a story of that emotional magnitude to earn worldwide distribution. That is not the case anymore. The hoax, once considered relatively rare by media professionals, has proliferated in the digital age as personal computers, laptops, tablets, smartphones and other mobile and wireless devices literally put the power of mass communication in the hands of people unaccustomed to media fraud or who have taken interest in perpetuating fraud. Phishing, check-kiting schemes and other electronic scams, warning of computer viruses or offering free giveaways, resemble the hoax but do not technically classify as such, as their intent is to manipulate others one-on-one and steal money or possessions. According to the website www.hoaxbusters.ciac.org, other motives include seeing how far digital chain letters will go in addition to harassing and bullying people, damaging reputations. Media hoaxes operate at another level. Their intent also may be motivated by theft or harassment but mainly perpetrators want to re-program content of news or reputation of corporate brands, often using social media to carry their fraudulent messages.

Hoaxes include false claims about products using mass media to indict and defraud a corporation, as we have seen with hoaxes alleging product tampering, from the 1993 "Pepsi scare," in which syringes were said to be found in cans of Diet Pepsi, to the 2005 "Wendy's chili scam," in which a finger was said to be found in a bowl of the product. These frauds were highly publicized, causing public relations practitioners at Pepsi in particular to metamorphose into investigative reporters in an attempt to manage the growing crisis spawning copycat hoaxsters nationwide—one at the *Journal/Sentinel* Inc. in Milwaukee (explored later). In the 1994 video with accompanying text, titled "What Went Right?," Craig Weatherup, Pepsi President and CEO in North America, noted that his public affairs division "mobilized to manage the scare ... responding to the press, coordinating with regulatory officials and giving customers, consumers and employees the facts." Pepsi's video showed how journalists and practitioners temporarily exchanged roles as the news media continued to perpetuate a false story while practitioners sought to refute it using the only arsenal at their disposal: *facts.*

In the 21st century, as platforms became interactive with corporations inviting feedback, a whole new generation of hoaxsters was born. These were so computer literate that they did not have to develop lavish interpersonal schemes, showing up in newsrooms or conference rooms with syringes in soda cans or meeting with reporters to share tales of woe or complaint; they merely had to send an email or text to a discussion group or organization, post a news release on a website (or create a fictitious news website or blog) and wait for an unsuspecting journalist or search engine to find and disseminate the digital bait worldwide.

One of the earliest examples occurred in 1996 when ABC news veteran Pierre Salinger reported that he had proof that a U.S. Navy missile was responsible for the crash of TWA 800, which investigators believed exploded because of a spark in a fuel tank. Salinger's so-called proof was an email distributed via the Usenet discussion network. He was taken in by a hoax. That a newsman as experienced as Salinger should fall prey to such manipulation continues to amaze media professionals. On the decade anniversary of the TWA tragedy, CNN reported:

> Bolstered by eyewitness accounts and the Internet, the explosion of TWA Flight 800 off the coast of New York 10 years ago spawned a slew of sinister conspiracy theories, most notably the belief that a missile from a U.S. Navy ship was responsible.
>
> So prevalent were these theories that the term "Pierre Salinger Syndrome"—the belief that everything on the Internet is true—entered the lexicon.[19]

In a widely distributed news article, observing the 100th anniversary of the press release, *The Christian Science Monitor* reported that

> lack of human involvement is a big part of why publicists and hoaxsters love Google News. Computer algorithms, not people, choose which news stories, blog entries, and press releases appear first when someone types in a term like 'iPod' or 'Dick Cheney.'[20]

Among the examples of hoaxes in the article was a New Jersey teenager's fabricating a news release about his hiring at Google News, using Google itself to spread the release—something that would be rare or impossible at a traditional news outlet.

Nevertheless, from Piltdown Man to Google, the intent of hoaxes historically has been to manipulate and program media for personal gain, exposure or some other self-serving motive.

That intent has become much easier across platforms because of internet and social media and the algorithms that empower both. In 2016, the British newspaper *The Telegraph* was among the first to chronicle the history of fake news as hoax, tracking it to the U.S. presidential election. According to its report, use of the term "fake news" was popularized by Republican presidential candidate Donald Trump to decry mainstream stories or media organizations that criticized him: "You are fake news!" he pointed at CNN's Jim Acosta while refusing to listen to his question.[21]

However, use of the term "fake news" to disparage journalists differs from internet outlets that intentionally disseminated fabricated news to sway votes in that election. That's a hoax and, in the past, before internet, using mainstream media to influence or undermine elections was nearly impossible to do. As *The Telegraph* states, distributing such a story would involve great cost; audiences generally believed news outlets of their choosing; and publishers of false stories could be sued for libel.

With internet, there is little cost of publishing a blog and distributing content via social media; algorithms can align content with political or personal beliefs, gaining trust; and legal risks are reduced because of the expanse and anonymity of the blogosphere. This is why journalists and practitioners must be prudent in accessing information from unreliable sources or worse, disseminating it without a thorough fact-check. This ability, by the way, was emphasized in the media literacy exercise in Chapter 1 to distinguish between "motive" and "motivation." In sum, deception lies at the heart of hoaxes and fake news. All deceptions are based on motives. Their cumulative manipulative effect undermines truth, and with it, trust in mass media.

MEDIA PULL STUNTS, TOO

Journalists and practitioners also manipulate sources, clients and consumers every day. They may lie to get an account or a story, go under cover or use a hidden camera, alter photographs or images, plagiarize copy, invent quotes or testimonials, deceive competitors, discriminate against others and exercise undue authority. These issues involve values of the individual journalist or practitioner and so are covered in chapters on falsehood, temptation, bias and power. Conversely, a hoax relies upon manipulation by *outside* sources whose motive is to program the media. For example, PR practitioners use the same internet methods as hoaxsters to disseminate news releases, posting them on corporate or business websites and waiting for search engines to carry them as news. In this manner, airlines and other companies earn millions in ticket sales through PR releases about special offers; those often are true, but use the same social media platforms rife with hoaxes.[22] Case in point: In 2006, Southwest Airlines had a genuine discount ticket offer using internet news releases; in 2017, the same airline was the target of a sweepstake scam offering free tickets, according to the fact-checking website Snopes.[23] The 2017 example was labeled a scam but the goal was the same as a hoax—manipulation—this time using the name of a trusted corporate brand to deceive customers.

Practitioners occasionally do publicity stunts as part of strategy to promote a service or product. These are not hoaxes. Stunts come with risks, and so they are relatively rare. But they do merit a mention. For instance, New York City coin dealer and author Scott A. Travers made several so-called "penny drops"—circulating rare, expensive coins worth as much as $1,000—at street vendor stands in Manhattan to publicize one of his books. He was invited to appear on ABC News, MSNBC, CNN and other television networks and was interviewed by international wire services.[24] Moreover, media were invited to some of his coin drops. There was nothing hoax-like about this. Travers simply used the stunt in a clever way to showcase his new book during the occasion of National Coin Week.

A few publicity stunts have spoofed the media, usually on April Fools, a day of reprieve. A company can claim "April Fools!" in response to whatever havoc emanates out of the stunt. On April Fool's Day, 1996, Taco Bell took out a full-page advertisement in *The New York Times* and four other city newspapers, titled—"Taco Bell Buys the Liberty Bell"—to announce that the Irvine, California-based fast food chain had purchased the historic treasure. A news release was distributed before the advertisement ran, noting that there was precedent for the acquisition in as much as companies had been adopting highways for years. Here is the text of the advertisement:

> In an effort to help the national debt, Taco Bell is pleased to announce that we have agreed to purchase the Liberty Bell, one of our country's most historic treasures. It will now be called the "Taco Liberty Bell" and will still be accessible to the American public for viewing. While some may find this controversial, we hope our move will prompt other corporations to take similar action to do their part to reduce the country's debt.[25]

As you can imagine, the public reacted with calls and complaints both to Taco Bell and the National Historic Park in Philadelphia, which oversees the Liberty Bell. To mitigate liability, Taco Bell waited until noon on April 1 before stating, in effect, "April Fools!," disseminating a release titled "The Best Joke of the Day." Mike McCurry, White House spokesperson then, reportedly took the joke in stride by suggesting that the federal government planned to sell the Lincoln Memorial to the Ford Motor Company, renaming it the "Lincoln-Mercury Memorial."[26]

The Taco Liberty Bell hoax was effective. Paine Weber, the PR company that helped execute the stunt, won a creativity award. On its website, the company recounts more details of the campaign, noting that

> Tom Brokaw gave the story four minutes on NBC "Nightly News," Taco Liberty Bell photos were splashed across the pages of hundreds of newspapers, "The Today Show" and CBS "This Morning" did live remotes and *USA Today* put the story on the front page ... not bad for a hoax![27]

In all, more than 1,000 print and broadcast outlets ran with or covered the stunt hoax, representing more than $25 million in free advertising—a temptation for any practitioner—and one, as well, to be resolutely resisted in the typical campaign. Better, instead, to put efforts in identifying those who would manipulate the news or tamper with your products and services.

EXPOSE AND DEFUSE MANIPULATION

Even though most media professionals are not trained to recognize and defuse a hoax, they often can be held liable because consequences can be quite severe. Two other situations are powerful enough to destroy credibility for *both* the individual and the company:

- **Plagiarism,** or the passing off of someone else's work as your own, to be covered in Chapter 7.
- **Litigation,** usually involving libel, extortion or discrimination, the latter to be covered in Chapter 8.

Plagiarism and litigation are important media topics covered extensively in classrooms and textbooks. They are intensely embarrassing for employees and companies, but they do not routinely violate the secret self, which may explain why journalists and practitioners are reluctant to discuss the consequences of a hoax.[28] Embarrassment accompanies the hoax because it:

- **Jeopardizes personal credibility.** The primary job of a media professional is to disseminate information according to precepts of social responsibility as discussed previously. A hoaxster usurps that duty and programs the media by making false claims.
- **Undermines corporate credibility.** Journalists and practitioners generally want to contribute to the good name of an employer, not detract therefrom, calling into question the competence of coworkers and/or the entire company.
- **Exposes personal beliefs.** As mentioned earlier, the hoaxster preys on the fears, desires, convictions and values of journalist and practitioner, exposing them for public scrutiny.
- **Exposes cultural beliefs.** The hoaxster preys on cultural fears, desires, convictions and social mores of society and so humiliates the audience, clients or consumers, who may cancel subscriptions or change channels, agencies or products.

Most hoaxes prey on social mores involving biases, fears, desires and convictions. But timing usually is a key component in any attempt to program media. Here are common elements indicating that a hoax may occur:[29]

1. When information about a sensational story, client or product seems to have reached a standstill.
2. When information about an event, incident, client or product threatens or supports a person's or a group's interests.
3. When a political candidate is running for office or an issue is being debated or considered for legislative action.
4. When society is consumed by a widespread fear or desire.
5. When society searches for a missing link, cure or other piece of evidence to advance learning, science or technology.
6. When a hoaxster needs the exposure or publicity.
7. When a media outlet has recently run a promotional campaign soliciting reader or viewer participation or feedback.
8. When a broadcast or other deadline or production schedule doesn't allow for research.
9. When the media outlet has a need for a certain type of story, client or product line.
10. When a story, client or product line is linked to a specific season, holiday or occasion.

These time elements can be combined, of course. For instance, a hoax can concern a sensational story at a standstill, play upon a fear, and be perpetuated near a broadcast deadline to circumvent research. There's no way to predict when a hoax will occur, but you can predict when one is *likely* to and be more apt to recognize it when it arrives.

In addition to sharing common time elements, most hoaxes fall into specific categories. As noted earlier, the motive of the hoaxster is to program the media, but his or her methods and goals may vary (along with consequences for the journalist and practitioner). Let's summarize all these particulars and illustrate them with a few examples of successful hoaxes over the years to show the prevalence in any technological era, past, present and future:

1. Activist Hoax

Method: Relying on the journalist to operate under predictable rules and modes of behavior.

Goal: To prove to the audience the bias/incompetence of the journalist and/or his or her story, product or client.

Example: In 2011, an anti-coal hoax website titled "Coal Cares" was offering free Justin Bieber and Dora the Explorer inhalers to children living near coal-fired power plants, in particular, Peabody Energy. The site stated: "Some environmentalists have suggested that coal companies should install an untested technology called 'scrubbers' atop coal plants to make them burn more cleanly, reducing coal particulate exposure as one cause of childhood asthma. For our part, Peabody has decided that reducing Asthma-Related Bullying (ARB) is the single most effective way to combat public misperceptions of our industry."[30]

Probable Time Elements

1. When information about an event, incident, client or product threatens or supports a person's or a group's interests.
2. When a political candidate is running for office or an issue is being debated or considered for legislative action.
3. When a hoaxster needs the exposure or publicity.

Consequences

The journalist, practitioner or his/her copy, product or client will be exposed as unreliable, often resulting in limited future coverage or promotion and/or loss of image or sales.

2. Impersonator Hoax

Method: Relying on the media's need to:

- Be informed or tipped about new stories.
- Use names, quotes, pictures, testimonials for developing stories or products.
- Accept information without verification as long as a name is associated therewith.

Goal: To become part of the news or campaign, to feel momentarily worthy or validated as a human being.

Example: An impersonator hoax involves someone claiming to be a celebrity, expert, eyewitness, victim or newsmaker. For instance, more than 50 people claimed to be eyewitnesses or victims finding syringes in the so-called "Pepsi Scare" in 1993. A telemarketer for *Journal/Sentinel* Inc. in Milwaukee claimed to have discovered such a syringe in a can of Pepsi purchased from a vending machine at a local Kmart. She opened the can in the newspapers' TV lounge and screamed. Later she admitted the hoax was "a quiet plea for attention."[31]

Probable Time Elements

1. When information about a sensational story, client or product seems to have reached a standstill.
2. When information about an event, incident, client or product threatens or supports a person's or a group's interests.
3. When society is consumed by a widespread fear or desire.
4. When a hoaxster needs the exposure or publicity.
5. When a media outlet has recently run a promotional campaign soliciting reader or viewer participation or feedback.
6. When a deadline or production schedule doesn't allow for research.
7. When a story, client or product line is linked to a specific season, holiday or occasion.
8. When a political candidate is running for office or an issue is being debated or considered for legislative action.

Consequences

The journalist or practitioner can be viewed as an opportunist or sensationalist, undermining credibility for the entire media outlet or company.

3. Personal Hoax

Method: Relying on the media's need to:

- Be informed or tipped about new stories.
- Use names, quotes, pictures, testimonials for developing stories or products.
- Accept information without verification as long as a name is associated therewith.

Goal: To generate evidence, bolster an alibi.

Example: In 1992, a man claiming to be a pregnant hermaphrodite (born with both sets of genitals) was interviewed by Bryant Gumbel on the *Today Show* and included in reports by such news agencies as Reuters and *The Washington Post*. Reporters and a gynecologist who felt the man's belly claimed to have sensed fetal movement. In truth, the man was a homosexual living in a southern Philippine town who wanted the media to document his case so that he could legally change his name and sex and marry his lover.[32]

Probable Time Elements

1. When information about an event, incident, client or product threatens or supports a person's or a group's interests.
2. When a hoaxster needs the exposure or publicity.
3. When a deadline or production schedule doesn't allow for research.

Consequences

In addition to loss of credibility, the journalist or practitioner risks being ensnared in the hoaxster's legal or personal problems.

4. Political Hoax

Method: Relying on the media's need to cover politics or public affairs, especially if individual outlets do so in an advocacy or adversarial manner.
Goal: To manipulate public opinion or focus attention on an already newsworthy person, topic or group.
Example: In 2016, a liberal activist who had worked for a Democratic candidate disseminated a fake public relations release before a special election in Connecticut, stating that a 19-year-old Republican candidate had dropped out of the race to focus on her studies. (The Republican nevertheless won, and the hoaxster was charged with suppressing voter turnout.)[33]

Probable Time Elements

1. When information about an event, incident, client or product threatens or supports a person's or a group's interests.
2. When a political candidate is running for office or an issue is being debated or considered for legislative action.
3. When society is consumed by a widespread fear or desire.
4. When a hoaxster needs the exposure or publicity.
5. When the media outlet has a continual need for a certain type of story, client or product line.
6. When a story, client or product line is linked to a specific season, holiday or occasion.

Consequences

The journalist or practitioner loses control of the message and risks becoming associated with the cause of the hoaxster and/or his or her personal problems and political agendas.

5. Sensational Hoax

Method: Relying on the media's need to provide blockbuster stories, products, services or testimonials.
Goal: To shock or wildly entertain, gaining exposure or sales.

Examples: The legendary Loch Ness monster photo published in the April 21, 1934 issue of the *London Daily Mail* was actually an altered toy submarine from Woolworth's Department Store. Three men were in on the hoax and in 1993, the surviving one confessed shortly before his death at age 90.[34]

Probable Time Elements

1. When information about a sensational story, client or product seems to have reached a standstill.
2. When society is consumed by a widespread fear or desire.
3. When society searches for a missing link, cure or other piece of evidence to advance learning, science or technology.
4. When a media outlet has recently run a promotions campaign soliciting reader or viewer participation or feedback.

Consequences

The journalist or practitioner loses control of the message; he or she (and/or the employer, product or client) is exposed as unreliable, unintelligent, fraudulent or unworthy.

6. Stunt Hoax

Note: *Stunt hoaxes differ from publicity stunts because they are perpetuated by people not associated with any agency, organization or outlet but intent on reprogramming media.*

> **Method:** Relying on the media's need to cover celebrities, scandals, oddities and wonder drugs/products.
> **Goal:** To generate publicity, outwit the journalist or cause general havoc.
> **Example:** Well-known stunt hoaxster Alan Abel spoofed *The New York Times*, *Daily News*, *Newsday*, *Post* and several metropolitan broadcast stations by doctoring a fake Lotto ticket and calling a press conference at a posh hotel. He hired an actress to pose as the sole owner of a $35 million jackpot ticket. Some TV reporters carried the session "live" from the suite of the "winner." A *Daily News* reporter uncovered the hoax by recognizing Abel as a lecturer in an adult-education class she attended on the art of practical jokes.[35]

Probable Time Elements

1. When information about a sensational story, client or product seems to have reached a standstill.
2. When information about an event, incident, client or product threatens or supports a person's or a group's interests.
3. When society is consumed by a widespread fear or desire.
4. When society searches for a missing link, cure or other piece of evidence to advance learning, science or technology.

5. When a hoaxster needs the exposure or publicity.
6. When a deadline or production schedule doesn't allow for research.
7. When the media outlet has a continual need for a certain type of story, client or product line.
8. When a story, client or product line is linked to a specific season, holiday or occasion.

Consequences

The journalist or practitioner not only is made to look the fool by the hoaxster but also must generate more attention to the stunt by acknowledging, disavowing and discrediting it. A well-timed hoax can be subtle or elaborate. But because its success relies on manipulation, you can take steps to defuse one by acknowledging your fears, desires, convictions and values.

Here are methods to spot and defuse hoaxes before they happen:

1. Always question the motive of the source

Nothing frightens a manipulator more than questions about "motive." In fact, use that word in your questions. Time your motive-based questions to catch the source off-guard. Space them out during the interview so that you can analyze the source's answers later to determine any wavering or inconsistent data.

Warning signs:

- *Does the source seem visibly uneasy or nervous upon being questioned on motive?*
- *How, if at all, is the voice or eyes of the source affected each time you return to the issue of motive?*
- *Do the source's answers to motive-based questions vary with each response?*

2. Always question your own needs

Determine whether the source knows how your media outlet operates. In fact, ask a question using a jargon word related to your outlet or newsroom. Assess your own eagerness to pursue the story. Find out if your media outlet has run a recent promotion soliciting a certain type of story, client or product.

Warning signs:

- *Does the source seem to know too much about media procedure for his or her occupation?*
- *Is the story, client or product falling into your lap precisely when you need it?*

- *Is the story, client or product coming to you so close to deadline that you must use it without doing the necessary research?*

3. Always question the impact on audience

Determine how the source's story, problem, discovery or product will affect your readers, viewers or customers. Assess how much the audience desires or fears what the source is peddling. Predict the reaction of audience if the story, indeed, turns out to be a hoax.

Warning signs:

- *Does the source's story, problem, discovery or product have the potential to harm or otherwise falsely raise hopes of your audience?*
- *Is the source empowering a case by playing off desires or fears of the audience?*
- *How vehemently will your audience respond if the story is a hoax and what will this mean to your media outlet?*

4. Always assess your own fears, desires, convictions or values

Ultimately hoaxsters rely on *you*, not your outlet, as the medium for manipulation. The more your beliefs go unacknowledged, the easier it will be for the hoaxster to prey on them to achieve his or her goal.

Warning signs:

- *Do you want to believe the source because of any fear, desire, conviction or value?*
- *In your past stories, press releases or campaigns, have you in any way communicated any such belief?*
- *Is the source the kind of person that you secretly loath or admire, fear or feel attracted to, a perfect example to support what you fervently believe in already?*

5. Always rely on media literacy to fact-check any report on social media, using multiple reliable sources to affirm or debunk an event, incident, purported fact, comment or topic

Social media, especially Facebook, has become the primary disseminator of false news reports, prompting the company and FactCheck.org to partner in an attempt to flag fabricated "news." The initiative was triggered by false news during the 2016 presidential campaign.[36] FactCheck.org recommends that reporters and viewers consider the source of information, read content carefully before jumping to conclusions, and verify the reputation of the author or group disseminating stories.[37]

Warning signs:

- *Did a reader or viewer send you a tip and social media link based on a bias that you both may share or that your media outlet has supported in the past?*
- *Is the headline or title of a report sensationalized with content about what might occur hypothetically if a sequence of events takes place?*
- *Is the content of an alleged news report undated or based on events that might have happened in the past, falsely depicted as happening in the present?*

The journalist or practitioner who outwits a hoaxster *enhances* his or her credibility, along with that of the employer. Public relations and advertising executives who defuse and expose a hoax often distribute news releases or promotional literature about the incident, gaining respect and attracting clients. News journalists who defuse and expose hoaxsters usually end up with bigger stories than the original suspect ones. That said, it is difficult to guard against the hoax given our ever-swifter media expectations, especially when deception often arrives in the form of a tweet or social media post. As media marketer Ryan Holiday correctly states in *Trust Me, I'm Lying: The Tactics and Confessions of a Media Manipulator*:

> You cannot have your news instantly *and* have it done well. You cannot have your news reduced to 140 [or 280] characters or less without losing large parts of it. You cannot manipulate the news but not expect it to be manipulated against you. You cannot have your news for free; you can only obscure the costs. If, as a culture, we can learn this lesson, and if we can learn to love the hard work, we will save ourselves much trouble and collateral damage. We must remember: There is no easy way.[38]

In the end, this is a sage warning. Time in the digital age is not on your side. Nevertheless, you have a big role in the outcome when it comes to media manipulation. The first requirement is to be skeptical, especially if content appeals to your own acknowledged biases, fears, desires and convictions about the world, people and social issues. The second requirement is to remember that news, public information and advertising must be based on verifiable fact. The last requirement is that you do your own research, fact-checks and analysis so you can discern the motives of sources as well as when, where, how and why a hoax might be perpetuated against you or your outlet.

"YOUR BIASES, FEARS, DESIRES AND CONVICTIONS"

Personal Journal Exercise

1. Research the topic of hoaxes online and find examples of six types presented in the text—Activist, Impersonator, Personal, Political, Sensational and Stunt. Then synopsize each hoax in the manner presented in the text, outlining specific methods, goals, summaries and consequences. (You may not use hoaxes discussed in the text, such as "The Pepsi Scare.") Save your research in a file or printout to be sent to your instructor or group leader for the "Communal Journal Exercise" explained later.

2. Make four lists (5–10 items each) based on the subjects below. **Note:** *Be sure to phrase your items appropriately without violating your or anyone else's privacy or damaging anyone's reputation, or simply eliminate items about which you feel uncomfortable sharing.*

   - **Personal biases, fears, desires and convictions.** (*Are you prejudiced against any ethnic group? Do you fear a mugging or an assault? Do you have a strong personal or religious belief?*)
   - **Social biases, fears, desires and convictions.** (*Do you think that a certain ethnic group gets special treatment? Do you fear that the moral fabric of your country is eroding? Do you believe in the death penalty?*)
   - **Sensational biases, fears, desires and convictions.** (*Do you believe that a certain ethnic group is subhuman or a super race? Do you fear ghosts? Believe in astrology? UFOs?*)
   - **Political biases, fears, desires and convictions.** (*Do you radically support, oppose or fear a specific politician, party or political issue?*)

3. Choose one item from each list that you prepared above in exercise No. 2 and create a 500-word journal entry or blog post or short podcast or multimedia presentation about how bias, fear, belief or conviction can be used against you in a hoax and how you might defuse it. **WARNING:** *As always, be careful not to violate your own or someone else's privacy or damage anyone's reputation and be especially appropriate and sensitive if you decide to cite bias against any ethnic group, sex, religion, lifestyle or race. (If you believe you may be disclosing information inappropriately, simply do not share the item.)*

Communal Journal Exercise

As instructor or group discussion leader, collect research about six types of hoaxes presented in the text—Activist, Impersonator, Personal, Political, Sensational and Stunt—from those who completed the first assignment in the "Personal Journal Exercise" above. Assemble that research in an online or printed document to be shared with the class or group. Then schedule a broader discussion about how media are manipulated based on biases, fears, beliefs and convictions.

NOTES

1 Uriah Kriegel, *The Varieties of Consciousness* (New York: Oxford University Press, 2015), 130.
2 Allen W. Wood, "Coercion, Manipulation, Exploitation," in *Manipulation: Theory and Practice*, eds. Christian Coons and Michael Weber (New York: Oxford University Press, 2014), 26.
3 Ibid., 45.
4 Malcolm Gladwell, *Blink: The Power of Thinking Without Thinking* (New York: Little, Brown; 2005), 11–12.
5 Pedro Blas Gonzalez, "Schopenhauer on Conscience as the Ground of Ethics," *Friesian Proceedings*, 2010; available from www.friesian.com/gonzalz3.htm
6 See Matthew Arnold's "Culture and Anarchy," *Selected Prose*, ed. P.J. Keating (New York: Penguin, 1982) and Stephen Covey's *7 Habits of Highly Successful People* (New York: Free Press; 15th Anniversary Edition, 2004).
7 Preston Ni, "14 Signs of Psychological and Emotional Manipulation," *Psychology Today*, October 11, 2015; available from www.psychologytoday.com/blog/communication-success/201510/14-signs-psychological-and-emotional-manipulation
8 George Simon, "Manipulation Tactics: A Closer Look," Dr.GeorgeSimon.com, April 5, 2013, www.drgeorgesimon.com/manipulation-tactics-a-closer-look/
9 Robert Schlesinger, "Fake News in Reality," *U.S. News and World Report*, April 14, 2017, www.usnews.com/opinion/thomas-jefferson-street/articles/2017-04-14/what-is-fake-news-maybe-not-what-you-think
10 Peter A. Hancock, *Hoax Springs Eternal: The Psychology of Cognitive Deception* (New York: Cambridge Univ. Press, 2015), 129.
11 Ibid., 180.
12 Ibid., 193.
13 See John Berendt, "The Hoax," *Esquire*, April 1994, 60.
14 Similarities between H.G. Wells' novel and the calamity sparked by Orson Welles' broadcast are discussed at length in "The Big Hoax" by Michael J. Bugeja in *Culture's Sleeping Beauty* (Troy, N.Y.: Whitston, 1993).
15 Donald McQuade and Robert Atwan, eds., *Popular Writing in America* (New York: Oxford Univ. Press, 1988), 127.

16 Dan Lynch doesn't identify the city but discusses the incident at length in "Guarding Against Hoaxes," *Editor & Publisher*, February 29, 1992, 44.

17 President Bill Clinton's 1998 claim—"I did not have sexual relations with that woman, Miss Lewinsky"—was made at a January 26 news conference that year with staff and spouse in attendance, with the intent to program media, qualifying it as one of the longest-lived hoaxes of all time.

18 "Blacks felt the heat in Dixie Town as alleged carjack suspect was sought," Associated Press report, in *The Newark Star-Ledger*, November 5, 1994, 4.

19 Jeffery Reid, "'Pierre Salinger Syndrome' and the TWA 800 Conspiracies," CNN, July 17, 2006, www.cnn.com/2006/US/07/12/twa.con spiracy/index.html?section=cnn_us

20 Randy Dotinga, "When Computers Do the News, Hoaxes Slip In," *USA Today*, March 28, 2006, www.usatoday.com/tech/news/2006-03-28-net-news-hoaxes_x.htm

21 James Carson, "What is fake news? Its origins and how it grew in 2016," *The Telegraph*, March 16, 2017, http://www.telegraph.co.uk/technology/0/fake-news-origins-grew-2016/

22 See Dotinga, "When Computers Do the News, Hoaxes Slip In."

23 See "Free Southwest Airline Scam," Snopes.com, no date, www.snopes.com/inboxer/nothing/southwest.asp

24 Dom Yanchunas, "Loose Change," *COINage*, August 2006, 50–51.

25 To see a picture of the advertisement and learn more about the stunt, visit www.museumofhoaxes.com/tacobell.html

26 See www.museumofhoaxes.com/tacobell.html, which also contains these related readings on the Taco Bell stunt: Robert Frank, "Taco Bell's Gag Over the Liberty Bell Doesn't Leave Philly Cracking Up," *Wall Street Journal*, April 2, 1996, B6 and Greg Johnson, "Taco Bell's Ad Was a Burrito Short of a Combination Plate," *The Los Angeles Times*, April 2, 1996, D2.

27 "Taco Liberty Bell," Paine PR; no date, www.painepr.com/case_studies2.asp?nav=quicktime&content=tacolibertybell

28 A case in point involves *The Milwaukee Sentinel*, a newspaper that enjoys a good ethical reputation. In its June 17, 1993 edition, the *Sentinel* featured a front-page story about and testimonial by an *employee* who claimed to have found a syringe in a can of Pepsi. In 1995, two editors at the *Sentinel* were contacted nine times by fax and phone message for comment about the incident. One said "no comment" and the other declined to return calls or answer faxes.

29 Based on content analysis by the author of some 100 case studies of hoaxes.

30 Brandon Keim, "'Coal Cares' Hoax Website backed by Science," *Wired*, October 5, 2011, www.wired.com/2011/05/coalcares/

31 Cary Spivak et al., "Woman Admits Story a Hoax," *Milwaukee Sentinel*, June 19, 1993, 1.

32 Howard Kurtz, "Yes, Sir, That's No Baby, 'Pregnant' Man Gave Birth to Hoax," *The Washington Post*, June 10, 1992, sec 8, B1-2.

33 Nick Reid, "Author of Hoax Special Election Email Fights Felony on First Amendment Grounds," *Concord Monitor*, February 21, 2016, www.concordmonitor.com/Archive/2016/02/gibson-cm-022216

34 "Fake in the Lake," *People*, March 28, 1994, 109.

35 Rocco Parascandola and Bill Hoffman, "A Lotto B.S.," *The New York Post*, January 9, 1990, 1.

36 Sydney Schaedel, "How to Flag Fake News on Facebook," FactCheck. org, July 6, 2017, www.factcheck.org/2017/07/flag-fake-news-facebook/

37 Eugene Kiely and Lori Robertson, "How to Spot Fake News," FactCheck.org, November 18, 2016, www.factcheck.org/2016/11/how-to-spot-fake-news/

38 Ryan Holiday, *Trust Me, I'm Lying: The Tactics and Confessions of a Media Manipulator* (London: Portfolio/Penguin, 2013), 235.

CHAPTER 7

Temptation: Brace for It to Strike

TEMPTATION STRIKES WITHOUT WARNING

Temptation is relative. What might tempt one employee—personal use of a company car, say—might not tempt another. That makes it a matter of choice associated with individual values. Simply defined, temptation is *the urge to reject or change one's value system because of pressure, competition, ambition, reward or conflict of two or more equally important interests.* But temptation, like the hoax, can catch us off-guard. In the aftermath of a decision we may feel guilt or regret because temptation often targets the value that brings the quickest short-term relief which, as we saw in the chapters on lying and manipulation, usually is the poorest ethical choice. In other words, when temptation strikes, we typically take advantage of a *sudden opportunity* to achieve a goal or solve a dilemma that we had yet to fully foresee or anticipate, prompting us to act on impulse.

Impulsiveness does not emanate from conscience but from pressure. We feel a sense of urgency to take action without fully evaluating priorities. Temptation stifles the inner voice of conscience, appealing to weakness of will. Philosophers call this *akrasia,* from the Greek meaning "lack of mastery" over impulse causing a person "to do what he or she otherwise appears to know is right."[1] Anita L. Allen in *The New Ethics: A Guided Tour of the Twenty-First Century Moral Landscape* notes that regret for our actions often occurs when we commit unkindnesses unthinkingly and later marvel at our lack of emotional self-control.[2] Often, lack of restraint in the wake of temptation—knowingly voiding the conscience or guilt pang by a choice—typically leads to regret. According to Daniel Golemon, in his masterwork *Emotional Intelligence,*

> The somatic marker [or "gut feeling"] is a kind of automatic alarm, typically calling action to a potential danger from a given course of action. More often than not these markers steer us away from some choice that experience warns us against, though they can also alert us to a golden opportunity.[3]

Goleman believes resisting impulse when temptation strikes "is the root of all emotional self-control, since all emotions, by their very nature, lead to one or another impulse to act."[4]

Increasingly in digital environments, we succumb to impulsiveness because technology offers instant communication to one or many individuals at the mere click of a mouse or tap of a texting thumb. Who has not sent an email or text to others on impulse, complicating rather than resolving a situation at home, school or work? Who has not felt pressure when an email or text pings our emotional buttons, tempting us to respond angrily in an electronic exchange that ruins relationships in the vacuum of cyberspace without participants being in the presence of each other so that interpersonal dialogue allows for an honest exchange of ideas and viewpoints?

As an example of how quickly temptation can strike, consider the case of a *Detroit Free Press* sportswriter covering the 1994 Winter Olympic Games in Lillehammer, Norway. At the time Tonya Harding, a skater under suspicion in the beating of rival Nancy Kerrigan, was the main focus of the Games and a global story that commanded much interest. (The 2017 film, *I, Tonya*, recounts the situation.) The *Free Press* sportswriter, witnessed by two other reporters, was not trying to violate Harding's privacy for a story but nonetheless gained access to the skater's electronic mail by chance, entering the skater's birth date as the password. "They were just goofing around, though we still, of course, think this was wrong," said Dave Robinson, deputy managing editor, adding: "There was absolutely no intention to use the information for a news story. [The reporter] was at the keyboard, someone read the number, they punched it in, it worked and it said 68 unread messages on the screen, and they immediately signed off."[5]

The reporter apologized in a letter to Harding. Even though the intent was to "goof around" with a computer, at Harding's expense—a wrong decision by the reporter who later felt regret—it is doubtful that she really believed the birth date would unlock the skater's email. Nonetheless, when it did, the temptation to access the unread messages must have been keen. But the reporter's values kicked in and prevented her from reading such mail. If she had and based a story on those messages, to beat the competition with a scoop, she also knew that this would have been a firing offense. Worse, the *reporter* might have become the focus of countless tabloid stories about "Tonya's E-Mail Secrets."

Keep in mind that yielding to temptation and then acknowledging the moral lapse differs greatly from intentionally hacking into private digital messages, images and content of other people. That is what happened between 2005 and 2007 in a scandal involving the now-defunct *News of the World* and other British publications affiliated with News International, a subsidiary of News Corporation. In this case, the motive of ever-higher ratings and readers tempted employees to hack phones and bribe officials to get access to celebrity and British royal family communications. Worse, in 2011 investigators discovered that similar practices had occurred with non-celebrities who happened to be in the news, such as a slain school-girl and families of fallen soldiers. Consequences of these actions over the course of several years led to resignations, closing of publications, loss of trust in media and, finally, an apology from News Corporation owner Rupert Murdoch, who noted that *News of the World*

> was in the business of holding others to account. It failed when it came to itself. We are sorry for the serious wrongdoing that occurred. We are deeply sorry for the hurt suffered by the individuals affected. We regret not acting faster to sort things out. ... Our business was founded on the idea that a free and open press should be a positive force in society. We need to live up to this.[6]

Here again was a clash of two values—the desire for greater ratings and revenue versus an open press and positive social force. In the Murdoch scandal, the latter was dismissed without contemplating consequences. The same process holds true for individuals as well as institutions. The process of changing or revising values is usually a slow and careful one, based on such concepts as influences, responsibility and truth. Typically, the key elements of temptation—sudden opportunity or unforeseen conflicts of interest—require that we make a quick decision and change or reject our values accordingly. Howard Buford, founder and president of the New York City advertising agency Prime Access, says, "Unless you think about ethics ahead of time, when faced with pressure, you're just going to do whatever is most expedient. My experience is that over time that ethical envelope gets pushed and there are definite situations which, if you think about them, you might say to yourself—*Walk away from it*. But that's not going to happen unless you have thought about ethics ahead of time."

TEMPTATION INVITES CONFLICT

Without a strong value system, you are more likely to yield to temptation. Conflicts are bound to ensue. True, there is little time in the workplace to analyze questionable situations. Journalists and practitioners often get themselves into ethical trouble unintentionally, as we have already seen in the chapter on manipulation. The hoax also tempts media professionals and preys on their busy schedules, offering itself close to deadline when there is little time to verify information. But there also exists a fundamental difference concerning the hoax and temptation: *intent*. Initially at least, most journalists and practitioners do not know that they are being hoaxed but they almost always sense when they are being tempted.

Here are situations in which temptation usually strikes:

- **Deadlines.** The media professional under pressure considers taking an ethical shortcut that entails falsehood or wrongdoing, plagiarizing a story or press release or someone else's ad campaign or artwork, compromising values simply to get the job done.

- **Competition.** The media professional wants to beat the competition so desperately that he or she takes ethical shortcuts that compromise values, such as exaggerating a rival's bad business record or stealing stories, clients or marketing research.
- **Ambition.** The media professional desperately wants to advance in the company or score a scoop or coup that he or she takes ethical shortcuts rather than earning a promotion or beating rivals according to competence and work ethic.
- **Reward.** The media professional so desires recognition (to feel validated) or money (to purchase items or ease debts) that he or she compromises values associated with work ethic or merit, such as honesty, honor, dedication and excellence.
- **Conflict of Interest.** The media professional's political, personal or moral interests suddenly clash with those of his or her employer, requiring the journalist or practitioner to compromise values or conceal intent.

Plagiarism is one of the most common types of temptation, associated with pressure, competition, ambition and/or reward. Conflicts of interest are among the most morally complex, often involving a clash of our own and/or other people's values with consequences spiraling out of our control when we respond on impulse instead of on our honor. Both will be discussed in detail later in the chapter.

At this point it is important to note that every journalist or practitioner is tempted at one time or another. You should not feel guilt or regret for contemplating ethical shortcuts because of deadlines, competition, ambition and rewards. But you have to remind yourself of the long-term consequences, which can be dire. As any media professional knows, deadlines can be impossible and competition, cut-throat. Ambition and reward can inspire an employee to set goals and achieve at higher levels. Contemplating shortcuts to beat deadlines and competition is an urge you may feel to offset the pressures of employment in an industry that prizes quick decision-making. The issue here concerns the choices you will make because of that urge. Will you take an ethical shortcut to get a story or an account—so as to advance your career or please your employer—or will you adhere to the motto, perhaps learned at home, that "hard work is its own reward"? Will you yield to temptation or reject it, postpone a decision about it, or amend or change your values to embrace it? In sum, feeling the urge and resultant pressure from the clash of equally important values, goals or priorities does not, in itself, make you an unethical person. It does indicate, however, that your value system may have a weak link or that your conscience needs to be amplified. As a result, temptation offers us opportunities to test our values and strengthen them.

Not all media professionals jump at the chance to write or shoot an award-winning story, photograph or video or secure a blue-chip client or account. Every day journalists and practitioners let opportunities pass because of consequences that might ensue, not only for them, but for others. For Lady Borton, writer and former field director for the American Friends Service Committee in Vietnam, that meant foregoing a global scoop that could have won her national acclaim and perhaps a top job as a reporter. "I was in Vietnam any number of times when the country was still closed" to the U.S. media, she says. "I could have gone out to the street, talked to the people about political issues and returned to the States or phoned in my story." But in the aftermath of a brutal war in the 1960s and 70s, sources who talked to Borton, an American, might have suffered harsh consequences.

"That time has passed." What hasn't, Borton adds, is the "great weakness of the news media (in) the push toward the *story* rather than the *people* of the story, and so the people often are violated. When you finally get the story, the story is not worth it. I'm not talking about investigative journalism," Borton notes. "I'm talking about day-to-day coverage" in which journalists seek sensationalism at all costs; even "if we obliterate people in the process, it doesn't matter because the journalist leaves and the people stay behind." Borton's value system weighed the potential consequences of her every interaction. She was conscious of the calamitous situations of war and conscientious about its victims and survivors. Thus, she was able to resist temptation to take advantage of her sources.

Here is a process to help you deal with temptation:

1. Consequences

Because temptation usually involves sudden opportunity, consequences can be greater than you initially anticipate.

Ask yourself:

- *What is the worst-case scenario I could suffer by yielding to the demands of deadlines, competition, ambition or reward?*
- *Am I willing to pay that price?*
- *How will yielding to temptation change me as a person? as a professional?*

2. Short- and Long-Term Effects

Because temptation usually offers immediate relief to a pressing urge or problem, the short- and long-term effects often differ greatly.

Ask yourself:

- *Is the relief that temptation offers worth compromising my values?*
- *If I yield to temptation now, what is to stop me from yielding again?*
- *How will my political, social or lifestyle agendas change over the short- and long-term if I yield to temptation?*

3. Sound Judgment

Because temptation usually involves sudden opportunity, you need to assess your current state of mind before acting.

Ask yourself:

- *Is the specter of deadlines, competition, ambition or reward causing me to respond in a way I normally wouldn't?*
- *Is the suddenness of the opportunity clouding my judgment?*
- *Am I imagining or overlooking consequences that are causing me to behave in a manner that I normally wouldn't?*

4. Independent, Voluntary Choices

Because temptation usually challenges basic values, you need to be sure that your choices—yielding, postponing the decision to yield, or refusing to yield—will be voluntary and of your own accord.

Ask yourself:

- *Is any other person or third party playing a role in or over-influencing my decision?*
- *Is any other person or third party clouding my judgment on this matter?*
- *Has any other person or third party influenced how I have gone through the above processes of establishing consequences, determining short- and long-term effects, and evaluating judgment?*

As noted earlier, temptation offers unique opportunities to test and strengthen personal and professional values. The more you deal with such issues by analyzing them in the above manner, the sounder your judgment will become. Now let's confront one of the most common types of temptation so potentially damaging to your career that we must focus on it separately.

RESIST THE URGE TO PLAGIARIZE

When journalists and practitioners steal from each other or outside sources and pass off that work as their own, they not only tarnish their own reputations but also that of their employers. The temptation to plagiarize has become particularly keen in the digital newsroom or agency because technology manipulates text, data and artwork with the ease of select, copy and paste functions. "Both the ease with which it is possible to quickly access such texts and the actual process of negotiating websites—clicking on links that take you to texts containing other links—gives students the sense that words are cheap and free, that words have equal value, and that origins are irrelevant," says Carolyn Kitch, educator and former magazine journalist. "Such an illusion leads to the legal problems of inaccuracy and plagiarism." Kitch reports that she has seen a spike in plagiarism cases due to the cut-and-paste mentality in reporting and research. "In some cases," she adds, "by the time that the student has a final product, he or she actually forgets where the information came from (because it never occurred to him or her to notice in the first place) and does not even fully realize that the resulting collage contains stolen goods." Intent aside, Kitch says, plagiarism now can be reliably *expected* in many journalism student papers. "In nearly every case, the student's response to being confronted with the plagiarism is astonishment or outrage, both reactions based not on denial of the act but on disbelief that it really matters—a response that reveals the ethical and moral dimensions of this legal problem." Kitch notes that these issues have arisen not only because of the ubiquity of digital technology in everyday communication but because projects often traverse platforms, especially in multimedia, morphing from the written word to the spoken word to the visual. Again, technological convergence requires a moral one. "More broadly," Kitch concludes, "what is lost is pride in practice" and "the inclination to pursue expertise and excellence in an area of work."

Plagiarism is associated with all platforms. It is defined as *stealing or closely imitating someone else's written, creative, electronic, photographed, taped, or promotional or research work, identifying it as your own without permission or authorization.* Plagiarism, once known as "cut and paste" journalism, has morphed into "select, copy and paste" journalism because of internet. Plagiarism continues to plague all media disciplines because of easy online access to source documents. Warnings came in the late 1990s. Writing in the December 1998 issue of *Prism*, published by the American Society of Engineering Education, Julie J.C.H. Ryan observed that before widespread use of internet plagiarism cases were difficult to expose, requiring diligence on the part of professors to track down source documents and ingenuity on the part of word thieves to dodge detection. "But today with the click of a mouse," she cautioned, "even technologically inept students have access to vast information resources in cyberspace without having to leave the comfort of their dorm rooms."[7]

Plagiarism continues to alarm educators and professionals because it usually is a firing offense across media platforms. An ill-famed example includes the May 2003 dismissal of *New York Times* writer Jayson Blair who stole others' words and invented information, leading to the resignations of executive editor Howell Raines and managing editor Gerald Boyd. Shortly thereafter *The Times* reported a study of 23 college campuses that found some 38 percent of undergraduate students responding to surveys noted that in the past year "they had engaged in one or more instances of 'cut-and-paste' plagiarism involving the internet, paraphrasing or copying anywhere from a few sentences to a full paragraph from the web without citing the source."[8] Journalism educators who utilize methods to identify and detect plagiarism, explained later in this chapter, confront students with evidence of plagiarism only to encounter a more frightening reality: *Many believe they have done nothing wrong. The New York Times* plagiarism report noted the same phenomenon: "Almost half the students [admitting plagiarism] said they considered such behavior trivial or not cheating at all."[9]

Before being able to address the issue of plagiarism, especially with respect to internet, it is important to define related concepts:

- **Copyright Infringement,** which involves using or disseminating a portion of or an entire document, research finding or statistics, still or moving images, software or computer programs, and/or sound files or recordings without the originator's permission or authorization. (It should be noted that plagiarism may or may not infringe on the copyright of a certain property, depending on the portion in question along with other factors, including loss of revenue in the original work.)
- **Proxy Plagiarism,** or "reverse plagiarism," which involves the creation of an original work or generation of research data with the specific intent of allowing another party to pass it off as his or her own. Examples are many but include doing a report for another person, out of friendship or profit; writing or producing a news story or video for another person's byline; adding a scholar's name to a submission without his or her knowledge or contribution, simply to increase chances of acceptance; or generating research in someone else's name, with or without permission, to gain favor or reward.
- **Matching Story or Research Assignment,** which entails using someone else's non-fiction work or research methodology as a template to generate an original authentic creation, typically by re-interviewing sources or retesting data. (This is usually not a violation of academic integrity as long as content remains original and format is used as a template, such as the inverted pyramid form for a newspaper article or a report format for a grant proposal.)
- **Invention,** which entails fabricating portions of or an entire document or image/video, sound file/recording, or research finding/statistic whose content is supposed to be based on quotations, testimonials, documentary images or video, survey responses or other purportedly true data.
- **Hoax,** a specific type of invention by a person or group making or disseminating a false claim with the intent to program or manipulate the news media or institutional policy or procedure for personal gain, exposure or some other motive.

The above definitions distinguish plagiarism from other, similar concepts that involve different motives and ethical lapses. For instance, the motive of *invention* is to circumvent the legwork or labor involved in generating an authentic document, image, sound or video, etc., rather than to program media or disrupt policy or procedure. An example of invention involves an incident that occurred in 1977 out of the St. Louis bureau of United Press International. Although the incident happened decades ago, it still serves as a prime example of temptation—in this case, invention—happening due to sudden opportunity. A photographer stringing for the wire service transmitted four dramatic purse-snatching photographs that had been staged several weeks earlier. The photographer reportedly wanted to prove that spot-news photos could be fabricated and still appear authentic. In a letter to *News Photographer,* the photographer explained why he invented the series of photos:

> It had always bothered me that as a photojournalist I was always at the mercy of most situations. ... Unfortunately, the shots turned out even better than I anticipated and on Oct. 28 the temptation to use them became too much to resist.[10]

Another journalist who could not resist the temptation to invent was Stephen Glass in articles for *The New Republic* and other publications before his deceptions were exposed in 1998. In a 2003 *60 Minutes* interview, Glass said his life "was one very long process of lying and lying again, to figure out how to cover those other lies,"[11] reminiscent of the lying syndrome discussed in Chapter 5. Glass said that he began making up details and quotations and soon found himself fabricating entire stories. To bypass the fact-checking process at magazines he invented fake notes, voice mailboxes and even a website, feeling confident because "I wrote fictional stories about fictional people at fictional times doing fictional things. And those people don't write letters."[12]

In that sense, invention circumvents the legwork of reporting. Plagiarism circumvents the legwork of *writing.* These observations are associated with the concept of a "matching story." Case in point: A former dean of Boston University's journalism school resigned when *The Boston Globe* reported that he may have plagiarized a commencement speech using material from a scholarly journal that also was reprinted in *Reader's Digest.*[13] However, in trying to match the story, *The New York Times* acknowledged that its account was "improperly dependent" on the original *Globe* article, or "essentially plagiarized," according to *Editor & Publisher.*[14] As this case illustrates, a matching story must be original and authentic. You may not simply "rewrite" portions of, or all of, a competing work—even if your media company owns both outlets—or rely on it for facts, quotations, citations, research and testimonials, passing it off as your own. By all means you can interview sources quoted in a competing story. You also should interview sources the competition has overlooked, putting those people high up in your article or highlighting them in a broadcast report, all the while being careful not to use a dateline if the match is made from another city using telephones or internet. In addition, refuse a byline.

As you can see, matching a story ethically involves legwork, which plagiarists routinely try to avoid. They not only take risks doing so, but also risk lawsuits, says Tom Hodson, former clerk to the U.S. Supreme Court and general manager of the public radio station, WOUB, associated with the journalism school at Ohio University. "The easiest of legal strategies involves proof of copyright infringement," Hodson observes. "All a plaintiff has to do in such circumstances is show that he or she owns the work in question and that it was used without attribution or permission. Then you can collect damages, court costs and even reasonable attorney fees. Other legal strategies include civil and criminal actions. It is a violation of common law for someone to take property of another and appropriate it for his or her purposes and profit. The plagiarist also may be committing a fraud upon the public for indicating certain works are his or her own. Also, the violator may have taken property of the author and converted it for his or her own purposes and made money on the use of the item or gained fame as a result of the use of the item. In such case you can receive even more monetary damages."

Perhaps one of the most embarrassing examples of a failed attempt to match a speech concerned Melania Trump's 2016 address to the Republican National Convention, which ended up plagiarizing a 2008 speech by Michele Obama who had campaigned against Donald Trump. Here are excerpts:

Michele Obama: "And Barack and I were raised with so many of the same values: that you work hard for what you want in life; that your word is your bond and you do what you say you're going to do; that you treat people with dignity and respect, even if you don't know them, and even if you don't agree with them."

"Because we want our children—and all children in this nation—to know that the only limit to the height of your achievements is the reach of your dreams and your willingness to work for them."

Melania Trump: "From a young age, my parents impressed on me the values that you work hard for what you want in life, that your word is your bond and you do what you say and keep your promise, that you treat people with respect. They taught and showed me values and morals in their daily lives. That is a lesson that I continue to pass along to our son."

"Because we want our children in this nation to know that the only limit to your achievements is the strength of your dreams and your willingness to work for them."

When initially discovered and brought to the attention of the campaign, former Trump top aide, Paul Manafort, dismissed the plagiarism claims, which only intensified media scrutiny. Once detected and documented, the specter of "coincidence" is difficult to believe and almost always easy to refute, as we shall learn later in this chapter. So was the case with this incident, which happened when speechwriter Meredith McIver admitted the mistake with this apology:

> In working with Melania on her recent First Lady speech, we discussed many people who inspired her and messages she wanted to share with the American people. A person she always liked is Michelle Obama. Over the phone, she read me some passages from Mrs. Obama's speech as examples. I wrote them down and later included some of the phrasing in the draft that ultimately became the final speech. I did not check Mrs. Obama's speeches. This was my mistake, and I feel terrible for the chaos I have caused Melania and the Trumps, as well as to Mrs. Obama. No harm was meant.[15]

After the apology, a British publication, *The Independent*, questioned whether McIver actually existed or whether she was an invention by the Trump campaign, prompting the suspicion to go viral on social media.[16] According to *Slate*, which confirmed McIver's existence, "The internet is fond of irrational conspiracy theories and portions of the internet embraced a particularly irrational one on Wednesday: That Meredith McIver, the long-time Donald Trump employee and ghostwriter who took the fall for the Melania Trump plagiarism scandal, might not be real." The publication then verified that McIver had been employed as a ghost writer for some books bearing Trump's name as author.[17]

Plagiarism and related concepts, such as invention and infringement, harm credibility to the extent that those who commit it may never work again in the profession. Plagiarism occurs across platforms. The theft and fabrication of data in a marketing report may seem a far stretch from the print cases discussed here, in as much as circumstances in an agency or corporation differ dramatically from those in a newsroom; but circumstances have little to do with theft: *values do*. The temptation to take shortcuts and the lack of resolve to do necessary legwork are usual factors in news, public relations, advertising and magazine, photo- and online journalism. While you may never commit plagiarism, you may be in a supervisory role and need to guard against it to protect the reputation of your outlet or company. Or your workplace or association rules may require you to report plagiarism or any other ethical wrongdoing.

YOU CAN DETECT AND PREVENT PLAGIARISM

To detect and prevent plagiarism, media professionals need to know precise terminology. The original work is called the *source* document. The plagiarized work is called the *target* document. These terms are used when significant portions of plagiarism occur in a target document. It should be noted that plagiarism also can entail technicalities such as citing a source without footnoting appropriately or using snippets of material without crediting it as someone else's except for a mention in an appended bibliography—infractions usually caused by oversight rather than by intent.

Intent is important when distinguishing between legal and ethical infractions. In other words, a person can commit plagiarism without intending to do so and can be held responsible by the person who created the original work. That is the legal consequence. Thus, in that regard, intent does not eliminate culpability. Intent is, however, a factor in ethical considerations, because making a choice to steal is a moral decision reflecting a person's value system.

Academic judiciary panels investigating allegations of plagiarism typically focus on intent. The professional world focuses on legal infraction, dismissing intent in the belief that journalists or practitioners should have learned about plagiarism in college. Internet has altered intent, especially as it concerns the concept of *plausible deniability*, an excuse that often justifies a person's actions based on *viewpoint* or *mindset*, which a third party can never fully ascertain. Plausible deniability is a common defense used to circumvent moral responsibility.

Before the advent of electronic publishing, when most plagiarists changed wording or paraphrased, plausible deniability usually involved "coincidence" to explain away similarities between source and target documents. As wording between such documents was similar but not always exact, coincidence may have been a suspicious but nevertheless plausible excuse in the absence of hard evidence. A case study involving plausible deniability occurred with passages lifted from a magazine article published in *Editor & Publisher* by Andrea Tortora, then editor of a student newspaper. The lead of a "Shop Talk at 30" essay stated:

> For the past 10 months, I've been racist, homophobic, sexist, biased and stupid. I've been exploitative and insensitive.
> I've been a college newspaper editor.
> At 22, I'm burned out, hardened and exasperated. As the editor of the *Post*, the independent daily student newspaper at Ohio University, I've defended my writers, my editors, and my newspaper to its patrons, many who do not understand journalism and its principles.[18]

A near-identical version of that lead appeared under the byline of the editor of another student newspaper. Upon discovering this, Tortora confronted that editor about suspected plagiarism and took notes in a telephone conversation during which the other editor claimed to have been "inspired" to write a near-exact lead based on a conversation he had in an internship. "Yeah," he reportedly stated, "it's a pretty amazing coincidence."[19] The claim of coincidence as a function of plausible deniability in the pre-internet era sent Tortora and her adviser to scientists on campus to calculate the odds of a 67-word passage occurring by coincidence in another person's story within months of the source document being published. Using the conservative figure of 800,000 words in the English language, a mathematician put the odds of a target document possessing the same excerpt as the source document as one in 800,000 to the power of 67'. Think about how difficult it is to win a lottery selecting seven numbers out of 50. Now imagine winning a lottery with 67 exact numbers out 800,000. Even this comparison does not fully represent odds in word theft, failing to take into account grammar, syntax, verb tense declination, slang and other factors. Thus, you can add a million more variations to your metaphoric lottery. But even these do not accurately represent the odds. There is the issue of sequence. Imagine the lottery now containing 1.8 million numbers and choosing 67 winning ones in sequence. That means the number "58," for instance, representing the word "the," must occur more than once in an exact position in your series of winning picks. "With respect to plagiarism the odds are very close to zero," Ohio University mathematics professor David Keck noted in an interview with Tortora's adviser.

Knowing these odds, many media professionals looked with suspicion on Kaavya Viswanathan's claim that she did not plagiarize intentionally in her novel, *How Opal Mehta Got Kissed, Got Wild, and Got a Life,* which contained passages similar to those in Megan F. McCafferty novels *Sloppy Firsts* and the 2003 novel *Second Helpings.*[20] The 19-year-old Harvard student had received a reported $500,000 in a two-book contract along with a DreamWorks movie deal. Viswanathan initially had no comment, then expressed surprise and finally exercised what journalist Chip Scanlon calls "the unconscious defense," stating that any similar phrasings "were completely unintentional and unconscious."[21]

Since most plagiarism cases now involve internet, where source documents are readily available and easily copied, "coincidence" no longer is a key factor, for the chances of randomly selecting identical wording—even for one paragraph—are, literally, astronomical.[22] Thus, plausible deniability has shifted from "coincidence" to "ignorance," which again involves viewpoint and which a third party can never fully ascertain. In other words, a person who claims not to know that copying someone else's work off the web and passing it off as one's own is, indeed, plagiarism, may or may not be telling the truth. One can always make that suspicious but nevertheless plausible excuse—*even in the presence of hard evidence.*

While some claims of ignorance may be true, especially if they involve inappropriate footnoting or referencing, few plagiarists evoke the "coincidence" defense in the digital age. "Ignorance" may be a plausible excuse for plagiarism, but it is not for the concept of "conscience," which indicates one's value system. Case in point: A senior journalism student at a major university who plagiarized a paper—by selecting, copying and pasting—asserted in a Judiciaries hearing: "I didn't know it was wrong." The professor who reported the student noted that such an excuse was negligent. The concept of "negligence," which involves whether one *should have known* that one's actions were wrong, often invites swift and severe consequences across media platforms. In fact, negligence can be so serious that it not only is illegal but also criminal in some cases. But even this does not get at the heart of the lie in this plagiarism case: The journalism student submitted plagiarized work in a writing assignment in which little writing was done. When this was explained, the student was found to have plagiarized despite her plausible denial.

Internet tempts students on deadline in a deceptive way associated with "the dorm room" effect. Before residence halls were wired, plagiarism was a public event. A student typically visited the library for a source document, which he or she photocopied in full view of others during hours of operation, hid the source document in the wrong stacks or even checked it out to avoid detection, and then retired to his or her residence hall to paraphrase language in a paper. The time it took to premeditate word theft was an essential component in this very public act. Students had time to ponder consequences—an act of consciousness—or to experience remorse, an act of conscience. Because of internet, the library is open at all hours electronically with source documents accessed on demand. Alone in their rooms, on deadline and feeling pressured, the temptation to plagiarize is simply too great for some students who might have thought better of the idea "in the light of day." Worse, selecting, copying and pasting content into a file called "My Documents" gives a false sense of ownership. Internet gives the impression that nobody else is looking through Windows when just the opposite may be true, especially when source documents are easily accessed by those who suspect plagiarism.

Internet makes it as easy to detect plagiarism as to commit it. There are dozens of fact-checking and plagiarism detection tools on the market. "With so many web pages produced daily, plagiarism is an evolving concern," states the technology weblog DigitalGYD, introducing the top detection software in 2017. "There are a lot of writers, bloggers who like to copy the writings of others and use them on their own blogs/essay assignments without giving proper credits." Increasingly, content creators as well as educators are using these tools to spot plagiarism and report it via social media. While you may never have the urge to steal someone else's copy, designs, photos or artwork, the real ethical issue is what action you would take if you found plagiarism in your work environment? That is important in the professional world. Suppose you discovered a colleague at your outlet was stealing the content of others? Would your value system be such that you would pursue the plagiarist, motivated not by pride but by integrity to protect the purity of the published or broadcast word? How would you react if someone stole *your* work? Would you believe that imitation is the sincerest form of flattery? If you made the latter choice, how would you respond should someone suspect *you* of theft merely because your work also appears under the byline of the plagiarist? What if you knew a student journalist had committed plagiarism and, years later, saw that person walk into your newsroom seeking a job at your place of employment? What, then, are your ethical obligations? What if you suspect that someone at your media company is plagiarizing and that *you* can be held liable for not reporting it to your supervisor, pursuant to human resources rules at your workplace?

As you can see, these questions imply that you should take a stance against plagiarism as a citizen of the media community, embracing social responsibility. Now a word of caution: Because plagiarism cases differ, from improper citations to outright theft, no one should accuse another of such theft until a case can be documented factually. Suspicion that plagiarism has occurred is insufficient. Accordingly, before taking any action against another, you should have solid evidence indicating plagiarism; otherwise you can expose yourself to counter charges or even legal action.

The best way to easily scan for plagiarism is to purchase or use free detection software. However, if you lack such software, you can gather evidence using methods below:

1. **Search via engines.** You have access to dozens of search engines, databases and archives to track down source documents. If one search engine fails, try another. Google is comprehensive but operates only if the source document is still on the web. An online archive like Wayback Machine, www.archive.org, takes periodic internet snapshots and so can enhance your detection.

2. **Start with the first paragraph.** Word-thieves often steal from the top of the source document. Enter into a search engine or databank a phrase from the first paragraph. There's another reason to start with leads: Many search engines, publication archives and library databases summarize them in abbreviated listings.

3. **Choose awkward or odd phrases.** If your search fails, using introductory paragraphs, enter awkward locutions into a search engine. An Ohio University student was caught plagiarizing because she used British spellings and these odd-sounding phrases in a final project: "indispensable guarantors" and "considering advertising's social impact." In seconds, a search engine generated addresses for five sites containing the source document.

4. **Use illogical word combinations.** The word "Boolean" means "logical word combinations," such as "advertising AND ethics." In August 2017, that combination produced 71,900,000 hits on google.com—far too many to weed through in a hunt for a source document. To catch a plagiarist, make Boolean searches *illogical*, taking a rare word or proper noun from the plagiarized document—" Skullbuster (a soap product)," for instance—and combining that with your operative word. By contrast, the combination "Skullbuster AND ethics" yielded 2,350 hits on google.com.

5. **Use library databanks.** Boolean searches are perfect if you are searching library databanks. Databanks often supplement information that search engines omit. Typically, though, you won't be able to access the source document but an abstract thereof (which should provide you with enough information to decide if you should access an article from an online newspaper or magazine— see No. 6 below).

6. **Access specific archives.** Boolean searches work exceptionally well with periodicals and newspaper archives that feature online search options. Some internet publications require subscriptions before allowing access to archives; others charge a fee per each downloaded article. Either way, both can be a good investment.

In the end, journalists and practitioners have an ethical responsibility to uphold high standards of originality. Without such standards, the written, digital or broadcast word is cheapened, values are compromised, and truth is undermined. To combat plagiarism in the digital age, it is essential for professors, editors and supervisors to inform interns and employees about consequences of committing this ethical infraction—from syllabi to ethics codes—and to distinguish it from other similar infractions, using correct terminology and detection methods as outlined here. Media professionals know that plagiarism wastes time and money and damages personal and corporate reputations, causing emotional and financial distress. The temptation to steal another's work can be keen in the hectic atmosphere of a newsroom or an agency but infractions are easy to prove through detection software, search engines and/or online archives. In essence, the digital deck is stacked against the plagiarist who relieves short-term pressure and then hopes in the long term that nobody recognizes the theft. Also, the onus is on you as an ethical journalist or practitioner to know in advance how you would respond if you witnessed plagiarism or related infractions. The ethical lessons are obvious—don't plagiarize and underestimate the intelligence or vigilance of your audience, colleagues, competitors or employers. Do investigate infractions and, if appropriate, report them.

AVOID CONFLICTS OF INTEREST

Other issues involving temptation are more complex, especially when they involve a clash of two equal but conflicting interests. Such conflicts often sharpen consciousness and deepen conscience, not because there are easy answers, but because the situation calls on us to choose one value, goal or desire over another equally alluring value, goal or desire. As Philip Patterson and Lee Wilkins note in *Media Ethics: Issues and Cases,*

> Ethics begins when elements within a moral system conflict. Ethics is less about the conflict between right and wrong than it is about the

conflict between equally compelling (or equally unattractive) alternatives and the choices that must be made between them.[23]

Let that observation influence our discussion here of conflicts of interest, which can be "monetary" or "non-monetary." The former is fairly easy to address ethically because it involves money or gifts or services given to journalists and practitioners for special favors. They include:

- **Junkets,** or an expenses-paid trip so that a journalist can cover an event. Officials at a ski resort, say, might offer a magazine editor a week at the resort to write a favorable review of the facilities.
- **Freebies,** or gifts like free meals or tickets, to befriend or influence a media professional. Officials at a new casino might invite a reporter to a banquet or send him or her tickets to see a top-name celebrity or even gambling chips to "try out" the new slot machines or tables.
- **Bribes,** or an outright payment or promise to buy services or goods from a media outlet in return for some favor. For instance, a lawyer can promise to purchase advertising from a TV station whose general manager cancels an investigative consumer segment about a product manufactured by the lawyer's client.

General rule: *Media professionals should not take junkets, freebies or bribes and agencies and companies should not offer them.*

Keep in mind, however, that magazine and book editors, along with advertisers and public relations practitioners, often solicit authors or clients over lunches and/or distribute free samples like back issues or promotional literature or products and host corporate visits or tours. These are typical business expenses. The best way to check the ethical nature of any suspected junket, freebie or bribe is to determine whether the item, function, service or tour in question is an attempt *to program media for personal profit*. If so, resist it.

That is often easier said than done until you experience the pang of conscience that informs you of a poor choice. Those incidents usually happen early in one's career. "I was fortunate to start my ad agency career right out of college, now more than 15 years ago," says Jason M. Boucher, vice president of client service for ZLRIGNITION, an Iowa agency. "Within a few months, my professional ethics were given the true test. A coworker and I were invited to an appreciation party at a casino restaurant. This kind of event was not foreign, a night filled with food and drink where the sales people could let all of us buyers know how much they truly 'liked' us. But then a few hours into the party, the radio company sales manager that was hosting the party grabbed the mic and informed everyone that they were getting a reward for being great buyers—a certain percentage of our previous quarter media buy back in casino chips, in my case about $500 in chips! What a fantastic thing for a 22-year-old who doesn't see that much from a paycheck. Except it wasn't fantastic. I was already over-served alcohol and only 10 feet from the casino floor."

Boucher knew instinctively that this was a kickback, and he shouldn't take it. "My job was simply to calculate math and negotiate buys with my clients' budgets. But for a brief moment, I didn't know any better and within 30 minutes I had gambled all of the money away.

"Shortly thereafter I discovered that I did in fact possess an ethical foundation. On the way home that evening I was able to secure a loan from my coworker for the full amount of what the radio company had given as a kickback. The next day at work I went straight to my ad agency CFO and explained the situation of the money that was given to us by the radio station and turned every cent over to him. We soon offered a credit to the client for which I had bought the original radio air time for. It turns out that the client was not able to accept the credit (as a government entity) and the CFO ultimately returned the kickback to the radio company.

"Looking back on those early months as a media buyer, $500 in poker chips doesn't seem like a very big deal. I've since been gifted more than that in my role as an account director; always to be shared with the client, office or returned. But I realize that night was my first true professional test, and at a time when my personal ethics were most likely to be defined.

"The pride that I took in ultimately doing the right thing has guided my career ever since."

Gifts or special favors usually have a monetary component. Veteran journalist Jackie Jones, chair of Multimedia Journalism at Morgan State University, was an assignment editor at *The Washington Post*. She has encountered several conflicts of interest during her 30-plus years as a reporter, copy editor, assignment editor, city editor and metro editor in a number of newsrooms, including *Milwaukee Journal Sentinel*, *Philadelphia Daily News*, *New York Newsday* and *Detroit Free Press*. Jones notes that conflicts of interest involving freebies can arise subtly over time. A source provides needed quotations on deadline or otherwise makes a journalist feel comfortable rather than inquisitive in his or her presence. "You begin to trust the source," she says, "and then you start overlooking his picking up the tab for coffee and drinks. An innocuous button or book becomes a more valuable gift, but no harm, no foul, it would seem. It's difficult, especially for a young reporter, to see the problem with any of that, but if you don't hold the line on the little things, the bigger things won't seem so big after a while."

Jones recalls a reporter at a suburban Washington, D.C. newspaper who went to lunch with a source. "He was handsome, smooth, well-dressed and, up to this point, had been an impeccable source. Everything he had ever told this reporter (all on background or off the record) checked out. He called. He had information that would be useful, he said, about a logjam with a major development project. It went downhill quickly. Before the waitress brought the check, the source—over the reporter's objections—gave the server his credit card and paid the bill." Outside the restaurant, the source pulled out a long white box, handed it to the reporter, hopped in his car and zipped away. The reporter approached Jones in the newsroom looking bewildered. "Inside the box were three dozen long-stemmed roses, in three different colors."

Those roses symbolized intent, as you learned in Chapter 5 about the ethics of gift-giving. "It turned out that he was trying to get her to report the story in a way that would allow him, and a few others, to get equity in the development project under the guise of a lack of substantial minority representation," Jones said. "He tried to get the story by wooing the reporter. He thought her youth and inexperience and his charm and good looks would guarantee a story slanted in the direction he wanted."

Jones told the reporter to send the source a check for the meal, give his flowers away and tell him that he had crossed the line ethically and, in doing so, put her in an untenable position. Further, she advised, the reporter should inform the source that this could not happen again and, if it did, her editor would contact him. The reporter put in extra effort to get an accurate story about closed-door negotiations concerning the development. "One by one," Jones said, "she got officials on the record who basically revealed that the dispute was linked to minority participation and how such participation would be defined." But the reporter did not immediately take Jones' advice about the source trying to influence her reporting with freebies. "He called her a few days later and asked what she was doing for lunch. She had not made the calls I instructed her to make the day of the fateful lunch. But she understood the problem now." The reporter informed the source that their lunches would cease unless he had legitimate newsworthy information to pass on to her. "Further, when they did meet, she would pay her own way or pick up the full tab, but he was not to pay." While Jones acknowledges that typically reporters are not manipulated by roses and lunches, journalists must be concerned about how this looks to others seeing them in public "An attractive reporter, an attractive source, a nice meal, an expensive, over-the-top gift and, volla, a reporter produces a story for a love interest—one who could walk away and say that it was all a misunderstanding. And a reporter is left with damaged credibility." In such a case, a monetary conflict of interest could metamorphose into a highly personal non-monetary conflict.

Non-monetary conflicts affect personal and professional relationships because of *values*. Possible conflicts are endless but mainly fall into three categories:

- **Personal vs. Personal Value.** This occurs when your personal value clashes with a personal value of a relative or other person outside your place of employment, such as might occur during a divorce or family upheaval. (While this type of conflict is important to note because it may indirectly cause ethical problems at work, it is beyond the scope of this book.)

- **Professional vs. Professional Value.** This occurs when one of your professional values directly conflicts with another of your professional values or when one of your professional values conflicts with that of your coworker, superior, client, source or employer.
- **Personal vs. Professional Value.** This occurs when one of your personal values directly conflicts with one of your professional values or when one of your personal values conflicts with the professional value of your coworker, superior, client, source or employer.

Essentially, such conflicts arise because the media professional did not foresee or prepare for the collision of two or more values. Or did not thoroughly adjust for the viewpoints and values of colleagues or constituents. For instance, in a "professional vs. professional" conflict, a reporter might be torn between a value that upholds free speech, even for white supremacists, while detesting their message. That is a genuine clash of personal values. However, this also can metamorphose into a different kind of "professional vs. professional" conflict if a supervisor is involved. Increasingly, this kind of conflict is amplified with social networks like Facebook and Twitter. The reporter who fervently believes in free speech might defend the supremacists' right to hold a rally, knowing such a stance would be controversial, not only on social media but also within newsrooms. Moreover, an assignment editor who sees that online might believe the reporter should not cover such a rally, creating a perception of bias and/or bad taste with the audience.

This type of conflict also can occur with practitioners. An example of a "personal vs. professional" conflict might involve a public relations employee who believes that climate change is a serious national concern and expresses that in her personal social media accounts while working on the political campaign of an organization that questions or denies climate change. The practitioner's supervisor or agency's client might discover this and lodge a complaint. As a result, the practitioner can be removed from the account or asked to take down her posts. That can lead to a deepening of the conflict.

Should practitioner and, in the earlier case, the First Amendment reporter accept reassignment to another account or story if their supervisors request that, questioning their professionalism? Should they take down their social media posts? Or should they challenge their supervisor's perception of their lack of professionalism and refuse to be reassigned, maintaining that they can still be thorough and objective?

On a personal and professional level, you usually have three options in non-monetary conflicts:

- **Choosing one value over another value.** In the two cases earlier, the reporter and practitioner can choose to take down their posts about free speech and climate change, satisfying concerns about perceived bias and/or bad taste. They can leave up their posts and accept reassignment and, potentially, career setback. Or they can refuse to change their deeply held beliefs, potentially risking their jobs. Of course, supervisors can allow the content to remain online and trust the professionalism of their employees. But there are consequences there, too, for both reporter and practitioner, along with their companies, if complaints are filed against them by viewers of their posts, advertisers of their outlets, or clients of their agencies.

- **Amending one or both values so that you can tolerate the troubling situation.** In the above cases, supervisors can make exceptions and negotiate with the employees so that potentially offensive material is blocked from public view, shared only with the reporter's private friends and personal acquaintances. Or reporter and practitioner can accept new assignments because that allows them to be even stronger advocates of their individual causes.

- **Coming up with one or more new values to deal with the troubling situation.** In the earlier examples, supervisors can adopt guidelines of semi-restricted online speech and incorporate that into their companies' ethics codes. A potentially radical solution for both employees might be to resist reassignment, suffer the consequences, adopting infrangible commitments to their causes and litigate against their employers because reassignment questions professionalism.

Also, it should be noted, professional vs. professional conflicts can occur across platforms, especially between journalists and practitioners. According to Martin and Wright in *Public Relations Ethics*, these two professions are suspicious of each other, and for good reason:

> The journalist wants a story; the public relations person wants it to be favorable to the client. Those do not have mutually exclusive goals; but they almost always get in each other's way. ... If journalists have a siege mentality toward public relations people, it may be because according to the U.S. Department of Labor, they're outnumbered nearly five to one. Plus, their salaries are an average 40 percent lower.[24]

Nevertheless, journalists and sources typically operate within the same social or political circles. "If you have covered a beat for a long time, your professional relationship with sources can start to feel personal," says Phil Elliott, Washington correspondent for *Time*. "In many cases, the reporters and the sources share an interest in the topic at hand, or else they wouldn't be spending their careers trying to understand the topics better and explain them to a wider audience." Reporters and sources often travel to the same cities or find themselves in the same hotels, airports and cab lines. "It's not an unreasonable inclination as a human to choose to share a meal rather than sit alone in a restaurant in a strange city, or to catch up over drinks around the corner from the office. Where it can get awkward is when one party decides the relationship is personal." When that happens, Elliott makes clear that he may find the company of sources enjoyable "but that won't keep me from writing about their mistakes." Moreover, he adds, "There's a reason I never accept anything more expensive than a cup of coffee and, when it wouldn't be awkward, my company picks up the tab. At times, sources find this overly fussy, but I explain it thusly: There will come a day when you're going to be deeply upset by something I write, and I don't want you to feel as if you've been misled about the nature of this relationship."

Elliott knows that he has to maintain long-term relationships with sources. "Even with sources I don't particularly enjoy working with, I always phone them before I publish something negative. That courtesy doesn't negate the hit they're about to suffer, but it preserves the working relationship."

Common conflicts of interest often occur in day-to-day assignments or activities. Some are personal, some are professional and others both. Some involve a clash of two ethical values held by different employees. Some involve a clash of an ethical value held by one or more employees and a corporate value. Because conflicts of interest are associated with temptation and, as such, are relative, each case will vary because situations do with people and companies. But a sampling of case studies in converged and traditional environments across platforms may help put into context some methods to recognize and resolve these moral dilemmas.

Digital Conflicts

In the past, a personal vs. professional conflict involved employees placing long-distance calls to family and friends while at work. Eventually, several media companies created policies that barred employees from using telephones for non-work-related calls, even in emergencies, and told them to bring personal cell phones to their places of employment for this purpose. Because cell phones were mobile, and employees were footing the bill, many soon became tempted to leave their work stations to use cell phones in restrooms and other areas of the workplace where a modicum of privacy was assured. In solving one problem with a policy, companies learned, they create another that cannot be policed without violating privacy because of the ubiquitous portability and access of digital gadgets.

More recently, however, companies are using social media monitoring tools to determine what employees are accessing on corporate IT systems. When you are hired by companies using these technologies, you will be asked to sign a document informing you that your supervisor will be able to see what you are viewing during work hours in addition to tracking your keystrokes. Some companies even monitor and fire employees based on what they may be viewing or posting even when not on company time.[25] Typically, personal vs. professional conflicts occur when employees browse shopping or hobby sites on internet rather than focusing on work during office hours. The temptation to browse beckons in any digital or mobile environment that relies on internet. After all, web use has become prevalent at home, school and work, with 84 percent of American adults going online daily, up from about 50 percent in 2000, when the Pew Research Center began tracking such usage.[26] Typical users spend more than $10\frac{1}{2}$ hours online each day, spilling over into work time and influencing work ethic because the allure of the web is omnipresent, especially with mobile technologies, owned by some 81 percent of adults.[27] Thus, it is imperative for employees to use discretion when accessing sites during work hours and to know privacy settings for social media and other online applications.

"In some companies, obscene email jokes are sent through the office and time is spent playing computer games with the sound turned off so as not to attract attention to how their time is actually being spent,"[28] writes Judy Allen in *Event Planning Ethics and Etiquette*. She notes that some employees are oblivious, playing games until management appears at their desks. While Allen believes that companies should have guidelines governing personal smartphone use, these also should be weighed against the fact that event planners on occasion work 14-plus hour days and so need to be in contact with family members. She also notes that new conflicts of interest arise when mobile phone users are contacted by supervisors or do business while driving in vehicles, causing accidents. "The company could face charges," she writes. "The same applies to personal injury. If an employee is injured while their attention is focused on text messaging or picking up emails in their line of work, they may be eligible for workman's compensation."[29]

Internet also is a font of opinions, from profiles on social network sites to personal blogs. From a traditional perspective, newspaper editors often express concern about reporters sharing private opinions about issues they cover. Doing so can hamper balance and fairness, or the public perception thereof. For instance, a newspaper publisher may not want the statehouse reporter proclaiming support for one political party and denouncing another. Increasingly, however, reporters using social media spout off passionately about political and other controversial issues. Online ethicists Robert I. Berkman and Christopher A. Shumway observe in *Digital Dilemmas* that blogging reporters enter murky territory, especially "if the blog is an 'unofficial' one, not sanctioned by the paper where the reporter has his or her 'day job.'"[30]

Andy Alexander, former ombudsman for *The Washington Post*, notes that such conflicts of interest have become subtler and complex in the digital age, associated with issues of influence and bias, real or perceived. "Does a business reporter have an obligation to interact with consumers, or does an economics reporter have an obligation to interact with the have-nots? Should journalists be active in groups—the Boy Scouts, for instance—that take positions on significant social issues like the rights of gays? Does casting a vote show partisanship, even though the ballot is secret?" All of these traditional issues have become more complicated when interactions are made public on omnipresent social media, not only resurrecting arguments about whether objective reporters may express personal opinions but also now lapsing into censorship or prior review involving the very outlets that (a) demand reporters be objective and (b) hold free speech sacrosanct.

Anita Bruzzese, a freelance writer and business book author who has written for national publications such as *USA Today*, recounts a digital conflict that arose when she was hired by a top news/popular culture site to write about workplace and career issues. "What I discovered while working for her is that she would often take quite a while to respond to my questions concerning a story. I assumed she was in a meeting or otherwise busy doing editor-type stuff. But I soon discovered this was not the case. She was on Twitter. Often ranting about politics, women's issues, the state of the world, etc. Obviously, it was her personal opinion, but her Twitter bio clearly stated where she worked and her job title.

"It made me uncomfortable."

Bruzzese clings to the ethical standards she learned at Oklahoma State's journalism school. "I don't talk or write about my personal beliefs or opinions, especially when it comes to politics. Before social media, that was usually the case for the editors at magazines or newspapers that hired me. With social media, that has all changed. So, while I still adhere to not stating my personal opinions online or trying to let bias color my work, I cannot say the same of editors like the one I mention."

Bruzzese was concerned about her editor's strong political views accessible by anyone online. "Will sources see that bias and not want to talk to me? Will they assume I have the same views? Will they consider me biased simply because I write for a site that lets their journalists do what they want online?"

Her dilemma was solved when the editor was fired, along with about 30 others staffers, in a layoff. "The editor has gone on to work for another site, but I've steered clear. It's definitely a lesson learned. I'm not sure how other freelancers deal with it, but I know that I am more careful these days about writing for those I believe have clear guidelines about what their writers and editors can and cannot do. As the old saying goes, 'You're often known by the company you keep.'"

These types of new conflicts are arising daily associated with internet. Traditional newspaper reporters are trained to let readers have the last word, especially in letters to the editor. Corrections and apologies aside, an opinion page editor would discipline any reporter composing a letter to the editor in response to reader criticism of his or her reporting. However, because newspapers have online editions encouraging interactivity in comments appended to coverage, with email addresses of reporters also shared for further digital interaction, journalists are tempted to "correct" opinions about their work. In doing so reporters may exercise poor judgment and respond personally, condescendingly or even offensively in emails or through the comments section. Many newspaper and broadcast ethics codes have no clauses providing guidelines in such cases, resulting in unforeseen professional vs. professional conflicts. For instance, the text of a reporter's email can be selected, copied and pasted to a blog for all to see. Reporters may claim that their message to a reader was personal and not intended for mass dissemination in a blog. However, a First Amendment purist might argue that if the journalist wrote what he or she wrote in an email, why shouldn't the blogger have the right to post that? As such, media professionals now have to ponder these new moral wrinkles because, frequently, the only gatekeepers in the internet age are one's conscience and awareness.

To guard against the temptation to reply digitally and aggressively, employees across media platforms have to ascertain the possible consequences, just as in any ethics issue. For instance, if a reporter responds to a blog critical of his or her work, would doing so make the reporter part of the story, traditionally taboo in the news media, depending on what was said? Sooner or later a journalist's comments are going to get back to an editor who usually wants reporters to stand by their words rather than stand up to readers who question them because the latter can end up maligning the audience. To further complicate the situation, typically reporters also are asked to maintain blogs and microblog during assignments when they are expected to interact with followers. The best advice is to read your outlet's or agency's guidebook on what is expected of you concerning audience interaction, especially on blogs and social media.

National Public Radio has published an *Ethics Handbook*, accessible online, that carefully spells out these expectations. The handbook asks reporters to use the same ethical standards in social media as on the NPR news site and warns against citing anonymous posts in any official report. According to the handbook, "When it comes to criticism of the work done by NPR's journalists, we treat our colleagues as we hope they would treat us. If we have something critical to say, we say it to their face— not on social media."[31] The handbook contains a wealth of information that applies not only to NPR but to journalism outlets (and even PR and advertising agencies) on internet etiquette involving potential conflicts of interest. In particular, a section focuses on audience criticism in comments or social media. While acknowledging that journalists are empowered by reporting news and commentary, NPR also cautions that its employees "do not have to put up being personally attacked because of our gender, race, religion or any other identifying factor."[32] The handbook notes two types of situations: an unpleasant but non-threatening comment directed at the employee; and one that actually does threaten the employee. In the first case, the employee should ask in a civil tone about any concerns a viewer or listener might have about content. Often, it states, a constructive exchange can ensue. In the second case, the handbook cautions the employee not to respond but forward the correspondence to NPR's internal distribution hub where it will be reviewed by the company's Legal, Security and News Operations personnel.

The internet can better fulfill its promise of being a medium of information rather than of distraction when basic ethics are followed. In sum, in the absence of any corporate guidelines, media practitioners must foresee the possible consequences of any online response by:

- **Determining whether the email or post will undermine your credibility.** It is better to stand by your facts and let them speak for you because they will do a better job.
- **Creating a conflict of interest (especially with your supervisor).** It is better to let the audience or clientele have the last word than escalate an exchange that ultimately will be reviewed by your supervisor.
- **Lapsing into unfairness through personal rather than professional rejoinders.** It is better to maintain your cool and credibility rather than lose them online. This tenet also applies to your personal exchanges on social media that may be shared by friends or followers.
- **Refusing to respond to threatening, sexist or racist comments directed at you or your company.** Immediately forward such correspondence to your supervisor for legal review.
- **Being wary about viewers who praise your work and especially ones who want to meet with you for useful tips.** Always maintain a professional, skeptical demeanor and never agree to meet with any unknown viewer no matter how tantalizing a news or client tip might seem to be. Your safety comes first. News and client tips can be shared in email or text. Gone are the days when reporters meet sources at 2 a.m. in empty parking garages.

Internal Legal Conflicts

Dan Winters, award-winning television anchor for NBC affiliate WHO-TV, describes a type of conflict of interest that regularly occurs within newsrooms and is seldom discussed. In the segment that follows, Winters recounts what occurred at another television station earlier in his career involving an investigative story about suspected malpractice of a local dentist.

"I had the documents, X-rays, and expert interviews that proved a local dentist was filling cavities that didn't exist. He was drilling holes in perfectly healthy teeth and billing the patients accordingly. I was all set to confront the dentist on-camera, until our station's corporate counsel at the time refused to allow it." Winters was instructed to present his findings to the dentist and request a sit-down interview so that he could respond. The dentist declined. "He later made a veiled threat of a lawsuit if we aired the story," Winters notes.

"Our attorney's reaction was to forbid me to publicly identify the dentist. At that time, the TV station I worked for was owned by a private equity firm. It was in the process of being sold. I was told litigation could have jeopardized the sale. I was dumbfounded. From my perspective, withholding the dentist's identity would allow him to continue harming unsuspecting patients and future patients. We had a duty to warn our viewers. We had information that could save them from irreparable harm."

When Winters was in college, he assumed threats to his stories would always come from external forces. "It didn't occur to me that journalism corporations have interests to protect, and that internal dilemmas can arise. I still don't like it, but it would be foolish to pretend it's not real. Fact: Reporters don't get to decide legal matters for their employers." Winters did have one decision to make. Should he scrap an important public health story? Or should he figure out a way to tell the dentist story so that his viewers would get valuable and actionable information? "I decided the story had to be told.

"With my news director's blessing, and that of our corporate counsel, I crafted a story that warned our viewers about a shady dentist we knew was practicing in our community. We called him 'Dr. Dozen,' based on the number of cavities he told a patient she needed to have filled. We presented the documentation and expert testimony from other dentists, including a dental school professor. We sent one of our producers to several local dentists, including Dr. Dozen, to receive treatment plans. We illustrated disparity among diagnoses, and the gray area that can arise when it comes to identifying cavities.

"The result? We started out with a story that mattered to patients and potential patients of 'Dr. Dozen.' We ended up with a story that affected everyone who watched it. By concealing Dr. Dozen's identity, we revealed to our viewers the importance of establishing a relationship with a trustworthy dentist, and the need to seek a second opinion if something doesn't seem to add up.

"I maintain that it would have been in our viewers' best interest for us to have exposed Dr. Dozen. Under different circumstances, I believe we would have had the attorney's blessing. This story taught me to find creative ways to broaden a story's appeal, to inform as many viewers as possible, and to never let failed attempts at perfection ruin stories that are still worthy of being told."

Compassionate Conflicts

Andy Alexander, quoted earlier in this chapter, says most reputable newspapers have written or online ethics policies and routinely enforce them. Acceptance of gifts in return for favorable stories is grounds for dismissal, he says. But that's an easy ethical call. Other conflicts are more complex, especially ones that might coincidentally appeal to the reporter's conscience.

During the course of a story, Alexander recalls, a veteran member of his reporting staff realized that an indigent couple may have been breaking the law to provide for their two children. The reporter had been working on a story about the debate over whether to raise the minimum wage. "In an attempt to show the struggles faced by minimum wage workers," Alexander says, "the reporter focused on an unskilled, under-educated low-income couple in Youngstown, Ohio. Our reporter worked hard to gain their trust, and in one heart-to-heart discussion the wife confided that the only way they stay above water financially is because she receives part of her salary 'under the table' from the donut shop where she works." This kept the couple's taxable income below a threshold enabling them to receive food stamps. "It's clearly illegal, and the donut shop owner is also operating outside the law," Alexander notes.

"I was relating this to a journalism class at a local university and asked what they would do if they were the reporter." The universal response was, *Expose the couple in print! Nail them for fraud!* But these were struggling parents of limited education and sophistication, Alexander countered, asking students whether there should be a newsroom discussion on the dilemma. "At what point does a reporter have an obligation to protect people who are not media-savvy? How might the children suffer if a prosecutor, reading this in a newspaper, decided to press charges?" These are questions associated with the value of compassion, to be covered later in *Living Media Ethics.*

In this case, the reporter and her editors, including Alexander, decided the proper course was to go back to the couple "and explain that it was important that we print this admission about 'under the table' income because it was true, and it also illustrated the dilemma faced by minimum-wage couples struggling to survive. We also explained the possible legal ramifications. In light of that, we asked, did they wish to continue co-operating on the story? They didn't, and we found another couple." As such, the conflict was resolved through transparency. However, the student responses disturbed in as much as "they saw no ethical question in any of this. They had a linear view of news, with no real concern of whether the reporter had any obligation beyond simply reporting what was said. I have to believe that they were being shortchanged in that their journalism education apparently did not sensitize them to ethical nuances like this."

Religious and Relationship Conflicts

Chris Thomas is the owner of The Intrepid Group and has managed more than a dozen crises for organizations ranging from non-profits to a large international corporation. His most high-profile work was for the Elizabeth Smart family. He began working as their official publicist shortly after 14-year-old Elizabeth was abducted at night from her home in front of her younger sister in June 2002. Feared killed, the girl was found nine months later in the presence of a couple who later were charged with the abduction.

"As for my own personal ethics and values," he says, "which I share from a religious standpoint as a member of the Church of Jesus Christ of Latter-day Saints, I do not partake of alcohol or drugs." His agency was contacted to handle an account for smokeless tobacco. "We were told, 'It's yours and for a lot of money.' We weren't interested even in talking about that account. We sure could have used the money, but we don't believe in the product." In this case, Thomas favored his religious-based value over the secular one of earning top dollar at his agency. He cites another example associated with his religious values. His agency handles tourism accounts and received a request for a proposal from a casino that seemed grounded in tourism rather than gambling. "But then the client made it clear that young single men were the target, and the objective was to get them drunk so that they could spend a lot of money. We resigned the account. We're not going to go there. Also, if I know a potential client is lying, I'm not going to take on that account, either."

In resolving conflicts, journalism students need not base decisions on religious values, Thomas says. But they should determine their ethical boundaries as soon as possible, knowing what they will and will not do in their chosen media profession. "There will be every temptation in the world at work," he says, and many will center on money. "Personally, and professionally, we have had situations where we realize that the almighty dollar is not the most important thing in the business. There have been times when the boundary of family comes first."

Typically, however, recent college graduates are striking out on their own, renting an apartment without roommates for the first time and relocating to a city where they have no family or friends. Jessie Opoien, political reporter for the *Capital Times* in Madison, Wisconsin, says just going about your normal social routine in a new city can bring you into contact with people who later become sources, or something more: dating prospects. "This is made even more difficult if you're single and looking to date," she says. "I've found myself jealous, at times, of my older colleagues who are already married or otherwise attached and don't have to worry about dating from a pool of people that could potentially create conflicts of interest. The one piece of advice I can offer on this is to be as open and forthcoming with your editors as possible if you see an issue like this presenting itself. When I developed feelings for a source to the point that we were considering dating, I talked to my editor about it. Having a chat with my boss about my love life isn't my idea of a good time, but by doing so, we were able to come up with a clear plan to approach the situation, and I was able to feel confident that I was acting appropriately." Opoien chose the correct route in being open and transparent with her editor.

Sometimes, however, couples who work for different companies encounter a more complex relationship conflict. Two public relations practitioners, Diana and Steve, worked for different firms in Cleveland, Ohio, and learned about the complexity of family conflicts before they had a family.[33] "One week before our wedding I was offered a new job," Diana says, "and Steve's firm offered him money to postpone our wedding. ... He was working on a deal and his employer didn't want him to leave for our honeymoon." Diana resolved her conflict by telling her new company that the wedding would come first. Steve, however, took more time to decide his conflict of interest. Some would argue that any decision to postpone the wedding depends on the amount of money the bridegroom was to receive from his firm. Others would criticize that criterion, opting for "family comes first"—in this case, the parents and relatives who had been planning the wedding for months. Many would say this is a test of how successful the new couple would relate to issues involving money and family. After all, money (or lack of it) ranks among top causes of martial strife. Shouldn't newlyweds ensure their bond monetarily as well as romantically? If so, do they have a price on any number of family issues—the postponement of events such as anniversaries, graduations and reunions? Moreover, if a company realizes that an employee can be bought off, will it continually violate family boundaries in favor of business ones? In Steve's case, Diana states, "he didn't take the money (I'm proud to say) and we went on our honeymoon to Hawaii." Doing so established a boundary for the couple, elevating the importance of their relationship, and like the religious boundaries of Chris Thomas, was a guide to resolve future conflicts.

Diversity Conflicts

Avelia Baya Sanchez-Crynes, a former minority relations analyst for a large petroleum company, had to reconcile her personal beliefs about diversity with her professional beliefs about fairness. At the time, her job responsibility was to establish a rapport with Women and Minority Engineering Programs across the nation. "Traditionally," she says, "the field of engineering has been dominated by white males. In addition, the working environment for women and minority engineers was somewhat hostile. My assignment was to devise a creative public relations plan that would give my organization credibility with the women and minority engineering students."

Sanchez-Crynes produced a video designed to appeal to a diverse audience. "The video opened with the vice president of the company who was Native American talking about value of diversity. The video portrayed the organization as a multicultural company. I purposely selected female and minority engineers for the video: a Hispanic male who spoke in Spanish and English, a Native American female who spoke in English and Navajo, and a white female and black male.

"My dilemma," Sanchez-Crynes continues, "was that the video portrayed the organization as a multicultural company that was committed to diversity." In reality, 6 percent of the company's employees were minorities and 16 percent were female. "The company was moving very slowly toward work force diversity," she adds. "So I had to ask myself, 'Is this video misleading?' I knew that as students viewed the video that they might get the impression that the organization would provide them with role models and mentors of like background. I also knew that women and minority engineering students looked for organizations that employed a significant number of women and minority professionals, to avoid a hostile work environment."

Sanchez-Crynes decided to discuss this conflict of interests with her supervisor in the Human Relations Division. Together they reviewed the contents of the video and redefined its objectives. They determined that the video's contents illustrated how other women and minority engineers obtained their professional goals. But the real objective of the video was to educate the students on how to conduct successful job interviews and succeed in industry. "We all agreed that the video would serve as an educational tool for the college students making the transition from academia to industry. We also felt that the video would serve as an educational tool for the company's managers and employees concerning the need for a diverse work force."

By discussing her concerns with her supervisor, Sanchez-Crynes was able to avoid a conflict of two equal but important values: her desire to succeed in her job vs. her commitment to diversity. Instead of initiating a confrontation about minority hiring at her company, Sanchez-Crynes was able to use the video to serve her target audience—college students—and educate managers about the positive aspects of diversity.

The lesson here involves discussing ethical concerns with an immediate supervisor and deciding how to revise the product so that its theme or message is clear and truthful, all the while cleaving to values—in this case, a commitment to diversity—which also guided her work ethic.

Figure 7.1 "Brian": Photograph by John Kaplan, reprinted with permission.

Visual Conflicts

John Kaplan, one of America's most accomplished photojournalists, has won the Pulitzer Prize for Feature Photography, along with other professional honors, including the National Photographer of the Year, the Overseas Press Club Award, two Robert F. Kennedy Awards and the Nikon Documentary Sabbatical Grant.

The picture titled "Brian" was part of the 1992 Pulitzer Prize-winning series for feature photography, "21: Age Twenty-One in America." Kaplan's goal was to follow the diverse lifestyles of young Americans. "Some I chronicled were the types of people we might dream about becoming as we grow up, such as a rock star, a New York model, a Harvard student and an NFL football player. Some were left behind by society such as an unemployed man in Appalachia, a Mexican immigrant mother without the benefit of citizenship, and Brian, who was born into a life of opportunity but made bad choices and became a prostitute in San Francisco."

Kaplan establishes a working relationship with the people whom he photographs. Before he begins a long-term photo project, he interviews potential subjects to learn about daily activities and motivations. He wants to account for their life choices and everyday perspectives, to avoid depicting them superficially. "Brian's tragedy was that his motivation was to find a way to get the money to buy Speed," Kaplan notes. "This was at the core of who he was, and he put himself on a cycle constantly spiraling down. He would sell himself as needed to get money to shoot up. He had a cheerful, outgoing personality but was an insecure person deep down. He looked well-dressed but only had a couple of changes of clothes and was essentially homeless.

"When he asked me if I wanted to see him shoot up, I worried that he was almost trying to please me. And I could have never dealt with the guilt if I thought I was encouraging him. What if I had said yes and he then died from an overdose?"

At this point Kaplan decided to tell Brian about photojournalism ethics. "This was the only time I can think of in my career where I felt I must explain the boundaries of my field," Kaplan notes, "and my own comfort level. He was an intelligent man and I think he appreciated that I was willing to talk with him about deeper issues. I always say to my subjects, 'In exchange for your time and your trust, I promise I won't exploit you.' When I say that, it's not some sales pitch or a slogan. I think long and hard to myself about what that really means." Because of this commitment, Kaplan says, his work has become known for its ability to depict the internal lives of people. So he had a long conversation with Brian about photographing him shooting up, "and I finally told him that if he was going to do it anyway, I'd photograph it. But only if he was not doing it for my benefit, I insisted."

Kaplan acknowledges that his choice was to photograph the situation or walk away, using the rest of the images without the one of him shooting up. "But I felt the picture was essential to the project because truly the most important thing to him was shooting up. He told me that day, 'I need to get high, high as a kite, and then deal with the world.'"

Kaplan's professional conflict was complex on several levels. He didn't want to suggest in the slightest what Brian should or should not do in his presence. Also, on a personal level, Kaplan had compassion for him. Professionally, he believed the tenets of social responsibility required him to document the scene. But he also was documenting a crime. Did that obligate him personally to ignore the crime, notify the authorities or get Brian help?

Here is how Kaplan explains it:

"I don't think it is the journalist's role to act as policeman. If I size up any given situation and believe a subject is in immediate danger, of course I would always act first as a person and try to get immediate help. But the journalist is not a social worker. In fact, social workers were aware of Brian and touched base with him regularly, along with the street walkers on San Francisco's Polk Street. In terms of responsibility, I felt for Brian's situation and believed he could really turn things around and make something positive of his life. Others did, too. He was a likeable person and I saw many try to help him.

"Brian is the only subject I've ever photographed that I actually sat down and said, 'Man, you are throwing your life away.' He thought he was just 'partying' and ignored the very real possibility he'd get AIDS or possibly overdose. Brian had a great deal of potential as a person and was from an upscale family in the Washington suburbs. But he was rejected by his parents after coming out to them. He left home, went to San Francisco, and unfortunately made some dangerous life choices."

Kaplan, a journalism professor at the University of Florida, advises students to ponder their commitment to truth and authenticity. "Are you being true to your subjects?" Kaplan asks. "Are you being fair? What is your responsibility to the greater good that journalism does in a free society? Are you seeking balance between doing your job well with doing the right thing for your own moral code?" Journalists and practitioners may have different answers to these questions, he admits. But contemplating them is vital in resolving conflicts. "In journalism," Kaplan says, "our collective diversity is our strength."

Here is a process to help you decide what action to take in resolving similar conflicts:

1. Consequences

Because temptation usually involves unforeseen conflicts, consequences can be greater than you anticipate.

Ask yourself:

- *What is the worst-case scenario I could experience by resolving conflicting interests or values by ...*

    (a) choosing one over the other?

(b)   amending one or both?

(c)   coming up with one or more new values?

- *In each case, am I willing to pay that price?*
- *How will each resolution change me as a person? as a media professional?*

2. Short- and Long-Term Effects

Because temptation usually offers immediate relief to a pressing conflict, the short- and long-term effects often differ greatly.

Ask yourself:

- *Is the relief that resolution offers worth ...*

    (a)   compromising one value for another?

    (b)   amending one value to keep another?

    (c)   coming up with new values to replace one or more of my old ones?

- *If I choose (a), (b) or (c), where will I draw the line the next time I have to resolve a similar conflict?*
- *How will my personal or professional interests change over the short and long term if I choose (a), (b) or (c)?*

3. Sound Judgment

Because temptation usually involves unforeseen conflicts, you need to assess your current state of mind before acting.

Ask yourself:

- *Are the unforeseen aspects of the conflict causing me to respond in a way I normally wouldn't?*
- *Is the pressure of the conflict clouding my judgment?*
- *Am I imagining or overlooking consequences that are causing me to behave in a manner that I normally wouldn't?*

4. Independent, Voluntary Choices

Because conflicts often pit personal and/or professional values against each other, you need to be sure that your choices—favoring one value over another, amending one or both values to resolve the situation, or conceiving new values—will be voluntary and of your own accord.

Ask yourself:

- *Is consideration for any other person or third party playing a role in my decision?*

- *Is any other person or third party over-influencing my judgment on this matter?*
- *Has any other person or third party influenced how I have gone through the earlier processes of establishing consequences, determining short- and long-term effects, and evaluating judgment?*

Finally, keep in mind that you may not be able to avoid consequences in any conflict of interest. However, by going through the above process, you will decide issues in a manner consistent with your values knowing that you did your best under trying circumstances according to the depth of your conscience and the breadth of your consciousness. That realization alone lessens the pressure associated with temptation and wrongdoing.

It also builds character.

"YOUR OWN CONFLICT RESOLUTION"

Personal Journal Exercise

1. Do two case studies based on your professional (or academic) experience involving:
   - A situation in which you were tempted to but did not compromise your values because of deadlines, competition, ambition or reward.
   - A conflict of two professional values or personal/professional values.

Without naming any individual or otherwise identifying anyone, write a brief summary of the situation for each of your case studies, explaining how you handled the conflict along with the outcome. **Note:** *If you cannot think of any examples from your professional or academic experience, do not invent them but research examples on the web and cite sources accurately.*

Example from personal experience

Situation: I was part of a campaigns class and a member of a student group. My contribution was supposed to be design. I procrastinated. The night before the design project was due, I browsed the internet and saw designs that I could easily adapt as my own.

Clash of values, goals or priorities: I didn't want to disappoint my group. I didn't want to steal a design that wasn't my own.

My choice: I stayed up all night and created my own design. It wasn't great, but at least it was original.

Outcome: My group was disappointed in my work but had suggestions about how I could improve it before deadline.

Note: *As you will be handing this in to your instructor or group leader, do not sign your name to the digital document or printout.*

2. Now run each case study above through the recommended processes concerning temptation (pages 189–90) and conflicts of interest (pages 217–19). Answer questions raised in those processes and record them in your notebook or ethics journal. Do not turn in your answers; analyze them.

3. Write two more summaries, based on the case studies completed in No. 1 above, explaining how, if at all, you would handle each situation *differently* after running them through the processes in No. 2 above.

4. Without referencing any situation that would violate your or someone else's privacy or reputation, create a 500-word journal entry or blog post or short podcast or multimedia presentation on any topic associated with this chapter, including plagiarism and conflicts of interest.

Communal Journal Exercise

Using a mailbox for confidential printouts or drop box for anonymous files, collect the examples from the first "Personal Journal Exercise" above. Assemble ones showing strong ethical values into a digital document to be shared with the class or discussion group. Do not discuss any example that showed poor ethics or in any way could violate anyone's privacy/reputation or disclose identity. Foster a class or group discussion about the wide range of conflicts, the role of temptation in them and the processes in this chapter that seek ethical conflict resolution.

NOTES

1 Anita L. Allen, *The New Ethics: A Guided Tour of the Twenty-First Century Moral Landscape* (New York: Hyperion, 2004), 10.

2 Ibid.

3 Daniel Goleman, *Emotional Intelligence* (New York: Bantam Books, 1995), 53.

4 Ibid., 81.

5 Dorothy Giobbe, "Unauthorized Entry," *Editor & Publisher*, March 5, 1994, 11.

6 Robert, Mackey, "Rupert Murdoch Apologizes to Victims of Phone Hacking," The Lede: *The New York Times* news blog, July 15, 2011, https://thelede.blogs.nytimes.com/2011/07/15/complete-text-rupert-murdochs-apology/?mcubz=3

7 Julie J.C.H. Ryan, "Student Plagiarism in an Online World," *ASEE Prism Magazine*, December 1998, www.asee.org/prism/december/html/student_plagiarism_in_an_onlin.htm

8 Sara Rimer, "A Campus Fad That's Being Copied: Internet Plagiarism Seems on the Rise," *The New York Times*, September 3, 2003, Section B, 7.

9 Ibid.

10 "Marc Kosa Responds," letter in *News Photographer*, March 1978, 38.

11 *60 Minutes*, "Stephen Glass, 'I Lied for Esteem,' interview with correspondent Steve Kroft, August 17, 2003, www.cbsnews.com/stories/2003/05/07/60minutes/main552819.shtml

12 Ibid.

13 See "J-School Dean Resigns in Plagiarism Controversy," *Editor & Publisher*, July 20, 1991, 11.

14 "Times Confesses: 'Improperly Dependent,'" *Editor & Publisher*, July 20, 1991, 11.

15 For the full apology by Meredith McIver, see "To Whom It May Concern," July 20, 2016, http://i2.cdn.turner.com/cnn/2016/images/07/20/meredithstatement.pdf

16 Rachael Revesz, "Meredith McIver: The Mystery of the Trump Employee Behind Melania's Plagiarised RNC 2016 Speech: A Ghost Writer or a Ghost?," *The Independent*, July 20, 2016, www.independent.co.uk/news/world/americas/meredith-mciver-rnc-speechwriter-melania-trump-donald-trump-allias-a7147081.html

17 Jeremy Stahl, "Yes, Melania Speech Fall Woman Meredith McIver Is Real. Here's Proof," *Slate*, July 20, 2016, www.slate.com/blogs/the_slatest/2016/07/20/yes_meredith_mciver_is_a_real_person_here_s_proof.html

18 Andrea Tortora, "What J-Profs Should Be Teaching You," *Editor & Publisher*, July 22, 1995, 48.

19 Andrea Tortora, notes from a telephone conversation provided to the author of *Living Media Ethics*. Tortora also observes that the editor in question later retracted his statement about coincidence and apologized for his mistake. Tortora adds in an interview: "My thoughts on all of this? I find it only fitting that I learned yet another valuable lesson and had another 'journalistic experience' from an article I wrote about what professors should be teaching you."

20 David Zhou, "Sophomore's New Book Contains Passages Strikingly Similar to 2001 Novel," *The Harvard Crimson*, April 23, 2006, www.thecrimson.com/article.aspx?ref=512968

21 Chip Scanlan, "The Tale of a Chick-Lit Plagiarist," Poynteronline, April 28, 2006, www.poynter.org/column.asp?id=52&aid=100604

22 According to Ohio University Physicist Ken Hicks, interviewed in 1995, "A 67-word plagiarism [coincidence] is theoretically possible but highly unlikely. ... [A] 3,000-word plagiarism is statistically impossible within the time-span of a typical human life."

23 Philip Patterson and Lee Wilkins, *Media Ethics: Issues and Cases*, 8th ed. (New York: McGraw Hill, 2014), 4.

24 D. Martin and D.K. Wright, *Public Relations Ethics: How to Practice PR Without Losing Your Soul* (New York: Business Expert Press, 2016), 18, 19.

25 Natalie Shoemaker, "4 Ways Your Employer May Be Spying on You," *Cheat Sheet*, November 30, 2016, available at www.cheatsheet.com/technology/4-ways-your-employer-could-track-you.html/?a=viewall

26 Andrew Perrin and Maeve Duggan, "Americans' Internet Access, 2000–2015," Pew Research Center, June 26, 2015, available from www. pewinternet.org/2015/06/26/americans-internet-access-2000-2015/

27 Jacqueline Howard, "Americans Devote More Than 10 Hours a Day to Screen Time, and Growing," CNN, July 29, 2016, available from www. cnn.com/2016/06/30/health/americans-screen-time-nielsen/index. html

28 Judy Allen, *Event Planning Ethics and Etiquette* (Ontario, John Wiley & Sons, 2003), 135–36.

29 Ibid., 136.

30 Robert I. Berkman and Christopher A. Shumway, *Digital Dilemmas: Ethical Issues for Online Media Professionals* (Ames, Iowa: Iowa State Press, 2003), 81.

31 No author, Social Media, NPR Ethics Handbook, July 2017 update, at http://ethics.npr.org/tag/social-media/

32 Ibid.

33 One of the practitioners was a former student of *Living Media Ethics* author Michael Bugeja and related the conflict of interest to him in letters.

CHAPTER 8

Bias: Recognize and Resist It

ARE YOU ACKNOWLEDGING DIVERSITY?

An irony exists about diversity in our technological age. Home offices are equipped with smartphones, tablets, desk- and laptops and all manner of digital devices able to access libraries, databanks and other information networks. Addresses for sources and clients are on internet rather than on streets. Since 2010, media corporations have been downsizing staffs because work can easily be outsourced to anyone who owns compatible hard- and software to create content or visuals and transmit them digitally at any hour, any day, in virtual space. While we cloister indoors at our work stations, communities are becoming more diverse. Are we acknowledging that? Even when in the company of others on the public street, we are apt to be texting and looking at smartphones rather than each other. As technology engages us, holding our attention, society in real place and time has changed. It's time we paid attention.

Audrey Singer, immigration fellow at the Brookings Institution, writes that the racial profile of the United States differs significantly from that of the past century. Forty years ago, most Americans could be easily categorized as white or black (even though such a depiction wouldn't apply in areas of the Southwest, for instance, which had significant Latino/a populations then, or the Plains states with American Indians and West Coast with generations of Asian Americans). In any case, Singer states, "The national portrait is being increasingly enriched with Asian, Latino, and multiracial people. High levels of immigration, intermarriage between groups, and the resulting offspring, as well as an important change in the methods by which the U.S. government collects information on its residents"—allowing them to check more than one racial box on Census forms—"all contribute to the incremental changes observed during the past few decades."[1]

It is increasingly as difficult to categorize people by sex as by race. As Gail Dines and Jean M. Humez observe in *Gender, Race, and Class in Media*, the term *gender* has acquired a new range of meaning in diverse society since 1990. "In queer theory," they write, "gender, sexuality, and desire are ambiguous, shifting, unstable, and too complex to fit neatly into a binary system."[2] The U.S. Census is including a new category in 2020 for same-sex marriage. People now will have a choice, filling out boxes for "opposite-sex" and "same-sex" spouses/unmarried partners. Approximately 0.6% of the U.S. population is transgender, experiencing health and medical disparities because their sex does not qualify them for inclusion or treatment in many venues; however, government and research organizations are addressing this and may expand documents, surveys and other sex/gender measures to be trans inclusive.[3]

Great disparities also exist in social class, as witnessed during the devastation of New Orleans by Hurricane *Katrina* (2005) and, later, the Houston area by Hurricane Harvey. A decade after *Katrina*, the Pew Research Center noted mass media's indelible impact: "From the start, the tragedy had a powerful racial component – images of poor, mostly black New Orleans residents stranded on rooftops and crowded amid fetid conditions in what was then the Louisiana Superdome."[4] A comprehensive study showed the almost half of the 971 deaths in Louisiana (49 percent) were the elderly age 75 and older; and while 51 percent of all victims were black as opposed to 42 percent for whites, "In Orleans Parish, the mortality rate among blacks was 1.7 to 4 times higher than that among whites for all people 18 years old and older."[5] A dozen years later, when *Harvey* hit, we were habituated to images of under-represented groups in urban areas suffering calamity. In a 2005 interview, Sidmel Estes-Sumpter, executive producer of WAGA-TV, Atlanta, and past president of UNITY: Journalists of Color, Inc., put the *Katrina* images in perspective. "We knew that poverty exists, but I don't think we knew the level of poverty because that topic was ignored by the media in New Orleans," she said. "The media didn't care. If poor people aren't able to buy their product, they were overlooked as part of the community."

Historically the elderly—who typically fall victim at greater rates in natural disasters—also had been overlooked because of decreased earning power due to retirement. While *Katrina* showed us images of African Americans, *Harvey* showed us images of the elderly. According to the Institute for Health Care Policy & Innovation at the University of Michigan,

> News and social media reports from coastal Texas have shown many striking images of Hurricane Harvey flood victims, but few were as arresting as a photo of older women in a Dickinson nursing home, sitting in waist-high water in their wheelchairs. Although the women were moved to safety, the picture highlighted how vulnerable older adults can be during and after major disasters.[6]

Meanwhile, the aging of America continues to spiral upward in large part because of increased longevity. A 2016 report by the Joint Center for Housing Studies at Harvard University noted the number of people aged 70 and over is anticipated to rise in the next few decades by 28 million at a growth rate of 90 percent, with one in five people aged 65 and older by 2035.[7]

Social class is showing wide gaps in disparity, too. The top 1 percent has been pulling away from the rest of the 99 percent in America for years now, according to the Brookings Institution. But that doesn't fully explain the disparity by social class, in as much as one group, the Upper Middle Class (top 20 percent by household income), has outdistanced itself from the rest of the country in earnings and influence. According to a Brookings Institution article titled "The Dangerous Separation of the American Upper Middle Class," mass media tends to focus on

> the impact of the super-rich on American politics, and rightly so. ... But while the Trumps and Kochs and Buffetts have the money to fund presidential campaigns, the upper middle class have plenty of political clout, too. They vote, they organize, they lobby, they complain: and their voices are heard.[8]

No matter how you view it, or what you think about it, our world is becoming more diverse ethnically, socially and longevously as it becomes more accessible electronically. Media professionals are working in narrower electronic spaces while communities outside Windows® are changing demographically and attitudinally. That places a big responsibility on professionals in digital and mobile environments at home, school or work. Journalists and practitioners utilize technology in almost everything they do. Even outdoors, they can be found using smartphones, multitasking on deadline "24/7," a symbol associated with round-the-clock cable TV coverage. Our audience or clientele may actually experience the richness of diversity in real places more often than professionals covering it in virtual spaces, especially since technology cuts into leisure time, which used to be spent in community with others without digital distractions.

RECOGNIZE MISPERCEPTIONS ABOUT RACE

Economic factors linked to downsizing may explain why some media professionals are tethered to computer cords at home and at work. Those factors will be explored in the chapter on power later in *Living Media Ethics*. For the moment, the issue concerns how media professionals depict society without fully experiencing the diversity of it. In *Blink: The Power of Thinking Without Thinking*, Malcolm Gladwell notes that absence from community can result in patterns of positive and negative associations based on race alone. For instance, people with a pro-white pattern of associations will behave differently among blacks:

> In all likelihood, you won't be aware that you're behaving any differently than you would around a white person. But chances are you'll lean forward a little less, turn away slightly from him or her, close your body a little bit, be a little less expressive, maintain less eye contact, stand

a little farther away, smile a lot less, hesitate and stumble over your words a bit more, laugh at jokes a bit less.[9]

As Gladwell notes, these things matter when an occasion such as a job interview requires face-to-face communication, during which words and gestures can influence hiring decisions, making a person seem less confident or more standoffish. The white person in such an exchange may not be racist but may come across as biased for the mere fact that he or she did not sufficiently experience diversity, leading to discernable racial associations.

Case in point: Avelia Baya Sanchez-Crynes, a skilled public relations practitioner, remembers how she felt applying for jobs shortly after graduating from college. "The posting of each job stated that women and minorities were highly encouraged to apply," she recalls. "During each interview, I would be asked if I could relate to African Americans or if I could relate to white females. After all, being a Hispanic female how could I possibly *not* relate to these individuals?"

Interviewers consistently overlooked her professional abilities, Sanchez-Crynes continues. "I distinctly remember one interview in which the interviewer had the audacity to ask if I could speak 'jive.' Not once did the interviewer ask if I could speak Spanish, so why did it matter if I could speak 'jive' as the interviewer so pathetically inquired?"

Sanchez-Crynes eventually secured a position with a major corporation based on her ability to address minority issues and recruit African, Hispanic and American Indians. "The interviewer was impressed and surprised that I had been raised and educated in a predominantly African American environment. Finally," Sanchez-Crynes says, "I had been given the chance to prove myself. After the first year of employment, I had broken every record held within the department and developed several new public relations campaigns, which were quite successful."

Stereotypes as expressed in Sanchez-Crynes' initial job interview also show how labels deprive others of opportunity so that minorities have to work doubly hard to prove themselves in settings that purport to follow equal opportunity procedures. That is why many ethicists and educators, along with media professionals, have committed themselves to end discriminatory or racist practices across platforms. One such industry leader is Mei-Mei Chan, now retired, who rose to the position of Florida Regional President at Gannett. She notes that once hired, people of color face challenges other new hires do not. "Because they stand out so visibly," she states, "they are held to higher standards. They are expected to be better than adequate, to prove they deserved being hired. 'Being average' is perceived by some observers as failure. Rather than taking time and effort to train minorities (and everyone else), managers are schooled in the 'sink or swim' method. When a white person sinks, it's just more driftwood. When a person of color sinks, it's an indictment of the whole race. Those minorities who do rise, and who are not prepared or trained for their new tasks, are viewed as another example of affirmative action at its worst."

These last observations are associated with racism. *The Random House Dictionary of the English Language* defines racism "as a belief or doctrine that inherent differences among the various human races determine cultural or individual achievement, usually involving the idea that one's own race is superior and has the right to rule others."[10] According to Jonah Berger in *Invisible Influence: The Hidden Forces that Shape Behavior*, "From an early age, middle- and upper-class American children are taught that they are 'special flowers' waiting to bloom," given the opportunity, autonomy and choice to control their destinies.[11] This is a kind of privilege that many people from under-represented groups seldom experience. Whether or not you believe that this is so, as a professional communicator your role is to acknowledge that the perception exists and then to engage others with sensitivity.

The desire to be associated with a race or ethnic group is a basic human instinct, according to Pat Shipman, author of *The Evolution of Racism: Human Differences and the Use and Misuse of Science*. "And it is in this instinct that racism is anchored," Shipman notes, "for racism is little more than a strong identification with one group, combined with fear and dislike of all others. Typically, the fear and dislike are fueled by unfavorable stereotypes, falsehoods, and half-truths, which serve to reinforce groups' boundaries."[12]

EXPLORE BIAS ACROSS PLATFORMS

Unfavorable stereotypes, falsehoods and half-truths are ethical issues across platforms. They not only apply to race but also to sex, social class, age, disability and other lifestyles and segments of society historically excluded from "shared community," an inclusive term associated with schools, churches, government, commerce, residential areas and other places where people gather or that they rely on in the course of living their lives. To explore bias across platforms, we should define other concepts, beginning with the philosophical term "tolerance," which has become pejorative, as in the sentence, "I will tolerate you at the workplace." Mahatma Gandhi and Martin Luther King, Jr. practiced tolerance because its antonym, "intolerance," defined how they were treated by the British in India and whites in North America. *The Random House Dictionary* defines tolerance as "a fair, objective attitude toward those whose opinions, practices, race, religion, nationality, etc., differ from one's own; freedom from bigotry. Interest in and concern for ideas, opinions and practices, etc., foreign to one's own; a liberal, undogmatic viewpoint. The act or capacity of enduring; endurance."[13] These definitions also happen to be ethical values across media platforms, illustrating the moral foundation that undergirds the practice of journalism and communication. As emphasized in the second chapter on influence, the ethical media professional tries to see the world as it actually is, adjusting for cultural, familial, personal and/or generational filters. The goal of tolerance is to see others as they actually are, too—members of the same species—with conscience and consciousness like yours, seeking a place in a shared community and world. Tolerance is an inclusive value. However, if the pejorative meaning of that term, "toleration," causes you to lose focus on the philosophical meaning, "tolerance," then substitute the term "inclusivity."

There are a few more concepts associated with bias:

- **Cultural exclusion** or the prevention or condemnation of certain viewpoints, ideas or practices in shared community.
- **Cultural inclusion** or welcoming diverse viewpoints, ideas or practices in shared community.
- **Racial inappropriateness** or using stereotypical behavior, language, content or images offensive to one or more individuals or groups in shared community.
- **Sensitivity** or an appropriate sense of occasion—behavior, language, content or images that takes into account the time, place, viewpoints, ideas or practices of one or more individuals or groups in shared community.

These definitions help us avoid easy rhetorical arguments about political correctness or other labels. For instance, a racially inappropriate person may or may not embrace racism or cultural exclusion but simply may lack sensitivity. A tolerant person may be insensitive on occasion because his or her consciousness is not yet fully developed or has been dulled by media consumption. (What you let into your ears—offensive lyrics, say—may come out of your mouth.)

"Bias is most often manifest in journalism education and industry as a lack of racial, gender, cultural, religious or intellectual diversity," says Shirley Staples Carter, journalism professor and former director of the School of Journalism and Mass Communications at the University of South Carolina. Carter, who has worked professionally in print and broadcast journalism, believes that educators and professionals have a social obligation to instill in students and employees "the values and competencies that allow them to gather and report news that reflects our increasingly diverse society." Carter agrees that the tenets of tolerance as stated earlier segue nicely into ethical journalism and media practice, and as such, should be emphasized across curricula in colleges and across platforms in media.

Diversity is a mindset, just like ethics. You practice it as a matter of conscience and a fact of consciousness. You commit to it regardless of skin color or locale. Carter, who has helped accredit journalism schools, says she is often "amazed at how creative some programs are in parts of the country that are less diverse than others in terms of populations served, but who have nonetheless developed courses or implemented programs and activities designed to expose their students to diverse perspectives and beliefs." Conversely, she observes, a journalism program in the South, while serving a more diverse population area, "may have problems dealing with racial issues that are less prevalent in other parts of the country. Yet, the very nature of that environment can provide a significant learning laboratory." For instance, students in her journalism program have a capstone experience that allows them to relive the history of place, learning first-hand about struggles of blacks on a number of topics, including an end to desegregation in public schools. Once again, this is sound journalism practice. Place inspires creativity as well as inclusivity. Historical events serve as powerful storytelling tools "and a method for students to learn fair and balanced reporting," Carter says. "This is an effective way to combat bias across platforms."

CULTURAL BIASES TAINT THE WORKPLACE

The U.S.–Vietnam War (1960–75) is a part of history. Journalist and author Lady Borton, who formerly served with the American Friends Service Committee, speaks about cultural bias tainting news reports during that war. "We all have our biases," she says, noting that reporters often disguise theirs or fail to take them into account. "You saw this especially during the Vietnam War," Borton adds. "Journalists almost never talked to the Vietnamese because they couldn't speak the language." Failing to interact with the people, journalists could not tell the entire story to the U.S. public. Once, Borton recalls, she took a reporter from a news magazine to Son My, site of the My Lai massacre in 1968, during which the U.S. military shot to death hundreds of unarmed men, women and children. The story broke in the fall of 1969 and seemed at the time an isolated incident to the audience in the United States. The reporter accompanying Borton was in a hurry so she lent him her typewriter and paper, which he used and then left the scene. Later she pulled the carbons out of the typewriter and read them. "I remember filing them away and being surprised that he was in such a hurry, because for me, this wasn't news. Things like this happened all the time—not to the extent of My Lai—but they happened. Yet these incidents never made it into the news because reporters had little contact with the Vietnamese." This lack of interaction affected reporting and how society back home perceived the war.

While the Vietnam War might seem distant, with respect to media coverage, the same issues as chronicled by Lady Borton have been leveled at U.S. media in the coverage of the Syrian War. According to a 2016 report in *The Boston Globe*, blame was leveled at media corporations that reduced the numbers of foreign correspondences, especially combat reporters. Without reporters in the field, U.S. society gets a Washington perspective with analysis by the Pentagon, State Department, White House and think-tank and cable-TV experts. "After a spin on that soiled carousel, they feel they have covered all sides of the story. This form of stenography produces the pabulum that passes for news about Syria."[14] The article does give credit to the handful of combat reporters on the scene but notes that their voices of reality are drowned out by official Washington sources. Thus, our perception of that conflict is skewed, just as it might have been during the Vietnam War.

Media create perceptions, for better or worse. When those perceptions are uninformed, assumptions abound, according to Lynne Choy Uyeda, founder of Asian American Advertising and Public Relations Alliance in Los Angeles. "When I first went into the business," she says, "nobody else was around and nobody knew there was an Asian market. Even within our industry, if we are Asian, the mainstream people tend to look at us not as real professionals. They assume that we all look alike and do not recognize the diversity within the Asian population. To them, Asian is a generic term." This attitude compounds problems associated with Asian cultural values, Uyeda notes. When Asian Americans apply for jobs, many personnel directors assume "we just got off the boat yesterday. They assume we don't speak English. They assume we are non-Americans and therefore would be very hard to deal with. They assume we don't know how to do business American-style. That may be true for the new arrivals," she adds. "But then these American companies forget that many of us have been here three to four generations. When interviewers speak to us, their first comment might be, 'My, you speak English so well.' They don't understand how insulting these things are."

Such attitudes may account for other, troubling statistics regarding race and mass media. Reports associated with bias also concern how mainstream media cover police shootings of African Americans, political parties, Muslim women and the LGBTQ (Lesbian, Gay, Bisexual, Transgender, Questioning) community. True or false, the reports focus on perception and indicate a level of bias by audiences and survey respondents across platforms. A 2016 Rasmussen survey found 71 percent of Americans "think that given two separate police shootings, the media would give more coverage to an incident in which a policeman shoots a black suspect," with only 11 percent believing "the media would give more coverage to a police shooting in which the suspect is white."[15] When it comes to politics, according to a 2017 Gallup poll, some 64 percent of those surveyed believe the media favors the Democratic Party, with only 22 percent stating the media favors Republicans.[16] *The Washington Post* reports a study in which stories "about women in the Muslim world are usually centered about one particular issue — namely, gender inequality — at the expense of topics like politics, art, fashion or sports," with "Muslim women who live in relatively equal societies" also covered in these terms.[17] Media coverage of the LGBTQ community also has come under scrutiny, especially when reports depict violence rather than everyday discrimination. The independent news site, *The Conversation*, states,

> For every highly publicized act of violence toward sexual minorities, such as the [2016] mass shooting at a gay nightclub in Orlando, there are many more physical and verbal assaults, attempted assaults, acts of property damage or intimidations which are never reported to authorities, let alone publicized by the media.[18]

Mercedes Lynn de Uriarte, former reporter and editor for *The Los Angeles Times* and associate professor emerita at the University of Texas, believes the environment of the newsroom—or any room, for that matter—has to foster intellectual diversity. "I argue that you cannot have integration without it because what you wind up getting is 'color-coded.' The distinction is this," she says: "When you don't have an intellectual environment in the newsroom where everyone feels obligated to be well-enough informed with different perspectives coming from different class, racial, ethnic, gender, age, sexual orientation, when everyone doesn't feel equally obligated— reading *from* that population *about* that population *to* that population, and making sure they spend time interacting in social settings *with* that population—then you have a limited newsroom and increasingly the burden for diversity falls on the shoulders of whatever management has declared as diverse: black reporter, Latina editor." This syndrome, she says, isolates, excludes and leads to burn-out. "A non-intellectually diverse newsroom environment requires that minorities carry the entire burden of producing diverse content against the grain of what is traditionally defined as professional coverage. Often, in the interest of keeping one's job, minorities comply. Integration then is color coded, but not diverse."

KNOW THE HISTORY OF INCLUSION IN MEDIA

Intellectual diversity takes history into account. One of the first documents to address this was the 1947 Hutchins Report advocating for a free and responsible press. The report speaks eloquently about the need for representative voices of all constituents in society. It came out strongly against stereotypes, as this passage illustrates:

> Today the motion picture, the radio, the book, the magazine, the newspaper, and the comic strip are principle agents in creating and perpetuating these conventional conceptions. When the images they portray fail to represent the social group truly, they tend to pervert judgment.
> Such failure may occur indirectly and incidentally. Even if nothing is said about the Chinese in the dialogue of a film, yet if the Chinese appear in a succession of pictures as sinister drug addicts and militarists, an image of China is built which needs to be balanced by another. If the Negro appears in the stories published in magazines of national

circulation only as a servant, if children figure constantly in radio dramas as impertinent and ungovernable brats—the image of the Negro and the American child is distorted. The plugging of special color and "hate" words in radio and press dispatches, in advertising copy, in news stories—such words as "ruthless," "confused," "bureaucratic"—performs inevitably the same image-making function.[19]

The excerpt anticipates race-based conflicts. In the 1960s riots broke out in Los Angeles, Chicago and Newark. During a 1967 Detroit riot, President Lyndon B. Johnson appointed a commission on civil disorders, led by Illinois Governor Otto Kerner, to investigate the underlying causes for such unrest. The Kerner Report, as it came to be known, also focused on minority depictions by the media, making these specific recommendations:

- Expand coverage of the Negro community and of race problems through permanent assignment of reporters familiar with urban and racial affairs, and through establishment of more and better links with the Negro community.
- Integrate Negroes and Negro activities into all aspects of coverage and content, including newspaper articles and television programming. The news media must publish newspapers and produce programs that recognize the existence and activities of Negroes as a group within the community and as part of the larger community.
- Recruit more Negroes into journalism and broadcasting and promote those who are qualified to positions of significant responsibility. Recruitment should begin in high schools and continue through college; where necessary, aid for training should be provided.
- Accelerate efforts to ensure accurate and responsible reporting of riot and racial news, through adoption by all news gathering organizations of stringent internal guidelines.[20]

Sidmel Estes-Sumpter, interviewed 25 years after the release of that report, when she was a planning manager at WAGA-TV in Atlanta, stated that the above terminology was archaic, "but if you substitute the words 'people of color' for the word 'Negro' or 'Negroes,'" you get a "blueprint" that the news media has yet to follow.[21] Estes-Sumpter believed the news media has wrestled with these issues, creating hundreds of diversity committees and task forces that "have yielded little progress and a lot of frustration." Estes-Sumpter, who passed away in 2015, made those comments in 1993. But little has changed, especially for minority women in newsrooms. As National Public Radio reported in 2017:

In many of today's newsrooms, women and journalists of color remain a sliver of those producing and reporting stories. According to studies from the American Society of News Editors, the Women's Media Center and the advocacy group VIDA, gender and ethnic diversity in newsrooms have hardly improved in the last decade despite increasing demand for more inclusive journalism in the current round-the-clock news cycle. ... Nationally, Hispanic, black and Asian women make up less than 5 percent of newsroom personnel at traditional print and online news publications.[22]

As history attests, issues involving media bias will not change substantially until more people of color are hired to add their perspectives to news, advertising, promotions and public relations campaigns.

DIVERSIFY NEWS- AND BOARDROOMS

One way to create intellectual diversity, dispel stereotypes and integrate newsrooms is to cover communities as they are found on maps rather than in marketing reports or big-data algorithms. "The mapmaker concept also helps us better understand the idea of diversity in news," write veteran journalists Bill Kovach and Tom Rosenstiel in *The Elements of Journalism: What Newspeople Should Know and the Public Should Expect.* "If we think of journalism as social cartography," they observe, "the map should include news of all our communities, not just those with attractive demographics or strong appeal to advertisers. To do otherwise is to create maps with whole areas missing."[23] Those areas typically delete minorities from the landscape.

Ziva Bransetter, who serves on the board of Investigative Reporters and Editors, believes media management must be willing to hire and train promising young journalists of color. "Citing a lack of 'qualified applicants' is a way to escape responsibility for running a diverse newsroom." Branstetter notes that the Center for Investigative Reporting has a program to train journalists of color working for other news organizations. "They work with our editors on a single investigative project that runs in their home news organization and on our website. Investing in the success of these young journalists even when it benefits other news organizations as much or more than our own is the kind of out-of-the-box thinking that needs to be done."

Philip Elliott, Washington correspondent for *Time*, notes serious barriers that hinder a more diverse journalism workforce. "When the lens pulls back, some of the fault lines are obvious, such as gender and race. But dig a bit deeper, and we tend to collect new hires from elite schools, pay them less than they are worth and count on their families' support to subsidize our journalism." Elliott says he could not have practiced journalism in his first few years after college if he didn't have help from parents. "Not everyone has that support, and we need to recognize many of our potential best recruits don't make it that far. At the same time, we need to be realistic about our self-selecting silencing. It's quite easy to stay in our newsroom bubbles, interact with only those of a similar background and share our views or beliefs. We need to be bringing in more voices from across the spectrum to challenge our own assumptions about the best way to practice journalism."

The best newsrooms emphasize diversity and promote inclusive viewpoints, especially when under-represented groups are depicted in stories. "Several times, I've had colleagues come to me when writing about LGBTQ issues to make sure they were as precise and respectful as possible," Elliott says. "When I've written stories that have race as a theme, I ask colleagues from all backgrounds to check my work to make sure it's as balanced as it can be. Having access to diverse colleagues makes journalism richer, expands our circle of sources and results in a more truthful version of the final product."

STEREOTYPES PERPETUATE BIAS

Another irony exists with regard to racism and media—the word "stereotype." It is a printing term depicting the outmoded practice of making a cardboard mold of a page of type and then pouring molten metal into the mold. This came to mean a "set form or convention." Metaphorically, media professionals are still creating cardboard characteristics and stamping molds on all who belong to a particular race or group or adhere to a certain lifestyle.

This can have a devastating effect, write Lee Wilkins and Renita Coleman in *The Moral Media: How Journalists Reason About Ethics*:

Stereotypes lead people to judge others—or the acts of others—based on the category of the actor, *not* the actions of an individual. Treating individual people based on some sort of general category that could represent them—all short people, all tall people, all women, all men, and so on—not only represents sloppy thinking, it is at its core unjust.[24]

Because stereotypes are unjust, they come with these consequences:

- **Mistakes.** Your report, photograph, advertisement, illustration or campaign will contain misperceptions and inaccuracies tarnishing your own and/or your company's reputation.
- **Substandard quality.** Your misperceptions and inaccuracies may cause your story or campaign to fall short of expectations, costing your outlet subscribers, patrons or contracts.
- **Professional embarrassment.** When your work is deemed racist, *you* become the focus of media attention and implicate your employer and coworkers by association.
- **Personal liability.** When your work contains race-related misperceptions and/or inaccuracies—such as believing allegations made by sources or over-billing or shunning clients because of their ethnic heritage—you or your firm can be sued, depending on factors involved in each case.

- **Undermined morality.** Even if your work succeeds, appealing to prurient interests who embrace stereotypes, you contribute messages to society that cause other people pain, suffering and humiliation.
- **Unanticipated disturbances.** The pain, suffering and humiliation caused by your report, photograph, illustration, advertisement or campaign can lead to protests against your employer or boycotts against your product or client.

These consequences typically spell failure for media professionals. More than counterparts of any other industry, employees across platforms should know that bias is wrong. They cover or deal with aspects of it every day, gathering information, creating business plans or resolving communication crises. Doing so, as a matter of course, they must embrace objectivity, fairness and truth and other core ethical values or lose out to competitors who do. Each journalist or practitioner is bound by tenets of social responsibility which, in part, protects freedoms and rights of the public. Given these factors, we must confront one undeniable truth: The media, more than any other industry, are responsible for generating stereotypes that dehumanize others, eroding their rights and privileges and depriving them of opportunities.

The injustice of stereotypes also is documented in reports by the Center for Integration and Improvement of Journalism at San Francisco State University. "Although they can cut both ways," one such report notes, "stereotypes frequently have been used to denigrate individuals because of race or ethnicity. Broad generalizations about a racial or ethnic population rob individuals of their uniqueness. To report with accuracy and comprehensiveness, journalists must be aware of, and avoid the use of, stereotypes."[25] The report provides many examples of stereotypes, several of which are mentioned in this section. One of the most common such labels, the assumption that "American means white," appeared in a story in *The San Francisco Chronicle* when a sportswriter called a white tennis star "an American in the strictest sense" because others, such as Michael Chang or Jennifer Capriati, either emigrated to the United States or their parents did. The CIIJ report concluded: "To stereotype U.S. citizens who emigrated to the United States as the other, or foreigners, is not only inaccurate but downright *un*American in a nation in which immigrants have played such a large role in history."[26] The sportswriter apologized for the stereotype, saying it in no way reflected his beliefs.

Another sports journalist, Anthony Federico, former editor for ESPN, was fired for the stereotypical headline, "Chink in the Armor," about the American NBA basketball player, Jeremy Lin, of Chinese descent. The ethnic slur, "chink," is particularly hideous (as are all such stereotypes). Federico maintained that his use of the term was an honest mistake in as much as he has used the phrase at least 100 times in the past.[27] The phrase dates back to the 15th century and refers to a vulnerable spot in a soldier's protective metal suit. However, when used in reference to a person of Asian heritage, the word takes on ominous meaning. As such, many journalists believe the phrase should not be used because of its now-racial overtones stemming from the Lin/ESPN incident.

In such cases, journalists often claim that they never meant to use a stereotype. Typically, as in the Jeremy Lin case, they apologize but also claim no ill intent. That's the danger of not being fully aware of slurs if you create content for a media outlet or agency. It's your responsibility to be aware of language. If you are negligent in this regard, you may be accused of being biased when you really are only echoing the misperceptions of the past.

Here are some stereotypes associated with American Indians published in metro newspapers: "Circle the wagons," "on the war path," "cavalry to the rescue," "ugh" (as in the *New York Daily News'* headline "Donald Says Ugh to Indian Gambling"), "smoking a peace pipe" and "going off the reservation." Mark Trahant, former executive editor of *The Salt Lake City Tribune* who now operates his own blog, "Trahant Reports," cites an 1867 editorial published in the *Idaho Statesman* that is indicative of that era. The article called for a feast to commemorate a grant treaty council of all Idaho Indians and recommended: "Then just before the big feast, put strychnine in their meat and poison to the death the last mother's son of them." Trahant, a member of the Shoshone-Bannock Tribe in Idaho and past president of the Native American Journalists Association, writes, "This may be ancient history to some—but to me, it's part of a continuing fabric of history that has not yet found the right pattern. The majority press still writes about American Indians with this misplaced passion—now it's found on the sports pages" in the nicknames of sports teams.[28] Responding to such stereotypes, the National Collegiate Athletic Association announced as early as 2005 that 17 colleges whose nicknames or mascots were based on American Indians "would not be permitted to hold tournament events unless they change their nicknames or eliminate images of American Indians in their facilities."[29] Some of the mascot names in the NCAA report included Braves, Redmen and Savages. (Ultimately, a handful of names were allowed primarily because of tribal sovereignty or permission by Native American nations for the teams to continue using the nickname.[30])

Gregory A. Reinhardt, a professor of anthropology and chairman of the department at the University of Indianapolis, researches stereotypes of American Indians. "I came to the conclusion that we put Indians on things to sell them. Plains Indians are the most common — anything with a war bonnet, the big feather headdress."[31] Reinhardt notes that company brands such as Land O'Lakes, Calumet baking powder and Argo cornstarch also use images of American Indians. So does the U.S. Mint in coins with a 2006 gold bullion piece replicating the Indian head nickel minted from 1913–38. Coins, of course, symbolize commerce. Reinhardt believes that stereotypes of American Indians also are associated with commerce, with the cumulative effect—from newspaper headlines to mascot nicknames to corporate brands and federal coins—implying that they are U.S. property, Reinhardt concludes.

Stereotypes associated with Latino/as include terms "illegal" and "alien." The National Association of Hispanic Journalists and other Latino/a groups has long maintained that such stereotypes are not only inaccurate but dehumanizing as well. A person may commit illegal acts, but how can he or she be an illegal person? Other similar hurtful stereotypes include content or depiction of Latino/as as barefooted and slovenly or taking a siesta and wearing a large sombrero, and these are found across media platforms in headlines, stories, slogans, advertisements, campaigns, photographs or illustrations.

Many whites see Latino/a Americans as one ethnic group. But Latinos comprise many racial populations—indigenous, African, Latino and white. The term "Hispanic" has been widely used since being adopted by the U.S. Census Bureau as a designation for citizens of Latin American ancestry. But what about ancestry that does not extend to Spanish origins? Even Latino/a may not accurately represent roots that trace back to Indian or African ancestry. Chicano/a, once a preferred term for Mexican Americans, also excludes ancestries. What about Cubans or Puerto Ricans? The point is, even within the so-named "single" ethnic group of "Hispanic," diversity exists.

April Hunt, board member of the Association of LGTBQ Journalists, worries about layoffs in newsroom that mean fewer women and people of color able to set ethical policies about stereotypes. Losing those voices has hurt diversity efforts, she says, and that affects newsroom practice. This should concern "all journalists and readers when so many voices and views are being kept out of the discussions in newsrooms. If nothing else, if you don't care about diversity, every journalist should care about accuracy.

"When I was in Orlando," reporting for the *Sentinel* newspaper, "we had an ongoing problem of police describing a suspect as 'Hispanic,' and the newspaper simply reprinted it. But there is no clear identifying mark of 'Hispanic.' You can be black, from the Dominican Republic and be, according to the U.S. Census, Hispanic. Ditto for Asians from places like Peru and very, very pale white folks like me with family in Cuba, Puerto Rico and Argentina." For accuracy's sake, Hunt convinced her editors to stop using the term Hispanic without a description. "If you don't have someone in the room who can explain that, the newsroom may become less accurate in how it covers the community."

Mercedes Lynn de Uriarte, formerly of *The Los Angeles Times*, notes that the publication's style book, rewritten in the 1980s, "mandated not to use the term 'Hispanic' unless it was the name of an organization or entity or the person self-identified as such. Otherwise the term was to be Latino/a."[32] De Uriarte and others in the newsroom argued that the term "Hispanic" should not be used in any other reference. "White-skinned upper-class Mexican-Americans and others of Spanish descent have often clung to the definition 'Hispanic' in order to make a race and class distinction between other Mexicans with indigenous backgrounds. But Mexico considers itself a 'mestizo' nation—or mixed ancestry—a term that acknowledges the blending of the races." Further, de Uriarte and others noted that the term Hispanic also was inaccurate. "If you walked up and asked someone 'Who are you?' a person would respond, 'I'm Guatemalan,' or whatever basic national heritage. That person would identify first by nation. And if you pressed for an umbrella term, they would use 'Latino.' No one whose country of origin was in Latin or Central America or Mexico would identify him- or herself as 'Hispanic,'" she says. "That is a U.S. imposed term."

Mei-Mei Chan, former Gannett news executive, relates to de Uriarte's experience, especially the labels and stereotypes. "Over the years," she writes, "I've been insulted because of my ethnicity—sometimes unintentionally. As a college student in Europe for the summer, an Austrian roommate said during a misunderstanding, 'that sneaky Chinese.' As a married adult, I walked into a grocery store in Washington, D.C., and was confronted by a coupon lady who asked, 'Do you speak English?' When I worked as executive editor of *The Post Register*, one caller quizzed me about my name. When I said I was Chinese, he paused and then said, 'Oh, you must be very smart.'"

Remarks such as these may be unintentional, a byproduct of labels shaping social mores. In America and Europe, stereotypes of Arabs and Muslim immigrants are associated with social mores due in part to wars in the Middle East. International public affairs journalist Teresa Krug is sensitive to stereotypes, especially labels that media often use when reporting in the Arab world. "When I was 25, I was hired to work at Al Jazeera English," she says, "a network that I had been taught to hate, growing up in the U.S., but came to adore when I finally sat down and watched it. The newsroom was incredible—far better than any graduate program—in which I worked alongside journalists from all different backgrounds, nationalities and religions who spoke what seemed like every language under the sun. We were encouraged to speak up, despite our position within the company, and voice an opinion on editorial content if we had one. As a result, when breaking news events happened, I found myself witnessing rigorous debates over email between correspondents in places like London and Paris and journalists throughout the Arab World, discussing whose lives matters, why an attack in the West should warrant more attention than one in say, Baghdad, and why someone might be compelled to inflict harm upon another human being." Krug gained incredible insight through these discussions and encounters. The saying—"one man's terrorist is another one's freedom fighter"—became ingrained in her psyche. "It didn't mean I had to agree with the motivations that drove the perpetrator, but it forced me to re-examine who gets labeled as a terrorist, and who gets to have the power to make those labeling decisions."

The old proverb "Sticks and stones may break my bones, but words will never hurt me" is a fallacy, writes ethicist Clifford G. Christians. Amplified across media platforms, offensive stereotypes hurt others when the people that they affect hear or see them and when the people that they do not affect use them in everyday discourse. Christians states that "cruel names and distorted pictures attack our very being. They go for the jugular emotionally."[33] Stereotypes attack the conscience and consciousness of people because humans are organized symbolically, Christians states.

As such, visual symbols of stereotypes often are powerful enough to ignite society, which we saw in 2005 in the riots that followed the publication in Denmark and elsewhere of a series of editorial cartoons depicting Islam stereotypically, including one panel with the Prophet Mohammad wearing a bomb-like turban. Most news reports about the controversy, like this one from the British Broadcasting Corporation, contained a statement maintaining that "Islam forbids any depiction of Muhammad or of Allah."[34] That, too, is a misstatement.

Reza Aslan, author of *No god but God: The Origins, Evolution, and Future of Islam*, is an authority on Islamic traditions and values and how they often clash with contemporary ideals of democracy and human rights. Aslan, born in Iran, has studied religions at Santa Clara University, Harvard University, and the University of California, Santa Barbara. At a roundtable discussion about the controversial cartoons,[35] Aslan shared an anecdote about visiting a Muslim country and seeing in a shop window a beautiful portrait of a young girl with light streaming all around her and with a shock of black hair peaking out from under her turban. "I thought this was Fatima, Mohammad's daughter," he said, "and while there are a few depictions of her, they are still quite rare." Aslan entered the shop and inquired about the portrait. The shopkeeper gave him a disgusted look. "This is not Fatima," the shopkeeper said. "It is the Prophet Muhammad."

The U.S. and European media have painted the controversy over the Danish cartoons as "a free press vs. religious dogma debate," Aslan said. "In the Muslim world, there is an equally black and white attitude that this is yet another attack on the Middle East by the West. Freedom of the press is depicted as dangerous, a Christian assault on Islam." These polar viewpoints only obscure the larger issue concerning depictions of the Prophet Muhammad. "The problem for early Muslims, who felt strongly against depicting the Prophet Muhammad, was the same as it was Christians, in the corruption of Jesus Christ, so that he, too, became a god apart from God." At the roundtable, Aslan showed a series of artwork and illustrations from the Muslim world depicting Mohammad. "In modern times, in images of the Prophet, the face is obscured in some ways, with shadows, for instance, but not always, as there is even a depiction of him and his wife holding hands in loving embrace," Aslan noted. "Many would object to this, but at the same time, not on a scale that we have been with the Danish cartoons, where there was such a furor. That is because the issue not only involved the depiction of Muhammad but also a noxious stereotype of Muslims as daft and dumb. As such the cartoons had one purpose—to offend. There were inflammatory depictions meant to insult in a manner that has oppressed Muslims for centuries. Also, and especially, these noxious stereotypes have been especially prevalent in Europe. Muslim immigration and the disturbances such as we have seen in France are fundamentally a socio-economic problem and not a religious one, because so many were brought to Europe to do work that Europeans didn't want to do after World War II." As an example of failed integration, Aslan stated, referring to 2005 riots in Paris, "Muslims have lived in France for decades, but were repeatedly told that they were not nor will ever be French. The history is shocking." But there was another issue associated with stereotypes and the Danish cartoons, Aslan noted: Several Muslim leaders asked for an apology. "But no one would meet with them at the newspaper or in the government." For five months their requests were ignored. "Finally, activists circulated the published cartoons with other (fabricated) radical cartoons—one, for instance, of Muhammad with a pig's snout. That ignited a lot of the violence."

No one in the Muslim world doubts that Western media have a right to publish cartoons. But they do object to the notion that freedom of the press "allows for the publishing noxious stereotypes," Aslan maintains. "Freedom of the press must be balanced by responsibility. The sad irony of this affair is that those who resorted to violence in the Muslim world only re-enforced the stereotype depicted of them in the cartoons."

Those stereotypes are blatant. Other stereotypical depictions are subtler, including those who suffer from obesity. Judith S. Stern, a distinguished professor in the departments of Nutrition and Internal Medicine at the University of California, Davis, co-directs the Collaborative Obesity Research Evaluation Team. She has published widely in both scholarly and popular periodicals and is an editorial adviser to *Prevention Magazine*. In the past, she said, emaciated women were depicted on the covers of magazines. "Women have become more muscular in current depictions," she said. "They are still very thin but not pre-pubescent." Nonetheless, media across platforms provide a steady diet of stereotypes in unbalanced stories and advertising campaigns. Concerning obesity, the coverage that upsets Stern most is the implication that obese people are at fault for their health. Other stereotypes include "fat people are ugly and weak willed." Journalists and practitioners should not perpetuate these stereotypes and should treat obese people with dignity and respect. "Obesity is a disease." Rather than treat the disease, we focus in media on treating the conditions of the disease such as heart problems, sleep apnea, diabetes and asthma. That's like living in a house with a hole in the roof, she says, and repairing or replacing the furniture each time it rains, rather than patching the roof.

Journalists and practitioners have an obligation to patch the media roof when it comes to stereotypes. Unjust depictions in news, advertising

and PR campaigns easily cross over to social media and infect other platforms. Eventually, the cumulative effect shapes social mores denigrating
thousands, if not millions of people, in the process. That is why we must
be sensitive to words, images, depictions and content that discriminatorily
casts any group in false, stereotypical light.

IDENTIFY AND RESIST STEREOTYPES

The best way to resist stereotypes across platforms is to be able to identify
them. Ask yourself:

- *Is the racial or ethnic angle in my story, photograph, illustration, advertise-
  ment or campaign absolutely necessary?*
- *If so, is it appropriate?*
- *If I am unsure, can I check with a member of that racial or ethnic group to
  determine appropriateness?*
- *Do I or my company have a resource list of experts on minority relations
  with whom I can regularly consult?*
- *Do I have access to handbooks that note offensive racial or ethnic terms?*
- *Am I reinforcing stereotypes by omission, eliminating people of color as
  sources for or subjects of non-racial stories, photographs, illustrations,
  advertisements or campaigns?*
- *Do I know enough about a particular culture to cover or target that culture
  without resorting to clichés or labels?*
- *Can the views, words or images in my work be misconstrued by people who
  do not share my own racial or ethnic type?*
- *Do the views, words or images in my work reflect my true beliefs or do they
  suggest a false racist or ethnic bias for which I may nonetheless be held
  accountable?*
- *Have I underestimated the intelligence or sensitivity of the audience, client
  or consumer in any way?*[36]

Keep in mind that anyone can make an innocent mistake regarding use
of stereotypes. Veteran journalist Mei-Mei Chan relates this compelling
anecdote: "Even in an ideal environment, we must take care we don't stay
trapped in ivory towers where we make lofty assumptions about knowing our readers. At *The Chicago Sun-Times*, a veteran, talented reporter
wrote a feature about raccoons becoming a big nuisance, cleverly com-
paring them to gangs in the way they intimidate, move in packs, shuffle
around. This story was read by a handful of editors, including myself and
a black colleague. A white female editor pointed out the historical conno-
tations of 'coons' and wondered if that might be a problem. We all said
no, our readers were smarter than that. We all were wrong, of course. The
story was blasted as intentionally racist by our large contingent of black
readers."

The moral here again relates to ethics across media platforms: *Don't make assumptions.* If you suspect a stereotype in a story, photograph, illustration, advertisement or campaign, eliminate it and revise more originally. If you are still accused of generating a stereotype, learn from the experience and practice another basic journalism tenet: *Do make apologies.*

It is important that you understand stereotypes on an emotional as well as intellectual level, especially if you are not a member of an underrepresented group. A useful exercise is to remember an event or situation about which you felt great enthusiasm and the urge to share that enthusiasm with a significant person, group or authority figure. Perhaps you were anticipating approval or even congratulations on the disclosure to a parent, mentor, sibling, relative, friend or other important person in your life. However, when you conveyed the news, that person not only disapproved but perhaps also berated you or in some way attempted to dampen your enthusiasm. How did that make you feel? When asked that question, white ethics students at Iowa State responded:

- *"You feel anger."*
- *"You wonder why you made the attempt in the first place."*
- *"You feel worthless or stupid."*
- *"You think, 'Why dream? Why care?'"*
- *"You cut off ties."*
- *"You feel broken, cast off. Useless."*
- *"You fight. You want to get to the bottom of it."*

That is how it feels to experience bias or the pain and humiliation associated with stereotypes. While you may not be a person of color, or experience racism every day, you can deal with it effectively as a journalist by being able to identify with it on this rudimentary level.

Then contemplate and practice these other recommendations from a *News Watch* report out of the Center for Integration and Improvement of Journalism, adapted slightly to suit all media platforms:[37]

Appropriate Descriptions

- Apply consistent guidelines when identifying people by race, sex, social class or other such category. Are the terms considered offensive? Ask individual sources how they wish to be identified and also consult with a supervisor, if appropriate.
- Only refer to the race, sex, ethnic heritage, social class or other such category of people when it is relevant. When it is, the identification needs to be sensitive.
- Consult a supervisor if you are unsure of the offensiveness or relevance of any term associated with race, sex, ethnic heritage, social class, etc.

- Use sensitivity in descriptions of rites and cultural events. Avoid inappropriate comparisons. For example, Kwaanza is not "African American Christmas."
- Be specific when using ethnic or racial identification of individuals. Referring to someone as Filipino American is preferred to calling that person Asian. The latter term is better applied to a group.

Appropriate Coverage

- Strive to present an accurate and full report to your readers, viewers, listeners, clients and customers.
- Don't overemphasize issues. For example, overemphasizing crime can perpetuate stereotypes, especially if minorities are depicted as the perpetrators.
- Do cover a variety of stories about minorities, not just those related to race, and depict or quote minorities in non-race related photographs, advertisements, illustrations and campaigns.
- Find out how issues affect different segments of society.
- Expand your contact lists and digital rolodexes. Include minorities who can provide authoritative opinions for a variety of subjects.

Appropriate Relationships

- With the help of a community member tour your city regularly, especially unfamiliar neighborhoods.
- Journalists, practitioners and their supervisors should educate themselves about the communities of people being covered or targeted. Cover them like a map to include all demographics in the shifting population.
- Work on building relationships with someone different from yourself. It can be a mentoring relationship.
- Ask yourself if you've allowed preconceived ideas to limit your efforts to include diversity.
- Take inventory of your circle of friends, coworkers, reading material, music and extracurricular activities and see how diverse they are and make some changes if diversity is limited.

Media professionals who follow such advice will have a personal edge over insensitive counterparts. The edge is two-fold. As noted at the beginning of this chapter, journalists and practitioners who reject bias also avoid errors associated with misperceptions. They write or document complete accurate stories or target consumers or publics with insight and precision. Perhaps more importantly, however, they learn different ways to solve problems, approach assignments, appreciate cultures, contribute to communities and, above all, disseminate appropriate and accurate information.

As Mei-Mei Chan concludes, putting these issues into perspective, "All of us have biases, that's a given. We need to be aware of the more damaging ones and be willing to overcome them. Every day, how we view the world is greatly colored and skewed by the powerful, pervasive media. That is a serious responsibility and a difficult undertaking. It's vital the media work at accurately and fairly portraying every aspect of the world, including people of color, whose numbers continue soaring. You cannot do that without a diverse staff collaborating to make thoughtful decisions. We need more young people of color to join the journalism profession so they can be part of that brain trust, to help present what is true, and break down barriers to understanding and mutual respect."

To accomplish these and other leadership goals, you need a solid ethical foundation that has been tested by challenges involving falsehood, temptation, manipulation and bias. We have covered that foundation and those tests in the first two sections of *Living Media Ethics*. In the final section, you will enhance your value system through fairness, discretion, compassion, empowerment and other ennobling ethical concepts, and learn about power, too, which is not a value but the force with which we assert our personal and professional values.

"TAKING STOCK: YOUR PERSONAL BIAS BAROMETER"
Personal Journal Exercise

1. List the highs, lows and turning points concerning *race*, *gender* and *social class* in your:
    *   Life
    *   Family
    *   Workplace
    *   Community.
2. Analyze your list by addressing the following:
    *   What epiphanies, truths, or lessons did you *learn* from each high, low and turning point?
    *   What *falsehoods*, if any, were associated with each?
    *   How do incidents, truths, lessons and falsehoods relate to *tolerance* (or lack thereof) within your life, family, work, town, country, world?
    *   How have they enhanced or biased your *conscience*?
    *   How have they enhanced or biased your *consciousness*?
    *   How can you *apply* lessons based on truth in your life?

3. Without identifying anyone by name or invading your own or another person's privacy or damaging anyone's reputation—referencing content of this chapter—create a 500-word journal entry or blog post or short podcast or multimedia presentation about truths and lessons that emanated out of this exercise.

Communal Journal Exercise

If you are the class instructor or group leader, do an assessment of your own perceptions about bias, diversity, stereotypes and methods to resist them. Contemplate these questions:

- When introducing truths about race, gender, social class and/or other such societal concerns, do you present your best or your ordinary self to others? For example, how do you introduce such material into your lesson plans if you are a teacher, into discussions if you are a group leader, or into daily interaction with others if you are a staff or business person?
- Are you avoiding discussion of sensitive or potentially controversial issues and if so, why? Peer pressure? Fear of mistakes? Anger? Approval-seeking? What can educators, colleagues and administrators, and/or coworkers and supervisors do to make you feel more comfortable engaging in discussions about race, gender, or social class?

Based on your truths and analyses, lead a class or group discussion about your own bias barometer and convey your own best practices and methods to resist bias associated with race, gender, social class or any other marginalized or under-represented group. As always, when doing so, do not violate your own or someone else's privacy or damage anyone's reputation and be especially sensitive to others during disclosures, as these are difficult discussions that often harken uncomfortable memories. However, not having these discussions only perpetuates intolerance.

NOTES

1 Audrey Singer, "The Changing Face of America," *eJournal USA: Society and Values*, December 2004, http://usinfo.state.gov/journals/itsv/1204/ijse/singer.htm
2 Gail Dines and Jean M. Humez, *Gender, Race, and Class in Media*, 2nd ed. (Thousand Oaks, Calif.: Sage, 2003), XV.
3 Greta R. Bauer, Jessica Braimoh, Ayden I. Scheim and Christoffer Dharma, "Transgender-Inclusive Measures of Sex/Gender for Population Surveys: Mixed-Methods Evaluation and Recommendations," *PLoS One*, May 25, 2017, www.ncbi.nlm.nih.gov/pmc/articles/PMC5444783/
4 Carroll Doherty, "Remembering Katrina: Wide Racial Divide Over Government's Response," Pew Research Center, August 27, 2015,

www.pewresearch.org/fact-tank/2015/08/27/remembering-katrina-wide-racial-divide-over-governments-response/

5 Joan Brunkard, Gonza Namulanda and Raoult Ratard, "Hurricane Kartrina Deaths, Louisiana, 2005," *Disaster Medicine and Public Health Preparedness*, Vol. 2, No. 4, April 1, 2013, https://doi.org/10.1097/DMP.0b013e31818aaf55

6 Sue Anne Bell, "Older Victims of Hurricane Harvey May Need Special Attention as Texas Recovers," Institute for Health Care Policy & Innovation, August 29, 2017, http://ihpi.umich.edu/news/older-victims-hurricane-harvey-may-need-special-attention-texas-recovers

7 See: "Projection of Older Populations and Households," Joint Center for Housing, Harvard University, 2016, www.jchs.harvard.edu/sites/jchs.harvard.edu/files/harvard_jchs_housing_growing_population_2016_chapter_1.pdf

8 Richard V. Reeves, "The Dangerous Separation of the American Upper Middle Class," Brookings Institution, September 3, 2015, www.brookings.edu/research/the-dangerous-separation-of-the-american-upper-middle-class/

9 Malcolm Gladwell, *Blink: The Power of Thinking Without Thinking* (New York: Little, Brown; 2005), 85–86.

10 *The Random House Dictionary of the English Language*, 2nd ed., unabridged (New York: Random House, 1987), 1591.

11 Jonah Berger, *Invisible Influence: The Hidden Forces that Shape Behavior* (New York: Simon & Schuster, 2016), 93.

12 Pat Shipman, "Facing Racial Differences—Together," *Chronicle of Higher Education*, August 3, 1994, B2.

13 "Tolerance," *The Random House Dictionary of the English Language* (New York: Random House, 1987), 1992.

14 Stephen Kinzer, "2016: The Media are Misleading the Public on Syria," *The Boston Globe*, February 18, 2016, available from www.bostonglobe.com/opinion/2016/02/18/the-media-are-misleading-public-syria/8YB75otYirPzUCnlwaVtcK/story.html

15 No author, "Most Say Media Inspires Attacks on Police," Rasmussen, July 13, 2016, www.rasmussenreports.com/public_content/politics/current_events/social_issues/most_say_media_inspires_attacks_on_police

16 Art Swift, "Six in 10 in US See Partisan Bias in News Media," Gallup, April 5, 2017, www.gallup.com/poll/207794/six-partisan-bias-news-media.aspx

17 Rochelle Terman, "The News Media Offer Slanted Coverage of Muslim Countries' Treatment of Women," *The Washington Post*, May 5, 2017, www.washingtonpost.com/news/monkey-cage/wp/2017/05/05/the-news-media-offer-slanted-coverage-of-muslim-countries-treatment-of-women/?utm_term=.84fe724aec26

18 Dominic Parrott, "Where Does Anti-LGBT Bias Come From—and How Does It Translate into Violence?," *The Conversation*, June 16, 2016, http://theconversation.com/where-does-anti-lgbt-bias-come-from-and-how-does-it-translate-into-violence-61001

19 Robert M. Hutchins, Chairman, *A Free and Responsible Press, The Commission on Freedom of the Press* (Chicago, Ill.: University of Chicago Press, 1947), 26.

20 See *Report of The National Advisory Commission On Civil Disorders* (New York: Bantam Books, 1968), 1–29.

21 Sidmel Estes-Sumpter, "Responding to a Revolution," *Kerner Plus 25 Report*, March 1993, 2.

22 Tal Abbady, "The Modern Newsroom Is Stuck Behind the Gender and Color Line," NPR, May 1, 2017, www.npr.org/sections/codeswitch/2017/05/01/492982066/the-modern-newsroom-is-stuck-behind-the-gender-and-color-line

23 Bill Kovach and Tom Rosenstiel, *The Elements of Journalism: What Newspeople Should Know and the Public Should Expect* (New York: Three Rivers Press, 2001), 165.

24 Lee Wilkins and Renita Coleman, *The Moral Media: How Journalists Reason About Ethics* (Mahwah, N.J.: Lawrence Erlbaum, 2005), 83.

25 *News Watch*, multiple authors, Center for Integration and Improvement of Journalism, San Francisco State University, 1994, 8.

26 Ibid.

27 Irving DeJohn and Helen Kennedy, "Jeremy Lin Headline Slur was 'Honest Mistake,' Fired ESPN Editor Anthony Federico Claims," *New York Daily News*, February 20, 2012, www.nydailynews.com/sports/basketball/knicks/jeremy-lin-slur-honest-mistake-fired-espn-editor-anthony-federico-claims-article-1.1025566

28 Mark Trahant, "Ethnic Media an Important Bridge to Minority Communities," *Kerner Plus 25 Report*, 25.

29 Brad Wolverton, "NCAA Restricts Colleges With Indian Nicknames and Mascots, *The Chronicle of Higher Education*, September 2, 2005, A65.

30 Mike Sorensen, "NCAA Says Tribal Approval is Key to Keeping Names," *Deseret News*, August 20, 2005, www.deseretnews.com/article/600157223/NCAA-says-tribal-approval-is-key-to-keeping-names.html

31 No author, "Feathers, Fierceness, and Stereotypes," *The Chronicle of Higher Education*, March 31, 2006, B21

32 Some publications now use the term "Latinix" rather than "Latino/a."

33 Clifford G. Christians, "The Sacredness of Life." *Media Development*, Vol. 2, 1998, 3–4.

34 No author, "Row Deepens Over Danish Cartoons," BBC, December 29, 2006, http://news.bbc.co.uk/2/hi/europe/4567940.stm

35 Reza Aslan spoke at Iowa State University on April 21, 2006 as part of First Amendment Day of the Greenlee School of Journalism and Communication.

36 These tenets are a composite of the author's and selected recommendations by the Center for Integration and Improvement of Journalism.

37 *News Watch*, 52–53.

PART III

Enhancing Your Ethical Base

Thus far in *Living Media Ethics* we have covered how consciousness and conscience work in tandem to shape values, foresee consequences and discern truth. Consciousness and conscience also inform each other to overcome challenges associated with falsehood, manipulation, temptation and bias. In this section, we utilize consciousness and conscience more selectively to enhance our values. Through case studies by and interviews with journalists and practitioners, we will deepen our intuition and sharpen our awareness to prepare for unforeseen conflicts, exercising fairness. We also will explore other fairness-related tenets such as corrections, apologies and discretion, and inspirational tenets such as forgiveness, compassion and empathy. We also will identify power bases leading to empowerment, overcoming challenge in everyday matters and even in actionable ones such as sexual harassment. Lastly media practitioners will discuss value systems across platforms, motivating you to create your own ethics code to include in your digital clipbooks or portfolios.

CHAPTER 9

Fairness: Level the Playing Fields

FAIRNESS MEANS CONTINUOUS IMPROVEMENT

Ethical journalists strive to achieve fairness and then assess whether they have, making adjustments to prepare for the next encounter. That makes fairness one of the most important values in any system. Embracing fairness, you live ethics. You eventually ensure ever-greater levels of ethical behavior because of the continual goal of self-examination and improvement. Fair-minded people know right from wrong. They commit to truth, especially to full disclosure, not only in what they disseminate but also about their own motivations and desires. They might be manipulated or tempted by others, but because they emphasize preparedness, they are less apt to be tricked or enticed the next time. Fair-minded people also promote inclusivity; they do not discriminate because racism is a lie. Moreover, they seek justice and a level playing field for themselves and others in society.

However, to embrace fairness and use it to enhance values, you also must have courage. You have to accept truth as you find it, even if that truth goes against everything that you have hitherto believed. You have to acknowledge, openly and freely, when you have been manipulated, tempted or biased; pride or ambition cannot stand in the way of such disclosures. For these and other reasons, we have postponed our discussion about fairness until this point. Fairness seems simple but assumes that we can foresee consequences, accept responsibility and admit and adjust for our biases. That requires commitment. Thus, before embracing fairness, media professionals must have good knowledge of influence, responsibility, truth, integrity, inclusivity and other concepts covered in previous chapters of *Living Media Ethics*.

Defined, fairness is *a continual process of improvement involving the evaluation of work and behavior to determine (a) whether the work is accurate or truthful, (b) whether the behavior is honest or appropriate, and (c) whether methods or values can be enhanced to meet those goals.*

"The most difficult issue I deal with is fairness," says Joe Mahr, investigative reporter for *The Chicago Tribune*. Before his present position, he worked at *The Blade* in Toledo, Ohio, where he shared in a Pulitzer Prize for reporting a string of atrocities by a U.S. battle unit in Vietnam. (More about that later in this chapter.) Mahr acknowledges that as an investigative reporter, he has to pursue "tough stories that invariably put people or institutions in a bad light. Somebody's screwing up. Somebody got away with wrongdoing. My goal is ensuring the story is more than simply accurate. It's that, and it's *fair*." To ensure fairness, Mahr puts his articles into proper context. In the course of an investigation into how a murder suspect reportedly evaded arrest, he learned "that the suspect didn't really evade arrest so much as the authorities screwed up 30 years ago when they failed to properly enter the murder warrant into a national fugitive database." The police on the force at the time of Mahr's investigation appealed to his sense of compassion, asking him not to use that information because it would tarnish the memory of former officers, several who had passed away or retired. Mahr knew that the information about the fugitive database was relevant. However, in honoring full disclosure, he says, there were other relevant facts, too. "It was equally important for me to put this in the proper context. At the time this screw-up occurred, the city was in the midst of one of its worst murder waves ever, as well as undergoing tough financial times. There had been cut-backs in the detective bureau, and detectives felt as if they were racing from call to call." While Mahr didn't dwell on these aspects in his story, he did include this information to reflect the context. "It didn't excuse the screw-up," he says, "but it helped explain why it happened." As a result, Mahr not only covered how a fugitive escaped justice, but did justice to the story by exercising fairness.

Justice is the byproduct of the fairness process. When performed impartially, the end result of fairness restores balance, makes things whole, sets things right. Many philosophers, not to mention media professionals, believe that life is unfair; truth, relative; and objectivity, impossible. But they still embrace justice whose roots trace back to Aristotle who professed that justice was the preeminent objective for humankind because our cultures and communities are inherently social.[1] In other words, to safeguard our communal way of life we have to get along, especially in a nation whose work ethic pivots on social mobility. Ethicist Anita L. Allen states that fairness has a basic requirement: "In the United States we are forced to compete with other people for many of the good and necessary things in life, so the playing field of competition should be level."[2]

News must be impartial, balanced and fair, or journalists do injustice to those they cover—so much so, at times, that outlets are sued for libel. Advertising and public relations also must take pains to be fair, especially when dealing with competitors or competitive bidding. Trade libel typically involves unfair, disparaging content leveled against a competitor; trade slander involves the spoken word, perhaps in an online video or broadcast. Advertisers commit libel or slander when they create unfair content that disparages competitors. Moreover, as communication agencies know, bidding processes and requests for proposals must be unbiased and "on the level" so that competition can flourish along with merit as part of our work ethic. According to the U.S. Justice Department:

> American consumers have the right to expect the benefits of free and open competition—the best goods and services at the lowest prices. ... The competitive [bidding] process only works, however, when competitors set prices honestly and independently. When competitors collude, prices are inflated and the customer is cheated. Price fixing, bid rigging, and other forms of collusion are illegal and are subject to criminal prosecution by the Antitrust Division of the United States Department of Justice.[3]

As you can see, the courts and Justice Departments hold media practitioners to higher standards of fairness than those in other professions because our words, images and sounds are transmitted via powerful technology to the public and influence culture and society.

FAIRNESS PIVOTS ON VIEWPOINT

Viewpoint is defined as *an event or opinion as experienced through someone else's eyes*. That is trickier than it sounds. Viewpoints vary because motives do. All you have to do is attend a trial (or watch one on television) to know that the defendant and plaintiff may have witnessed the same event or act but perceived it in remarkably opposite ways, according to each person's personality, morality and/or special interests. Journalists and practitioners must factor that into their work and campaigns. You learned about motives in the very first journal exercise in *Living Media Ethics*, and we're still discussing it as a primary factor in almost every chapter.

Viewpoint is especially vital in social marketing campaigns whose goal is to raise awareness. "Social marketing has been an important cause for us that taps into our hearts and minds, as well as our professional skills," says Marcie Brogan, founder and chair of Brogan & Partners, a marketing agency that began with a four-woman staff in 1984 and now has expanded with offices nationwide. "The agency's social marketing work is often aimed at balancing other messages in the interest of fairness." One such issue concerned gambling in the wake of three new casinos meant to boost Detroit's economy. Brogan & Partners' research indicated that nearly 5 percent of Michigan residents were considered compulsive gamblers. The agency intervened with a campaign on behalf of the Michigan Department of Community Health. Deploying broadcast, print and guerilla marketing—a tactic aimed at using unconventional strategies that reap high results on low budgets—"the campaign targeted audiences that were at risk of developing a gambling problem," Brogan said. Her staff investigated perspectives of target groups and "offered a frank, objective view of gambling and directed compulsive gamblers to professional help." Members of her creative team may never have gambled, but still had to create a campaign for constituents of diverse demographics (age, household income, ethnicity, etc.) and psychographics (attitudes, lifestyle preferences, consumer behavior, etc.). Likewise, the creative team not only had to be aware of its own viewpoints about gambling, so as not to be biased by its use as an economic stimulus, but also those of audience, sources, clients and/or competitors.

Situations arise daily across platforms that require fairness. Nancy Vonk and Janet Kestin discuss this in *Pick Me: Breaking into Advertising and Staying There*, a title that alludes to the competitive nature of media and the values needed to succeed in the profession. The authors note that issues of fairness often involve ideas in advertising—"where they come from, what gets put before the public eye, and how far you will go to make a name for yourself."[4] Vonk and Kestin present a case study that illustrates how responsible practitioners use ethics to guide them in unanticipated situations where impulse control should be exercised. They write that two creative teams had been assigned to the same project and had not been consulting with each other because the best concept was supposed to prevail. One team outdistanced the other and went home for the evening while the other team struggled. As they labored over their stalled project, the art director went to the rival team's office to fetch a pen and saw thumbnail designs of the rival team's concept. He was tempted to look, and he liked what he saw. But he also realized that by changing one component he could make the rival team's idea spectacular. Instead of waiting until the next day and practicing full disclosure, telling his colleagues what happened and sharing his idea, he stole and modified the concept and presented it to his creative director. Authors Vonk and Kestin ask,

> Should the art director have saved his revelation and shared it with the other team the next day? Yes. So, who owns our ideas? Once presented to clients, neither we nor our agencies own our ideas. Our clients do. They pay us to come up with ideas—for them.[5]

But that is not the only moral bottom line in this scenario. Let's consider viewpoints of all involved in the case study and the unforeseen consequences of stealing a rival team's idea. Do you tell members of your own team what happened and get them to collude and conspire with you? Or do you let them think you came up with the new concept entirely on your own? Can you manipulate them to deceive the very coworkers on the rival team with whom they may work in the future? What if someone reports the theft to the creative director? Suppose members of the rival team members express outrage, rejecting the excuse that this was a sudden opportunity that transpired in pursuit of a pen and claiming that you purposely broke into their office with intent to steal? After all, they saw you struggling as they happily left the office for home. Your reputation can be damaged, perhaps irreparably. And even if the case study were altered so that it occurred outside of the agency, involving a rival agency's thumbnail forgotten in a potential client's conference room, the consequences in the long term can be just as severe concerning your status as a professional. Successful people also are mobile. Today's competitor can be tomorrow's coworker. But there are even more unforeseen consequences to the theft of an idea as presented in this case study which, by the way, applies across platforms because ideas do, from enterprise stories in news to enterprises in business: *The creative director has to clean up the mess.* Sure, she may want a winning idea. What she doesn't want is a parade of complainants in her office with low morale—deadly in the creative business. She may even decide to fire the employee who stole the idea, and that involves another kind of due process concerning severance pay, budgets and other personnel issues. Finally, she will have to report all this to her own superior who may question why this situation happened under her watch.

"Firing offenses include stealing," says Carolyn Lewis, educator and former general manager of the WOUB Center for Public Media at Ohio University. "I can overlook a 5-cent copy on the copy machine, but you cannot take what isn't yours. Also, you can get fired for coming to work and not doing the work. If you report to work, your supervisor expects work. And while you are here, you should give it your all for eight hours." That said, Lewis believes the most difficult task is firing an employee, even if that is the end result of the fairness process. "Will they be able to pay the bills? Will they land on their feet? I wonder about this even if the person isn't talking to me. Does he or she have children and mouths to feed?" In those cases, she shows compassion, to be covered in more detail in the next chapter on power.

Fair-minded managers assess all viewpoints before taking action and share certain traits:

- Their value systems are strong enough to serve as touchstones for others.
- They evaluate their actions, admit errors and provide access or opportunities for wronged parties to express their viewpoints or truths.
- They enhance their values by analyzing (a) unforeseen conflicts of interest before those conflicts occur, (b) evaluating their performance to determine whether it meets their standards, and (c) assessing whether they have treated others fairly or whether others have treated them fairly.

FAIRNESS MAKES LASTING IMPRESSIONS

Journalists and practitioners often develop the above traits by experiencing a defining moment while on assignment or working on a PR or advertising campaign. When Dan Horn, long-time reporter for *The Cincinnati Enquirer*, was a student intern at a large city newspaper, he was assigned to interview the parents and sisters of a high school student named John who committed suicide. At the time, Horn believed the assignment might win him an award or a position upon graduation at a major newspaper. However, while interviewing the family and learning more about John (including details in a suicide note), he had to deal with his own emotions and influences, confront the concepts of right and wrong, and begin enhancing a value system to guide him in his career. He wrote an essay about the experience in an ethics class at Ohio University and published it soon after in a newspaper trade magazine. Here is an excerpt:

> Every teen-age boy gets stood up by his friends, breaks up with a girl, gets teased in school for stupid superficial reasons and disagrees with his elders once in a while. Every teen-age boy doesn't commit suicide because of it, and the whole world doesn't need to make judgments about what pushed John over the edge.
>
> I wasn't going to tell John's grandfather that an argument he had with his grandson triggered the suicide, I wasn't going to tell a 17-year-old girl that John killed himself because she wouldn't go out with him, and I wasn't going to tell a bunch of high school students who didn't know any better that their name-calling may have convinced John to swallow a bottle full of pills. ...
>
> John taught me something about journalism I'll always value more than a clip I can dangle in front of prospective employers. He showed me that sometimes stuffy textbooks don't have all the answers and sometimes reporters must do what they think is right, not just what they think will win them an award or get them an interview with the *Washington Post*.
>
> As reporters, we tell ourselves all too often that we can print whatever we're allowed to print and do whatever we're allowed to do. Every once in a while, somebody comes along and reminds us that it isn't always so simple.[6]

Dan Horn, who shared in a 2018 Pulitzer Prize awarded to *The Enquirer*, reflected on his early experience in the newsroom. "John's story taught me the importance of fairness. It's a simple lesson, one that should have been obvious to me before I ever wrote that original news story about John. But I've learned over the years that fairness is a tricky concept. For reporters, it requires a delicate balancing act: *Be aggressive but sensitive, be tough but reasonable.*" Horn acknowledges that his motto seems oxymoronic. "But that's the nature of the job. Reporters who do the job well ask themselves every day if this story, this sentence, this *word* is fair. Am I explaining this person's point of view as clearly as I can? Is this quote in the proper context? Would someone be needlessly hurt if I include this bit of information, even though I know it to be true?"

Notice that none of these questions concern whether the information is right. Accuracy is an entirely different issue. You can't be fair if you are inaccurate, that's a given. But you can be unfair and accurate at the same time. The quote can be right and an important fact can be clearly stated, and yet the story may still mislead or confuse readers. "Horn adds that each new story comes with its own set of issues involving fairness. "It's a daily battle—one that we don't always win. But we can give ourselves a chance every day by asking two questions," he adds: "'Is it right?' and 'Is it fair?' John's story taught me that those two questions don't always have the same answer."

Answers to such questions apply across platforms. They not only entail your own work but that of your creative team, newsroom, agency, organization and colleagues and the multitude of viewpoints of your audience and clientele. To make lasting impressions on the job, follow this process to evaluate your own or others' work and/or behavior:

1. Ascertain Preconceived Notions

To practice fairness, you have to determine what, if any, presumptions may influence your or other people's judgment.

Ask yourself:

- *Am I willing to approach specific people or issues with an open mind or do I have any preconceived notions that may lead to a conflict or dispute?*
- *Are others willing to approach me with an open mind or do they seem to have preconceived notions that may lead to a conflict or dispute?*
- *Have both parties listened carefully to each other to dispel any such preconceived notions?*

2. Balance Viewpoints and Differing Interests

To promote fairness, you should be able to identify, evaluate and balance viewpoints and interests.

Ask yourself:

- *If I were the other party and held an opposite opinion or lifestyle, how would I view this particular issue or dispute?*
- *How are others viewing me, based on my opinions or lifestyle?*
- *Are there any misperceptions in viewpoints that need to be identified, addressed and/or balanced by one or both parties?*

3. Seek Bonds or Advice

To ensure fairness, the parties involved should seek common bonds or opinions and/or contact impartial advisers to help resolve issues or disputes.

Ask yourself:

- *What experiences or values do I and the other party share so that we can identify common bonds?*
- *What interests or activities do I and the other party share so that we can identify like opinions?*
- *What specific concerns shall we bring to the attention of impartial experts so that we can overcome basic obstacles and try one more time to reach a decision or resolution?*

4. Evaluate Actions or Treatment

To enhance fairness in the future, you need to evaluate the above processes to determine whether you have learned anything from the issue, dispute or resolution.

Ask yourself:

- *How could I have been treated more fairly?*
- *How could I have treated the other party more fairly?*
- *How has the process affected or enhanced my values on fairness?*

After evaluating responses to those questions, consider whether you acted improperly. If so, consider taking preventative measures to ensure that this or similar incidents do not recur. Also consider whether you should apologize to the other party in a timely manner without preconditions or justifications. You have no control over whether your apology will be accepted. The goal of any apology or correction is to make amends and make whole, setting the record straight.

FAMILIARIZE YOURSELF WITH FAIRNESS CONCEPTS

Corrections and Apologies

All journalists and practitioners must correct the record and apologize when they make mistakes. This is a fundamental requirement of fairness. One website was among the first to hold media outlets accountable— "Regret the Error," founded by Canadian freelance writer Craig Silverman. The site catalogued corrections across media platforms. "Corrections are part of the fabric of journalism," Silverman states. "Yet they have become so entrenched that no one thinks to question their efficacy. It occurred to me that they were ripe for scrutiny, and a blog would be the perfect format to reprint the best/worst and start a discussion about errors, accuracy and corrections." Silverman's blog eventually resulted in a book by the same title, which won the National Press Club's Arthur Rowse Award for Press Criticism.

Silverman believes most media practitioners are aware that they should apologize for mistakes, but many do not. Some outlets publish corrections in a prominent place, others in the section or segment where the error occurred, and still others elsewhere in the publication, broadcast or post. Some outlets explain why a timely apology and correction was not rendered; others ignore this. The end result is a haphazard process, which in itself violates the standards of fairness expressed in the previous section. Silverman has called for a wholesale revaluation of policies to discern universal standards that apply across media platforms.

In response to that challenge, researchers from Iowa State University did a study that identified these core components of a correction:[7]

1. *Identify the error (what it was, when/where it occurred).*
2. *Correct the record.*
3. *Do so as soon as possible.*
4. *Do so prominently.*
5. *Provide an explanation to the audience or clientele.*
6. *Disclose how the error could have been avoided and/or how it will be prevented in the future.*
7. *Issue an apology to those damaged by the false disclosure.*

Those researchers also used Silverman's blog to compile and evaluate newspaper corrections posted by Regret the Error. They analyzed 631 corrections from 70 newspapers. Their study yielded a range of results verifying many of Silverman's suspicions. They broke their data down into several categories, including objective mistakes (errors in fact or design or print flaws) and subjective mistakes (errors of faulty judgment or omission). Objective errors happened most often, accounting for 83.7 percent of the sample. The others were subjective. Here are some results:

- Only 30 percent of the corrections identified the date of the error.
- About one-fifth (19.2 percent) omitted referencing the original mistake in the correction.
- About three-quarters (71.6 percent) presented the right information, as it should have been published.
- Surprisingly, almost 5 percent of the corrections neither included the right information nor provided a clarification, simply identifying what was wrong.
- Only 25 percent of the corrections explained why errors occurred.
- Out of the entire 631 corrections, only 1.5 percent (10) included how the error could have been avoided and only 1.4 percent (9) how the error could be prevented in the future
- Only 4.3 percent expressed an apology for the mistake.

Because of the tenets of social responsibility, covered in Chapter 3, it is clear that editors must practice fairness not only to serve and inform the audience but also to build credibility. While the study focused on newspapers, the lesson applies to all platforms. Just as in any transaction, even between two individuals, falsehoods need to be corrected in a timely manner without justification and genuine apologies need to be expressed. Otherwise, people lose trust in each other. Credibility is based on trust and once again applies to platforms as well as to people. Without trust and credibility, people stop speaking to each other. Without trust and credibility, people also stop reading, subscribing, listening to or viewing media.

Jerry Ceppos, former dean of the Manship School of Mass Communication at Louisiana State University, recalls learning that lesson as a young journalist at the *Miami Herald*. Then-executive editor Larry Jinks introduced the idea of regular, anchored corrections under a logo stating "Setting the Record Straight." This made "an indelible impression" on Ceppos. "Probably it was floating around in my head many years later when the *San Jose Mercury News*, which I edited, went too far on an investigative series. After we re-reported the series and verified the flaws, it was obvious that we should run a nuanced column reporting what we did right and what we did incorrectly." According to Ceppos, the column turned out to be controversial, "but the idea of explaining mistakes to readers, and how they happened, never struck me as worthy of debate. It's just what you should do."

Chris Adams, who shared in a Pulitzer Prize at *The Wall Street Journal*, directs training at the National Press Foundation, a Washington-based non-profit for working journalists. He poses an interesting question about corrections: *Are errors unethical?* "Most journalists would say no, of course not. They are the result of a mistake—an honest one at that," he states. "And certainly, most newspapers appear to make it a point to correct the record on any mistake, no matter how small. That's why you'll see a newspaper's taking up valuable newsprint to fess up that John Smith's middle initial is 'B' not 'D.' All of that is good. But what I've seen over the years is a resistance on the part of many reporters to correct the record unless their arms are twisted," Adams says. He acknowledges that even editors and reporters whom he respects occasionally adopt "the stance that they'll correct a mistake only if an aggrieved party specifically asks for a correction. ... I've seen reporters who essentially negotiate *out of* corrections, sweet-talking a long-time source to not ask for a correction, figuring that lets them off the hook. Obviously, they then owe that source a favor. If a regular reader points out an error, the observations are often dismissed." These practices may or may not happen weekly in every newsroom, but when they happen too often, as Adams indicates, credibility is compromised along with ethical values. Moreover, the scenario that he describes can happen in an agency as well as a newsroom. True, the circumstances may differ dramatically but the motivations of the practitioner do not: Attempts to sweet-talk out of errors and apologies happen not only with clients but among colleagues as well, with one asking the other to ignore a wrongdoing or mistake in a campaign or an account. Adams' recommendation to prevent errors also applies across media platforms: *Rigorously fact-check content.*

Traditionally, newspaper editors and educators have cautioned reporters not to fact-check their quotations with sources, fearing that the source will argue about an assertion or otherwise compromise the reporter. In some newsrooms today, this is taboo. Nevertheless, reporters concerned about accuracy and fairness usually feel socially responsible to get accurate quotes. When Adams worked as an investigative reporter at *The Wall Street Journal,* he would not show the full story to his sources. But he would show them "a numbered, point-by-point summary of every fact and item in the story that dealt with them," requesting that they inform him if anything was inaccurate. "If something wasn't inaccurate but the source objected to its thrust or inclusion, I'd hear their argument out," he notes, adding that he rarely changed anything. "But I'd rather have had the debate before the story ran than after." Moreover, to ensure fairness to all parties, including his newspaper, Adams cleared his fact-checking strategy with *Journal* editors and the newspaper's attorney, ensuring that they had no concerns with it. According to Adams, "It actually meshed with the philosophy an editor of mine at *The Journal* who taught me—no surprises—as in, 'A source shouldn't be surprised by anything he sees when he picks up a story about him.'"

Note at this point our earlier discussion about the ethics of quote-making in public relations. Adams fact-checks quotations with sources, even though the news industry has various standards associated with that practice. Point being, if news journalists are taking steps to ensure the accuracy of interviews, practitioners should be doing the same when quoting executives and clients in news releases. A word of caution, however: Checking quotations with sources differs from *fact-checking* what they asserted. Once a reporter is certain about what a source claims, especially if that claim was affirmed in a phone call, email or text, the next step is to verify the truth of the assertion. This practice proved especially significant in the wake of lies, half-truths and exaggerations associated with the 2016 presidential campaign. There are reliable websites devoted to fact-checking, such as FactCheck.org, a project of the Annenberg Public Policy Center. Using research to verify or dispute claims by sources is a routine aspect of the fairness process.

Discretion

Discretion involves the power to act on one's own judgment, relying on *perception.* Like fairness, this is associated with consciousness. Discretion also is about self-awareness, knowing seemingly insignificant character traits, such as when you are at your sharpest and at what tasks as well as knowing when you are at your dullest and/or most reactive. For instance, if you are a morning person, you might schedule creative projects then and less creative ones, such as fact-checking, later in the day. Or perhaps you savor the hour in the evening set aside for a hobby, exercise or other favorite pastime. Knowing that, you might want to shut off your cell phone or allow voicemail to take a call from a source or client. Of course, on some assignments, you will be interrupted at inopportune times and occasions. If you must do a task or take a call then, acknowledge and adjust for your limitations and emotions.

Journalists and practitioners also use discretion when determining what information should be excluded or kept confidential. *The Chicago Tribune*'s Joe Mahr uses discretion every day. "Just how much information do you need to put in a story?" he asks. "As an investigative reporter, it is easy to fall into a mindset of dumping your notebook containing all the bad or juicy tidbits on whoever is being exposed at the time. But is it relevant? Does it advance the story? If not, it shouldn't be a part of the story, no matter the temptation to put it in." Mahr cites as an example his work with others at *The Blade* in Toledo, Ohio, in the Pulitzer Prize-winning series, "Buried Secrets, Brutal Truths," published in 2003. The series by Mahr, Mike Sallah and Mitch Weiss concerned how the U.S. Army kept secret a string of battle atrocities in Vietnam. "I wrote about those atrocities committed by an elite unit in Vietnam, and how the government covered it up for more than three decades," Mahr states. "One of the main suspects had been arrested a couple years before the series publication for soliciting a prostitute and, later, for shoplifting meat. These are sensational tidbits about the person which, if published in a profile about him, "would seem like further ammunition that the person is 'bad.' But are these tidbits relevant? Do they help explain why this person helped commit atrocities? Do they, in any way, show the difficulties of living with committing those atrocities? Our answer: No. They simply were tidbits that didn't fit into the context of our story, so we didn't use them."

Confidentiality also requires discretion. Journalists who quote anonymous sources should follow internal policies concerning to whom anonymity should be granted and how that should be explained in news stories. Almost all news organizations have policies on the topic, shared with readers, particularly when changes are made, as a matter of transparency. *The New York Times*, whose reporters at times have been jailed for refusing to reveal anonymous sources or been criticized by readers and media critics for use of such sources, tightened standards for anonymous sources in 2016. In a memo to the newsroom, Philip Corbett, the standards editor, stated:

> At best, granting anonymity allows us to reveal the atrocities of terror groups, government abuses or other situations where sources may risk their lives, freedom or careers by talking to us. In sensitive areas like national security reporting, it can be unavoidable. But in other cases,

readers question whether anonymity allows unnamed people to skew a story in favor of their own agenda. In rare cases, we have published information from anonymous sources without enough questions or skepticism—and it has turned out to be wrong.[8]

The new policy requires a top editor to review and approve articles that rely on information from unnamed sources. The policy, among other things, also requires any use whatsoever of anonymous sources to be approved by the reporter's supervisor.

Policies on confidentiality apply across media platforms, especially in public relations, advertising and event planning agencies. Practitioners attend meetings in clients' companies or organizations and learn sensitive information about finances, personnel and proprietary information. Often, because of their presence at sessions when these matters are discussed, clients forget that they are not official members of the firm. As Judy Allen writes in *Event Planning Ethics and Etiquette*, when practitioners overhear such information, it should never be repeated or discussed. "Maintaining client confidentiality is an ethical part of doing business. What happens inside the company stays there and is not taken or talked about outside."[9]

However, in some situations, what a practitioner hears or is instructed to do may be especially upsetting. In one case, an Iowa State University intern working for a world-famous non-profit organization, bearing the name of a deceased icon, was told to make up quotes and literally put them in the mouth of the famous founder. This is not quote-making; it is sheer invention with huge consequences for the organization if someone investigated and disclosed the fabrication. She did as her supervisor instructed, but later regretted that to such extent that she decided to seek a career in investigative journalism. At the time she might have practiced discretion and refused to follow orders, based on her own moral value of truth-telling. This was covered previously in the chapter on temptation, under professional conflicts of interest. The case is included here because discretion also is at the heart of fairness, defusing such conflicts. According to Patricia J. Parsons in *Ethics in Public Relations*, practitioners will

> have to make a choice between what the employer or client is asking of them and what they as individuals, and based on their own personal value systems, know to be right. Clearly, then, as a public relations practitioner, you have duties to yourself, your employer or client, your profession and to society as a whole.[10]

Sometimes practitioners have a duty to understand different cultures, not only in the United States, but across the world. Cultural norms play a big role in ethical decision-making, says Donna Ramaeker Zahn, global outreach strategist for the International Food Policy Research Institute, Program for Biosafety Systems. To understand those norms in her travels,

Ramaeker Zahn practices two aspects of discretion: She seeks counsel from those in a specific city, country or region and then seeks to understand culture before making a decision on behalf of her organization. This requires multiple layers of information about the local environment, she says. "Is what you observed even actually what happened? Is a male reporter's refusal to shake the hand of a woman who is a source and of higher political status sexist, disrespectful, offensive or wrong? Should the reporter be thrown out of a meeting? It depends," she observes. "Who are the individuals? Who else was present at the time? What are their beliefs? Could devotion to a specific religion play a role?" Until she has sufficient information, she listens and seeks insight, practicing discretion.

Ramaeker Zahn witnessed what appeared to be an unprofessional situation. It happened in a country where "day-to-day survival consumes a majority of waking minutes." She observed a college professor there take graduate students to a three-day scientific meeting even though the students had no means to pay for housing and had to sleep outside on the ground. In the United States, such a scene "would likely be met with gasps, horror or quick judgment that the professor should be disciplined, or at the very least called out by others attending the meeting. In this cultural setting, the answer again is: It depends." This is what she learned. For students, attending the conference was a rare opportunity to gain access to brilliant minds, the latest scientific findings and new contacts who can help chart a career path for them in the future. Discretion allowed her to adjust her viewpoint and see the situation as potentially positive rather than entirely offensive.

Journalists and practitioners also interact with sources and clients about relatively routine matters. Even in these mundane matters, discretion is important as are Ramaeker Zahn's recommendations to seek counsel when uncertain about a situation and then analyze the setting and situation before making a decision on behalf of your organization. When communicating with sources and clients, should you use email, text, social media, write a memo, schedule a teleconference, or travel across or out of town for an interpersonal consultation? The temptation in the wireless news- and boardroom is to use technology because it is quick, efficient and convenient. However, over-reliance on digital communication can lead to unanticipated problems when we lack "interpersonal intelligence," or the ability to know when, where and for what purpose technology may be appropriate or inappropriate.

John Paluszek, senior counsel at Ketchum, notes that agencies use email much more than telephone calls, a past practice that also had a richer interpersonal element. "It is true for most of us that email is obviously more immediate. A simple message or question can be answered promptly. But then you have to decide if it's a discussion where give and take must take place over a conversational period of time. Then you shouldn't use email." Paluszek also acknowledges that email can be especially beneficial when used appropriately, to fact-check a quotation, say, or verify an appointment or distribute attachments for a project. But like any other convenience, the medium also can be misused. "I think that people get so hung up on the immediate, efficient concentration of language that we're all tempted to take shortcuts," Paluszek says, "and shortcuts in language can lead to misunderstandings" internally with coworkers and externally with clients or even the news media. "The old adage that what you write can wind up on the front page of *The New York Times* also applies to email in spades."

There are as many risks responding to emails and texts as creating them. Again, discretion comes into play. When you lack answers to an inquiry or read a sarcastic or inappropriate message, you need to pause, resist the temptation to respond and think through the situation. "After years in the business you do get a 'smell sense' about what could boomerang and hurt somebody or yourself," Paluszek says. "It's worth stepping back a few hours before you move ahead with some messages." He also adds that discretion matters in such seemingly minor tasks as composing an address list. Some people are offended when they are not copied on an email and others may not merit access to privileged information. "Young practitioners who are unsure of what is the right thing to do in such cases should consult a senior colleague," Paluszek says. "That takes time, but it's time well spent. All in all," he concludes, "communications technology is what it has always been—a valuable tool subject to human intelligence."

Retractions

The Committee on Publication Ethics was formed in 1997 by a group of editors concerned about accuracy, fairness and author misconduct. Its code of conduct addresses such issues as intellectual property, corrections and retractions. COPE defines retraction as "a mechanism for correcting the literature and alerting readers to publications that contain such seriously flawed or erroneous data that their findings and conclusions cannot be relied upon."[11] It recommends issuing a retraction if there is evidence that findings are erroneous or unreliable, if content was previously published elsewhere or without permission, or if there is evidence of plagiarism or unethical research. Those decisions typically are made by supervisors in advertising, journalism and public relations. Reporters and corporate communications officers on occasion issue retractions themselves if they or sources intentionally or unintentionally provided unreliable information. (Before doing so, they consult with supervisors and explain why such a retraction may be necessary.)

Accurate, fair and balanced perspectives are especially important to Clarence Page, the 1989 Pulitzer Prize winner for Commentary and member of *The Chicago Tribune*'s editorial board. He also was a regular contributor of essays to *The News Hour* with Jim Lehrer and has been a regular on The McLaughlin Group, NBC's *The Chris Matthews Show*, ABC's *Nightline* and BET's *Lead Story* news panel programs. With respect to fairness, Page recalled correcting the record in one of his columns, which he voluntarily retracted. He followed the fairness tenet of accepting truth as you find it, even if that truth goes against everything you have hitherto believed. Page came to see that he had overlooked an important viewpoint in his original column and, out of a sense of fairness, corrected the record in a new column that contained an apology. In the case study below, provided for *Living Media Ethics*, he discusses aspects of corrections, discretion and email correspondence that led to the apology.

"TO ERR IS HUMAN"

By Clarence Page, The Chicago Tribune

Too many facts can get in the way of a good story, according to an ancient nugget of cynical newsroom wisdom. But what do you do when the story gets out before facts catch up to it?

Or, in the case of a columnist like me, what do you do when the story on which you have based your strong opinion turns out to be woefully incomplete?

My most memorable example occurred in 1998 after the U.S. Department of Transportation directed the airlines to establish "peanut-free zones."

Their aim was to protect passengers who have nut allergies. A departmental directive called for airlines to interrupt their usual offerings by providing three peanut-free rows upon a passenger's request. Any peanut fans who happen to be seated in those rows would be out of luck when flight attendants offer the goobers.

Airline executives, according to news accounts, responded with "You've got to be kidding" when the DOT guidelines came out. They weren't alone. What a nutty idea, I thought—expressing the sort of shameless pun that leads to catchy, if groan-inducing, headlines.

After all, I reasoned, if peanuts are that bad, why not ban them from the entire flight? What, I wondered, will the big government herd us into next? Helpfully I suggested a no-talking zone for those of us who want to avoid overly chatty seat-mates. Even minor issues start to look more outrageous at deadline time.

I enjoyed writing that column—until the emails came in.

One particularly bracing message came from a Charlotte, N.C., reader whose two-year-old had a peanut allergy. He described in heartbreaking detail how a year earlier his son reacted after eating a cookie with a peanut fragment in it. His little throat and lips swelled up and he broke out in hives. Similar attacks can cause the child's throat to swell up until air is shut off, sending the child into a fatal coma.

"You may be surprised to know that I, too, thought it was 'nuts' for the DOT to adopt rules creating peanut-free zones in airplanes," my reader's email said. But he was no longer scoffing at those rules. Instead he and his wife had to always carry a pen-like syringe to give their son a quick shot if he has an attack and rush him to an emergency room. None of that is easy to do aboard an airplane.

Unfortunately, my commentary, he wrote, had "piled another brick on the wall of ignorance that families like ours will be running into just to protect our children and give them the basics: a safe home, an education and a chance to pursue their dreams."

As a fellow father, I was touched so deeply by those words that I decided to do something that I usually find to be about as appealing as oral surgery: I wrote another column on the peanuts regulation to retract and apologize for my earlier snark.

It is humbling to face one's mistakes, but we all need to be humbled sometimes. Most important, I felt I needed to do what countless editors had advised me in my years as a reporter: Tell the whole story.

The government, for all its other mistakes, was not quite as dumb as I made it out to be. I needed to remove my brick from "the wall of ignorance."

In the end, my second column generated more responses than my earlier one did. Most of it was not only favorable but appreciative. For all the criticism they may have of the media, news consumers tend to recognize another reality.

Some news consumers may think that corrections and clarifications are a sign of weakness. But most news consumers in my experience find them to be reassuring. In their search for reliable media, they find journalists who admit their mistakes to be more trustworthy than those who try to pretend that they never make any.

"DO YOU OR OTHERS PLAY FAIR OR FOUL?"

Personal Journal Exercise

1. Without violating your own or someone else's privacy or damaging anyone's reputation, recall a professional or academic situation, incident or event in which you believe you were treated unfairly. Describe details in a digital file but do not identify people involved in those situations, incidents or events.

2. Without violating your own or someone else's privacy or damaging anyone's reputation, recount a professional or academic situation, incident or event in which you believe that *you* treated someone else unfairly. Describe details in a digital file but do not identify people involved in those situations, incidents or events.

3. Review your digital files in Nos. 1 and 2 above. Now put each example through the fairness process on pages 257–58, ascertaining conflicts, balancing viewpoints and differing interests, seeking bonds or advice. Take notes to be used in No. 4 below.

4. Review your notes in No. 3 and make a determination about whether you were treated fairly (Exercise No. 1) and whether you treated another fairly (Exercise No. 2). Contemplate and take notes associated with these questions:

   - *How you could have been treated more fairly?*
   - *How you could have treated another person more fairly?*
   - *How the process has affected or enhanced your values on fairness?*

5. Without violating your own or someone else's privacy or damaging anyone's reputation, create a 500-word journal entry or blog post or brief podcast or multimedia presentation about what you learned from the above exercises. Also, send that assignment in to your instructor or group leader.

Communal Journal Exercise

As class instructor or group leader, you will have received journal entries, blog posts, podcasts or multimedia presentations from participants who did the "Personal Journal Exercise," No. 5, above. Code those exercises, focusing on the concept of viewpoint and lessons learned from the fairness process. Schedule a discussion about that. When possible, also note how discretion could have helped resolve fairness conflicts.

NOTES

1 Anita L. Allen, *The New Ethics: A Guided Tour of the Twenty-First Century Moral Landscape* (New York: Hyperion, 2004), xxxii.

2 Ibid., 39.

3 See "Price Fixing, Bid Rigging and Market Allocation Schemes," U.S. Department of Justice, June 25, 2015, www.justice.gov/atr/price-fixing-bid-rigging-and-market-allocation-schemes

4 Nancy Vonk and Janet Kestin, *Pick Me: Breaking Into Advertising and Staying There* (Hoboken, N.J.: Wiley, 2005), 139.

5 Ibid., 140.

6 Excerpt is from the student paper, not the published article.

7 Michael Bugeja, Jane Peterson, Rut Rey and Fernando Anton, "Rating the completeness of newspaper corrections in 2005 as compiled by 'Regret the Error,' presented August 2, 2006 at the Association for Education in Journalism and Mass Communication annual convention, San Francisco," study.

8 Margaret Sullivan, "Tightening the Screws on Anonymous Sources," the Public Editor newsblog, *New York Times*, March 15, 2016, https://public editor.blogs.nytimes.com/2016/03/15/new-york-times-anoymous-sources-policy-public-editor/?mcubz=0

"Confidential News Sources," The New York Times Company, February 25, 2005, www.nytco.com/company-properties-times-sources.html

9 Judy Allen, *Event Planning Ethics and Etiquette* (Ontario, John Wiley & Sons, 2003), 99.

10 Patricia J. Parsons, *Ethics in Public Relations: A Guide to Best Practice* (London: Kogan Page Ltd., 2016), 25.

11 Elizabeth Wager, Virginia Barbour, Steven Yentis, Sabine Kleinert, Council on Publication Ethics, "Retraction Guidelines," September 2009, https://publicationethics.org/files/retraction%20guidelines.pdf

CHAPTER 10

Power: Apply As Needed

POWER EXPRESSES VALUES

Power is not a value but the force that we use to put forth our values or the reputation that we earn because of those values. When we exercise too much power, we risk oppressing others. When we exert too little, others can take advantage of us. The objective is to apply only as much power as needed to address or resolve an issue without causing harm to innocent others. According to the book *The 48 Laws of Power*, "Power is essentially amoral. ... Half of your mastery of power comes from what you do not do, what you do not allow yourself to get dragged into."[1] Power is indirectly referenced in all of the chapters discussed previously in *Living Media Ethics*—in addition to all of the values, principles and processes—thereby making the concept the capstone consideration of any value system. How we express power is a function of leadership, credibility, trust, courage and other moral badges. We reveal our character via power and the choices that we make. If, for instance, the challenge is unemployment and the problem, financial, we can apply for a job or rob a bank. We can solicit a recommendation from a mentor or a bank sack from a teller. Then power goes passive. We bask in its glow or sweat in its glare.

Ethics has two primary components: values and power. Think of the term "values" as the numerator and "power," the denominator. As in math, if the denominator is zero, you have nothing, no matter how enormous or insignificant the numerator. You may decide to rob a bank, but first you have to get off the couch. No action, no choice. (*Deciding* to take no action—ignoring an error or overlooking sexual harassment—is a *choice*.) Without choices, our values are not on the line. When they are, power puts them there.

Power is a broad topic, particularly across media platforms. It applies to employees, their positions and their corporations—even to governments doing business with or regulating them. Those are professional considerations. Power also is intensely personal, associated with how you treat others and how they treat you as you perform your duties. In such light, some ethical issues involving power and media are omnipresent at the workplace. Those include business practices, censorship and self-censorship, restraint, taste considerations, hidden messages and harassment. In this chapter, we will investigate the power of the press vs. profit. You should know about the financial practices of media conglomerates and how you might respond to them. Budgets and earnings affect everyone across platforms, often forcing journalists and practitioners to do more with less, a pressure that can invite ethical shortcuts. You also should know about censorship and self-censorship and be able to distinguish them from standards of taste and free expression—what the public will or will not allow, from depictions of grief to use of profanity—so that you can serve your audience, clients and constituents with insight and discretion. You should know when to harness your own personal power at the workplace to prevent or report harassment, realizing just how powerful you actually are, even if you sometimes do not feel so, informed by consciousness and guided by conscience. Finally, you should know when to exercise the most powerful moral value of all, compassion and related ethical principles—including forgiveness, sympathy and empathy—all of which inspire us not only to follow the Golden Rule, but also to transcend it.

Media Power vs. Profit

Many professions are powerful. Business influences the economy and that, in turn, affects everyone because of the cost of living. Superstores like Wal-Mart affect communities, literally revamping hometowns. To explain how, journalist Charles Fishman has written a book titled, *The Wal-Mart Effect: How the World's Most Powerful Company Really Works—and How It's Transforming the American Economy*. Fishman uses analytical and verbal skills to take on one of the world's most powerful companies. He also has reported for *The Washington Post*, which took down the Richard Nixon administration in the 1970s Watergate series by Bob Woodward and Carl Bernstein. Obviously, there are talented, even powerful, employees at Wal-Mart with salaries comparable to Fishman's at *Fast Company* magazine, where he is a senior writer. But none that can take on *The Post*. Concerning money, revenue for Wal-Mart as reported in 2016 was $133.6 billion, an increase of 3 percent. That's about 80 times more than that of *The Washington Post*. So which company is more powerful—Wal-Mart or *The Post*—and why?

"Journalists have influence disproportionate to their pay sometimes," Fishman says, but so do Wal-Mart's ordinary front-line buying staff—the people who pick the varieties of dog food and clothes and cordless phones to stock in the stores. "They can't 'take on' *The Washington Post*," but the retail staff at Wal-Mart has more power to determine what we buy every day "than any business section reporter at *The Post* or *Fortune* or *The Wall Street Journal*."

Fishman's reporting skill stands as testament to the power of the press. "The most remarkable thing about *The Wal-Mart Effect*," he states, "is that a single person, with a telephone, a computer, a stack of notebooks and pens, a set of fairly urgent questions, and a credit card, was able to dig in and write what has turned out to be an important book about the largest, most powerful company currently operating in the world. From the second-floor office of my home outside Philadelphia, I took on the task of trying to understand Wal-Mart. Despite its culture of secrecy, despite its size and impact, the company couldn't stop me." Fishman adds that he was supported by his publisher, Penguin, which bought the book before it was written and provided an advance that allowed him to live for the 15 months it took to complete the work. "That is a remarkable testament to the power, protection and nurturing effect of the First Amendment," he says, adding that in recent years there has been a series of books by reporters who have taken on "the entirety of the American government, with great courage and honesty." From an ethical perspective, Fishman says, journalists have a responsibility to hold institutions accountable, "and while some stories and projects require huge resources, many do not." All that those stories and projects require, he notes, is determination, honesty and an ethical framework.

So which is more powerful, Wal-Mart or *The Washington Post*? It depends on how you define power. As Fishman puts it, Wal-Mart is clearly more powerful than he or *The Post, Fast Company* or Penguin Press, if you consider that decisions made by Wal-Mart's staff shape the world every day. "Reporters have the opportunity to shape how people *understand* the world."

That differs from the direct, immediate power that managers and executives at a company like Wal-Mart wield. Without media professionals like Fishman, that power would be unrestrained and business institutions would not be held accountable for their actions in pursuit of profit.

Revenue-minded media companies also focus on earnings. Increasingly, media conglomerates larger than *The Post* are demanding ever higher profit margins, often at the expense of news gathering. That can undermine not only the power of the press but of the people, too. In arguing against the concentrated ownership of media outlets, ethicist Clifford G. Christians notes that democratic nations prize a diversity of opinions and access to the marketplace of ideas. For democracy to thrive, citizens need both education and information. "When the media fail in their mission, civic life is stymied. Time Warner manufactures social resources, not something secondary such as silver doorknobs for Corvettes or swimming pools for the world's Hollywood stars."[2] Christians cites philosophers Martin Heidegger and Jacques Ellul in contending that a technological society is at odds with human freedom because its efficiency breeds normlessness. "The overwhelming power of means buries a consideration of ends," Christian writes, noting that the "critical challenge is not the immoral decisions of corporate leaders, but amorality in our culture."[3] In other words, the undue emphasis on technology as a means of revenue as well as of ends not only undermines the media's power to do social good but also dissolves ethical norms.

"When profit motive trumps truth, we dilute our journalist values," says David T.Z. Mindich, author of *Tuned Out: Why Americans Under 40 Don't Follow the News*. "Then people start to wonder what the value of journalism is in the first place." That can spark a media chain reaction. "If you don't have a good source of facts to help you become a good and active citizen, then you start to forget the purpose of the First Amendment and that, in turn, weakens journalism and it's a downward spiral from there."

Even in the large corporate environment, media professionals still have amazing powers. Phil Elliott, Washington correspondent for *Time*, says many of his sources have tremendous importance and influence. Some are captains of industry or government officials with industry ties. All have a say, directly or indirectly, about corporate profit and the U.S. economy. "They have power to shape a debate, to wield control over a federal budget or to upend diplomatic norms. But their power over me is limited. They cannot tell me what to ask, what to write and what to publish. In their act of speaking with me, they give up tremendous power, and they give it up to me. Once their words are in my hands—in my notebook, on my recording, on my screen and on my pages—there is relatively little that they can do." Nevertheless, Elliott admits to getting flustered before interviews with significant people or those his questions are likely to irk. "But I also take small comfort in the fact that, in this relationship, I hold the upper-hand because it is within my power to convey the contents of our conversation to the wider public. And, for many sources, they need the public to be brought into the conversation more than I need to have it."

One of the "power tools" for journalists is the Freedom of Information Act, signed into law in 1966 by President Lyndon Johnson. Government entities often resist FOIA requests for information "by either refusing to provide properly requested records or ignoring the requirements that the documents be made available within specified time periods,"[4] according to the FOIA Project, funded in part by Syracuse University. If a FOIA request is denied, the Freedom of Information Act allows reporters and news organizations to sue. *The New York Times* filed some 36 federal FOIA lawsuits in the past 16 years. David McCraw, *The Times'* vice president and assistant general counsel, states: "Simply, we feel that using this law is an essential part of our mission."[5] That attests to the ethical value that *The Times* places on responsible reporting.

Other news outlets also place a premium on truth and the means to obtain it, using the Freedom of Information Act and in-depth investigations. "Truth and the press have never been under greater threat," says Pulitzer Prize finalist Miles Moffeit, investigative reporter for *The Dallas Morning News*. Moffeit notes that investigative reporting has become more difficult as business and government try to withhold information from the public and even malign journalists for trying to access the data. Again, as is often the case, profit and economy are considerations. "We have to double down on our mission to hold public servants accountable," Moffeit states. "That means being dogged—yet relentlessly polite—in challenging those who are abusing the public trust. Are they following laws and regulations? Are they profiting from their public service? Are they twisting or hiding facts?" Unfortunately, he adds, because many news organizations have been grappling with resources, they have cut back on investigations. "Reporters have a huge responsibility now to stretch ourselves as watchdogs, and to champion the vulnerable, as well as ourselves as guardians of democracy."

We began the chapter asking which was more powerful, *The Washington Post* or Wal-Mart? We end this section by noting how *The New York Times* utilizes federal law to obtain information that the government withholds from the public, even though taxpayer dollars fund government. We also witnessed the power of media outlets like *Time* in Phil Elliott's viewpoint on dealing with influential sources and the commitment of investigative reporters like Miles Moffeit of *The Dallas Morning News* who holds officials accountable in a dogged pursuit of truth. Sometimes, though, governments resort to censorship to control public access to the truth.

Censorship vs. Self-Censorship

Censorship speaks to the power of government, and self-censorship to that of lobbyists. The government can conceal policies from the media by labeling them secret or restrict access to sensitive areas, especially during war, acting in the national interest. But in times of peace, censorship is primarily a concern of journalists working for U.S. companies operating in foreign countries with stricter laws regulating the media. Leaders of certain countries know the maxim "Knowledge is power" and so silence their media to protect their policies. This not only relates to news coverage but advertising and public relations campaigns as well. As David B. Ottaway has written as a State Department correspondent for *The Washington Post*, oppressive regimes often worry about their political *and* economic health, suggesting a correlation: the weaker that health, the stronger the censorship.[6] Typically these leaders restrict markets or campaigns promoting products or services that their citizens cannot afford or might want to adopt. According to editors of *The Quill*,

> Worldwide press censorship is the rule, not the exception. The Divine Right of Kings is a half-forgotten, even quaint notion. But Reasons of the State is alive and well and dwelling nearly everywhere. In much of Africa—black Africa as well as South Africa; in parts of Europe; in the Middle East; in the Far East; in Asia; in Mexico; in Central America; in South America—reasons of state are used to squeeze and channel and even shut down the flow of information.[7]

The specter of censorship is rampant in these countries. According to Sir John Tusa, former executive of the British Broadcasting Corporation, or

BBC, "Censorship has a thousand faces—openness only one, whichever country you are in. Of all its masks, self-censorship can be as bad as any, the willing decision not to report something you know is happening."[8]

Corporations may refuse or agree to government demands. In 2006, the search engine company Google did both. Early in that year Google declined to hand over data to help revive a child protection law that had been struck down by the U.S. Supreme Court. The law would have punished operators of child pornography sites that can be accessed by minors. Google, which voiced First Amendment concerns, resisted the federal subpoena because it would violate rights of its users. This was in keeping with the company's brand, no longer used, of "Do no evil," which has a Kantian ring, elevating the duty to serve clientele via unrestricted access to information. However, shortly after embracing free speech and rebuffing the U.S. government's demands, Google negotiated a deal with China to limit access and censor certain searches done in that Communist country. A fact in the equation might have been that the U.S.-based search engine had competition in China from Baido.com, whose market share at the time rose from 33.1 percent to 46.5 percent compared with Google's 22.4 percent to 26.9 percent.[9] Nevertheless, the U.S. company opted to justify censorship, even though that business decision conflicted with its "Do no evil" mission—which, for better or worse, branded Google as ethical. This decision was questionably so and hence raised questions among clientele. In the wake of criticism, the company issued this explanation:

> In order to operate from China, we have removed some content from the search results available on Google.cn, in response to local law, regulation or policy. ... While removing search results is inconsistent with Google's mission, providing no information (or a heavily degraded user experience that amounts to no information) is more inconsistent with our mission.[10]

In essence, the company indicated that censorship might be inconsistent with its mission *but lack of information was even more inconsistent*. Google might have been embarrassed by the timing of two news reports that seemed to contradict each other ethically along with the corporate motto of "Do no evil." Although the company justified its actions, the contract to serve China inherently was a business decision, not a moral one—at least that was the perception. Acknowledging that, however, would have compelled Google to wrestle with its brand identity, which guided the company in resisting the U.S. government on First Amendment grounds. Yielding to China seemed based on revenue projections.

That was to change in the years ahead. In 2010, Google terminated its Chinese search engine, essentially losing an enormous market for its services. In the future the company may return to the Chinese market, but the reason for shutting down services was based on a distinct ethical reason: *censorship*. In 2016, according to *The Atlantic*, "Google found that the Gmail accounts of a number of Chinese human-rights activists had been hacked," indicating some sort of government surveillance.[11] One year earlier, Google dropped its "Do no evil" mantra from its conduct code. Its parent company, Alphabet, noted that employees of all its companies, subsidiaries and affiliates "should do the right thing—follow the law, act honorably, and treat each other with respect."[12] Both actions had to do with corporate ethics.

Media professionals, including those at Google, derive their power from the First Amendment. It is important to note that whenever discussing the state of media across platforms. The U.S. system of government is based on that premise, assuring free speech, free press, freedom of and from religion, assembly and petition. Those five rights make censorship and self-censorship significant social as well as media concerns. However, too often, companies as well as citizens take First Amendment freedoms for granted. Andy Alexander, former ombudsman for *The Washington Post*, says, "In talking about the First Amendment with young journalists, I am struck by their passive reaction to restrictions that could profoundly affect them as professionals and as citizens. They seem undisturbed by the campaign to reduce transparency in the way government officials conduct the peoples' business. They seem not to be worried by harsh criticisms (often by elected officials) intended to silence those who utter statements that do not echo the party line. And they appear utterly incapable of articulating a defense of why the First Amendment matters."

A survey of 1,002 respondents conducted by the Newseum Institute affirms Alexander's views. Conducted in 2015, those surveyed were asked to name the specific freedoms of the First Amendment. While 57 percent of Americans named freedom of speech, only 19 percent cited freedom of religion, with 10 percent naming freedom of the press and the right to assemble, with only 2 percent citing the right to petition; worse, some 35 percent of Americans could not name any of the rights.[13] The inability to embrace freedoms of the First Amendment affects the practice of advertising, journalism and public relations. It is one thing to know your rights as a creator of content; it is quite another to know what your audience or clientele will prohibit or allow.

Prior vs. Personal Restraint

Government censorship, covered in the previous section, also is called "prior restraint." Defined, such restraint involves *public officials trying to prevent media from disseminating sensitive or embarrassing information*. Legal analyst Douglas E. Lee notes that this is extremely difficult to do because "limits on prior restraint (as such censorship is also known) have been firmly in place for more than 70 years."[14] Lee references how prior restraint was tested in 1971, "when the government attempted to prevent *The New York Times* and *The Washington Post* from publishing the Pentagon Papers, a classified study of U.S. decision-making in Vietnam."[15] The media's right to publish was affirmed by the U.S. Supreme Court in "New York Times Co. v. United States." That benchmark ruling was the subject of the 2017 film, *The Post*, starring Meryl Streep as then publisher Katharine Graham and Tom Hanks as editor Benjamin Bradley.

Defined, personal restraint means *postponing the decision to respond with an appropriate amount of power to a perceived threat until you can ascertain whether that threat actually exists and, if so, whether it is potentially minor, significant or catastrophic.*

Personal restraint is difficult to practice without a strong value system. Studies have shown people typically believe they have a greater capacity for restraint than they actually do. Researchers call this tendency "restraint bias," or an inflated sense of "impulse-control beliefs" that prompt people "to overexpose themselves to temptation, thereby promoting impulsive behavior."[16] While such studies address potentially addictive behaviors, such as hunger or drug cravings, they also apply to journalists and practitioners operating in tense, tempting, deceptive, manipulative and dishonorable situations.

A common situation across platforms is how to deal with internet trolls, a specter that any journalist and practitioner faces daily in digital environments. A 2015 study out of Stanford and Cornell universities analyzed 40 million posts on news, political and gaming websites, focusing on two distinct groups: future-banned users and never-banned users. Banned users were designated as trolls who often went off topic and posted more comments per day on each thread, with many of those deleted. In reporting the study, *Time* noted that trolls typically posted surly comments banned by the website, making those individuals "get even crazier—a cycle that gradually spins out of control, until they're ultimately shut down."[17] As you might anticipate, the study recommended that the best way to discourage trolls is to ignore them.

Some media websites encourage journalists and practitioners to engage with people who post comments on social media. Those policies differ from company to company with policies explained in employee manuals. One study found that most respondents on news sites want journalists to explain content and respond to comments. According to the Center for Media Engagement at the University of Texas-Austin, some "81 percent of survey respondents at each news site would like it if journalists clarified factual questions in the comment section," with the percentage varying between 71 percent and 87 percent across the news sites.[18] If your newsroom or company encourages comments or clarifications, you will need to practice restraint, especially if your person or your professionalism is sullied in an online comment. A reliable method of disempowering trolls is to startle them with professionalism. Focus on content and ethical standards and let facts speak for themselves. One note of warning, however: Be sure to check with your supervisor if you receive threatening comments about your post or on your company website. This has become all too common an occurrence. A 2014 Pew Research Center report noted that 40 percent of all internet users are harassed online, with men trolled more often than women, except in journalism, where women also were attacked personally, including "sexual harassment and threats of violence."[19]

Personal restraint also involves your interactions at the workplace or in group settings, such as classes, meetings or even parties and other social events. Often others at those gatherings might say something or profess a personal or political belief that unnerves you to such extent that you are tempted to respond angrily. During those occasions, you should respond with the proper amount of power to address the situation while maintaining your integrity and professionalism.

One of the ways to do that is to ascertain the levels of your offense-taking. Ask yourself:

- What are my "trigger words"—words or phrases that cause a positive or negative response in me and cloud my perception and discernment—precisely when I need both to represent my views or ideals as powerfully and appropriately as possible?
- What are the issues or behaviors that do *not* concern me or my unit but nonetheless annoy (slight irritation), anger (moderate irritation), or outrage me (substantial irritation)?
- What are the issues or behaviors of that *do* concern me or my unit and annoy me (slight irritation), anger (moderate irritation), or outrage me (substantial irritation)?
- Am I responding with similar or varying levels of offense-taking at slight, moderate, or outrageous issues and behaviors?
- Is there any difference in the levels of offense-taking between issues or behaviors that (a) concern me or my unit and (b) do not concern me or my unit?

After analyzing your answers, determine whether you are satisfied with your levels of offense-taking and decide whether you should (a) speak up less or more powerfully when situations warrant, (b) lower your levels to maintain your perception and discernment or (c) raise them to safeguard your values and ideals. There is an ethical reason why you should make such an evaluation. If too many voices express outrage over issues of slight impact on your workplace, others may not be fully able to discern legitimate voices of complaint.

Taste vs. Free Expression

In many respects, self-restraint also is a matter of taste. Defined, taste is *the suppression of images or messages in a specific medium by authorized representatives of that medium, usually with a goal of appropriateness in response to privacy or community and customer standards or with respect to budgetary concerns.* Taste differs from self-censorship because supervisors are responding to standards set by audience, clientele and communities. Depending on values or corporate policies, journalists and practitioners restrict or transmit images and/or messages in the interest of (or without regard to) taste. That makes it an ethical issue associated with responsibility, manipulation, temptation, conflicts of interest and fairness (among other values). Admittedly, taste usually is a function of discretion and included here because:

- Content reviewed for taste often is powerful in itself, involving grief, pornography, profanity, etc.
- Software and multimedia applications typically amplify such content through photo-enhancement, music, voice-overs and videos, often converging at once.
- Such content in a digital environment may reach unintended readers, viewers, listeners, publics, constituents and consumers.
- Gatekeepers of content (in-house attorneys, editors, managers, agency owners, etc.) determine taste based in part on the power of their positions.

The decision to create, gather, report, restrict, ban or disseminate questionable material is a function of power that can consume an entire outlet. Arguments in favor of disseminating such content typically rely on the First Amendment. Arguments against such content can involve government regulation, restricting profanity over public airwaves, for instance, or forbidding tobacco products in advertising. Media professionals also realize implications concerning taste after the fact through loss of subscribers, clients and consumers and, as a consequence, even loss of employment. In addition, there can be lawsuits, boycotts and protests—not to mention political and financial pressure from elected officials to stockholders. That can affect business. Moreover, standards of good taste vary from media outlet to media outlet, market to market, town to town, region to region, industry to industry. In other words, what one radio talk show host will allow, another might not, depending on audience standards; what an advertising director at a newspaper might allow to illustrate an "R"-rated movie, a photo editor might reject at the same newspaper on the same day, according to standards about the use of sexually suggestive images in ads vs. news.

Such standards can be shaped by the individual publisher, agency owner or media executive. Sometimes taste is a function of budgets or work schedules, with editors or managers opting not to pursue a story or a campaign because of liability or risk or because they lack the financial or human resources to execute the project. Typically, taste standards are put into place by supervisors with the audience, consumer, client or budget in mind. But management's intentions at times also may be suspect.

When editors or supervisors reject a high-risk story or campaign proposal, a journalist or practitioner may accuse them of self-censorship. It can go the other way, with management seeking sensation or hype, demanding that the journalist or practitioner do a high-risk project that violates ethical standards.

Taste also can be exercised by the individual journalist or practitioner without his or her employer or supervisor even knowing about it. Often, media professionals are made to cross the line in documenting what they feel may be indecent. For instance, a photographer was asked to cover a funeral of a teenage boy found in the basement of his home hanging from the ceiling. "There was a sexual component to the story," the photographer observes, which he learned from an emergency service worker at the local hospital. "It was tragic and worth addressing, but I did not think that the family needed more attention drawn to the event by having a photograph in the newspaper. My editor did not agree, and I was sent to make photographs of crying teenagers at the boy's funeral. I did attend but decided to leave my camera in the car." The photographer decided to lie rather than confront his editor. "When I got back to the office, I claimed to have not loaded the camera properly and lost all the photos as a result." Perhaps the photographer should have confronted the editor about the decency of the coverage. By not doing so, this type of taste-related conflict of interest (professional vs. professional, as discussed in the chapter on temptation) is sure to emerge again. However, his choosing not to do the assignment and then to lie about it indirectly speaks to the power and fear of management.

"Taste and decency do each other a disservice when they appear linked together as a single phenomenon. The law distinguishes them,"[20] writes Colin Shaw in *Deciding What We Watch: Taste, Decency, and Media Ethics in the UK and the USA*. Shaw states that the law does not punish bad taste, which is a product of civility, manners or social mores subject to rapid change. "On the other hand, an issue of decency touches on something more profound and permanent, recognition of common humanity, preservation of individual human dignity through the regard owed by one human being to another."[21] In this sense, the photographer who lied about his camera disagreed with his editor on two counts involving the taste and decency of publishing the funeral photo. The term "decency" literally means conforming to social norms as to what is morally acceptable. The problem here, however, concerns where one draws the line on what is decent or indecent content in a report or campaign.

Standards of decency may differ legally from taste in the courtroom but not in the news- or conference room. Decency plays a role in taste considerations, and that is determined by audience and clientele. However, two factors have complicated standards of decency across media platforms. Increasing use of technology homogenizes community standards over time. Before network and cable television, people in different parts of the United States dressed, spoke and ate according to cultures of their region. Now we tend to don the same brand-name clothes, speak the same lingo and consume the same fast foods. Technology, including text messaging, smartphones, social media and mobile devices, has added to that effect. Internet has homogenized us even more by blurring boundaries of what constitutes a community. Geographic and community standards used to play a larger role in determining standards of decency. What used to be decent in New York City often was indecent in Iowa City. That no longer is the case. A "community" can be Iowa City. It can also be the social network Instagram accessed in Iowa City but distributed throughout the world. In the digital age, we lost physical place and, with it, clear designations of what is tasteful, decent and respectable within particular geographical regions. In some sense, this compels journalists and practitioners to be as ethical as possible in what they say or show via the internet because the content can be viewed everywhere by groups who might take offense at what you post.

Time and technology change standards at ever faster rates, not only in communities but also in industries. The late Hugh Sidey, native of Greenfield, Iowa, and former White House correspondent for *Time*, had access to presidents who had personal habits that pushed the envelope on taste and decency. In a 2005 speech at Iowa State University, Sidey noted that after the 1961 Vienna summit President John F. Kennedy invited him to dinner to give him his personal impressions of Soviet Premier Nikita Khrushchev. "Kennedy was with two gals from the White House. Right off you could see that Kennedy had a sex problem. But I didn't report that. I was more interested in Khrushchev." On another occasion at the White House, Kennedy invited Sidey to go for a swim. "I told him, Mr. President, I came here to interview you. I don't have a swimming suit. And he said to me, 'You don't need a swimming suit in this pool.' So there I was teetering on the edge of the pool, wondering what the etiquette was. Who should take off his pants first, the President or the visitor? The President beat me to it." Sidey noted that this was his first and last underwater interview. "My editors wanted me to describe that," he said, "but I didn't mention it." Sidey believed the description exceeded standards of decency and taste. Since then, of course, dozens of books have been written about or mention the sex life of Kennedy. Moreover, if a reporter was put in the same situation today as Sidey was at the swimming pool, the president's dip rather than his comments would have been banner news.

In the past, journalists like Sidey could make determinations about what they would or would not put into a story because of taste considerations. That has changed with digital media. According to journalists Bill Kovach and Tom Rosenstiel, the notion of press as gatekeeper—"deciding what information the public should know and what it should not—no longer strictly defines journalism's role." They write: "If *The New York Times* decides not to publish something, at least one of countless other websites, talk radio hosts, and partisans will. We now see examples of this regularly."[22] This effect allows more judicious consideration of taste without fear of self-censorship in that other media inevitably will cover content that exceeds the bounds of audience or target market; however, it also allows more questionable content into the public domain, altering social mores and homogenizing morality.

Issues of taste in news coverage can have great impact on society. One of the most mundane tasks is gathering information from police reports or court documents, often the source of taste-related privacy problems in the newsroom. The task may be mundane but the details in such reports or documents often are stark. When published, they can cause great pain to family and friends of crime victims. Such was the case with an Ohio University student whose friend was murdered along with another woman acquaintance near Akron. The story was covered in detail by *The Akron Beacon Journal*. **WARNING: Content that follows concerns violence and descriptions of sexual assault.**

The OU student felt the information that area newspapers published about the murders violated the privacy of the victims and that of family and friends. "I know my friend's death was brutal and painful," she says. "I know she suffered more horror than I can ever imagine in my life. However, thanks to the newspaper's vivid description, images of her death fill my mind. Did I need to know, let alone the public, that Wendy was found naked from the waist down, with her top pulled up and her bra torn in half? Was it necessary to print that she was raped twice, by two guys? Or that her face was covered with 'inch-deep lacerations' from a knife? Or that they were 'killed with a blunt instrument smashed against the right sides of their heads.' Or that the weapon 'crushed (Wendy's) skull' and that 'both died of brain injuries.'

"I did not. These descriptions have caused nightmares and unnecessary horror. When I think of Wendy I no longer think of the beautiful model she was. It's hard to get the image of her bloody, mutilated body out of my mind. It's hard to stop picturing her being raped in this 'field of tall cattails.' And it is hard to realize that her death was slow and painful. Did the paper have to mention that before she was beaten to death, the guys tried to kill her by strangling her with a shoelace?"

The student believes that newspapers should have eliminated those details from their reports in the interest of privacy and community standards. Some editors might argue otherwise, however. According to their values, they accept the risk of hurting or offending some individuals in the name of the public good or the community's right to know. The details of the Akron murders illustrate the brutality and violence of rape, a hideous abuse of power; they may influence citizens or their representatives to take a stronger stance on crime, for instance. A classmate of the OU student who complained about the coverage happened to be an intern at *The Akron Beacon Journal* when editors there decided to cover the murders in depth.

April Hunt, who went on to work for *The Atlanta Journal-Constitution* and *The Orlando Sentinel*, did not participate in the coverage but remembered it well. Hunt, communication manager at Emory College, says, "Sadly, while I don't think each detail was completely necessary, the stacking of such detail does serve a purpose: to explain the magnitude of the crime. More seasoned now, I would hope to be a little less graphic, say about the facial lacerations by calling them mutilations. But I do think that the attempt of strangling by shoelace shows the horror of what these women endured, and that will be part of the record as the assailants go to trial, potentially to prison and, under Ohio law, could be eligible for parole."

John Cádiz Klemack, a general assignment reporter for NBC4 in Los Angeles, recalls an incident that occurred earlier in this career when on assignment for KSTU, the Fox News affiliate in Salt Lake City, Utah. He rushed with his crew to the scene of a head-on car crash in which a driver crossed the center line and collided with a car driven by a teenage girl. "The girl died. We were there as police told the girl's mother and our camera was the only one rolling," Klemack recalls. "The mother's scream was chilling. She fell to the ground screaming and crying as police surrounded her to hold her from hitting her head on the pavement. She was yelling out, 'Not my baby! Not my baby!' The video is haunting. But we had it. And would have made for a gut-wrenching story on the accident. But we didn't use it. Not one frame."

Klemack cites an example where KSTU *did* use graphic video. "We happened to be shooting video of a horse race when the lead horse tumbled and began having a seizure. I had never seen anything like it. It wiggled and turned and moved so fast, the horse's neck broke and it died on the track. Even after its apparent death, the horse was still shaking in the dirt. But we showed it. We had a disclaimer on the story warning about its graphic nature but explained that we needed to show it because it was part of a conspiracy to improve horse strength and speed. The trainer had been injecting the horse with chemicals, and it's possible that's what led to the horse's seizure and death."

In the first instance, concerning the car accident, Klemack and crew decided not to air the emotional video of the mother's grief, because of privacy concerns. In the second, they aired the graphic video because of newsworthiness, usually a determining factor in the decision to publish, broadcast or post graphic details that might offend the audience. Note, too, that the station ran disclaimers warning viewers about what was to be aired. That also is standard and shows respect for the public.

The decision to use or edit potentially inappropriate material is a function of fairness as well as taste. **WARNING: Racial slurs and profanity present a special challenge. Because we have to use them in this text, illustrating standards of morality, we caution you with this disclaimer about content in the next several pages using the n-word and other vulgar terms.**

Occasionally, journalists and practitioners have to deal with an abhorrent word like the n-word that will offend, hurt or humiliate almost everyone in the audience but also indicate the severity of the offense or bigotry by a source or client. Kenn Venit, a television news consultant, believes, "No news organization wants to offend its audience, but no one wants to censor, either."[23] Media and HBO publicists had to deal with that in 2017 when late-night host Bill Maher spoke with Republican Senator Ben Sasse of Nebraska, discussing how adults in California still dress up for Halloween. Senator Sasse said that didn't happen in this state, prompting this exchange:

> **Maher:** "I've got to get to Nebraska more."
> **Sasse:** "You're welcome. We'd love to have you work in the fields with us."
> **Maher:** "Work in the fields? Senator, I'm a house nigger. No, it's a joke."[24]

Maher apologized for the remark. Note in this case that *The New York Times*, which reported the exchange as printed above, used the racial slur rather than "n-word."

Sometimes an editor's impulse to protect readers from slurs or profanity undermines the primary duty to inform them, which in this case might mean using the offensive word without substituting hyphens or euphemisms. The latter can be especially confusing. Venit cites a newspaper trying to avoid the word "fuck" in a piece discussing former President Richard Nixon's use of "the most common four-letter barnyardism" and asked: "How am I supposed to know what barnyardism we're talking about here?"[25]

"Fuck," as broadcasters know, is one of the notorious seven profane words generally banned from public airwaves during restricted hours when children are thought to be awake. (Others are "cocksucker," "cunt," "motherfucker," "shit," "piss" and "tit," although the latter three are not nearly as subject to self-censorship as the others.) The Federal Trade Commission does not keep a list of profane words; neither does it have jurisdiction over subscription-based cable and satellite services. Magazines print these words regularly as long as they do not exceed the bounds of taste of the target audience. An ethical issue arises, however, when editors have to make a judgment call, which happened at *Writer's Digest*, a freelance and creative writer periodical. Its editor at the time, Bruce Woods, encountered the term "fuck" when preparing for publication an interview with world-renowned author Stephen King. King, discussing slow days at the typewriter, said:

> I had this tense scene where there were a lot of sexual politics involved, and I wanted to do it right and I didn't know if I could. And what that means is that I dallied by the teapot, and I read the sports twice and I said to myself: "Well, you shouldn't be doing this, you shouldn't be reading anything right now, because when you read, it fucks you up.[26]

Dealing with the word "fuck" is a "balancing act," Woods said. On the one hand, you try to maintain "the integrity of the piece" and on the other, make it suitable for the audience. "This is sometimes not simple," he adds. "Do you risk running an article that nobody—because of the offensive material it contains—will finish, purely in the name of editorial integrity? Do you run a piece that nobody will finish—because the life has been taken out of its voice—in order to kowtow to what you suppose are the sensitivities of your audience?" Woods decided to use "fuck" in the King interview "because it is a part of King's voice and also because, I felt, readers expect King to be a bit dangerous." Woods did eliminate one or two earlier uses of "fuck," however, "both to avoid chasing readers away before they could be hooked by the piece and because we felt that the impact of the remaining usage would be most dramatic in the article's conclusion."

A handful of readers objected. Woods published a letter from an anonymous reader who wrote,

> Well WD, you finally did it. You've stooped to the low level of pornographic writing. I was shocked to see the use of an offensive four-letter word in the Stephen King interview. I will no longer purchase your periodical, and I will be sure to tell others of my reason for this decision.[27]

The vast majority of readers did not complain about the use of "fuck" in the King interview. But the reader's canceling of her subscription is the typical response, a consequence that all editors weigh before approving use of profanity. Utmost in mind is the reputation of the outlet.

Several journalists working at traditional outlets have been fired or reprimanded for views expressed on blogs or social media. This has complicated ethical issues concerning taste, which previously were handled internally between employee and supervisor about content under consideration for publication, broadcast or public release. Internet separates the employee from both the outlet and the supervisor, with one usually working at home and the other in the office or newsroom, creating a situation in which the blogger may be held accountable for personal views in posts, especially if they offend others or are directed at the place of employment. One of the earliest such offenses happened in 2005. A reporter, formerly of the *Dover* (Del.) *Post*, was fired after his editor learned that the reporter's "MySpace" site had made certain negative references about African Americans, Martin Luther King Day and James Earl Ray, King's assassin. The reporter maintained that his firing violated his free speech rights, but as he worked for a private employer, and government did not interfere, any First Amendment legal action likely would prove futile.[28]

More recently, veteran broadcaster Valerie Hoff, formerly of WXIA, Atlanta, was looking for a source who had a video of white police officers assaulting an African American. She located the video in a Twitter feed whose owner had remarked that "news niggas" were contacting him for the footage. Hoff contacted him privately, stating: "'Please call this news nigga. LoL I'm with 11alive."[29] The source soon discovered that Hoff was a white woman using the term, and that offended him. Initially, he felt that Hoff was calling him the racial slur. She explained that she was referring to herself and apologized. The conflict then escalated when the reporter's use of the term was documented in a screenshot and shared on social media. The station suspended Hoff for two weeks. Reportedly, media then became interested in the incident and, according to a lawsuit filed by Hoff, she was forced to resign. This is a complicated but important case in documenting how journalists and practitioners have to be professional at all times, even when sending private messages.[30]

As you can see, digital and social media quickly escalate misjudgments in taste both in the public and private arenas. Companies are cautious about how they are depicted across platforms because of the global and occasionally inflammatory reach, undermining their brands. Nonetheless, because digital and social media pit free speech and press against media practices pertaining to taste, the topic can become inflammatory. Case in point: In 2005, an associate beauty editor at *Ladies' Home Journal* tendered her resignation at the Meredith Corporation's magazine, planning to take a job at *Seventeen*, when she was identified as the blogger of a site that had discussed her workplace. *Ladies' Home Journal* asked her to leave before her two-week's notice had expired, and *Seventeen* rescinded its job offer.[31]

Meredith Corporation, like several other media companies, includes information in its employee handbook under the section, "Blogging and other forms of online discourse":

Whether or not you choose to create or participate in a blog or other form of online publishing or discussion is your own decision. Your online activities in or outside of work that affect your job performance, the performance of others, or Meredith's business interests are a proper focus for company policy. Accordingly, if you do participate in online discussions, make sure you know and follow Meredith's *Code of Business Conduct & Ethics* guidelines. Pay particular attention to what the code has to say about confidential or proprietary information, about avoiding misrepresentation and about competing in the field. If, after checking the code, you are still unclear as to the propriety of a post, it is best to refrain and seek the advice of management. You are personally responsible for your own posts, and your postings are not corporate communications. Be mindful of what you write. If you can be identified as a Meredith employee in your online discussions, you should make it clear that you are speaking for yourself and not on behalf of Meredith. Be respectful of the company, employees, clients, partners and competitors. Ensure that your online activity does not interfere with or detract from your work commitments or the company's interests.[32]

The policy allows blogging. However, it also reminds employees that online activities have the potential to affect the company, recommending that bloggers consult the ethics code and a supervisor on any issue that might violate standards. Further, the policy asks blogging employees to be mindful of what they post in a converged media environment. After all, content from blogs appears regularly in traditional outlets such as *The New York Times* and *Washington Post*. A 2006 study by Marcus Messner and Marcia Watson presented at a national journalism conference examined 2,059 newspaper articles and found that they routinely use blogs as sources and that blogs heavily rely on traditional sources, too.[33] That creates a "cycle of sources," allowing ever stronger opinions and responses. As we saw in the Valerie Hoff example, even private text messages and responses from journalists and practitioners can be copied, selected and posted on a blog or social media site. In sum, what appears via one medium on one platform soon can appear across a multitude, requiring media professionals to think critically before posting impulsively.

Journalists and practitioners not only must be aware of the digital media environment but also the shifting demographics of U.S. society. No longer can they make broad cultural generalizations about taste. "Taste in advertising really goes back to a basic premise of knowing your market," says Connie Frazier, executive vice president of the American Advertising Federation. "What may be okay for one subset of the market may not be okay for another subset. So *where* you place the advertisement is important in that taste and tone must be consistent with the target subset." However, problems arise when advertisements intended for one target market cross over to and offend another market because of convergence. "In a world of converged media what might appeal to one subset might increasingly be exposed to other subsets." Advertisers must be aware of that fact. "You can no longer box people," Frazier says. "Even though ideally we as advertisers would like to be able to say—'All these people who have these characters utilize these media venues'—we can't. We're diverse people. The advertising industry has to be respectful of that." This differs from the 1960s. Back then, Frazier says, the mass market was primarily white. "Now we have multiculturalism. I have within my own market, for example, people who are Caucasian, African American, Hispanic and Asian, and if I'm a small advertiser, then I may not have the budget for each of those subsets.

"In some instances, if a large share is targeted toward a specific ethnic group it behooves us develop a campaign for that group." However, she notes, if advertisements are going to be read or viewed by various segments of the populace, then advertisers "have to rise above mass marketing through the use of universals rather than generalizations or even stereotypes. We should seek common bonds. Advertising should be inclusive." Because of that, we must rethink taste and decency standards. "The advertising of the future will have to be universal. The key, then," she adds, "is to develop critical thinkers, strategic thinkers. That goes for large advertisers, too."

Finally, a word about "trigger warnings." You will have noticed that such warnings were used in this section because content can spark intense emotional reactions in individuals who have suffered from assault, violence, stereotypes, racism and other traumatic events or experiences. While the subject of trigger warnings has been controversial in higher education—see Michael Bugeja's essay "The Fuss: Teaching in an Age of Trigger Warnings and Micro-Aggressions"[34]—such "viewer discretion" alerts are routine across platforms in media. Failure to use that message in potentially offensive material can be grounds for disciplinary action, especially for broadcast producers.

Latent vs. Manifest Messages

Taste, with regard to advertising, concerns the message as much as the product. An ad has two goals: to inform and to influence. When it informs, it sends a manifest (or obvious) message: "Buy this toothpaste because it prevents tooth decay." When an ad influences, it sends a latent (or hidden) message: "Buy this toothpaste and experience love because a beautiful woman or handsome man will kiss you." Taste can involve one or both messages or how those messages are used in tandem with images or illustrations. It's easy to spot questionable taste in a manifest message. Typically, the product may violate social mores or community standards, including solicitations for pyramid schemes or escort services, for instance. Questionable taste in latent messages can be easy to spot, too.

One such notorious message went down in the annals when *The Minneapolis Star Tribune* published an advertisement at the height of a widely publicized controversy concerning two rival Olympic skaters. The latent message alluded to figure skater Tonya Harding's role in a conspiracy that led to the baton-beating of rival Nancy Kerrigan after a practice session at the U.S. Figure Skating Championship before the 1994 Winter Olympic Games. Harding's husband hired a man to attack Kerrigan with a metal baton, and the advertised product was based on that incident. Harding had no role in the actual beating; nonetheless, a company took advantage of the media coverage and billed the product "The Tonya Tapper" with the slogan: "You've Seen How It Works/Now Get One for Your Protection." In this case, the manifest message was: "Buy this product to protect yourself against crime." The latent message was "You've Seen How It Works." What the audience saw on television news was Nancy Kerrigan doubled up and crying from pain on a rink floor after being beaten by a baton. That made the latent message questionable, if not offensive. After the ad ran, *The Star Tribune* received about 20 calls from readers who thought it was in poor taste; nonetheless, it met in-house standards because the product was legal. "The ad didn't say anything about [Harding's] guilt or innocence," a newspaper spokesperson said. "If it had, it would have changed the way we looked at it."[35]

In some cases, the manifest and latent message are fine but become questionable in tandem with an image or illustration. For instance, an advertisement for a gas chlorinator in a trade magazine informed the audience that "it's simpler—it works better—it costs less." The latent message stated that the product is "built right (half the story)/and backed right (the other half)." The ad was in poor taste, though, because the photograph illustrating it had nothing to do with the product: an apparently naked model with her hand on the chlorinator. A text bubble covered her breasts and pubic area and inquired whether the reader planned to buy or shop for a chlorinator within the next year. Customers could check a "Yes" or "No" box. Another box stated: "I want photo only."

Sometimes ad copy alone can be controversial. A billboard ad by Labatt USA, which distributes Mexican beer, featured the headline, "Finally, A Cold Latina." The ad's latent message stereotyped women of that heritage as sexually loose. It didn't matter the ad was created by an agency specializing in the Latino/a market or that a purported 92 percent of those surveyed by the company failed to find the slogan offensive.[36] Those arguments no longer matter when a potential stereotype is disseminated in a multicultural community accessing a multitude of media platforms. After complaints about the stereotype, those billboard ads came down.

Some might find these advertisement examples clever, crude or coy but fundamentally *harmless*. They are not. The proliferation of such messages in a culture adds up, shaping social mores and stereotypical attitudes. As these case studies, interviews and examples also document, the power of the media across platforms is great. To operate ethically in such an environment, and take part in the decision-making process, you must realize the power that *you* possess and learn how to apply it appropriately.

EMPOWERMENT: *YOU CAN CLAIM IT*

The word "empower" is more elusive than it seems at first glance. You can "empower" another person by relinquishing your own authority or abilities, as in this sentence taken from *The Random House Dictionary of the English Language*: "I empowered my agent to make the deal for me."[37] Or the word can mean "to enable," as in another sentence from the same dictionary: "Wealth empowered him to lead a comfortable life." The word "empowerment," associated with gender equity, is based on both meanings, implying that one should not blindly relinquish authority or abilities and instead claim them for one's self.

Empowerment takes many forms at the workplace. As stated earlier, power concerns the force that we exert expressing our values or the confidence that we gain because of our values. When so defined, it is near impossible to be powerless because almost everyone has values and aspires to have confidence in his or her abilities. People who claim otherwise may not be aware of or have made a choice not to acknowledge their power. Conversely, you may not realize how much power you actually possess, especially if you have decided to practice or pursue a career in mass communications. Such an aspiration assumes that you like to communicate with others via words or images or already are working in or studying mass media and using powerful technology, such as computers, smartphones and virtual reality platforms. That suggests you are more powerful than ordinary consumers because you are using techniques and technology to inform an audience or serve a clientele.

Add to this the incidentals of your life or your background that enhance your power base. Perhaps you were reared in an affluent family and have access to powerful individuals who can promote your interests or advise you. Or perhaps you were reared in a less fortunate environment and have encountered challenges along the way, sharpening your awareness or independence. There are simply too many variables to address theoretically when it comes to establishing the scope of each person's power. To exercise it, however, each person has to analyze those variables. Otherwise you may be prone to empowering others, sacrificing your values or beliefs, or too uncertain about how to apply them in a crisis. Remember that power is a force, not a value: too little force, and your beliefs will be overridden; too much force, and they will offend others. Thus, ascertaining how much force to apply in each situation requires that you know how and when to tap your power bases.

Let's illustrate that, listing the power bases of a typical journalism professor. In most cases, the person:

- Will have had a good education in the United States or abroad.
- Will have had professional media experience.
- Owns computer, communication technology and video equipment and can send or transmit messages or images instantaneously almost anywhere 24 hours each day.
- Influences readers, viewers or listeners with published or broadcast works, papers or talks.
- Has access to powerful people in publishing, media and education.
- Is a member of influential academic/professional associations.
- Is employed and earns a decent wage.
- Has or is on the path toward tenure and so cannot easily jeopardize his or her job.
- Can exert authority over children, spouse and partner.
- Can exert authority over students and staff.

As you can see, there is real potential for abuse here. If the professor wanted, he or she could take advantage of less-educated people, to feel superior, or use experience or contacts cynically, to dull the dreams of others. He or she could tell aspiring journalists and practitioners that they should use their skills to advance causes serving his or her political, personal or financial interests. The professor could prevent the hiring or promotion of others to lessen competition in his or her discipline. The person can use blogs to ridicule rather than to inform. He or she could use professional contacts and associations to find jobs for ingratiating graduates, practicing favoritism to boost ego. He or she also could abuse children or a partner or a spouse, to control their behavior, or students and staff, to make teaching less demanding. As a professor, the person could claim the First Amendment or academic freedom to take on any challengers.

But if the professor resists those self-serving temptations, he or she can add one more item—more powerful than the sum total of all others—to his or her power list: *credibility*. Nothing is more important for a teacher, especially a teacher of media and communication. Remember the question that began this chapter: Who is more powerful—Charles Fishman, author of *The Wall-Mart Effect*, or Wal-Mart, one of the most powerful companies on earth? We concluded Wal-Mart had more direct power than the journalist, but that the journalist helped the public understand the limits of that power by holding big business and government accountable. The teachers of media professionals like Charles Fishman have immense power, too. When teachers are credible and trustworthy, their influence is literally incalculable.

"Every young person needs an engaged adult in his or her life," says Judy Clabes, former president and chief operating officer of The Scripps Howard Foundation. Clabes, herself inspired by teachers, credits them with the success that she has enjoyed as an industry leader. Students need credible teachers who show care and compassion and who can inspire them to become "journalists and communicators who will put their knowledge to work in only the *most exemplary way*."

Teachers also are responsible for directing students to proper resources, not only to advance their careers but also to help them seek necessary counsel, especially in the wake of sexual harassment. Educators are bound by Title IX, which requires schools to take steps to prevent and remedy sex- and gender-based harassment, including sexual violence that occurs within its educational programs and activities. A Title IX coordinator investigates alleged violations and directs those who suffer harassment to myriad resources, including counseling, medical attention and guidance on judicial processes. After a student graduates and secures employment, he or she is covered by Title VII of the Civil Rights Act, a 1964 federal law that prohibits companies from discriminating against employees on the basis of sex, race, color, national origin and religion.

What happens if harassment associated with race, religion, age or sex happens while a student is on internship with a media company? That is a difficult legal question involving such factors as whether the internship is paid or unpaid; whether internship provider was screened by the college or university, signing a contract with a clause associated with harassment; and where the internship was located, as some states have extended harassment protection to unpaid interns. Unpaid interns are generally not protected by the federal Civil Rights Act, exempting them from protection by the U.S. Equal Employment Opportunity Commission. The U.S. Department of Labor has guidelines to determine whether an internship qualifies as unpaid:

1. The internship, even though it includes actual operation of the facilities of the employer, is similar to training which would be given in an educational environment.
2. The internship experience is for the benefit of the intern.
3. The intern does not displace regular employees, but works under close supervision of existing staff.
4. The employer that provides the training derives no immediate advantage from the activities of the intern; and on occasion its operations may actually be impeded.
5. The intern is not necessarily entitled to a job at the conclusion of the internship.
6. The employer and the intern understand that the intern is not entitled to wages for the time spent in the internship.[38]

The U.S. Congress has been trying with varying degrees of success to close the loophole that creates this unprotected class of "volunteer" workers, especially those working in federal government. In any case, it is important to know your rights when it comes to harassment as *a component of your own empowerment*. That means determining whether your state or educational institution extends protection to you in unpaid internships and what recourses you have at your disposal if any incident occurs while you are on the job.

Concerning any type of harassment, be sure to know your rights, especially ones associated with retaliation. Harassers count on fear and initial confusion, causing self-doubt. Manipulative people who oppress others know that fear momentarily silences the conscience and confusion clouds awareness, giving harassers an opportunity to take advantage of others during any hesitation. That is why it is important to know all you can about the specter of harassment at the workplace by voluntarily doing intake training or by asking your employer to provide it, if that isn't routinely offered at your place of employment. Before accepting any position, you also might want to check the company's ethics code to see if it includes strongly worded statements about harassment and provides clear procedures that lead to effective reporting and prevention.

Professional associations that oversee each industry, such as The Public Relations Society of America, set standards dealing with improper behavior. The PRSA code of ethics requires practitioners to report ethical violations such as harassment, "whether committed by PRSA members or not, to the appropriate authority."[39] The public relations industry historically has been aware of the specter of harassment and has taken strong stances on the topic. For instance, *Public Relations Journal*, under the editorship of Susan Fry Bovet, asserted:

Public relations practitioners have a duty to protect their organizations and clients from sexual harassment charges by establishing policies and procedures for dealing with such incidents in the workplace. ... [S]exual harassment is really about power, rather than sex. Its tactics and goals vary, but it usually involves the threat of job or account loss. Often, women who leave jobs that have become "impossible" or are fired or forced out before retirement don't even realize they have been victims of sexual harassment, which is covered in the discrimination provisions of Title VII of the Civil Rights Act of 1964.[40]

The Civil Rights Act of 1991 imposes stiff penalties in sexual harassment cases when the employer knows about but does not correct behavior or take adequate steps to remove the abuse. Many companies require employees who observe discrimination to report it. (Read the employee manual to learn about requirements.) A word of caution: It is important to practice restraint until you are sure that another employee or manager has harassed you or another colleague. Amy Pyle, editor-in-chief of the Center for Investigative Reporting, suspected that she may have been treated unfairly when early in her career, on her first day at work, an editor called her "kiddo." Pyle is quoted as saying, "It upset me but then I learned he called everyone kiddo. It was just his way of speaking. It's important not to overreact. The key for women is to recognize when something is important enough to take action."[41]

In the example below, one woman shares an account of what happened to her shortly after she graduated from college. While you may have handled the situation differently, it is important to allow her to tell her story without undue criticism, for no one really knows how he or she will respond to sexual harassment until it happens to him or her. Empowerment, however, also concerns knowledge of workplace laws and procedures to report harassment to the appropriate authorities, not only when it happens to you but also when it happens to a colleague. Often the question is not whether you will or won't commit a serious offense, such as harassment; it concerns what you might do if you witness it at the workplace. The account below shows how devastating the experience can be. The woman sharing her story did so here in the hope that you will make a commitment to combat discrimination at the workplace. **WARNING: Descriptions in her account may evoke traumatic emotions, especially if you have experienced assault.**

"A CASE OF SEXUAL HARASSMENT"

Anonymous, former account executive

My first position out of college was as an advertising account executive with small-town daily newspaper. My responsibilities included selling and designing advertising campaigns for local businesses. One of my accounts was a jewelry store owned and operated by a father and son team. The father became a problem.

The trouble began almost immediately. The father would tell me dirty jokes and make lewd comments. He would comment on the way I dressed and eye me up and down. Needless to say, the situation was uncomfortable, but as a very green sales person I was at a loss what to do. Because he was my client, and I very much needed his business, I was wary about telling him how I felt. Besides, it was not as if I had never heard dirty jokes or off-color remarks before. I found myself laughing self-consciously at his remarks and then vainly trying to change the subject back to the business at hand.

The situation did not improve. In fact, it went from bad to worse. I became so uncomfortable that I started to avoid the father completely, which was difficult because he ran the show. At the very least I tried to never be alone with him in the store. Unfortunately, this strategy did not always work either.

One day I walked into the jewelry store and the father was by himself. I was there to pick up an ad. He told me it was in his office and asked me to follow him. I did. Once inside the small room, he stepped behind me, closed the door, turned off the light and grabbed me. I was in shock.

I remember feeling his lips on my face, searching for my mouth. His whiskers were rough on my skin. He was not gentle. I finally got my wits about me enough to push him away and scream. He let me go and I lunged for the light switch. I will never forget the humiliation I felt standing in that office staring into the face that moments ago had been smashed against my own. The first thing that entered my mind was that somehow, I was at fault. If only I had not laughed at his jokes and remarks, I kept thinking. If only I had had the courage to tell him his comments embarrassed me. I felt completely ashamed.

He began mumbling that he was sorry and didn't mean anything. He said he thought it would be best if we didn't mention the incident. Just pretend it didn't happen. I never did mention it, until years later to very good friends. In fact, I continued on as his account executive, although our relationship was definitely different after that episode. But forget it I never will.

NURTURE COMPASSION

Empathy, forgiveness, sympathy and compassion all hinge upon the human condition (interaction between conscience and consciousness). John J. Ratey, Harvard Medical School psychiatrist, believes conscience "is a wisdom whose origin and practice are as puzzling as they are precious," with the word "*conscience* easier to illustrate than define."[42] Nevertheless, he adds, conscience is the wellspring beneath law, theology and ethics.

Earlier in *Living Media Ethics*, we defined "conscience" as an intuitive knowledge of right and wrong, involving how we choose to live among and view others. Conscience, we said, is a tiny voice inside us, informing us intuitively what to do and avoid and when and how to act under pressure. We defined "consciousness" as a sense of awareness, involving how our interactions affect or influence others and ourselves. By expanding our awareness, we can foresee consequences of our actions before taking them and minimize harm. Both concepts define the human condition, and the goal of ethics is to harmonize our dual nature so that conscience informs consciousness and vice versa, allowing us to intuit right and wrong and then act ethically with others according to our own and shared values at home, school and work.

Philosophically, we strive to master higher moral concepts as we live our ethics. Those values are similar in nature because they involve harmonizing the conscience and consciousness, not always easy given the struggles and rigors of daily life. These related concepts, often confused with each other, cannot be explored theoretically in depth in a media ethics book, but for purposes of discussion, they are:

- **Forgiveness:** The decision to let go feelings of anger or resentment against a person, thing or group that has harmed you, whether or not the other is worthy of it, without forgetting the harmful or hurtful act. The German word for forgiveness, *vergeben*, literally means to "let go." We practice forgiveness because anger and resentment blunt the conscience so that we cannot hear that still, small voice inside us. As such, consciousness must let go for us to go on. By pardoning the acts of others, as an act of conscious will, forgiveness might seem directed outward at people, places and things; actually, we forgive others for ourselves, in order to live a fulfilling life.

- **Sympathy:** An expression of sorrow or pity on account of some negative occurrence that has befallen an individual. The German word for this concept also is telling: *mitfühlen*. Literally, it means to feel with and for someone else, sharing in the grief, sorrow or loss of another person as if it were our own. To do so, the conscience senses the pain of another person. As we gain in experience, that pain is balanced by consciousness, which stills our emotions so that we can adequately express our condolences and articulate a lasting expression. Humans sympathize. According to Daniel Goleman in *Emotional Intelligence*, "Developmental psychologists have found that infants feel sympathetic distress even before they fully realize that they exist apart from other people. Even a few months after birth, infants react to a disturbance in those around them as though it were their own, crying when they see another child's tears."[43]

- **Empathy:** A feeling of awareness of the everyday human experience and an understanding that we are fellow travelers in a world of good and evil. Once more, the German word for the concept is lucid and illuminating: *einfühlen*. To feel "at one" with someone else. To express empathy, consciousness detects an issue of the human condition, and the conscience atones, or becomes one, with that person. The conscience of both individuals atones or unifies to such extent that the other's life is as precious as one's own. Goleman notes that empathy leads to moral action "when a bystander is moved to intervene on behalf of a victim; the research shows that the more empathy a bystander feels for the victim, the more likely it is that she will intervene."[44]
- **Compassion:** The ability to respond to the suffering of others in such a way as to bestow grace—a momentary unification and acknowledgment of the human condition—to mitigate their physical, spiritual or emotional pain. The German word for this concept is *mitleid*, or to "suffer with." The conscience senses the pain, as it does with forgiveness, sympathy and empathy; but unlike those other concepts, compassion offers transcendence, a momentary glimpse into a world of immensurable community that arrives just when we need it most. The word "transcendence" comes from a Latin base, with the prefix *trans* meaning "beyond" and *scandare*, meaning to climb. In extreme situations, as we will discuss momentarily, compassion moves us beyond the real-world situation that has generated suffering.

Compassion, among the highest values that humans embrace, is rarely discussed in employee handbooks. Yet journalists and practitioners, especially in news covering crises and in public relations managing them, are exposed to situations where compassion is present or noticeably absent. During such times, you may be asked to speak with victims of violence, natural disasters, accidents or other tragedies. In doing so, says Miles Moffeit of *The Dallas Morning News*, it is essential to take a delicate, compassionate approach:

> Put yourself in the victim's situation. How would you want to be treated, tone-wise, manner-wise? Allow yourself to empathize, to search for common emotional ground. Let the victim "invite" you into her story. Ask, "where would you feel most comfortable starting?" Then, before the interview process is over, take her through events chronologically to nail down the sequence. If one experience is too painful to relate, stop the interview and give her the option to take a break or to come back to that detail later.[45]

Pulitzer Prizes are won when reporters master the art of storytelling, documenting compassion and related ethical concepts. Photographers, especially, capture moments of forgiveness, sympathy, empathy and, again most powerfully, compassion. There is an ethical reason behind this. These higher concepts are intricately linked to explain the human condition. Sympathy, for instance, triggers concerns for others, nurtures community and, most important, signifies what actions, outcomes and motives are moral or not.[46] Philosophers also have held that sympathy and compassion help us understand such concepts as respect, humility, pride, envy and hatred.[47] We know these tenets not by studying them, but by feeling them—and this is vital—when events, situations or incidents happen to others.

Nonetheless, compassion often is misunderstood. According to the American Buddhist nun Pema Chodron,

> When we talk of compassion, we usually mean working with those less fortunate than ourselves. Because we have better opportunities, a good education, and good health, we should be compassionate toward those poor people who don't have any of that. However, in working with the teachings on how to awaken compassion and in trying to help others, we might come to realize that compassionate action involves working with ourselves as much as working with others. Compassionate action is a practice, one of the most advanced. There's nothing more advanced than relating with others. There's nothing more advanced than communication—compassionate communication.[48]

Chodron's definition indicates that compassion is internal, something we nurture through the conscience. Journalists and practitioners can be thrust on any day out of their impersonal worlds of computers and smartphones into a real world of pain. Broadcasters and photographers get to document that pain, often at great personal risk. Such was the case when Pulitzer Prize-winning photographer John Kaplan covered a domestic violence situation in a Pittsburgh office building. "I had never before been in such a dramatic situation," he recalls. His photo (see page 299) was taken literally 15 seconds after police officer Victor "Kojak" Balsamico had fired the fatal shot to subdue a gunman who had shot his estranged wife in the leg. "She ran, injured, down the hallway to hide. The gunman holed himself up in the room. Kojak and the other officer, a motorcycle cop, had each arrived independently, answering the call for help on the police radio.

"When I look at the picture now, I see his remorse, a trait that is often not associated with police work. He knew he had a job to do but had never shot a man before. He clearly regrets that he took a life, even though he believed there was no other way." The motorcycle cop is showing his deep sense of compassion to Balsamico, and that was captured, too. Concerning compassion, Kaplan says, "Amazingly, Balsamico went to visit the mother of the man he had killed that very evening. To me, that says so much about the character of the man. Perhaps that's a level of bravery even more dramatic than the picture itself."

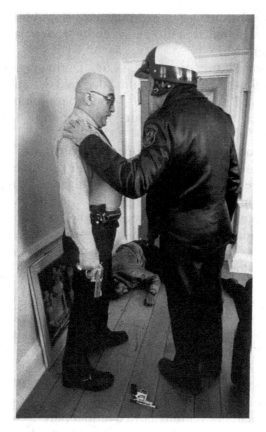

Figure 10.1 "A Policeman's Torment": Photograph by John Kaplan, reprinted with permission.

The photo was published on front pages around the world and was the first of Kaplan's to appear in *Life Magazine*. "It has since been used in several police science textbooks as an example of the proper way to comfort a fellow officer after a shooting," Kaplan notes. Balsamico and Kaplan would become friends and would meet a few times a year after the tragic day in 1985 that brought them together. "I think we had mutual respect for the challenges and ethical dilemmas of each other's profession. Although it's not a pleasant picture to look at, I keep a copy of it on the wall of my home office, thinking often about Kojak." In providing the above interview for *Living Media Ethics*, Kaplan noted that when he moved from Pittsburgh in 1996, he lost touch with Balsamico whose telephone number had been disconnected. "I often wonder if he is still alive and how he is doing."

In 2008, Victor "Kojak" Balsamico was doing fine in retirement when contacted for an interview for the previous edition of this book. "I think of the shooting every day," Balsamico said, "and I pray for the man twice a day. Every night before I go to bed I say prayers for him and his mother and his brother who hated me so badly. All he knew was that I was a cop who killed his brother."

Balsamico was on the force for 35 years. "During my career, I fired my weapon several times," he says, "but this (depicted in Kaplan's photo) was the only time that I hurt someone. If I could have jumped in quicker, it wouldn't have occurred. But he pointed his weapon right at me. I almost talked him out of it."

There are good cops and bad cops, Balsamico said, just as there are good journalists and bad journalists. "About 20 percent of cops shouldn't be on the job," he stated. "They succumb to anger and temptation. About 80 are decent cops. They have compassion. They show empathy. They believe in God or mankind. Their strongest values are knowing themselves and their limitations and doing unto other as they wish done unto them. As for journalists," he added, "they also need to have compassion and show understanding. When covering police, they need to walk in their shoes to understand their viewpoint."

Balsamico passed away in 2014. His obituary was titled, "Officer guided by a lifelong compassion for youths," noting how he would work with troubled teens in Pittsburgh. The word "compassion" again described his essence, which Kaplan captured in his telling photo so many years before.

Sometimes journalists do walk in the shoes of police, and everyone else, when disaster strikes, as was the case in New Orleans during the tragedy of Hurricane *Katrina*. One of the world's chief sources of information was the staff of Charlotte Porter, former bureau chief for The Associated Press in Louisiana and Mississippi. In 2005, she and her 18 New Orleans-based staffers had to overcome harsh realities to report the news when faced with an unprecedented natural disaster. "The AP threw more resources at this story than any domestic news event I had seen in almost 30 years with the company," Porter says. "Reporters, photographers, TV and radio crews, technicians and human resources personnel were flown in from across the country. Trauma counselors were called in. A carefully crafted corporate budget went out the window. For weeks, it was the biggest story we covered.

"The hardships were unlike anything we had ever faced," Porter adds. "For weeks, those of us who were outside the city, living in a no-frills motel and commuting long distances to a makeshift newsroom, it was days or weeks before we knew if we had homes to return to." News is difficult to gather on any day, but especially so during *Katrina*. "For the staffers inside the city, conditions were a nightmare," Porter says. "All power was gone. The roof was ripped off a hotel where many stayed. City water quickly became undrinkable. And then there was the work of wading through stinking, verminous, contaminated water to cover death and destruction on a scale unseen in this country in decades. Staffers flying in to help with the story trucked in gasoline, antibacterial hand wash, rubber boots, even a boat.

"Getting the story out was a different kind of nightmare. In an age when even cruise ships have internet services, it's almost impossible to imagine being isolated. But as power went out, so did phone service. Cell towers went down. Unless you had access to a generator, there was no way to charge batteries once cell phones and laptops ran out of juice. And even with a charged phone, getting a call in or out of the 504-area code was a matter of perseverance and luck. Mary Foster, our reporter who stayed at the Superdome for a week in horrifying conditions, found a working pay phone in a hallway of a ruined hotel, and managed to get out a few collect calls. Kevin McGill, who had been working out of the *Times-Picayune* office until that newspaper was forced to evacuate, found the only way to communicate with his wife 350 miles away was via text messaging on his cell phone, which takes less bandwidth than voice.

"With all this," Porter notes, "the basics of good journalism didn't change, nor did the debates with which every newsroom is familiar." During this horrific event, Porter realized the role of compassion in her reporting. That moment came on the day the levees broke, flooding much of the New Orleans area. An editor in New York asked Porter to write a story "about what it was that made us love the quirky, bawdy, desperately poor town." Rather than a story, Porter decided to write an "Ode to New Orleans," describing the quirky compassion of the port city. "I wept like a child as we put the ode together. I've never found a story harder to do," she recalls. Here's an excerpt:

There's a whole new meaning today to that old Louis Armstrong favorite, "Do you know what it means to miss New Orleans?"
We know all too well.
As we write this, we don't know if our homes are standing, what has happened to many of our friends or what is left of our city. Should we write its obituary, or just a love letter to a city that despite poverty and decay, despite corruption and decadence, was always so vital and carefree?[49]

Compassion happens on smaller scales every day in the aftermath of traffic fatalities, which journalists usually cover. "Traffic fatalities—there were 43,220 in the United States in 2003—leave families with the pain of unexpected loss,"[50] writes John P. Ferré in "Last Words: Death and Public Self-Expression," an entry in the book, *Quoting God: How Media Shape Ideas about Religion and Culture*. Ferré notes that wakes, funerals and burials sometimes fail to meet the needs of those who grieve,

So every year, thousands of people who have lost loved ones to traffic accidents take matters into their own hands—literally. They fashion crosses, gather keepsakes, and return to the site of the fatality to memorialize the person whose life was cut short at that place. Only through such participation do they feel satisfied with their response to the needless and unforeseen death.[51]

Figure 10.2 "Roadside Memorial": Photograph by Diane Bugeja, reprinted with permission.

There is a problem with that, however. "Crosses may be a recognizable sign of memorials, but they are also Christian signs, and that fact angers some people who object to religious symbolism on public property."[52]

Media professionals usually support separation of church and state because of the "establishment clause" of the First Amendment: "Congress shall make no law respecting an establishment of religion or prohibiting the free exercise thereof." But roadside markers, especially Christian ones as depicted by photojournalist Diane Bugeja usually are overlooked in coverage as a matter of compassion—which may or may not be ethical, depending on whether you believe it is socially responsible to urge townships to take down such markers because of the establishment clause. Bugeja's picture has two Christian symbols in it—a cross and a Christmas tree.

We'll end the section on compassion with another depiction and accompanying essay by Therese Frare, a Seattle-based photojournalist, who discusses the personal and ethical aspects of her award-winning photo "Final Moments." The portrait documenting the death of an AIDS activist originally appeared in *Life* magazine and later was picked up by Benetton in an advertising campaign emphasizing social issues. Frare's photo was at the center of a debate about the appropriateness of such a private moment being used in an advertisement. In her essay here, she explains how she decided to allow such use. She also discusses several aspects of power and addresses an important issue regarding taste. Ethicists often argue against staged photographs in the news. But Frare poses the question "Is it okay to use real photos in advertising?"—a medium that typically uses "staged" or set-up illustrations in campaigns. That simple but powerful question expands the boundaries of ethical debate, not only with regard to Benetton, but to photojournalism in general.

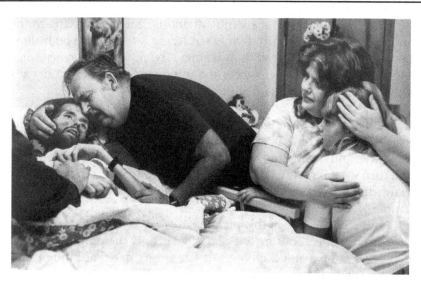

Figure 10.3 "Final Moments": Photograph by Therese Frare, reprinted with permission.

"LASTING MOMENTS"

Therese Frare, photojournalist

When I think of power in regards to the "Final Moments" photograph, I am reminded by the sheer power of death as the final experience of this life. I think of the power of family and the incredible love parents feel for their children. I think of the power of a moment—a real moment of intense emotion—a moment so personal and so raw that it overwhelmed the senses.

It is impossible, actually, for me to discuss this photo without discussing the Kirby family to whom I am forever indebted for inviting me into their lives. David was an AIDS activist and had spent the last several years of his life trying to educate people about AIDS. When he met me, as a volunteer at the hospice-approach home he was living at, I believe that he saw me as a vehicle for his message—that people with AIDS need care and love.

His father Bill is among the most loving people I have ever met and his mother Kate (not pictured; that's his sister and niece) is a strong, quiet woman who is dedicated and wise. Anyway, every week for a couple of months I visited David and his family and by luck or fate I happened to be visiting a caregiver friend of mine on the day that David died.

Knowing that it was a serious situation, I sat in the living room and my friend and David's family tended to David in the bedroom. I remember sitting there with my cameras by my feet and consulting a higher power, looking upwards and thinking, "This one is your call. I need a sign if I am to take photographs here."

Within seconds David's mother emerged and said, "Therese, we would like you to photograph people saying their final good-byes to David." I got up, quietly walked into the room, positioned myself in the corner and did not move. I made perhaps less than a dozen frames and then went back into the living room, cried with my friends, eventually drove home in a daze, slept for a day, and processed the film a couple of weeks later.

Power, in the case of this picture—

I cannot talk about my power. There is only the power of death, the power of love and the power of fate—the force that brought me to David and his family in order for me to tell their story.

Several months after David's death and with the permission of his family, I submitted the photo to the "moments" section of *Life* magazine where it received a double truck spread. After that success I sent a copy of the photo to the World Press Photo Competition, where it ended up winning two awards in the 1991 competition. With the award, it traveled to many countries and was picked up by various AIDS shows.

Eventually Benetton saw the image in the World Press Yearbook and requested it for an issue-oriented campaign. Once again I left the decision to a more knowledgeable source—in this case David's family. They agreed to the photo being used and even during the controversy, maintained that Benetton did not take advantage of their son's death but had instead sponsored the photo to be seen by billions all over the world. Like I said, those Kirbys are amazing people.

Which I suppose brings us to another power—power of the press and power of advertising. The same photo used in different ways brought about entirely different reactions. Is it okay to use staged photos in the news? Is it okay to use real photos in advertising?

In the end, the image has the power to move the audience—whether in a gallery, a magazine, or an advertisement—but the reaction to it is different depending on the context in which it is seen.

If people are offended by its use, does that diminish its power or add to it? These are all questions to which I do not have the answer. I only know what happened and why.

Power. As a photojournalist people lend you their power when they invite you in their lives. It is important to respect that. But the minute you take the photos out from the box under your bed and show them to the world, you lose your power to protect them. You cannot explain to a billion people what an image means. Like a child that grows you can only put it out in the world and hope for the best.

"YOUR PATH TO EMPOWERMENT"
Personal Journal Exercise

To determine how to use your power effectively when a situation is important enough to take action, follow the guidelines below. As you go through the guidelines, take notes in response to questions in each section of the power process described below.

1. Ascertain your personal and professional power

Ethical journalists acknowledge their power so they can tap or restrain it during suspected challenges or crises. To acknowledge your power base, make a list of items—one list for yourself and another anonymous one for your instructor or group leader doing the "Communal Journal Exercise."
  Ask yourself:

- *Am I intellectually or physically powerful?*
- *Do I have access to powerful tools or technology like cameras or computers?*
- *Can I communicate powerful ideas?*
- *Do I know or have access to honest mentors and/or powerful people?*
- *Do I supervise or have authority over others?*

2. Evaluate your personal or professional power

After you have acknowledged your power base, determine how you have been employing that power. Analyze each item on your list.

Ask yourself:

- *Do I usually abuse this type of power when I have the opportunity?*
- *Do I usually exert the appropriate amount of this power to meet each challenge or problem? Or do I usually over- or underestimate situations?*
- *Do I usually avoid using this type of power at all costs?*

3. Take prudent action or practice restraint

Identify items on your power list that are reliable or need improvement. The goal is to meet each challenge or problem with the appropriate amount of power to suit the occasion. Each time you exert power, record the results in your journal.

Ask yourself:

- *When I feel the urge to take action, do I usually (a) suppress that urge when the stakes or consequences warrant a response, (b) act on behalf of others for whom I have no responsibility, or (c) act in my own interests?* **Note:** If (a) or (b), seek advice from a mentor or role model whose judgment you trust to determine how to proceed or whether your participation is really required.
- *What are the usual results of my taking action: (a) bigger or more complex problems, (b) symbolic but important participation, (c) compromise to resolve a situation or dispute, or (d) total resolution of a situation or dispute?* **Note:** If (a), practice restraint until you can determine how your participation will be helpful.
- *If I take action, who else might be affected: (a) innocent individuals or groups, (b) individuals or groups indirectly associated with the situation, or (c) only those directly associated with the situation?* **Note:** If (a) or (b), practice restraint until you can determine whether your interests are greater than the effect your actions may have on other innocent or indirectly related persons or parties.

4. Take responsibility for your actions

Once you have ascertained and evaluated your power, you need to accept consequences for your actions. This will help you maintain or restore your personal integrity and/or professional credibility.

Ask yourself:

- *Do I have anything to apologize for or correct? For instance, did I misperceive a threat or make a hasty judgment based on faulty information?* **Note:** If so, apologize or correct errors to match the degree of misperceptions or mistakes ... without unduly damaging your own or other parties' interests.

- *Does another party have anything to apologize to me for or correct? For instance, did someone else misperceive a threat by you or make a hasty judgment based on faulty information?* **Note:** If so, you may decide to demand an apology or a correction or some other resolution to off-set the misperception or mistake.
- *Are the consequences a direct result of (a) my actions, (b) part my and part someone else's actions over which I had no influence or control, or (c) someone else's actions over which I had no influence or control.* **Note:** If (b) or (c), assume responsibility for your part in the situation and/or inform other affected parties about the actions over which you had no influence or control.

Review your notes generated by the exercise above. Without violating your own or anyone else's privacy or damaging anyone's reputation, create a 500-word journal entry or blog post or a brief podcast or multimedia presentation about your power bases and whether you typically utilize those attributes, showing proper restraint and accepting consequences for your choices.

Communal Journal Exercise

As instructor or discussion leader, devise a confidential method for the class or group to drop off printouts or send documents to a digital drop box so that you can collect lists of individual power bases as described in No. 1 of the "Personal Journal Exercise" earlier. Once you have all lists, create a master list of power bases representing the class or group and have a discussion about how they can embrace *collective* empowerment if they worked together on a team project such as exonerating wrongly convicted people or on a political aspiration such as legislation restricting assault weapons. Be sure to ask the class or group to practice restraint and be mindful of their trigger words if discussion happens to focus on a topic in which they have strong personal beliefs or distressing experiences.

NOTES

1 Joost Elffers and Robert Greene, *The 48 Laws of Power* (New York: Viking, 1998), xxi.
2 Clifford G. Christians, "Social Ethics and Mass Media Practice," in *Communication Ethics in an Age of Diversity*, eds. Josina M. Maukau and Ronald C. Arnett (Urbana, Ill.: University of Illinois Press, 1997), 93.
3 Ibid.
4 "About the Freedom of Information Act," FOIA Project, no date, http://foiaproject.org/about/aboutfoia/
5 Ibid.

6 David B. Ottaway, "Gathering String," *The Quill*, March 1987, 29.
7 "Censored, By Reasons of the State," no author, *The Quill*, March 1987, 23.
8 John Tusa, "When Donkeys are Tractors," *The Quill*, March 1987, 25.
9 Kevin J. Delaney, "Google Introduces Service in China," *The Wall Street Journal*, January 25, 2006, B2.
10 Ibid.
11 Kaveh Waddell, "Why Google Quit China—and Why It's Heading Back," *The Atlantic*, January 19, 2016, www.theatlantic.com/technology/archive/2016/01/why-google-quit-china-and-why-its-heading-back/424482/
12 Tanya Basu, "New Google Parent Company Drops 'Don't Be Evil' Motto," *Time*, October 4, 2015, http://time.com/4060575/alphabet-google-dont-be-evil/
13 Newseum Institute, "2015 State of the First Amendment Survey," July 2015, www.newseuminstitute.org/wp-content/uploads/2015/07/FAC_SOFA15_report.pdf
14 Douglas E. Lee, "Prior Restraint," First Amendment Center, September 13, 2002, www.newseuminstitute.org/first-amendment-center/topics/freedom-of-the-press/prior-restraint/
15 Ibid.
16 Loran F. Nordgren, Frenk van Harreveld and Joop van der Pligt, "The Restraint Bias: How the Illusion of Self-Restraint Promotes Impulsive Behavior," *Psychological Science*, December 1, 2009, http://journals.sagepub.com/doi/pdf/10.1111/j.1467-9280.2009.02468.x
17 John Patrick Pullen, "Science Says You Should Ignore Internet Trolls," *Time*, April 20, 2015, http://time.com/3827683/internet-troll-research/
18 Natalie Jomini Stroud, Emily Van Duyn, Alexis Alizor and Cameron Lang, "Comment Section Survey Across 20 News Sites," Center for Media Engagement, January 12, 2017, https://mediaengagement.org/research/comment-section-survey-across-20-news-sites/
19 No author, "Chasing Stories, Women Journalists Are Pursued by Trolls," Freedom House, April 26, 2017, https://freedomhouse.org/blog/chasing-stories-women-journalists-are-pursued-trolls
20 Colin Shaw, *Deciding What We Watch: Taste, Decency, and Media Ethics in the UK and the USA* (New York: Oxford, 1999), 32.
21 Ibid., 32–33.
22 Bill Kovach and Tom Rosenstiel, *The Elements of Journalism: What Newspeople Should Know and the Public Should Expect* (New York: Three Rivers Press, 2001), 23.
23 Tony Case, "Publishing Profanities," *Editor & Publisher*, November 6, 1993, 11.

24 Dave Itzkoff, "Bill Maher Apologizes for Use of Racial Slur on 'Real Time,'" *New York Times*, June 3, 2017, www.nytimes.com/2017/06/03/arts/television/bill-maher-n-word.html

25 Case, 11.

26 W.C. Stroby, "Interview with Stephen King," *Writer's Digest*, March 1992, 27.

27 "Digging at the King," anonymous letter, *Writer's Digest*, June 1992, 4.

28 For a fuller treatment, see "Fired Reporter Says Blog Meant as Joke," NBC10.com, February 3, 2006, www.nbc10.com/news/6667658/detail.html, and Workplace Prof Blog's February 21, 2006 post, http://lawprofessors.typepad.com/laborprof_blog/2006/02/another_blogger.html

29 See "Valerie Hoff, Plaintiff, vs. Pacific and Southern, Llc, dba TEGNA, a Licensee of Television Broadcast Station WXIA-TV, Atlanta," https://cmgajcradiotvtalk.files.wordpress.com/2017/07/valerie-hoff-lawsuit.pdf

30 Ibid. This is the lesson no matter what the outcome of Hoff's case, which you should read in its entirety at: https://cmgajcradiotvtalk.files.wordpress.com/2017/07/valerie-hoff-lawsuit.pdf, from which details here have been paraphrased.

31 Jeremy Blachman "Job Posting," *The New York Times*, 31 August 2005, Final, Section A, 19.

32 Policy provided by Meredith Corporation to Michael Bugeja and is reprinted with permission.

33 Michael Bugeja attended the presentation of this paper at the 2006 convention in San Francisco of the Association for Education in Journalism and Mass Communication. An abstract of this paper is available from www.aejmc.org/convention/06convention/06abstracts/part1.htm

34 Michael Bugeja, "The Fuss," *Inside Higher Ed*, October 25, 2016, www.insidehighered.com/advice/2016/10/25/teaching-controversial-topics-age-microaggressions-trigger-warnings-and-tweeting

35 Dorothy Giobble, "'Tonya Tapper' Ad Creates A Stir," *Editor & Publisher*, February 26, 1994, 11.

36 "'Cold Latina' Billboards Coming Down at Month's End," *The Business Journal of Phoenix*, May 18, 2004, http://phoenix.bizjournals.com/phoenix/stories/2004/05/17/daily14.html

37 *Random House Dictionary of the English Language*, 2nd ed., unabridged, 638–39.

38 "Fact Sheet #71: Internship Programs Under the Fair Labor Standards Act," U.S. Department of Labor, April 2010, www.dol.gov/whd/regs/compliance/whdfs71.htm

39 PRSA, Code of Ethics, "Enhancing the Profession," no date, http://prsa.org/_About/ethics/enhance.asp?ident=eth5

40 Susan Fry Bovet, "Sexual Harassment," *Public Relations Journal*, November 1993, 26.

41 M.L. Stein, "Unwelcome Gender Politics," *Editor & Publisher*, September 11, 1993, 13.

42 John Ratey, *A User's Guide to the Brain: Perception, Attention and the Four Theaters of the Brain* (New York: Vintage Books, 2002), 5.

43 Daniel Goleman, *Emotional Intelligence* (New York: Bantam Books, 1995), 105–06

44 Ibid., 98.

45 Miles Moffeit, "Ethics and Practice: Interviewing Victims," Dart Center for Journalism and Trauma, January 19, 2012, https://dartcenter.org/content/ethics-and-practice-interviewing-victims

46 Eric Schliesser, *Sympathy: A History* (Oxford: Oxford University Press, 2015), 210.

47 Ibid., 215.

48 Pema Chodron, *When Things Fall Apart* (Boston, Mass.: Shambhala, 2000), 78.

49 Charlotte Porter, "Ode to New Orleans," NBC News, August 31, 2005, www.nbcnews.com/id/9138529/ns/us_news-katrina_the_long_road_back/t/locals-love-new-orleans-vivid-ever/#.WbwDPsiGO1s

50 John P. Ferré, "Last Words: Death and Public Self-Expression," in *Quoting God: How Media Shape Ideas about Religion and Culture*, ed. Claire H. Badaracco (Waco, Texas: Baylor University Press, 2005), 132.

51 Ibid., 132–33.

52 Ibid., 136.

CHAPTER 11

Value Systems: Create Your Own

COMMIT TO ETHICAL LIVING

Aspiring journalists and practitioners can base their value system on what they have learned thus far in *Living Media Ethics*:

1. **Acknowledge the influences in your life** that may affect judgment, for better or worse, in an attempt to make independent choices.
2. **Develop the strong work ethic** required for most media jobs to safeguard the principles of the First Amendment and social responsibility.
3. **Know right from wrong** and consider long-term consequences of actions before taking them, accepting responsibility for those actions no matter if the outcome is good or bad.
4. **Embrace the values of role models and mentors** rather than the fame of media idols and icons because values endure and fame is fleeting.
5. **Commit to truth**, shunning falsehoods of every stripe, from exaggeration to invention, safeguarding your own and your company's reputation
6. **Do not intentionally manipulate others** or allow others to manipulate you out of respect for your audience, clientele and/or constituents.
7. **Do not yield to temptation** by taking shortcuts to achieve goals and resolve conflicts of interest in your own and your company's best interests.
8. **Do not discriminate against others** because you have committed to truth, and discrimination, inherently, is a lie.
9. **Exercise fairness**, accepting truth where you find it, even if that truth goes against everything you hitherto have believed.
10. **Practice discretion** in matters small and large, from being mindful about use of technology to honoring confidentiality.

11. **Practice restraint**, knowing when, how and on what occasion to tap your power, applying only as much as needed to address a situation or resolve an issue.
12. **Develop a value system** based on the above tenets, so that each one is enhanced and empowered by the other, living their ethics throughout their careers.

That last tenet, developing a value system, is what this final chapter is about: all about *you*. Unlike other media ethics text, *Living Media Ethics* asks you to apply your knowledge—perhaps even your journal entries, blog posts, podcasts and multimedia presentations—in a digital portfolio with professional ethics code that you will update throughout your career. You may not have been aware of a value system built into the design of this text, with subheads used in each chapter representing a motto-driven comprehensive code of conduct:

- Aspire to Live Media Ethics
- Ethics Are Not in the Cloud
- Emphasize Motives over Medium
- Make Platforms Truthful Again
- Commit to Truth Now, Not Later
- Know Standards Across Media
- Moral Literacy Enhances Credibility
- Develop Ethical Values
- Shortcuts Compromise Ethics
- Ethics Can Be Taught
- Revisit "Family Values"
- Learn a Few Philosophical Tenets
- Know Right From Wrong
- Remember Who Molded Your Morals
- History Matters More Than You Think
- Language Shapes Perception, Too
- Sharpen Insight and Attain Balance
- Right and Wrong Differ from Good and Bad
- "Justification" is Just an Excuse
- Be Accountable for Behavior
- Accountability Means Having to Say You're Sorry
- Seek Role Models and Mentors
- Recognize Responsibilities

- Responsibility Creates Trust
- Some Things Are Almost Always True
- Be a Font of Truth
- Objectivity is a Process
- Truth is Subject to Proof
- Truth Should Be Transparent
- Make Appropriate Disclosures
- Exercise Good Judgment
- Satire is Truth Everyone Knows but Won't Admit
- Truth Can Be Mythic, Too
- Lies Undermine Trust
- Lies Have Consequences
- Detect the Many Types of Lies
- Quote-Making Can Be Untruthful
- Pictures Can Lie, Too
- Question Every Lie
- Remember How Manipulation Feels
- Manipulators Violate Conscience
- Manipulators Exploit Media
- Hoaxes Rewrite History
- Media Pull Stunts, Too
- Expose and Defuse Manipulation
- Temptation Strikes Without Warning

- Temptation Invites Conflict
- Resist the Urge to Plagiarize
- You Can Detect and Prevent Plagiarism
- Avoid Conflicts of Interest
- Are You Acknowledging Diversity?
- Recognize Misperceptions About Race
- Explore Bias Across Platforms
- Cultural Biases Taint the Workplace
- Know the History of Inclusion in Media
- Diversify News- and Boardrooms
- Stereotypes Perpetuate Bias
- Identify and Resist Stereotypes
- Fairness Means Continuous Improvement
- Fairness Pivots on Viewpoint
- Fairness Makes Lasting Impressions
- Familiarize Yourself with Fairness Concepts
- Power Expresses Values
- Empowerment: *You Can Claim It*
- Nurture Compassion
- Commit to Ethical Living
- Values Reinforce Work Ethic
- Our Rights Have Historic Roots
- Values Foster Teamwork

The key to success as a journalist or practitioner is a strong value system, according to Jennifer McGill, longtime executive director of the Association for Education in Journalism and Mass Communication. She has specialized in leadership development, especially diversity and inclusion, and implements strategies of the various divisions of her organization, which not only cover advertising, journalism and public relations, but also subgroups such as Media History, Communication Technologies and Media Ethics. "One of the central qualities for a future employee in any field should be a deep-seated belief in fairness and truth in all that he or she does," McGill says, emphasizing the importance of a personal value system. A graduate of the University of South Carolina, she learned "the first week of my first journalism class that things are always more complicated than they seem. There are two sides to every story or issue and you have to consider both sides." A well-honed value system helps you do that, to such extent, that you rely on it every day, living your ethics. "Then you take a breath and learn more." As a former newspaper reporter, and in her AEJMC leadership role, McGill asks this question "every day—and sometimes more than once a day—'What am I missing?'" The question reminds McGill to find additional sources and ask more questions before deciding how to proceed on any issue. That, she says, builds leadership potential.

McGill has a motto that has guided her as an executive: *Integrity is your most important quality. Period.* "You need to understand what ethics are and how they relate to the work you do. It does not matter what your job is or what you do in your off hours." Embrace your conscience. "A clear sense of right and wrong and your own worth can help you navigate those 'gray' areas that crop up," she says. "The good thing is that you get to practice those positive moral values every day. If you get it wrong one day, you still have the next day to get it right."

That is how you live your ethics.

VALUES REINFORCE WORK ETHIC

Value systems enumerate workplace responsibilities and clarify mission. You express your moral standards in a code of ethics, which usually has a preamble, stating why the document is important, followed by an organizational statement of core principles. A code can even contain a pledge or an oath. These three components often reinforce the corporate or organizational mission statement, which differs from a code. A mission statement can have ethical components, but its intent is to state why a company or organization exists strategically and to state shared goals pertaining to all constituents, from employees to stockholders. Codes concern the behavior of those constituents. A good code also should have a central theme—an overriding principle of service or duty that guides and motivates an employee, an outlet or an entire company. In Jennifer McGill's case, hers was a commitment to integrity. Value systems may emphasize excellence, optimism, curiosity, collaboration or a combination of tenets that represent equity, equality, quality, fairness or discretion. Codes of ethics document corporate or organizational culture.

In their book about the ethics of persuasion, Missouri professors Margaret Duffy and Esther Thorson note that codes remind us about what should be important to us as communicators. "Codes of ethics must become a balanced part of a complete ethical framework for individual practitioners. To be truly ethical, practitioners must move beyond blind obedience, a technocratic allegiance to rules, and reliance on the industry's long-standing conventions."[1] This is an especially important concept as we come to understand our own values and to search for companies that may share them. Our values not only help us pledge allegiance to truth, fairness, responsibility and other moral concepts. They also give us the courage and confidence to resolve conflicts of interest or report bias or other violations at the workplace. According to Duffy and Thorson, a code of ethics helps you think for yourself, "making decisions that may go against the status quo or cost an account, and commitment to living up to your decisions."[2]

True, there are problems with codes—ethical ones, namely—in that some companies herald their standards as part of a marketing or brand-name promotion. Others have codes that are on the books but not necessarily enforced. Some codes neglect to include statements about competence or work ethic, especially a commitment to research. As ethicist Claude-Jean Bertrand states in *Media Ethics & Accountability Systems*, codes often do not recommend that journalists and practitioners "do some homework before going on an assignment, dip into archives (or data banks), and consult experts."[3]

There can also be legal concerns about codes. Gene Policinski, CEO of the Newseum Institute and of the Institute's First Amendment Center, says, "There is a traditional objection, often voiced by lawyers, that you cannot be sued—or lose a case—on the basis of an ethics code you don't have. If newspapers say 'thou shalt not steal' and someone on the staff does, you have violated at least your own guideline as well as any applicable law. In a sense, you're neutral if you don't have any guidelines. At the least it's more difficult to hold you accountable on so-called ethical grounds." Conversely, it can be argued, especially in court, that the lack of an ethics code is evidence that management has not properly advised its employees about moral infractions. Because of this and other factors, Policinski's "personal view is that you are better armed to go to court" if your company ensures that "the staff is fully informed about the code, that it is fully explored with every one to whom it applies and that it is fully-implemented—that it applies fairly and evenly across the staff—and is consistently applied."

Policinski's view is also that of *Living Media Ethics*. Codes are not self-serving advertisements for clipbooks, resumes, websites, employee handbooks and annual stockholder reports. They are serious agreements about community and organizational standards. They require regular updating to take into account provisions that are unclear, underdeveloped or antiquated technologically. Many media companies were not prepared for social media proliferation and blogging, for instance, and had to update their codes to articulate standards in digital media and how they might apply across platforms.

OUR RIGHTS HAVE HISTORIC ROOTS

No matter how one feels about codes of ethics, they are part of U.S. culture and history. Our charter documents, in a large sense, constitute a code with the Declaration of Independence as the mission statement, stating the country's purpose for being:

> We hold these truths to be self-evident, that all men are created equal, that they are endowed by their Creator with certain unalienable Rights, that among these are Life, Liberty and the pursuit of Happiness.—That to secure these rights, Governments are instituted among Men, deriving their just powers from the consent of the governed,—That whenever any Form of Government becomes destructive of these ends, it is the Right of the People to alter or to abolish it, and to institute new Government, laying its foundation on such principles and organizing its powers in such form, as to them shall seem most likely to effect their Safety and Happiness.

The Constitution contains the code, and it begins with this preamble:

We the people of the United States, in order to form a more perfect union, establish justice, insure domestic tranquility, provide for the common defense, promote the general welfare, and secure the blessings of liberty to ourselves and our posterity, do ordain and establish this Constitution for the United States of America.

The seven articles of the Constitution articulate organizational structure with the Bill of Rights stating core principles, beginning with the First Amendment:

Congress shall make no law respecting an establishment of religion, or prohibiting the free exercise thereof; or abridging the freedom of speech, or of the press; or the right of the people peaceably to assemble, and to petition the government for a redress of grievances.

Finally, to become a citizen, a person must take the U.S. Oath of Citizenship, which requires, among other things, that those seeking "membership" renounce allegiance to foreign states and support the Constitution.

The value of a personal or professional code of ethics, on a much lesser scale, of course, involves the same level of commitment. Again, this applies historically to our charter documents whose core principles—equality, liberty, pursuit of happiness and more—were not applied fairly, evenly and consistently across the U.S. population. Moreover, there have been those who argued fervently against putting into law many of these core principles on the grounds that mentioning them would create liabilities, including amendments that abolished slavery (Article XIII), or granted equal voting rights to men regardless of race (Article XV), or that granted equal voting rights to women (Article XIX). Again, from a legal perspective, once a country, company and/or person formally commits on paper to a code, they can be held liable for infractions—not necessarily a bad thing, for sooner or later, as we have seen in history, we may be made to live up to lofty aspirations. In the end, the Constitution is a living document and amendments thereto, living ethics. Clauses have inspired and motivated millions, so much so, in fact, that the Statue of Liberty's pedestal inscription, written by the U.S. poet Emma Lazarus, serves as our motto:

Give me your tired, your poor, your huddled masses
yearning to breathe free, The wretched refuse of your
teeming shore, Send these, the homeless, tempest-tossed,
to me: I lift my lamp beside the golden door.

Whether we live up to that motto, whose golden door alludes to the Golden Rule, is subject to debate. That happened on a national scale in 2017 during a White House press briefing on immigration reform. Presidential aide Stephen Miller was asked whether a restrictive immigration bill violated the spirit of the Lazarus poem. Miller stated, "The Statue of Liberty is a symbol of liberty enlightening the world. The poem that you're referring to was added later, it's not actually part of the original Statue of Liberty."[4] He noted that the Statue of Liberty was given to the country in 1886 and the poem inscribed on the pedestal in 1903. Nevertheless, some would argue that the poem is as powerful as the statue because it was embraced as America's motto of optimism and hope, enduring values.

VALUES FOSTER TEAMWORK

"This is going to sound terribly Pollyannaish, but the value—personal and professional—that has served me best is hope, or optimism," says journalism professor Carolyn Kitch, former senior editor for *Good Housekeeping*. "While I make sure I am always prepared in case the worst happens, I go into any project or relationship with the attitude that the best will happen." Just as Kitch now motivates students at Temple University, she also was known for motivating trainees in the editorial office at *GH*, a Hearst publication with a long-standing ethical reputation, extending limited warranties on products that carry its "seal of approval." According to Kitch, "Part of being successful is motivating colleagues to produce their best work. To do that, you have to believe they're capable of it, and you have to convey that belief to them." Hope has its consequences, Kitch observes. "Yes, there are 'professionals' who ultimately don't merit your trust and respect, and yes, there are people who will try to walk all over you. You have to be prepared for those people and able to deal with them; you have to be ready to put out fires, and you have to know how to protect yourself. But I think it's worth it to take the risk of assuming the best about people at the start. For most people, confidence, appreciation and even basic courtesy are tremendous motivators (and components of hope)."

Karol DeWulf Nickell, editor-in-chief of *Phoenix Home and Garden* and former editor of *Better Homes and Gardens*, also believes the best about people, especially when they are under pressure. She shares an anecdote about her time as editor of *BH&G* when the value of collaboration, or teamwork, helped her overcome great professional odds.[5] "In our profession," she says, there is a motto that applies across media platforms: *Count on yourself, but commit to the team.*

"These words are true of many experiences in my career, but in the summer of 1993, they were put to a test I could never have imagined." During that time, Nickell says "the perfect storm hit Des Moines and the flood of the century turned downtown into a no-man's land. Our water supply was wiped out and our lives were turned upside down." Nickell worked then at Meredith's turn-of-the-century corporate building on the bank of the Skunk River, opposite the water plant. The facilities "took a direct hit when the flood ravished the area."

Nickell had to work under pressure, if not underwater, to meet her deadline, two weeks away. "We were told to gather our staffs at a temporary location in West Des Moines," she said. "We didn't know what to expect, but I know I expected more than what we found there. The entire magazine group, *BH&G, Midwest Living, Successful Farming, Special Interest Publications, Country Home, Traditional Home* and *Wood* was there, probably around 180 of us. We were told each magazine would be given a desk and phone area. I had a staff of 14 and we were given two folding tables, a couple chairs and one phone.

"We were told that the situation at 1716 Locust, our corporate address, was dire and dangerous. Mud, water, and debris filled our two lower levels." Later Nickell learned that snakes were swimming among the tables, chairs and china that filled their lower-level photography studio. "The EPA had registered potentially dangerous gases in the air, so no one would be allowed in the building for more than 15 minutes. This news was daunting, but the worst was yet to come. All our electronic files had been destroyed by the flood waters. Our servers were on the lower levels and all attempts to revive them and retrieve their precious content had failed. I think my heart literally stopped as I tried to grapple with this information."

Then Nickell and her staff learned about more technical problems and new computer applications that were instituted before the storm hit Des Moines. "Not only were we to create our next issue on deadline out of thin air, we were to learn a completely new computer and production system while we did it!" Nickell and team rose to the challenge. "For the next bleary two weeks, we worked like dogs—and because many of us didn't have running water at home, we also smelled like dogs." Because of teamwork, the staff met their deadline and produced the magazine. "I really don't remember all the details," she says. "I just remember the collaboration, the strong sense of team and the feeling of pure joy when our November 1993 issue made it into the hands of our readers."

The *Better Homes and Gardens* audience appreciated the efforts. "Our readers responded with such generosity and care because of our long-standing commitment to them. ... When they asked for help, we were there. And when the roles were reversed, the readers' response was overwhelming. This," Nickells adds, "exemplifies the magic, power and good business in the bond between journalists and readers."

Newcomers to the work force are often surprised about the emphasis that many media companies place on ethics. Value systems are increasingly important in the business world where many public relations and advertising students will work. Consider how *Business Week* described the corporate philosophy of Robert D. Haas, chief operating office from 1984 to 1999 for Levi Strauss, in a cover story titled "Managing by Values":

Haas believes the corporation should be an ethical creature—an organism capable of both reaping profits and making the world a better place to live. ... Haas is out to make each of his workers, from the factory floor on up, feel as if they are an integral part of the making and selling of blue jeans. He wants to ensure that all views on all issues—no matter how controversial—are heard and respected. The chairman won't tolerate harassment of any kind. He won't do business with suppliers who violate Levi's strict standards regarding work environment and ethics.[6]

Haas built trust along with brand loyalty, which also is based on trust. But he is among thousands of business executives committed to ethics in large corporations and small. One such executive is John Arends, president of Arends Integrated Communication, a family-owned branding and marketing agency. "Living ethics is not a nine-to-five job," he says. "It's a five-to-nine job." In other words, ethical practitioners contemplate their actions during off-hours, preparing for new challenges the next day and communicating strategies to the team. Arends confronts what he calls "the daily realities—choices that help shape and define who we are as a business." Often, he says, these choices take the form of questions that shed light on the ethical factors defining client-agency relationships.

Here is a representative sample of choices that practitioners make in the course of doing business:

- "Am I prepared at a level that will make the next two hours worth the client's investment in time and budget dollars?" *Ethical factor: responsibility.*
- "Will I be honest and generous with this client in a demonstrable way, expressing both doubt and delight as we lean over the Arthurian round table that dominates our conference room?" *Ethical factors: fairness, honesty.*
- "When the client reviews a new ad campaign and says, 'My wife likes purple and hates red, so let's change the headlines to purple,' will I defend the original choice made by a seasoned graphic designer steeped in a deep understanding of color theory and brand identity standards? Or will I cave and make it purple?" *Ethical factor: influence.*
- "Would I make the same choice with a client whose annual billings were ten times larger? Smaller?" *Ethical factor: temptation.*
- "Will I be fair in distributing credit to my team of writers, strategists, designers and account execs?" *Ethical factor: fairness.*
- "When I challenge a client to 'have courage' and embrace a new strategy that could put his or her career at risk, will I bolster that decision with courage and risk of my own?" *Ethical factors: courage, responsibility.*
- "When I feel we're being treated with less respect than our work and our commitment deserve, will I be able to articulate that frustration in a constructive way, that saves face for the client, deepens mutual respect and elevates the relationship?" *Ethical factors: respect, discretion.*
- "Have we prepared the creative brief with enough insight, or do we need to ask more and better questions? Are we short-changing

the client? How do I respond when a member of my agency team, fatigued by frustration, declares that the client deserves to be short-changed?" *Ethical factors: leadership, discretion, accountability.*

- "The brochure just delivered had a typo everyone missed. Our initials are on the sign-off slip stapled to the proof. Right next to the client's initials. Do we pick up the entire cost of the fix? Share it? Duck it entirely?" *Ethical factor: fairness.*
- "When our largest client asks us to utilize the same layout and graphic concept we've created for another client—and then suggests the agency only charge him half price for the creative execution—will I find the ethical chops to refuse and reprimand him? Educate him? Fire him?" *Ethical factors: responsibility, discretion.*
- "When we fact-checked a brochure with one of the product engineers, we discovered the marketing coordinator, in his brief to the agency, had overstated a benefit by stretching a feature's true performance. The marketing guy tells us to ignore the concern and 'go with what I gave you.' Do we ignore him, make the change and print it, knowing that it stretches the truth? Do we go over his head to his boss, a move that could get both of us fired, or cost us sizeable billings when the acrimony occurs?" *Ethical factor: manipulation.*

Clearly, Arends says, morning team meetings at his agency usually aren't filled with such daunting questions. "For the most part," he says, "we're fortunate to have solid, ethically sound clients, mostly manufacturers dominated by engineers who have had their professional ethical standards codified at top engineering schools. And as in most things, there is a hereditary factor at the root of our integrity as a business. Our founders, my parents Don and Martha Arends, have always been intensely honest. My father could no more change his high ethical standards than change the color of his eyes or the size of his ears." Arends says that the reference to his late father's ears are not only affectionate but symbolic "in a business where listening accurately and truly to client problems can head off 99 percent of misunderstandings or ethical dilemmas."

CREATE A CODE YOU CAN LIVE BY

When it comes to your own personal ethics code, create one you can live *by*—not live *with*. In other words, you not only should explore and articulate rigorous moral standards; you will want to commit to and nurture them conscientiously throughout your career. Don't express values that you have questioned while reading *Living Media Ethics*. For instance, you may truly believe that objectivity does not exist or that moral relativity does exist; if that is the case, don't embrace objectivity or moral absolutes in your ethics code. It is essential, however, that you create a code that applies equally in the digital and interpersonal world and that you do embrace some ethical principles such as truth, responsibility, tolerance and fairness. Amorality (having no moral standards or restraints), however, will not serve you well in any media position.

"In a high-tech world enamored of machines, there is immoral behavior to be sure, but even more worrisome is amorality," says ethicist Clifford G. Christians, who believes that when societies pour resources into means, "the ends shrivel away. ... The moral life is alien. Moral vocabulary isn't heard or understood. We are without moral bearings and devoid of moral categories."[7] Ethics codes remind us about moral vocabularies and categories, especially when we compose codes for clipbooks and portfolios. Doing so is a commitment that can ensure job success, particularly in amoral environments where values-driven leadership usually stands out, even during interviews.

During such interviews, applicants often emphasize words like "ambition" or "objective." An ambition is not a value but a desire. An objective is not a value but a goal. The words are often synonymous. In fact, you can plug "ambition," "objective," "goal," "desire" or "dream" into the following sentence and still mean the same thing: *My _____ is to replace the anchor for NBC "Nightly News."* When you can substitute words like that with little or no change in the meaning, the sentence lacks substance. It can mean the person works hard and achieves or takes shortcuts and deceives in pursuit of success. Unethical people can have ambitions and objectives, too. Recruiters know this. But you cannot substitute the word "value" for any of the terms in the above sentence because a value has substance. If you told that recruiter *I have made a commitment to integrity in all that I do*, you just might get a call-back for a second interview. Such a comment suggests that you have skills in addition to the maturity to use them responsibly on the job.

Having a job objective on your resume is not important. Having a values statement, however, is. David Peasback, president of Canny Bowen Inc., a New York City recruiting firm, says objectives on resumes "sometimes do more damage then good. Have you ever seen a job objective that said 'I want an unchallenging job with unlimited career potential'?"[8]

Imagine this. You and another mass communication graduate from a rival school have equal talent and experience and find yourselves as finalists for a public relations position at a prestigious agency with a well-known ethical reputation. The recruiter hands your rival a copy of the Public Relations Society of America ethics code, informing her, "I have read these. Have you?" Your rival has not read PRSA code but promises to do so. In your interview, the recruiter asks you the same question, and you showcase your digital portfolio with your *own* code of ethics. You inform the recruiter, "I have read your company's code of ethics online. That's why I applied for a position. I also created my personal ethics code as a tab in my portfolio because I feel strongly about ethics. My code also is in line with the PRSA code, but more personal, discussing how I feel about responsibility, truth, fairness, discretion and other values."

Who makes the better impression?

You do. Does that mean you'll get the job? That is neither the point nor the objective. You will have shown interest in the agency's culture and standards, showing a commitment to research. The recruiter, more than anyone, also knows that applicants almost always possess the skills for entry-level jobs but few have the maturity and ethics to remain in those jobs. "In speaking to fellows in our Diversity Institute, who hope to go into journalism as they make a mid-career switch, I recommend that they begin formation of what I call a 'moral compass' or code of ethics for themselves—and then compare that with the employers they hope to work for," says Gene Policinski, CEO of the Newseum Institute. Policinski asks fellows to write down in spiral notebooks two or three things that as journalists they hope they always do, and two or three things they hope they never would do, and then build on those notes throughout their careers. "Over time," he says, "I hope those notes evolve into an independent, self-sustaining set of guidelines—or moral or ethics code, if you wish." Policinski prefers the word "guidelines" to "code" because the former "should be alive and breathing—recognizing that circumstances will differ and a personal view may change with experience and learning." Moreover, he advises, you don't need many or complex guidelines to represent your value system. "They should be general," he says. "We have the Ten Commandments as a guide many people accept for a moral life. We could have 200,000 Commandments with all the nuances needed to accommodate potential occurrences in one's life." More effective is a generic guide about moral decision-making. "Codes that become too specific just complicate the issue of ethics." Policinski concludes, "Regardless of whether or not you are a believer, it seems to me that the 'Ten' in the Ten Commandments is about right—it covers the areas broadly and leaves the nuances up to you."

At Iowa State University's Greenlee School of Journalism and Communication, every student in advertising, journalism and public relations must have a digital portfolio that features a personal code of ethics. The portfolio with accompanying code has been cited by the Accrediting Council on Education in Journalism and Mass Communications as a chief reason for the School's near 100 percent placement rate.[9]

At this point we want to note that codes of ethics by the various journalism and communication associations are as important as your own. You will want to review codes across platforms and ensure that your standards also are embraced by the industry. You can access examples online for almost every media industry. Go to a search engine and name the organization plus "ethics code" and you can find samples from such organizations as The American Advertising Federation, The National Press Photographers Association, The Public Relations Society of America, The Radio-Television Digital News Association, The Society of Professional Journalists and the Online News Association.

As interviews and citations indicate in this chapter, successful careers are based on a balance of values—yours, your supervisor's and your employer's. Those avenues must intersect. Job failure often has little to do with competence or competition. You may have strong values but work for a supervisor and/or company with weak ones. Or you may have weak values and work for a supervisor and/or company with strong ones. Or everyone's values may be strong (or weak) but essentially different on important issues or actions. Your goal upon graduation or re-entry into the work force may be, simply, to find a job. Salary levels and advancement opportunities are factors you'll want to weigh, of course. But job dissatisfaction and termination are almost always based on value conflicts when they aren't based on financial ones. A good way to determine your compatibility is to research ethics codes as well as the mission statements and corporate philosophies of potential employers. Contact the company and request a copy of the employee handbook if the handbook isn't online. Read all those documents and decide whether you might like to work for that company. You can also pattern after that company a values document to accompany your resume, portfolio or clipbook.

Here are general tenets as found in some 100-plus codes of ethics across media platforms:

1. **What Codes Should Promote**
   - Truth in all actions and interactions.
   - Discretion in determining actions and interactions.
   - Responsibility for all actions and interactions.
   - Fairness as a means of continuous improvement.
   - Quality service and/or production to build corporate trust or brand loyalty.
   - Teamwork, sensitivity, collegiality, inclusivity.
   - Resolution of problems via transparency (openness), fairness and other shared values.
   - High, consistent standards of conduct.

2. **What Codes Should Prevent**
   - Temptation, taking shortcuts to attain goals.
   - Deception, cheating to attain goals.
   - Manipulation, deceiving or treating others like objects.
   - Bias, dealing unfairly with others based on race, sex, social class, lifestyle or religion.
   - Self-gain, using corporate resources for personal benefits.
   - Incivility, reacting to rather than resolving challenges.

3. Touchstones
    - Is it legal, honest, responsible?
    - Does it improve teamwork, morale, communication?
    - Does it enhance internal culture and external image?
    - Is it sensitive toward others and diverse viewpoints?
    - Does it resolve problems without creating new ones?

Adding a personal ethics code to a digital portfolio is an important step in preparing for your future across media platforms. You should begin the portfolio as early as possible, preferably in your first year of college, and then document year-by-year your professional growth, adding content from student media and organizations. You can choose from the many blog template and support providers on internet, including WordPress, Tumblr, Weebly and Wix, among others. Media outlets typically prefer WordPress because you will be able to manipulate design via HTML and other coding. Templates from some other providers often do so much for the blogger that everyone's site seems to have the same theme, color patterns and functions. That might not distinguish you from others. Perhaps the best choice is to try a few and see which ones you prefer.

After you register for a blog, it will be important to choose the best name. Typically, in student portfolios, you will want to use your name or a variant of your name, such as janesmithportfolio, jsmithportfolio or janesmithportfolio824. If you can use your name or a close variant thereof, it might be best to buy the domain so that it will remain yours for years to come. Here's how a sample free Wordpress URL looks: janesmithportfolio824.wordpress.com. Buy the domain name and it's simply: janesmithportfolio824. (The 824 here might be the month and day of your birth, as in "August 24.") After you register your blog, select and activate theme and design and be sure to check how it appears so that it represents your work professionally. Then fill out settings noting, among other things, who can comment, what links to share, posts, feedback and other particulars. You should also add pages such as "home," "resume," "work samples," "videos," "multimedia," "campaigns," "internship work" and "contact data." As a safety precaution, you might want to delete your physical address from resumes and contact data. Typically, all you will need is an email address. Consider adding widgets such as search functions, calendar, archives and blog stats. Finally, learn basic HTML and coding to enhance your blog so that it is a comprehensive, interactive website. Easy guides are available on internet.

Keep your portfolio active after graduation, too. This can be useful in promotions and new positions. Also, don't discard your ethics document but update it in the spirit of *Living Media Ethics*. Changes in values can be signs of growth or decline requiring amendments and/or revisions. The longer you work in mass media, the more apt your values are to metamorphose as you adapt to your working environment or work across platforms.

But the beauty of living media ethics across platforms is in the amending so that your standards increase in proportion to your influence at work.

In the end, no one can predict the changes that will occur in your value system during your career. But there is also good news. You may not have control over budgets, benefits, contracts, assignments, mergers, buyouts, closures, office moves, promotions, demotions, reprimands, awards, hirings, firings, layoffs and management restructures. You may not have control over deaths, births, marriages, divorces, illnesses, relocations and myriad other highs, lows and turning points that may affect your performance at work. By exercising your values, however, you will *always* determine your response to pressures and pleasures ... and learn and grow in the process.

"YOUR OWN CODE OF ETHICS"

Personal Journal Exercise

1. Write a brief separate statement about your own values concerning such concepts as influence, responsibility, truth, falsehood, temptation, manipulation, bias, fairness, discretion and taste. Length: 25–75 words.
2. Find similar statements in online codes of ethics from a media organization or firm where you would like to work.
3. Compare your statements with ones in the codes and revise, if appropriate, clarifying terms or harmonizing content in keeping with industry standards.
4. Re-evaluate each of your statements, circling key words and terms and listing them on a separate sheet.
5. Now condense each statement and keep or combine as many of those key terms as possible—about 10–50 words per item in your short statement on each value.
6. Assemble your codes in the same document and revise the wording of each so that all codes are similar in length and read in a consistent and parallel manner. (Common style errors include using the first person, "I," in some codes and not in others and switching verb case or tense.)
7. Decide on the format in keeping with your employment interests or disciplines. (Many opt for a resume-like document or brochure, although successful codes have been displayed on websites and posters, in videos and podcasts, and in an array of creative or product-oriented designs.)
8. Show a draft of your code to a mentor or role model and/or share yours with peers in a study group or workshop. Ask for a critique and then revise your document so that it lacks embarrassing misspellings or grammatical mistakes.

9. Include your code in a portfolio of professional work or projects completed during an internship or temporary position. Lacking these, include academic assignments that meet industry standards, perhaps ones generated by the "Personal Journal Exercises" in this text, as long as you are sure to protect your own and others' privacy.
10. During job and internship interviews, wait until the personnel manager asks a "responsibility"-related question ... and then refer to or display your code.

Communal Journal Exercise

Assemble a website with links to all of the digital portfolios and/or ethics codes created by your class or group. Be sure to ask permission from individuals in the class or group so that you can share their links on internet or social media. Devise a formal signed permission form that allows you to do that. Finally, make sure that your institution or organization supports that and that it does not violate any policy or procedure, especially ones associated with the Family Educational Rights and Privacy Act of 1974, a federal law that protects the privacy of student records.

NOTES

1 Margaret Duffy and Esther Thorson, *Persuasion Ethics Today* (New York: Routledge, 2016), 276.
2 Ibid.
3 Claude-Jean Bertrand, *Media Ethics & Accountability Systems* (New Brunswick, N.J.: Transaction Publishers, 2000), 61.
4 Alana Abramson, "White House: Statue of Liberty Doesn't Represent U.S. Immigration Policy," *Time*, August 2, 2017, http://time.com/4884808/stephen-miller-immigration-policy-jim-acosta/
5 Karol DeWulf Nickell's comments are excerpted from an April 15, 2005 speech at Iowa State University.
6 Russell Mitchell and Michael Oneal, "Managing By Values," *Business Week*, August 1, 1994, 46.
7 Clifford G. Christians, "Philosophical Issues in Media Convergence," *Communications and Convergence Review* 1, No. 1 (2009): 4.
8 "Is a Job Objective Essential on a Resume?," no author, *New Woman*, June 1992, 38.
9 To view online examples of student portfolios with ethics code, visit: https://myethicsclass.com/portfolios/

Selected Bibliography

Alia, Valerie. *Media Ethics and Social Change*. New York: Routledge, 2004.

Allen, Anita L. *The New Ethics: A Guided Tour of the Twenty-First Century Moral Landscape*. New York: Hyperion, 2004.

Allen, Judy. *Event Planning Ethics and Etiquette*. Ontario: John Wiley & Sons, 2003.

Badaracco, Claire H. *Quoting God: How Media Shape Ideas about Religion and Culture*. Waco, Texas: Baylor Univ. Press, 2005.

Bagdikian, Ben H. *The New Media Monopoly*. Boston, Mass.: Beacon Press, 2004.

Berkman, Robert I. and Christopher A. Shumway. *Digital Dilemmas: Ethical Issues for Online Media Professionals*. Ames, Iowa: Iowa State Press, 2003.

Berkowitz, Peter, ed. *Never a Matter of Indifference: Sustaining Virtue in a Free Republic*. Stanford, Calif.: Hoover Institution Press, 2003.

Bernstein, R.B. *Thomas Jefferson*. New York: Oxford Univ. Press, 2003.

Bertrand, Claude-Jean. *Media Ethics & Accountability Systems*. New Brunswick, N.J.: Transaction Publishers, 2000.

Bizzell, Patricia and Bruce Herzberg. *The Rhetorical Tradition: Readings from Classical Times to the Present*. New York: St. Martins, 1990.

Bok, Sissela. *Lying: Moral Choice in Public and Private Life*. New York: Vintage Books, 1999.

Bok, Sissela. *Lying: Moral Choice in Public and Private Life*. New York: Pantheon, 1978.

Bonhoeffer, Dietrich. *Ethics*. New York: Touchstone, 1995.

Bugeja, Michael. *Culture's Sleeping Beauty*. Troy, N.Y.: Whitston, 1993.

Bugeja, Michael. *Interpersonal Divide: The Search for Community in a Technological Age*. New York: Oxford Univ. Press, 2005.

Campbell, Joseph. *The Hero With a Thousand Faces*. Princeton, N.J.: Univ. of Princeton, 1973.

Chadwick, Ruth, ed. *The Concise Encyclopedia of Ethics in Politics and the Media*. San Diego, Calif.: Academic Press, 2001.

Chodron, Pema. *When Things Fall Apart*. Boston, Mass.: Shambhala, 2000.

Christians, Clifford G., Mark Fackler, Kim B. Rotzoll and Kathy Brittain McKee. *Media Ethics: Cases and Moral Reasoning*, 6th ed. New York: Longman, 2001.

Cialdini, R.B. *Influence: The Psychology of Persuasion*. New York: Harper, 2007.

Coons, Christian and Michael Weber, eds. *Manipulation: Theory and Practice*. New York: Oxford University Press, 2014.

Covey, Stephen. *7 Habits of Highly Successful People*. New York: Free Press; 15th Anniversary edition, 2004.

Day, Louis Alvin. *Ethics in Media Communications: Cases & Controversies*. Belmont, Calif.: Wadsworth/Thomson Learning, 2003.

DeLapp, K. and J. Henkel. *Lying and Truthfulness*. Indianapolis, IN: Hackett Publishing Company, 2012.

Dines, Gail and Jean M. Humez. *Gender, Race, and Class in Media*, 2nd ed. Thousand Oaks, Calif.: Sage, 2003.

Duffy, Margaret and Esther Thorson. *Persuasion Ethics Today*. New York: Routledge, 2016.

Eichenwald, Kurt. *Conspiracy of Fools: A True Story*. New York: Broadway Books, 2005.

Elffers, Joost and Robert Greene. *The 48 Laws of Power*. New York: Viking, 1998.

Erman, David M. and Michele S. Shauf, eds. *Computers, Ethics, and Society*. New York: Oxford Univ. Press, 2003.

Fallows, James. *Breaking the News: How the Media Undermine American Democracy*. New York: Vintage Books, 1997.

Fraser, Jill Andresky. *White-Collar Sweatshop: The Deterioration of Work and Its Rewards in Corporate America*. New York: Norton, 2001.

Galician, Mary-Lou, ed. *Handbook of Product Placement in the Mass Media: New Strategies in Marketing Theory, Practice, Trends, and Ethics*. Binghamton, N.Y.: Haworth, 2004.

Gladwell, Malcolm. *Blink: The Power of Thinking Without Thinking*. New York: Little, Brown; 2005.

Glasser, Theodore L., ed. *The Idea of Public Journalism*. New York: The Guilford Press, 1999.

Guelzo, Allen C. *Abraham Lincoln: Redeemer President*. Grand Rapids, Mich.: William B. Eerdmans, 2003.

Gurak, Laura J. *Cyberliteracy: Navigating the Internet with Awareness*. New Haven, Conn.: Yale University Press, 2001.

Hancock, Peter A. *Hoax Springs Eternal: The Psychology of Cognitive Deception*. New York: Cambridge Univ. Press, 2015).

Holiday, Ryan. *Trust Me, I'm Lying: The Tactics and Confessions of a Media Manipulator*. London: Portfolio/Penguin, 2013.

Hutchins, Robert M. *A Free and Responsible Press*. The Commission on Freedom of the Press. Chicago, Ill: University of Chicago Press, 1947.

Iggers, Jeremy. *Good News, Bad News: Journalism Ethics and the Public Interest*. Boulder, Colo.: Westview Press, 1999.

Isaacson, Walter. *Benjamin Franklin: An American Life*. New York: Simon & Schuster Paperbacks, 2004.

Jones, John Philip, ed. *The Advertising Business: Operations, Creativity, Media Planning, Integrated Communications.* Thousand Oaks, Calif.: Sage, 1999.

Keating, P.J., ed. *Matthew Arnold: Selected Prose.* New York: Penguin, 1982.

Kovach, Bill and Tom Rosenstiel. *The Elements of Journalism: What Newspeople Should Know and the Public Should Expect.* New York: Three Rivers Press, 2001.

Kriegel, Uriah. *The Varieties of Consciousness.* New York: Oxford University Press, 2015.

Kurtz, Howard. *Media Circus: The Trouble with America's Newspapers.* New York: Times Books, 1994.

Lumby, Catharine and Elspeth Probyn, eds. *Remote Control: New Media, New Ethics.* Cambridge: Cambridge Univ. Press, 2003.

Martin, D. and D.K. Wright. *Public Relations Ethics: How to Practice PR Without Losing Your Soul.* New York: Business Expert Press, 2016.

McQuade, Donald and Robert Atwan, eds. *Popular Writing in America.* New York: Oxford Univ. Press, 1988.

Merrill, John C. *Journalism Ethics: Philosophical Foundations for News Media.* Boston, Mass.: Bedford/St. Martin's, 1997.

Merritt, Davis. *Knightfall: Knight Ridder and How the Erosion of Newspaper Journalism is Putting Democracy at Risk.* New York: AMACOM, 2005.

Mindich, David T.Z. *Just the Facts: How "Objectivity" Came to Define American Journalism.* New York: New York University Press, 1998.

Overholser, Geneva and Kathleen Hall Jamieson, eds. *The Press.* New York: Oxford Univ. Press, 2005.

Parsons, Patricia J. *Ethics in Public Relations: A Guide to Best Practice.* London: Kogan Page Ltd., 2016.

Patterson, Philip and Lee Wilkins, *Media Ethics: Issues and Cases*, 8th ed. New York: McGraw-Hill, 2014.

Rabaté, Jean-Michel. *The Ethics of the Lie.* Suzanne Verderber, trans. New York: Other Press, 2008.

Rakove, Jack N. *James Madison and the Creation of the American Republic*, 2nd ed. New York: Longman, 2002.

Randall, Willard Sterne. *Alexander Hamilton: A Life.* New York: Perennial, 2003.

Retief, Johan. *Media Ethics: An Introduction to Responsible Journalism.* Cape Town: Oxford Univ. Press, 2002.

Ridley, Matt. *The Origins of Virtue: Human Instincts and the Evolution of Cooperation.* New York: Penguin, 1996.

Rosen, Jay. *Getting the Connections Right: Public Journalism and the Troubles in the Press.* New York: The Twentieth Century Fund Press, 1996.

Roszak, Theodore. *The Cult of Information.* Berkeley, Calif.: Univ. of California Press, 1994.

Sandefur, Timothy. *The Conscience of the Constitution: The Declaration of Independence and the Right to Liberty.* Washington, D.C.: Cato Institute, 2015.

Schliesser, Eric. *Sympathy: a History.* Oxford: Oxford University Press, 2015.

Schulweis, H.M. *Conscience: The Duty to Obey and the Duty to Disobey.* Woodstock, VT: Jewish Lights Pub, 2008.

Searle, John R. *Seeing Things as They Are: A Theory of Perception.* New York: Oxford University Press, 2015.

Seib, Philip and Kathy Fitzpatrick. *Journalism Ethics.* Fort Worth, Texas: Harcourt Brace, 1997.

Seitel, Fraser P. *The Practice of Public Relations.* Upper Saddle River, N.J.: Prentice Hall, 1995.

Shaw, Colin. *Deciding What We Watch: Taste, Decency, and Media Ethics in the UK and the USA.* New York: Oxford Univ. Press, 1999.

Siebert, Fred and Theodore Petersen and Wilbur Schramm. *Four Theories of the Press.* Urbana, Ill.: Univ. of Illinois, 1974.

Singer, Peter. *Practical Ethics*, 2nd ed. Cambridge: Cambridge Univ. Press, 1993.

Sorabji, Richard. *Moral Conscience Through the Ages.* Chicago, Ill.: University of Chicago Press, 2014.

Spence, Edward and Brett Van Heekeren. *Advertising Ethics.* Upper Saddle River, N.J.: Pearson, 2005.

Stahr, Walter. *John Jay: Founding Father.* New York: Hambledon and London, 2005.

Strohm, Paul. *Conscience: A Very Short Introduction.* New York: Oxford University Press, 2011.

Van Creveld, Martin. *Conscience: A Biography.* London: Reaktion Books, 2015.

Vonk, Nancy and Janet Kestin. *Pick Me: Breaking Into Advertising and Staying There.* Hoboken, N.J.: Wiley, 2005.

Warner, Charles and Joseph Buchman. *Media Selling: Broadcast, Cable, Print, and Interactive.* Ames, Iowa: Iowa State Press, 2004.

Wilkins, Lee and Renita Coleman. *The Moral Media: How Journalists Reason About Ethics.* Mahwah, N.J.: Lawrence Erlbaum, 2005.

Woodward, Bob. *The Secret Man: The Story of Watergate's Deep Throat.* New York: Simon & Schuster, 2005.

Index

48 *Laws of Power* 271, 328
"60 Minutes" 81
"60 Minutes Wednesday" 81–2
1765 Stamp Act 52
1994 Winter Olympic Games 186, 289
2016 U.S. presidential election 154–5; and fake
    news 65, 93, 138, 170

A

Abakanowicz, Magdalena 120–1
Abby [John Jay slave] 55
ABC television xiii, 169, 171
Abel, Alan 177
accountability 58, 79–86; defined 80
Accrediting Council on Education in Journalism
    and Mass Communications xi, 322
Acosta, Jim 170
Adams, Chris 260–1
Advertising Age 89, 108
*Advertising Business: Operations, Creativity, Media
    Planning, Integrated Communications* 9, 329
Advertising Ethics 39, 330
ADWEEK 32
Afghanistan 30
agora 52, 59
akrasia 185
Akron (O.H.) Beacon Journal 283–4
Al Jazeera 8, 238
Albany (N.Y.) Times Union 167
aletheia 103
Alexander, Andy 207, 211–12, 277
Alia, Valerie 36, 327
All the President's Men 152
Allen, Anita L. 252, 327
Allen, Judy 311, 388
Allyn & Bacon xv, xvii
alternative facts 94, 113, 138
American Advertising Federation xiii, 12, 92,
    288, 323
American Friends Service Committee 189, 229
American Greeting Cards 123–4
American Psychological Association 30
American Society of Engineering Education 191
American Water Works Association 109
Amico, Sam 2
Anderson, Michael, C. 104
Anderson, Terry 55
Anheuser-Busch 62
Annenberg Public Policy Center 261
Anthony, Susan B. 50
appropriate disclosure 114
Arends Integrated Communication 319
Arends, John 319–20
Aristotle xxi, 29, 62, 74, 252; and Golden Rule
    135
Aristotle's Mean 37, 95, 105
Arnold, Matthew 163
Asian American Journalism Association 54
Asian American Advertising and Public Relations
    Alliance 230
Aslan, Reza 239–40
Associated Press xiii, 8, 55, 116, 152, 168; and
    Hurricane Katrina 300
Association of LGTBQ Journalists 237
Atlantic 277

B

Baby Boomer 62
Bagdikian, Ben H. 58, 327

Balsamico, Victor "Kojak" 298–300
Barkley, Charles 89
Baum, L. Frank 127
Bausch & Lomb 143
Baya Sanchez-Crynes, Avelia 214–15, 226
BBC *See* British Broadcasting Corporation
Benoit (John Jay slave) 56
Bentham, Jeremy xxi, 95
Bergen, Candice 32–33
Berger, Jonah 227
Berkman, Robert I. 207, 327
Bernstein, Carl 152–3, 272
Bernstein, R.B. 55, 327
Berry, Stephen 12
Bertrand, Claude-Jean 96, 314–15, 327
Better Homes and Gardens xiii, 317–18
Bewitched! 32
Bill of Rights 56–7, 97, 316
Bishop, Bojinka 109–10
Black Community Information Center 168
Blackstock, Ben 41–2
Blair, Jayson 191–2
Blink: The Power of Thinking Without Thinking 16,
    161–2, 225, 328
Bok, Sissela 78–9, 105, 136–40, 327; and
    questionable lies 153–4
Bonhoeffer, Dietrich 43–4, 327
Booker, Hester 168
Boolean 199–200
Borg, Lindsey 113
Borgman, Jim 224–5
Borton, Lady 189, 229
Boston Globe 193, 229–30
Boston University 50
Bosworth, Andrew 19
Boucher, Jason M. 201–2
Bovet, Susan Fry 293–4
Bovsun, Mara 111–12
Boyd, Gerald 193
Bransetter, Ziva 8–9, 233
British Broadcasting Corporation xiii, 239, 275
Brogan & Partners 253–4
Brogan, Marcie 253
Brokaw, Tom 172
Brookings Institution 223, 225
Bruzzese, Anita 208
Buchman, Joseph 15, 330
Buford, Howard 16–17, 187
Bugeja, Diane xiii, xv, 150–1, 302
Burr, Aaron 58
Bush, George W. 81–2
Business Week 318

C

Campbell, Joseph 126, 327
Canny Bowen Inc. 321
Cusanus, Nicolaus 51
Capital (W.I.) Times 16, 213
Carrington, Edward 54
Carruth, Hayden 138–9
Carter, Hodding III 13
Carter, Betsy 92–3
Carter, Shirley Staples 42–3, 228–9
Castells, Manuel 95, 98
Castle Underwood Agency 142
Castle, Grant 142
CBS xiii, 8, 31–2, 81–3, 142, 172
Center for Integration and Improvement of
    Journalism 235, 242
Center for Investigative Reporting 8, 233, 294

Center for Journalism Ethics 3
Ceppos, Jerry 260
Chamberlin, Dennis xv, 117–22
Chan, Mei-Mei 226–7, 238, 241, 244
Cheney, Dick 170
Chicago Sun-Times 241
Chicago Tribune xiii, 10, 251, 262, 265–6
Chodron, Pema 298
Chris Matthews Show 265
Christians, Clifford G. xi, 36, 46, 59, 96, 98, 103,
    239, 273, 321, 327; and common good 34;
    and moral literacy 13
Cialdini, R.B. 141, 327
Cicero, Marcus Tullius 52, 55
Cincinnati Enquirer 255
Civil Rights Act of 1991 294
Clabes, Judy 292
Clinton, Hillary 79, 154–5
CNN xiii, 19, 46, 170–1
CNN's International Newsource 46
Coca-Cola 60–2
Cochran, Jean 115
Cohen, Richard 153
Coleman, Renita 234, 330
Collaborative Obesity Research Evaluation Team
    240
Columbia Broadcasting Company 166
Columbia University 14
Committee on Publication Ethics 265
compassion 295–7
Confucius xxi, 37
conscience 3, 8, 24–6, 28, 31–2, 45, 56, 75–9,
    103, 135, 137–8, 185, 188, 200, 209, 211, 219,
    239, 244; and Abraham Lincoln 95–6; and
    compassion 295–7; defined 13; and Dietrich
    Bonhoeffer 15; human condition xvii, 106,
    228; informing consciousness 23, 26, 28, 31,
    38, 75, 133, 249, 272, 295–6; lapses of 17,
    77, 201; listening to 33; and Martin Luther
    51; and manipulation 162–4, 293; and moral
    convergence 13–17; in philosophy 35–7; and
    public relations 10; and remorse 197–8; and
    value systems 312–13; violation of 161–2;
    and *Wizard of Oz* 127
*Conscience: The Duty to Obey and the Duty to
    Disobey* 76, 330
consciousness 3, 35–7, 41, 51, 76–7, 95, 130,
    137, 162, 164, 198, 200, 219, 239, 244, 261;
    and Abraham Lincoln 95–6; as awareness
    13, 25, 296; and science 37, 106; defined 13;
    human condition xvii, 106, 228; impaired 44;
    informing conscience 23, 26, 28, 31, 38, 75,
    133, 249, 272, 295–7; and moral convergence
    13–17; and philosophy 103–5
Conversation 231
Conway, Kellyanne 94
Cooper, Anderson 89
copyright infringement 192
Corbett, Philip 262
Cosby, William 58
Country Home 318
Covey, Stephen 163, 328
Culbertson, Hugh 114, 140
cultural exclusion 228
cultural inclusion 228
Cunningham, Peggy H. 9, 39, 80
Curtis, Michael Kent 40
CVS Health 66
Cyberliteracy xvii, 328

D

Dallas Morning News 274–5, 297
Dan Pinger Public Relations 146
Davis, Kim 64

Day, Louis Alvin 91, 94–5, 328
de Uriarte, Mercedes Lynn 231, 237–8
*Deciding What We Watch: Taste, Decency, and
    Media Ethics in the UK and the USA* 281, 330
Declaration of Independence 53, as charter
    document 52, and Enlightenment 55; and
    happiness; as mission statement 315
DeLapp, K. 135, 328
Democratic National Headquarters 152
Denver Post 8, 117
deontology 34, 36
Des Moines Register viii, 4
Detroit Free Press 186, 202
Detroit News 125
Die Zeit 8
Digital Dilemmas 207, 327
DigitalGYD 198
DiJohn, Linda xix–xx, 7, 115
Dines, Gail 223, 328
discretion 261–5
disinformation 154–5
Donne, John 106
Douglass, Frederick xxi, 14, 50
Dover (Del.) Post 286
DreamWorks 197
Duffy, Margaret 10, 314, 328
Dunn, Anne 11–12

E

E.T., The Extraterrestrial 126
Economist 155
Edelman xiii, xix
Editor & Publisher xv, 193, 196
Eiler, Terry 149–50, 152
*Elements of Journalism: What Newspeople Should
    Know and the Public Should Expect* 233, 329
Elliott, Deni xix
Elliott, Phil 205–6, 233, 274
Ellul, Jacques 273
Emancipation Proclamation 95
emeth 103
Emory College 284
Emotional Intelligence 185, 296
empathy 295–300
Energizer Bunny ® 125
Engel, Allison 9
Englehardt, Elaine E. 145–6
Enlightenment 51, 53–6
Enron 6
Enteron *See* Enron
epiphany 127–8
Erdely, Sabrina Rubin 84
ESPN 235–6
Esquire xiii, 92
Estes-Sumpter, Sidmel 224, 232
Ethics Handbook 209
Ethics in Public Relations 263, 329
Ethics of the Lie 136, 329
ethnic cleansing 113
Evans, DeAnn 145–6
Event Planning Ethics and Etiquette 207, 263, 327
*Evolution of Racism: Human Differences and the Use
    and Misuse of Science* 227

F

Facebook 19, 142, 179, 204; and 2016 U.S.
    presidential campaign 154–5
FactCheck.org 179–80, 261
fake news 4, 108, 155; 2016 U.S. presidential
    election 65, 93, 138, 154, 164; and alternative
    facts 94, 113; as hoax 166, 170–1
Fallows, James 78, 88, 328
family values 29–34, 42

Fast Company 272–3
Federal Trade Commission 107, 285
Federico, Anthony 235
Felt, Mark 153
Ferré, John P. 301
First Amendment 40, 43, 156, 204, 209, 273–4, 277, 280, 286, 192, 311; and Bill of Rights 56–57, 315–16; and Establishment Clause 302; and Google 276–7
Fishman, Charles 372–3, 292
Flintstones 32
Flournoy, Eli 46
FOIA Project 272
Ford, Henry 50
forgiveness 295–8
Fort Wayne News-Sentinel 117
Foster, Scott 20
Four Theories of the Press 90, 330
Franklin, Benjamin xxi; and family values 30–1, 34, 50; and free press 53–4, 57; and hoax 145
Frare, Therese 302–5
Fraser, Jill Andresky 27, 328
Frazier, Connie 12, 288
Freedom Forum xiii
Freedom of Information 9, 274–5
full disclosure 111–13, 251–2, 254

G

Galileo Galilei 104
Gallop 32, 136–7
Gandhi, Mahatma 103, 227
Gannett xiii, 226, 238
Garland, Judy 127
Garrett, Melissa xiii
Gates, Bill 50, 89
Gender, Race, and Class in Media 223, 328
Gettysburg Address 95
Giangrande, Gregory 143
Gingrich, Newt 64
Gladwell, Malcolm 161–2, 225–6, 328
Glass, Stephen 193
Glen Falls (N.Y.) Post-Star 64
Golden Mean 37, 95
Golemon, Daniel 185–6
Gonzalez, Pedro Blas 162
Good Housekeeping xiii, 12, 317
Google News 170
Google 170, 199 and "Do No Evil" 276–7
Great Chain of Being 126
Greeley, Horace 96
Greenwald, Marilyn 88
Greeting Card Association 124
Griffin, Dustin H. 122
Guardian 8
Guelzo, Allen C. 96, 328
Gumbel, Bryant 175
Gurak, Laura J. xvii–xviii, 328
Gutenberg, Johannes 51
Gyekye, Kwame xxi

H

Hamilton, Alexander xxi, 50, 54, 57–8
Hamilton, Andrew 58
Hancock, Peter A. 165, 328
Harding, Tonya 186, 289
Harlan (I.A.) Tribune 42
Harper's Bazaar 92
Harvard Medical School 76, 295
Harvard, University 52, 224, 239
Hass, Robert D. 318–19
Hearst xiii, 317
Heekeren, Brett Van 39, 330
Heidegger, Martin xxi, 273

Henkel, J. 135, 328
Hero with a Thousand Faces 126, 327
Hitler, Adolf 166
Hoax Springs Eternal 165, 328
Hochstein, Peter 104
Hodges, Lou 79
Hoff, Valerie 186–7
Holiday, Ryan 180, 328
Hopkins, Budd 168
Horn, Dan 255–7
Houston Chronicle 2
How Opal Mehta Got Kissed, Got Wild, and Got a Life 197
Howard, Josh 82
human condition xvii, 13, 23, 30, 106, 295–6, 298; and compassion 297; and empathy 297; dual aspects of 25, 37, 51
Humez, Jean M. 223, 328
Hunt, April 237, 284
Hurricane Harvey 224
Hurricane Katrina 224, 300–1
Hutchins Commission 75
Hutchins Report 231

I

I Love Lucy 32
I, Tonya See Tonya Harding
Idaho Statesman 236
inappropriate disclosure 114–15
Independent 195
Influence: The Psychology of Persuasion 141, 327
Institute for Health Care Policy & Innovation 224
Intel 84–86
International Communication Association 95
International Food Policy Research Institute 263
Internet Galaxy 95
Interpersonal Divide in the Age of the Machine i, xi, xxi
Intrepid Group 212
Intruders 168
invention 191–3, 195, 311
Investigative Reporters and Editors 8, 233
Invisible Influence: The Hidden Forces that Shape Behavior 227
Iowa State Daily 6, 116
Iowa State University i, xi, xiii, xvii, 63, 66, 259, 263, 282
Iraq 30, 87, 142
Isaacson, Walter 53, 328

J

J. Walter Thomson 136
Jackson, Patrick 91
James Lange theory 161
James, William 161
Jay, John xxi, 50, 55–6
Jefferson, Thomas xxi, 50, 54–6, 58
Jensen, Jeff 89
Jinks, Larry 260
Johnson & Johnson 109
Johnson Foundation 97–8
Joint Center for Housing Studies 224
Jones, Jackie 202–3
Jordan, Michael 88–9
Journal of Media Ethics 10
justification 77–9

K

Kambom, Sadiki 168
Kant, Immanuel xxi, 25, 38, 153; and deontology 35–6

Kaplan, John xv, 9, 93, 152, 215–17, 298–300
Kasell, Carl 115
Keck, David 197
Kelly, Megyn 89
Kennedy, Anthony, M. 144–5
Kennedy, John F. 50, 282
Kerner Report 232
Kerrigan, Nancy 186, 289
Kestin, Janet 254, 330
Ketchum xiii, 146, 264
Khrushchev, Nikita 282
Killian, Jerry 81
King, Martin Luther xxi, 44, 63; and tolerance 227
King, Stephen 285–6
Kitch, Carolyn 12, 166, 190–1, 317
Klemack, John Cádiz 284
Knight Foundation xiii, 13
Knudson, Tom 66
Korean War 167
Kosovo 113
Kovach, Bill 233, 282, 329
Kraft USA 62, 109
Kreis, Steven 50
Krile, Angela 43
Kruckeberg, Dean 60
Krug, Teresa 8, 238
KSTU 284
Kunerth, Bill 66
Kurtz, Howard 138, 151, 329
Kwaanza 243

L

Labatt USA 290
Ladies' Home Journal 287
Carl Lange 161
Lao Tzu xxi
Lee Enterprises xiii
Lee, Douglas E. 277–8
Lenger, John 64
Leo Burnett xiii, xix, 48
Lewis, Carolyn 255
LIFE 299, 302
Lin, Jeremy 235
Lincoln, Abraham xxi, 50; and Gettysburg Address 95; and slavery 95–6
Loch Ness monster 177
Locke, John xx–xxi, 50–1; as America's philosopher 25, 52; and natural law 53
London Daily Mail 177
Los Angeles Times 39, 231, 237; and photojournalism 151–2
Louisiana State University 260
Luther, Martin 51–2
Lying and Truthfulness 135, 328
Lying: Moral Choice in Public and Private Life 105, 139, 327
Lynch, Dan 167

M

Madison, James xxi, 50, 57–8; and Bill of Rights 56
Mahawinney, George M. 167
Maher, Bill 285
Mahr, Joe 10, 251–2, 262
Malcolm X 50
Manafort, Paul 194–5
Manning, Morris L. xv, 116
Mansfield, Harvey C. 52
Manship School of Mass Communication 260
Mapes, Mary 82
Marvin, Carolyn 112

Massachusetts Institute of Technology's Media Lab 138
Masson v. The New Yorker, Alfred A. Knopf, and Janet Malcolm 144–5
matching story 192
McCafferty, Megan F. 197
McCarthy, Joseph 167
McCraw, David 274
McCurry, Mike 172
McGill, Jennifer 313–14
McGill, Kevin 301
McIver, Meredith 195
McLaughlin Group 265
Media Circus 138, 329
Media Ethics & Accountability Systems 314, 327
Media Ethics: Cases and Moral Reasoning 35–6, 327
Media Selling: Broadcast Cable, Print, and Interactive 137, 330
Meredith Corporation xiii, 287
Merrill, John C. 104, 329
Merritt, Davis 59, 329
Messner, Marcus 288
Meyer, Philip 112
Miami Herald xiii, 260
Michigan Department of Community Health 253
Microsoft Word® 81–2
Midwest Living 318
Mill, John Stuart xxi, 38, 50; and "Principle of Utility" 34
Millennials 2, 27, 48
Miller, Stephen 316–17
Milwaukee Journal Sentinel 202
Mindich, David T.Z. 274, 329
Minneapolis Star Tribune 289
Missing Time 168
Missouri School of Journalism 78, 135
"Morning Edition" 115
Moffeit, Miles 274–5, 297
moral absolutes 95–8, 106, 136, 320
Moral Media: How Journalists Reason About Ethics 234, 330
Moran, Mia xiii
Mores, Steve 42–3
Morgan State University 202
Morgantown (WV) Dominion Post 44
Morrow, Lance 32
MSNBC 142, 171
Murdoch, Rupert 187
Murphy Brown 31–3; *See also* Candice Bergen
Murphy, Mary 82
Muslim 237–8; depiction of women 39–40, 229–30 and stereotypes 239–40
My Lai 229

N

National Association of Black Journalists 54
National Association of Hispanic Journalists 54, 237
National Collegiate Athletic Association 236
National Geographic
National Lesbian and Gay Journalists Association 54
National Press Foundation 260
National Public Radio xiii, 209, 232
Native American Journalists Association 54, 236
NATO 113
NBC xiii, 172, 210, and Brian Williams 142–3
NBC4-Los Angeles 284
Neikirk, Barbara 43–4
Neill, Marlene S. 10
Nelson, Colleen McCain 93
New Coke 61

New Ethics: A Guided Tour of the Twenty-First Century Moral Landscape 185, 327
New Republic 193
New York Daily News 142, 236
New York Newsday 202
New York Post 58, 143
New York Times Magazine 117
New York Times xi, xiii, 4, 15, 29, 117, 143, 154, 171, 177, 193, 282, 285, 288; and anonymous sources 162–3; and Freedom of Information Act 274–5; and Jayson Blair 191–2; and Supreme Court 278; walkout 108
New York Tribune 96
New York Weekly Journal 52, 58
New York Woman 93
New Yorker xi, 143–4
News Corporation 186–7
News International 186
News of the World 186
News Photographer 193
News Watch 242
Newseum xiii, 277, 315, 322
Newsweek xiii, 33, 92, 166
Ni, Preston 163
Nickell, Karol DeWulf 317–18
Nieman Foundation xiii
"Nightline" 265
Nike 6, 89
Nixon, Richard 152, 272
No god but God: The Origins, Evolution, and Future of Islam 239
Noe, Tracey 66–67
Noel-Russell, Michael 116
Noles, Pam 141–2

O

O, The Oprah Magazine 92
O'Leary, George 143
O'Reilly, Bill 86
Obama, Michele 194–5
objectivity xviii, 5, 53, 103–4, 137, 154, 235, 252, 320; defined 65–6; as process 104–11
"Ode to New Orleans" 301
Ohio University 47–8, 63, 88, 109, 140, 152, 183–4, 194, 196–7, 255–6
Oklahoma Press Association 41
Oklahoma State University i, xix
Omaha World-Herald 8, 67
Online News Association 92, 323
Operation Iraqi Freedom 113
Opoien, Jessie 16, 213
Orlando Sentinel 284
Ottaway, David B. 275
Overholser, Geneva 4, 329
Oxford University Press i, xi, xv, xvii

P

Page, Clarence 265–7
Paluszek, John 146–7, 264–5
Parks, Rosa 50
Parsons, Patricia J. 263, 329
partial disclosure 111–14
Patterson, Philip 200–1, 329
Payne, Henry 125
Peabody Energy 174
peak experience 128–30
Peasback, David 321
Penguin Press 273
Pennsylvania Gazette 53–4
Pentagon Papers 278
People v. Croswell 58
Pepsi 61, 109, 169, 175, 261
personal restraint 277–9; definition 278

Persuasion Ethics Today 10, 328
Pew Research Center 12, 207, 224, 279
Phair, Judy 91, 143
PhairAdvantage Communications 9, 143
Philadelphia Daily News 202
Philadelphia Inquirer 167
Phoenix Home and Garden 317
Picard, Robert G. 52
Pick Me: Breaking into Advertising and Staying There 254, 330
Pinger, Dan 146
plagiarism xviii, 41, 172, 188, 190–200, 265
Planned Parenthood 47
Plato xxi, 37, 50
plausible deniability 196–7
Policinski, Gene 315, 322
Poor Richard's Almanac 30
Porter, Charlotte 300–1
Porter, Sue 112
Power of Identity 95
Practice of Public Relations 145, 330
Prevention Magazine 240
Prime Access 17, 187
Prism 191
Program for Biosafety Systems 263
Project for Excellence in Journalism 57
proxy plagiarism 192
Psychology Today 163
Public Relations Ethics 205, 329
Public Relations Journal 293
Public Relations Review 145
Public Relations Society of America 92, 144, 293, 321, 323
Pulitzer Prize Board 4
Pyle, Amy 294

Q

Quayle, Dan 31–3
questionable lies 153, 156
Quill xv, 275
Quorum Consulting 17
quote-making 144–8, 263
Quoting God: How Media Shape Ideas about Religion and Culture 301, 327

R

Raasch, Chuck 155, 164–5
Rabaté, Jean-Michel 136, 329
Rachels, James 36
racial inappropriateness 228
Radio-Television Digital Directors Association 92
Raines, Howell 191
Rakove, Jack N. 57, 329
Randall, Willard Sterne 58, 329
Random House Dictionary of the English Language 39, 87, 227, 290
Ranly, Don 135–6
Ratey, John J. 76, 295–6
Rather, Dan 81–3, 85
Raytheon xiii, 113
Reader's Digest 29, 193
Reagan, Ronald 50, 146–7
Reese, Cassandra 62, 109
Regret the Error 258–9
Reinhardt, Gregory A. 236–7
Remote Control: New Media, New Ethics 11, 329
Reuters xiii, 144, 175
Richwine, Lisa 144
Ridley, Matt 106, 329
Rigney, Melanie 108
Robinson, Dave 186
Roe v. Wade 63

Rolling Stone 83–4
Roosevelt, Eleanor 50
Roosevelt, Franklin D. 50
Rosen, Jay 59, 330
Rosenberg, Julius and Ethel 167–8
Rosenstiel, Tom 233, 282, 329
Ross, William David 36
Roszak, Theodore 59, 330
Ryan, Julie J.C.H. 191

S

Sacramento Bee 66
Saint Louis Post-Dispatch 155, 164
Salinger, Pierre 169–70
Sallah, Mike 262
Salt Lake City Tribune 236
San Francisco State University 235
San Jose Mercury News 260
Sands, Deanna 8, 67
Sasse, Ben 285
Satire: A Critical Reintroduction 122
Saudi Arabia 96
Schmuhl, Robert 52
Schopenhauer, Arthur xxi, 38
Schulweis, H.M. 76, 330
Science 138
Scripps Howard Foundation xi, xiii, 112, 292
Searle, John 13–14, 330
Second Helpings 197
Secret Man: The Story of Watergate's Deep Throat
    153, 330
Seitel, Fraser P. 145, 330
Serbia 113
Seventeen 287
Shaw, Colin 281, 330
She Beverage 62
Sheppard, Dan 104
Shipman, Pat 227
Shoshone-Bannock Tribe 236
Shumway, Christopher A. 207, 327
Sidey, Hugh 282
Silverman, Craig 258–9
Simon, George 164
Simpson, Nicole Brown 86
Singer, Audrey 223
situation ethics 95
Skullbuster 199
Slate 138, 195
Slater, Jan 109
Sloppy Firsts 197
Smart, Elizabeth 212
Smith, Susan 168–9
social mores 42, 46–9, 56, 58–9, 61–3, 67, 103,
    142, 281–3; and advertising 289–90; and
    cultural beliefs 173; and perception 65; and
    stereotypes 238–41
social responsibility 32, 90–4, 111, 173, 199, 217,
    234, 259, 311
Socrates 39, 75
Sommers, Christina Hoff 17, 94–5, 97–8, 102
Sorabji, Richard Rustom Kharsedji 14, 330
Southwest Airlines 171
Speakes, Larry 146–7
Special Interest Publications 318
Special Olympics 6–7
Spence, Edward 39, 330
Sports Illustrated 89
Stahr, Walter 56–330
Standage, Tom 155
Starck, Kenneth 60
Stars and Stripes 142
States News Service 144
Statue of Liberty 317
Stern, Judith S. 240

Strohm, Paul 14, 330
Stuart, Charles 168
Successful Farming 318
Sullivan, Teresa A. 84
Sunday Times of London 166
Superman 126
Swift, Jonathan 122–3
sympathy 272, 295–8
Syracuse University 274

T

Taco Liberty Bell hoax 171–2
Tao 39
taste xviii, 114, 272, 325; and advertising
    289–90, 302–3; and free expression
    279–89
Taylor, Gail 44–6
Telegraph 170
teleology 33–4
Temple University 12, 166, 317
Ten Commandments 39, 322
Thomas, Chris 212–213
Thorson, Esther 10, 314, 328
Time Warner 273
Time xiii, 32, 117, 205, 233, 274–5, 278, 281;
    "Man of the Year" 64
Times-Picayune 301
Title IX 292–4
Title VII 292–4
"Today Show" 172, 175
tolerance 58, 98, 112, 227–8, 321
Tortora, Andrea 196–7
Traditional Home 318
Trahant, Mark 236
Travers, Scott A. 171
trigger warnings 289
trigger words 44, 62–9, 81, 84, 279, 307
Trump, Donald 4, 64, 86, 154, 195 and fake
    news 155, 170, 194
Trump, Melania 4, 194
*Trust Me, I'm Lying: The Tactics and Confessions
    of a Media Manipulator* 180, 328
truth® campaign 48
Tulsa World xix
Tumblr 324
*Tuned Out: Why Americans Under 40 Don't Follow
    the News* 275
Turner, Ted 89
Tusa, John 275–6
TWA "Flight 800" 170
Twitter 143, 204, 208, 286; and falsehood 138

U

U.S. Census 223, 237, 327
U.S. Constitution 52, 54, 56, 97, 316
U.S. Department of Labor 205, 292
U.S. Equal Employment Opportunity
    Commission 292
U.S. Justice Department 253
U.S. Supreme Court xx, 55, 63, 144–5, 148, 194,
    276, 278
United Press International i, xi
UNITY 53, 223
University of California, Davis 240
University of California, Santa Barbara 238
University of Florida 93, 217
University of Illinois 109
University of Indianapolis 236
University of Iowa 12, 64
University of Michigan 224
University of South Carolina 228, 313
University of Texas 231, 278
University of Virginia 83–4

University of Wisconsin-Madison 3
US News and World Report 164
USA Today xi, 142, 172, 208
Usenet 170
utilitarian 34–8, 95
Uyeda, Lynne Choy 230

V

*Vanishing Act: the erosion of online footnotes
    and implications for scholarship in the digital
    age* xi, xvii
Vanity Fair 27, 489
Vedas 39
Venit, Kenn 285
viewpoint 196–7, 252–4, 268
Viswanathan, Kaavya 197
Vonk, Nancy 254, 330

W

WAGA-TV 224, 232
Wake Forest University 40
Wall Street Journal 84, 260–1, 272
*Wal-Mart Effect: How the World's Most Powerful
    Company Really Works—and How It's
    Transforming the American Economy* 272
Wal-Mart 271–5, 292
War of the Worlds 166–7
Warner, Charles 15, 78, 330
Washington Post xi, xiii, 4, 8, 20, 83–4, 87, 108,
    138, 151, 175, 202, 207, 230, 271–2, 275,
    277, 288; and Pentagon Papers 278; and
    Watergate 151–2
Watson, Marcia 288
Wayback Machine 199
Weatherup, Craig 169
Weber Shandwick xiii, xix

Weebly 324
Weiss, Mitch 262
Welles, Orson 166–7
Wells, H.G. 166–7
Wendy's 169
West, Betsy 82
Wetter, Erica xiii
*White-Collar Sweatshop: The Deterioration of Work
    and Its Rewards in Corporate America* 27, 328
WHO-TV 210
Wilbanks, Jennifer 86–7
Wilkins, Lee 200–1, 234, 329, 330
Williams, Brian 142–3
Williams, Cindy 84
Wilson, Woodrow 50
Winters, Dan 210–11
Wiredu, Kwasi xxi
Wix 324
Wizard of Oz 127
Wood, Allen 161
Woodward, Bob 152–3, 272, 330
WordPress 324
WOUB 194, 255
Writer's Digest xv, 285–6
WXIA 286–7

Y

Y2K 64

Z

Zahn, Donna Ramaeker 263–4
Zarrella, Ronald 143
Zelizer, Barbie 50
Zenger, John Peter 51–2
ZLRIGNITION 201
Zuckerberg, Mark 19